Sébastien Tremblay
A Badge of Injury

Transnational Queer Histories

―――

Edited by
Bodie A. Ashton and Sabrina Mittermeier

Volume 2

Sébastien Tremblay

A Badge of Injury

The Pink Triangle as Global Symbol of Memory

DE GRUYTER
OLDENBOURG

ISBN 978-3-11-221505-0
e-ISBN (PDF) 978-3-11-106771-1
e-ISBN (EPUB) 978-3-11-106831-2
ISSN 2750-6096

Library of Congress Control Number: 2023943020

Bibliographic information published by the Deutsche Nationalbibliothek
The Deutsche Nationalbibliothek lists this publication in the Deutsche Nationalbibliografie; detailed bibliographic data are available on the internet at http://dnb.dnb.de.

© 2025 Walter de Gruyter GmbH, Berlin/Boston
This volume is text- and page-identical with the hardback published in 2024.
Cover image: Memorial wall painting "The UNforgotten" that shows the Auschwitz detainee Walter Degen by Nils Westergard, Bülowstraße 94 in Berlin-Schöneberg, Photo: Sébastien Tremblay, 2023
Typesetting: Integra Software Services Pvt. Ltd.
Printing and binding: CPI books GmbH, Leck

www.degruyter.com

Throughout this book I have capitalized Pink Triangle when discussing the concept or the symbol, whereas I use lowercase when discussing the actual badges worn in the Nazi camps.

Throughout the book, I have used common denominations for North American cities. I did so for clarity. I would like to invite readers to reflect on the fact that names such as Montréal, New York or Boston are but one aspect of North American settler-colonialism. Like symbols and pictures, geographical names are indicators and factors of historical change.

For Guy and for TT

Acknowledgements

Like the Pink Triangle, the journey behind this book also took me across many continents. This story started in Canada before evolving into a dissertation project financed by the DFG Graduate School, "Global Intellectual History," at Freie Universität Berlin before being finally completed in the north of Germany between the chants of seagulls and the smell of Danish pastries. It seems natural to start by thanking my primary PhD supervisor, Sebastian Conrad, for his patience, dedication, continuous support, and for welcoming me into his office every month to go through my now-legendary lists of questions. His input in these meetings always helped me decide which paths I should follow in my research. I am equally grateful for my secondary supervisor, Martin Lücke, who likewise sat down with me and allowed me to pick his brain on multiple occasions. Thank you for motivating a quirky French-Canadian scholar to dive into the political meanderings of German queer history. Going back to the drawing board and rewriting this dissertation into a book was not always an easy task. I would like to thank Sabrina Mittermeier and Bodie Ashton for opening the door to their new series on transnational queer history, as well as Rabea Rittgerodt at De Gruyter for making this episode another story of kinship. No one should underestimate the power of emojis in professional emails!

I am similarly thankful for the support of the Ernst-Reuter-Gesellschaft, the Halle Foundation, and the Deutsche Forschungsgemeinschaft, for their funding of my research, archival stays, and numerous opportunities to cross the Atlantic multiple times in order to share my ideas with colleagues on both continents. I would also like to extend my gratitude to Camilla Bertoni, Sebastian Gottschalk, and Julia von der Wense for their help in navigating the troubled waters of bureaucracy. I am additionally thankful to Kristine Schmidt and Peter Rehberg, as well as Birgit Bosold, Ben Miller, and the team of the Schwules Museum in Berlin, who manage to keep one of the best queer archives in Europe afloat. I am similarly in debt to Caitlin McCarthy from the LGBT Community Center National History Archive in New York City, Nicholas Maniu at the Forum Queeres Archiv München, the personnel of the Manuscripts and Archives Division at the New York Public Library, Jake Newsome and Klaus Müller for their perspective at the US Holocaust Memorial Museum, and especially Albert Knoll of the archives at the Gedenkstätte Dachau for going the extra mile as archivist and opening his personal papers to me.

Global historians are trained to understand the value of teamwork and the potentiality of collaboration. Queers have known for decades the necessity of developing a broader network for support and inspiration. I was privileged to find both in the solace of Freie Universität Berlin and Humboldt Universität zu Berlin. These three years of solidarity, mutual aid, and respect have been sprinkled with the fabulous comments and feedback from a rich community of scholars. I am especially obliged to the weekly criticism of my brilliant writing group: Cecilia Maas and Luc Wodzicki. At SCRIPTS, I am grateful to Christian Volk, Gülay Çağlar, Marianne Samaha, Alexandra Paulin-Booth, and Friederike Kuntz. Likewise, I have been able to surround myself with other scholars working on queer and gender studies/issues during these years at the Friedrich Meinecke Institute. I am therefore indebted to the words of encouragement and constructive criticism of Merlin Bootsmann, Adrian Lehne, Lukas Herde, Andrea Rottmann, Nina Reusch, Ulrike Schaper, Veronika Springmann, and Lorenz Weinberg.

The last miles of this journey have unexpectedly taken place in the north of Schleswig-Holstein where I am now happy to evolve. I wrote this book with the Baltic Sea as a soundtrack, inspired by the ground-breaking research of my new colleagues. I am grateful to Christiane Reinecke for welcoming me with open arms at the Europa Universität-Flensburg. It is a joy to discuss and work with her week after week. This second home in the north has been a fertile ground intellectually. I thank my colleagues at the Seminar for History and History Didactics the people of the Interdisciplinary Centre for European Studies, the International Staff Network, and all of those who have joined me for walks around campus. I especially want to thank Anna Kompatscher, Sophie Costanza Bleuel, Lara-Sophie Hoeren, Michelle Witen, Inken Carstensen-Egwuom, Anna Katharina Mangold, Maria Schwab, as well as Nelo Schmalen and Tamás Jules Fütty.

If this book is my own, it is also anchored in a wonderful and stable network. Like the Pink Triangle's journey, my writings are the result of numerous formative key moments and encounters. I would first like to thank Margrit Pernau of the Max Planck Institute for Human Development in Berlin for believing in me and turning my incessant questions about conceptual history and memory studies into a productive and insightful collaboration. Furthermore, I extend my appreciation to Jani Marjanen, Pasi Ihalainen, and Martin J. Burke of the History of Concepts group for thought-provoking sojourns in Finland. I would also like to thank Justin Bengry, Benno Gammerl, Tara Povey, and John Price for a welcoming extended stay at the Centre of Queer History at Goldsmith, University of London. It was a delight to exchange ideas with you and your students. In the United Kingdom, I thank Mirjam Brusius, Craig Griffiths, and Anna Hájková for their important research and for their support and feedback. In North America, I would especially like to thank Christopher Ewing and Jennifer Evans who not only inspired this research but are people I am now lucky enough to call friends. The same can be said for the time and dedication given to me by all participants of the 2019 Tokyo Summer School of the Global History Collaborative, the members of the NYLON Berlin group at the Humboldt Universität zu Berlin, the Doctoral Lab of the John F. Kennedy Institute for North American Studies, and the *Berliner Colloquium zur Geschichte der Sexualität.*

I would like to separately underline the respect and gratitude I have for a circle of scholars. Lisa Hellman, Lea Börgerling, Michael Facius, Nadja Klopprogge, Sonja Dolinsek, Pascal Siegrist and Sarah Bellows-Blakely have been like older academic siblings over the past few years. Scholarship should not only be seen as the sum of the accumulation and circulation of knowledge, but also the necessity to offer care to each other during difficult times. This global septet found the perfect way to go along with the music, gifting me with advice and feedback beyond all expectation. Similarly and as importantly, I extend my profound thanks to my dear friend Alexandra Holmes who spent hours correcting much of the French charm out of my prose.

At home on both continents, my story of migration and this scholarship is finally linked to an extensive chosen family waltzing with me through the hurdles of life and jumping with me through the hoops of uncertainties and anxiety. My mental health and strengths lay upon the shoulders of this global story of emotional intelligence and communication, my own community. This cluster goes beyond national borders and two urban settings. Nonetheless, in Montréal, I would like to thank Catherine Lefrançois, Gabrielle Provost, Andréann Cossette-Viau, Roxanne Mallet, Émilie Roberge, Anaïs Michaud, Guillaume Cyr, Vanessa Gauthier Vela, Émilie Gendron, and Florence Payette for following me since the start of this German chapter and waking up daily to my virtual rants and soothing my qualms. Distance has nothing on our friendships. In Berlin, I would like to start by thanking my sisters of the 'Grufti Squad,' Daniela Turß, Julia Föll, and Sarah Christoph for providing me with music, love, and comfortable darkness. Laja Destremau and Flora Petersen, thank you for gifting me with a francophone bubble and a possibility to grow. Hannah Geiger, Ed Greve, Nora Huberty, Miriam Zimmermann, Janis Humann, Saleema Adu Smith, Yener Bayramoğlu, Maddalena Arosio, and Minas Hilbig, thank you for being friends and allies, bringing friendship and politics together, and making this city my home. To Giulia Mandelli, Barbara Uchdorf, and my dance family, thank you for offering me a stage and a studio to dance my worries away and create something with you every week. To my old family and partners in crime at the former Café Chaos in Montréal, thank you for convincing me a decade ago during a particularly emotional shift at the bar to follow my dreams of writing books, being a historian, and finally to go back to university. Who would have thought that this journey would lead me to migrate and learn another language? On this note, *dankeschön* to Paule Desormeaux, my first German teacher, who made me fall in love with the language almost 20 years ago.

In the middle of this project, I was lucky enough to cross paths with a wonderful otter who is even more multi-layered than the symbol I've spent the last years seeing everywhere. Tilo Patrick Kochs has not only debated some of the arguments of this book with me over lengthy breakfasts, he has also provided me with a safe space to write it. I am grateful every single day for his presence by my side and without his care, this book would not have been written. For all the talk in *A Badge of Injury* regarding the potential of the negative for queer collective memory, Tilo is an example of the importance of queer joy.

Lastly, I would like to finish with a somewhat cliché *merci* to my mother, Francine Contant. Scholars, and dare I say especially queer scholars, are often inclined to write long articles and monographs about the body and the aspirations of the working class. What constitutes the working class? What does the working class want? My mom, a strong woman raising me and my brother on her own, a nurse exploited under capitalism, has filled my childhood with books and culture. Through her ceaseless sacrifice she enabled me to finish school and supported me through university at the expense of her health and her financial well-being. The completion of this book inside a classist system is not due to my successes alone, but the resilience of a woman who dared to dream for her children. My introduction to class struggles and feminism came not during a lecture in my first year at university, but through the realization that my deeds today have only been possible due to the labors of one woman. For that, I am in her debt.

Contents

Acknowledgements —— IX

List of abbreviations —— XVII

List of figures —— XIX

Introduction – There and back again: A Pink Triangle's journey —— 1
    1   The visual history of the Pink Triangle —— 5
    2   Global queer history —— 6
    3   Nazi atrocities and the Pink Triangle —— 9
    4   Queering gay history —— 11
    5   Provincializing queer history —— 13
    6   Memory and victimhood —— 15
    7   Feeling the Pink Triangle —— 15
    8   Searching for the Pink Triangle —— 20
    9   Mapping the Pink Triangle's journey —— 23

1   A badge of continuities – Pink radical politics and identification with the Nazi past —— 27
    1.1   Emancipation on paper —— 30
    1.2   Wearing Pink Triangles, showing Pink Triangles —— 32
    1.3   Remembering the men with the pink triangle —— 38
    1.4   Collectivizing the triangle —— 46
    1.5   The power of images —— 49

2   A badge of narratives – Pink Triangles, written communication networks, and the Queer Atlantic —— 55
    2.1   Pink Triangles over the Atlantic: Narrating victimhood in the press —— 57
    2.2   Writing a play, sharing a myth: *Bent* and collective memory —— 63
    2.3   A man with a mission: Richard Plant and transatlantic gay historiography —— 71
    2.4   Pink Triangles against the grain: Lesbian symbolism and memory —— 79
    2.5   From narratives to the streets —— 84

3 A badge of memory – Defining and remembering victimhood in the queer Atlantic —— 86
    3.1   Americanizing and globalizing the Holocaust —— 88
    3.2   Remembering the injury —— 95
    3.3   Pink Triangle injuries, Pink Triangle warnings —— 103

4 A badge of inclusion – Carving Pink Triangles into stone and shaping the queer subject —— 106
    4.1   Of triangles and reliefs —— 108
    4.2   Seeking justice for the community: Working out trauma at the site of injury —— 114
    4.3   Getting a seat at the table: Transatlantic official Holocaust memory and queer activism —— 125
    4.4   Same triangles, different triangles: Transatlantic inclusions —— 132
    4.5   The cohesive potential of the triangle —— 135

5 A badge of exclusion – Pink Triangle frameworks and the limits of collective memory —— 137
    5.1   The men without the Pink Triangle —— 139
    5.2   The men not just wearing the Pink Triangle —— 144
    5.3   The women with[out] the Pink Triangle? —— 148
    5.4   Memory with or without solidarity —— 156

6 A badge of universalization – Pink Triangles and the limits of Euro-American queer suffering —— 158
    6.1   Carving Pink Triangles in Schöneberg —— 159
    6.2   Patent of nobility: The International Lesbian and Gay Association and the universalization of suffering —— 165
    6.3   Pink Triangles against homophobia: International victimization in official political memorialization —— 174

7 A badge of survival – AIDS activism, Pink Triangles, and an aesthetic of injury —— 181
    7.1   Act up! coalitions, direct action and emancipation —— 186
    7.2   AIDS activism and international knowledge transfers —— 189
    7.3   A queer trivialization of genocide? Dystopian visions of an epidemic —— 197
    7.4   Still a badge of survival —— 208

8 A badge of temporalities – European time and asynchronous Pink Triangle modernities —— 211
     8.1   Looking back at whiteness in the Euro-American world —— 214
     8.2   A badge of European modernity? —— 218
     8.3   A badge of homosynchronism —— 221
     8.4   Different timelines, same triangle —— 225

9 A badge of visibility – Branding Pink Triangles for emancipation —— 229
     9.1   Branding Pink Triangle bridges: Capitalism —— 231
     9.2   Pictorial agency —— 236
     9.3   The potential of objects —— 239

Epilogue – The Pink Triangle in homonationalist times —— 243
     10.1   Many Pink Triangles —— 244
     10.2   Memory culture and victimhood in the transatlantic world —— 246
     10.3   A visual history of the Pink Triangle —— 248
     10.4   Global queer history and provincialized gayness —— 249
     10.5   Beyond homonationalist triangles? Beyond the rainbow? —— 251

Bibliography —— 257

Index —— 279

List of abbreviations

ACT UP	AIDS Coalition to Unleash Power
AHA	*Allgemeine Homosexuelle Arbeitsgemeinschaft e. V* (General Working Group for the Homosexual Community)
AHB	*Arbeitsgruppe Homosexualität Braunschweig* (Working Group Homosexuality Brunswick)
CBST	*Congregation Beit/Beth Simchat Torah*
CDU	*Christlich Demokratische Union Deutschlands* (Christian Democratic Union of Germany)
CID	*Comité International de Dachau* (International Dachau Committee)
CSU	*Christlich-Soziale Union in Bayern e. V.* (Christian Social Union in Bavaria)
FDP	*Freie Demokratische Partei Deutschlands* (Free Democratic Party of Germany)
FRG	Federal Republic of Germany
GLF	Gay Liberation Front (of Cologne)
GDR	German Democratic Republic
HAW	*Homosexuelle Aktion Westberlin* (Homosexual Action West Berlin)
HOSI Wien/ HOSI Linz	*Homosexuelle Initiative Wien/Linz* (Homosexual Initiative Vienna/Linz)
HuK	*Ökumenische Arbeitsgruppe Homosexuelle und Kirche e.V* (Ecumenical Working Group on Homosexuals and the Church)
ILGA	International Lesbian and Gay Association
PDS	*Partei des Demokratischen Sozialismus* (Party of Democratic Socialism)
SA	*Sturmabteilung* ('Storm Detachment,' paramilitary organization of the Nazi Party)
SAK	*Schwule Aktion Köln* (Gay Action Cologne)
SPD	*Sozialdemokratische Partei Deutschlands* (Social Democratic Party of Germany)
SS	*Schutzstaffel* ('Protection Squadron,' paramilitary organization of the Nazi Party)
TBP	The Body Politic
USHMM	The United States Holocaust Memorial Museum
VSG	*Verein für sexuelle Gleichberechtigung* (Association for sexual equality)
VVN	*Vereinigung der Verfolgten des Naziregimes* (Association of the Persecutees of the Nazi Regime)

List of figures

Figure 1 The Dachau so-called 'Triangle Relief' in 2018. Photo taken by the author —— **110**
Figure 2 The Pink Triangle memorial stone on the so-called 'Wailling Wall' of the former concentration camp of Mauthausen in 2019. Photo taken by the author —— **116**
Figure 3 The Pink Triangle memorial stone in Dachau in 2018. Photo taken by the author —— **121**
Figure 4 The Pink Triangle monument at Nollendorfplatz in the Berlin borough of Schöneberg in 2023. Photo taken by the author —— **157**
Figure 5 Two different views of the Pink Triangle monument in Cologne in 2017. Photos taken by the author —— **162**
Figure 6 "SILENCE = DEATH Poster," New York Manuscripts and Archives Division, NYPL Digital Collection, accessed November 1, 2022, http//digitalcollections.nypl.org/items/510d47e3-3ec0-a3d9-e040-e00a18064a99/ —— **203**

Introduction – There and back again: A Pink Triangle's journey

While sitting in an MA seminar on the West German history of homosexualities almost a decade ago at *Freie Universität Berlin*, I took part in a vehement debate on the uses of a symbol beloved by many members of the queer community in North America: the Pink Triangle. Originally used by the Nazis to brand non-heteronormative men – or men deemed to be non-heteronormative – in death and concentration camps, the Pink Triangle was later recuperated in the long postwar era for various emancipatory purposes in Europe, North America, and Australia. Now in a seminar room in the Berlin borough of Dahlem, I could still picture myself a decade earlier, at the height of puberty, unveiling a poster in my bedroom with the symbol plastered on its center. The poetry behind the gesture is not lost on me nowadays, but after years of hiding the poster in my closet, I was ready to hang it beside my bed.

Uncomfortably deskbound years later, the dismissal of my defence of the Pink Triangle by my peers similarly marked me out, this time as a migrant and as a political activist. I was part of a group of about 20 students discussing a text by James Steakley on the exaggeration of a presupposed Homocaust: the now debunked idea that the Nazi persecutions of queer men had been more important than the Shoah.[1] As one of the only non-German nationals in the room, I was opposed by a group of German students who fervently condemned all uses of the Pink Triangle in queer activist circles, going as far as to consider its recuperation as a form of trivialization of Nazi atrocities, and even as a relativization of the genocide of the European Jewry.[2]

---

[1] James D. Steakley, "Selbstkritische Gedanken zur Mythologisierung der Homosexuellenverfolgung im Dritten Reich." In *Nationalsozialistischer Terror gegen Homosexuelle: Verdrängt und Ungesühnt*, ed. Burkhard Jellonek and Rüdiger Lautmann (Padeborn: Verlag Ferdinand Schöningh, 2002), 55–68. Massimo Consoli coined the term 'Homocaust' in 1981 and published his own book discussing the idea in the 1990s. See: Massimo Consoli, *Homocaust* (Milan: Kaos, 1991). For more on the topic see Jake W. Newsome, *Pink Triangle Legacies: Coming out in the Shadow of the Holocaust* (Ithaca, NY: Cornell University Press, 2022). In this book I use the term 'Homocaust' analytically to refer a long list of narratives representing the Nazi persecutions of queerness as a genocide, comparing the regime's queerphobia with its antisemitism, falsely equating the Shoah with queerphobic atrocities.

[2] Throughout this book, I exclusively use the term Holocaust when discussing the Shoah, the Nazi genocide targeting European Jews. I do so while acknowledging that experts have discussed the need to understand the complexification of violence behind the Holocaust, and also focus on other entangled forms of violence of the era. As this book deals with concurring discourses of

The experience scorched me – I could clearly remember the provocative writings of queer Jewish men I used to devour during my undergraduate years in Canada and the Pink Triangle on the walls of the queer organizations I used to campaign with. These associations had helped me find a place in a heteronormative world. Surely, I thought, they could not be deserving of all these criticisms? I remained there aghast, hearing about how "we" North Americans were "in the wrong." Yet I also tried somewhat to understand the position of my fellow students in Dahlem. I just could not paint the situation to be so black and white.

Assuredly, the history of the Pink Triangle could not be boiled down to a dichotomy between so-called good or bad usages of history. I knew that a collective memory of National Socialism was different on both sides of the Atlantic. Was the Pink Triangle on the walls of the queer committee at the *Cégep du Vieux Montréal*[3] the same as the one worn by victims of the Nazis? Was the separation of national histories of queerness really a useful framework to understand the journey of a symbol now that it seemed to be so global? And most importantly, how did this symbol of fascist queerphobia make its way across space and time to become a visual statement of queer identity?

The Pink Triangle appeals to individuals as a statement about the historicization of queerness. Compared to the rainbow flag, or other known symbols of queer history connected to the feeling of pride, the triangle appeals to negative episodes of history, legitimizing struggles in the present by looking at a past of injury, of violence, and of suffering. Both the rainbow flag and the Pink Triangle are symbols of temporality, of a before and after. However, the Triangle does not necessarily mark the transformation of shame into a proud coming-out narrative. Instead, it ascertains struggles in the present, looking at the past, imagining the future.

Although much more prevalent at the end of the twentieth century, the symbol is still used by organizations in the Euro-American world – where it once dominated – but also on a more extended scale beyond the Atlantic.[4]

---

victimhood and memory debates in the second part of the twentieth century, I do this for clarity to distinguish between the Holocaust and other persecutions and genocides committed by the Nazis: the Porajmos, queer persecutions, etc. For a recent discussion on the complexification of violence, see Michael Wildt, "Was heißt: Singularität des Holocaust?," *Zeithistorische Forschungen/Studies in Contemporary History* 19, no. 1 (2022): 128–147.

3 In the Canadian province of Quebec, a CÉGEP – *Collège d'enseignement général et professionnel* – is a public educational institution where the first level of higher education between high school and university is provided.

4 See for example the official logo of the Australian Queer Archives in Melbourne (AQuA): "About us," Australian Queer Archives, accessed January 16, 2023, https://alga.org.au/about-us.

The use of the Pink Triangle is also still alive and well in the academic world. During the last weekend of June 2019, as Europe and North America were celebrating the fiftieth anniversary of the Stonewall uprising in New York, one of the founding myths of queer liberation, the *Haus der Kulturen der Welt*, 'House of the Cultures of the World,' and the *Magnus Hirschfeld Gesellschaft*, 'Magnus Hirschfeld Society,' were hosting the *Archives, Libraries, Museums and Special Collections Conference* in Berlin, focusing on the thematic of queer memory and exploring "the potential of generating audiences for queer archives, libraries, museums and special collections, with a special focus on the arts and artistic interventions."[5]

By hosting the conference in the German capital, the conveners were also putting forward an additional narrative to the events in New York. Indeed, they were offering a German extension to World Pride; they connected the event with the centenary of Magnus Hirschfeld's *Institut für Sexualwissenschaft*, 'Institute for the Science of Sexuality,' destroyed by the National Socialists in 1933, which used to stand on the location of the *Haus der Kulturen der Welt*.[6] By linking Stonewall to Berlin, the conference metanarrative anchored queer activism between the emancipation of the east coast of the United States in the second part of the twentieth century and the early emancipation of queerness in *fin de siècle* Berlin and its destruction by the Nazis. As I show in this book, this entanglement and universalization of German-US American queer history is the basis of most of the historical awareness expressed by queer activists in the second part of the twentieth century, a historical narrative bringing its own inclusions and exclusions.[7]

The conference's waltz between US American and German queer history was not the only entanglement between this book, Euro-American queer liberation, and National Socialism. Between interesting panels, networking, and new promising research, I was able to sit down and interrogate some of my international colleagues walking through the space with a pink triangular brooch secured on their outfits. Coming from cities such as Copenhagen or Melbourne, many of these white cis gay men told me how they were wearing it as a badge in order to remind everyone present at the conference of the radical potential of queer history. Sitting around a table and presenting my analysis of the symbol as a vector of

---

[5] See the official press communiqué of the *Schwules Museum* 'Gay Museum' in Berlin: "ALMS Conference Berlin," accessed January 16, 2023, https://www.schwulesmuseum.de/presseaktuell/alms-conference-berlin-2019/?lang=en.

[6] Rainer Herrn, *Der Liebe und dem Leid: Das Institut für Sexualwissenschaft 1919–1933*. (Berlin: Suhrkamp, 2022); Laurie Marhoefer, *Sex and the Weimar Republic: German Homosexual Emancipation and the Rise of the Nazis*. (Toronto, ON: University of Toronto Press, 2015).

[7] For a good example of this German–centric history of homosexuality, see Robert Beachy, *Gay Berlin: Birthplace of a Modern Identity* (New York, NY: Alfred A. Knopf, 2014).

identity for gay men and other members of the queer community in the Euro-American world, I could not help but search for further explanations for the ubiquity of the Pink Triangle. Were the men talking to me all wearing the same triangle, saying the same thing? Were they using the same triangle as the one forced upon the men in the camps? Was it possible – is it possible – to disentangle all the various layers of history and of memory attached to one symbol? All in all, was the Pink Triangle a vector of historical change or is it its indicator?

A Badge of Injury aims to answer some of these questions. It maps the Pink Triangle's transatlantic voyage and identifies the various paths followed by this symbol at the crossroads of memory studies, queer theory, and a transregional history of queerness. Thus, it intersects queer temporalities, queer history, and queer memory. It studies the ways in which the Pink Triangle became a symbol of historical awareness, but also how its uses conceptualized, framed, and universalized Euro-American forms of queerness. It reflects on the importance of National Socialism for queer utopianism. It analyses the Pink Triangle's dialectical journey across the Atlantic to demonstrate the link between emancipation and victimhood. In so doing, it simultaneously sheds light on the way the symbol has influenced discursive exclusions in the queer present, that is, tensions and power asymmetries between cis gay men and other members of what is commonly referred to as the queer community.

What can a study of the key moments of a symbol like the Pink Triangle tell us about the intersection of temporalities and memory studies? *A Badge of Injury* argues that transatlantic entanglements of a queer memory culture of National Socialism and a circulation of knowledge in the queer transatlantic press forged modern queer readings of the long postwar era, anchoring queer politics in narratives of victimhood. Consequently, a dialectical exchange on both continents paved the way for a visual culture based on tropes of survival. This visual culture is intrinsically linked to the Pink Triangle, is not necessarily based on historical facts, and played an important role in constructing the queer subject and its relationship to the writing of queer history. In other words, *A Badge of Injury* argues that by looking at the formation of a collective memory of Nazi persecutions as they were – and are – remembered in the Euro-American world, it is possible to identify how the adoption of one dominating historical narrative influenced the historicization of queerness.

By investigating the functions of the Pink Triangle for queer collective memory, this book establishes the important and active roles of images in the construction of historical narratives, revealing how social movements are influenced beyond the textual, and how they use visuals to frame their past, consider their present, and imagine their future. Simply put, the Pink Triangle started its journey as an icon, being simultaneously used as an instrument on both sides of the

Atlantic, especially in the Federal Republic of Germany (FRG) and the United States of America. These uses of the icon were accompanied by new understandings of the queer self, pushed internationally, and contributed to the erasure of other forms of queerness. Studying visuals is therefore not only necessary to identify historical change, but also to understand how visual concepts manifest and influence historical change.

1 The visual history of the Pink Triangle

The Pink Triangle is an interesting case study of the possibility of using images and symbols as third idioms to map the circulation of memory and knowledge. *A Badge of Injury* offers a new perspective on queer history by looking at global conceptual history and by also going beyond the textual. It exposes how looking at visual concepts, in this case the Pink Triangle, historians can synchronically and diachronically analyze the intellectual history of social movements, mapping transfers of ideas while drawing from various semantic fields in multiple languages.[8]

Throughout the various chapters, I demonstrate how images carry numerous layers that survive over time and how they offer ways to represent a multitude of narratives.[9] Through a plurality of case studies, the three parts of the book show how political symbols such as the Pink Triangle can represent a particular discourse, but also how a symbol's various layers and significations can be received

---

[8] Martin Fuchs, "Reaching out or Nobody Exists in One Context Only Society as Translation." *Translation Studies* 2, no. 1 (2009): 21–40; Dorna Safaian and Susanne Regener, "Lebenswelten als Protest. Fotografische Praktiken der deutschen und dänischen Schwulenbewegung seit den 1970er Jahren." *Beiträge zur Geschichte und Ästhetik der Fotografie* 39, no. 154 (2019): 15–24; Dorna Safaian, "Why Images? The Role of Visual Media in Protest Movement Research", *History | Sexuality | Law*, 13/10/2019, accessed January 16, 2023, https://hsl.hypotheses.org/995.

[9] Sébastien Tremblay. "Der Rosa Winkel: Vielschichtige Symbolik und Erinnerung in der Schwulenbewegung beiderseits des Atlantiks / The Pink Triangle: Multilayered Symbolism and Memory in the Queer Atlantic." In *Queer Lives 1900–1950*, ed. Karolina Kühn and Mirjam Zadoff (Munich: Hirmer Verlag, 2023), 328–341. The use of visuals and the history of sexuality has a long tradition. See for example Katie Sutton, "Sexology's Photographic Turn: Visualizing Trans Identity in Interwar Germany." *Journal of the History of Sexuality* 27, no. 3 (2018): 442–479; Jennifer Evans, "Seeing Subjectivity: Erotic Photography and the Optics of Desire." *American Historical Review* 118, no. 2 (2013), 430–462. On the importance of pornography and erotica for queer history, see Jonas Nesselbauf, "Was Sie schon immer über Pornographie wissen wollten, aber nie zu fragen wagten: Eine Annäherung in sechs Schritten." In *Ästhetik(en) der Pornographie: Darstellungen von Sexualitäten im Medienvergleich*, ed. Norbert Lennartz and Jonas Nesselbauf (Baden-Baden: Nomos, 2021), 9.

plurally and intersectionally according to context, space, and time. Some have called this kind of analysis the "agency of images";[10] this book explains how this is also a form of conceptual interpretation triggered by the senses.[11]

A *Badge of Injury* ascertains the necessity of considering and researching visual concepts to understand discourses existing simultaneously, side-by-side at the core of historical narratives shared by social movements. For instance, some German gay historians still pretend that lesbian women are falsifying history by appealing to the structural Nazi oppression of queers.[12] The book argues that the materiality of images lies at the core of these controversies. Instead of adding new case studies to the research on other queer experiences of German fascism, it follows the path of visual intellectual history, deconstructing the claims of recent gay scholarship and gay historiography, and underlining the materiality of the Pink Triangle – that is to say, the tension between its history and mythology circulating in activist circles. Moreover, its visual history exposes gay and lesbian historiographies, showing not only how the Pink Triangle became a symbol of legitimization and memory, but how its adoption influenced the building of tensions inside queer communities. In this regard, *A Badge of Injury* avoids lionizing queer liberation and many recuperations of the symbol, yet also refrains from endlessly discussing the ethics of its usage.[13]

2 Global queer history

The journey of the Pink Triangle is a transregional story with entanglements on many continents and repercussions across the world. Following its journey across the Atlantic, *A Badge of Injury* opens a much-needed dialogue between queer history and global history. Through various case studies, it not only shows how diffi-

---

10 Alfred Gell, *Art and Agency: An Anthropological Theory* (Oxford: Clarendon Press, 2007).
11 I was inspired by recent research on visual conceptual history: Margrit Pernau and Imke Rajamani, "Emotional Translations: Conceptual History Beyond Language." *History and Theory* 55 (February 2016): 46–65.
12 Alexander Zinn uses an alarmist tone and denounces as unscientific and ideological the alleged dangers of opening categories of analysis. Alexander Zinn, "Gefühlte Wahrheiten: Wie LGBTI-Aktivismus die Wissenschaftsfreiheit bedroht." In *Wissenschaftsfreiheit: Warum dieses Grundrecht zunehmend umkämpft ist*, ed. Sandra Kostner (Baden-Baden: Nomos, 2022), 165–182.
13 The focus of this project was not an ethical analysis of the various recuperations of the Pink Triangle or of the ways comparisons between the Nazi persecution of queerness and other Nazi atrocities were discussed on both sides of the Atlantic. These would be fascinating conversations and are beyond the scope of this book.

cult it is to disentangle the Pink Triangle from its transatlantic voyage but also how various national actors were part of a transregional conversation on the symbol, influencing the construction of memory on both sides of the ocean. This back and forth between local gay and lesbian communities moulded both a cultural memory of National Socialism and a basis for the imposition of Euro-American narratives on the world stage, for example, in international organizations.

Consequently, *A Badge of Injury* underlines the problem of writing national queer histories without considering a transregional transfer of ideas. Emphasizing how local or national contexts are still relevant to the interpretation of discourses and symbols, it also maintains that these national contexts cannot be isolated. The following chapters remind us that it is necessary to go beyond the nation-state and take broader communication networks into consideration, especially while writing a queer history establishing the fluidity of identities and memory. For instance, I emphasize the shared assumptions of transnational AIDS activism in the FRG and the United States in chapter seven, at the same time analyzing its diverse national manifestations and the way in which they interacted with local contexts.

In order to analyze the journeys of an icon and intertwine its key moments, I have limited the scope of this project to the Euro-American world, to Western European democracies and the east and west coasts of North America.[14] The narratives offered in this book therefore need to be balanced and pitched against other

---

14 With brief excursions on the outskirts of the northern Atlantic in Israel, Uruguay, etc. Atlantic/Euro-American history has a rich historiography. My cartography of the northern parts of the transatlantic world, that is, connections between North America and Europe as broader cultural spheres of influence, was inspired by my lecture of: Alison Games, "Beyond the Atlantic: English Globetrotters and Transoceanic Connections." *The William and Mary Quarterly* 63, no. 4 (2006): 675–692; Jessie Labov, *Transatlantic Central Europe: Contesting Geography and Redefining Culture Beyond the Nation* (Budapest: Central European University Press, 2019); Mireille Rosello and Sudeep Dasgupta, "Introduction Queer and Europe: An Encounter." In *What's Queer About Europe? Productive Encounters and Re–Enchanting Paradigms*, ed. Mireille Rosello and Sudeep Dasgupta (New York, NY: Fordham University Press, 2014). Julia Straub, "Introduction: Transatlantic North American Studies," in *Handbook of Transatlantic North American Studies*, ed. Julia Straub (Berlin: De Gruyter, 2016); Omise'eke Natasha Tinsley, "Black Atlantic, Queer Atlantic: Queer Imaginings of the Middle Passage." *GLQ: A Journal of Lesbian and Gay Studies* 14, no. 2–3 (2008): 191–215; Jerry H. Bentley, "One Regional Histories, Global Processes, Cross-Cultural Interactions." In *Interactions: Transregional Perspectives on World History*, ed. Jerry H. Bentley, Renate Bridenthal and Anand A. Yang (Honolulu, HI: University of Hawai'i Press, 2005), 1–13; Martin W. Lewis and Kären E. Wigen, *The Myth of Continents. A Critique of Metageography*. Berkeley, CA: University of California Press, 1997.

less canonical spaces, including the Midwest, the southern parts of the United States, and the Canadian prairies. The same can be said about Europe, where, as with North America, I focus on largely populated areas, namely big cities such as Berlin, Cologne, Frankfurt (Main), Munich, Paris, and Amsterdam.[15] It is therefore essential to consider this study as a transregional or translocal examination in a global perspective and not as a story between nations or a world history of the Pink Triangle as a symbol. This is partly due to space, but also because these numerous regional foci tend to entwine local, national, and international aspects. Each national discourse present in this context influenced actors at play, but I concentrate the inquiry on activist discourses and the circulation of knowledge produced by grassroots organizations and civil actors, not necessarily on the level of the state.

My story of the Pink Triangle is still a contribution to global history. Breaking free from diffusionist models of queer history, *A Badge of Injury* moves further from the idea that world history consists of national moments exported to elsewhere in the world. Echoing my reflections on the conference in 2019 at *Haus der Kulturen der Welt*, it is an answer to German-centrist narratives or North American diffusionist models. It is part of a new endeavor to assess in-betweens and transregional entanglements, identifying global or transnational moments in history.[16] As many before me have shown, global history is not *per se* a history written on the global scale, but an analysis of entanglements that underlines how national or regional contexts are not independent from each other but are actually embedded spaces of contact.[17] It is also an inquiry into discussions happening on the world stage, an investigation of in-betweens and international brokers, and a focus on connections and disconnections. All these aspects are at the core of *A Badge of Injury*.

---

15 As previously mentioned, Australia will need to be added to the equation in a future project as the Pink Triangle is still widely being used 'down under.' Similarly to the whiteness of this story, I decided to focus on spaces already touched upon to deconstruct the narrative, allowing me to dig deeper in the material and show the 'provinciality' of dominant actors and voices.
16 It is following other monographs going in the same directions: Tiffany N. Florvil, *Mobilizing Black Germany. Afro-German Women and the Making of a Transnational Movement* (Champaign, IL: University of Illinois Press, 2020).
17 Sebastian Conrad, *What is Global History* (Princeton,NJ: Princeton University Press, 2016).

3 Nazi atrocities and the Pink Triangle

The Nazi regime was not always consequent in its view on sexuality yet moved fast against queer individuals.[18] This took many forms, including the execution of Ernst Röhm, a close ally of Hitler but known to be a queer man.[19] The regime also closed, sacked, and burned the *Institut für Sexualwissenschaft*. The institute's archives and papers, the world's largest collection of work on sexualities at the time, were burned in 1933 on the *Opernplatz* (now *Bebelpatz*) in the center of Berlin under the encouragement of Joseph Goebbels and ecstatic students.

National Socialism's persecution of non-heteronormativity did not stop at book burning and destroying renowned research on homosexualities and trans* studies. §175 StGB – part of the German penal code that criminalized male non-heteronormative sexualities – precedes the Nazi Party and finds its origins in the adoption of Prussian Law by the German Empire following German unification in 1871.[20] However, the Nazis' seizure of power remains an unequivocal milestone in the history of persecution of male-male sexualities in Germany.

For the Nazis, male-male sexuality was considered on the same level as venereal diseases.[21] Seen as an affliction, it could be treated; it could be violently forced out of German men. Consequently, it also meant that the *Volksgemeinschaft*, 'the people's community,'[22] allegedly needed protection from the dangers of such a so-called infection. Nazi officials modified the law in June 1935, extending the definition of an act of intercourse or anal sex "contrary to nature" to encompass an act of simple lewdness between two men.[23] Moreover, this newly reinforced law considered an attack on "society's general sense of shame" or the intention of debauchery as a felony. Queer men were then harassed, surveilled, and persecuted, based on lists compiled during the Weimar era or following de-

---

18 Dagmar Herzog, *Sex after Fascism: Memory and Morality in Twentieth-Century Germany* (Princeton, NJ: Princeton University Press, 2005).
19 Michael Schwartz, "'Herrschaft der Homosexuellen': Die Röhm–Skandale 1932 und 1934 als öffentliche Provokation." In *Homosexuelle, Seilschaften, Verrat*, ed. Michael Schwartz (Oldenbourg: De Gruyter Oldenbourg, 2019), 160–211.
20 Jens Dobler, *Wie öffentliche Moral gemacht wird: Die Einführung des § 175 in das Strafgesetzbuch 1871*, Queer Lectures 14 (Berlin: Initiative Queer Nations, 2014). Clayton J. Whisnant, *Queer Identities and Politics in Germany: A History 1880–1945* (New York, NY: Harrington Park Press, 2016).
21 Herzog, *Sex after Fascism*, 35.
22 This word is inseparable from its Nazi connotation.
23 Susanne zur Nieden, "Der homosexuelle Staatsfeind: Zur Radikalisierung eines Feindbildes im NS." In *Homophobie und Devianz: Weibliche und männliche Homosexualität im* Nationalsozialismus, ed. Insa Eschebach, (Berlin: Metropol, 2012), 23–34.

nunciations by their fellow citizens. Thousands of them were deported in concentration camps where they were often branded with a pink triangle stitched on their uniforms.

In Austria, queer women were also persecuted under a different part of the penal code.[24] If they were not legally persecuted in Germany, the historiography of the last decades has demonstrated how women desiring women were also structurally oppressed, living in fear and in hiding, and often labelled as "antisocial" elements of society.[25]

Same-sex sexualities were not the only aspect of queerness to be persecuted by the regime. Recent research has shown how trans* men and women were also the target of Nazi heteropatriarchy.[26] It is therefore more accurate to discuss the persecution of queerness as a whole and not only focus on juridical categories created by the perpetrators.[27] As the history of the Pink Triangle highlights and as I will attest in this book, this tension between an analysis of the structures of violence and cases anchored in the perpetrator's vision is at the center of historiographical debates raging to this day, where certain scholars wrongfully dismiss lesbian and trans* suffering during the era, clinging to §175 StGB as a sort of *sine qua non* for victimhood.[28]

---

[24] Johann Karl Kirchknopf, "Die strafrechtliche Verfolgung homosexueller Handlungen in Österreich im 20. Jahrhundert." *Zeitgeschichte* 43, no. 2 (2016): 68–84; Jens Dobler, "Unzucht und Kuppelei: Lesbenverfolgung im Nationalsozialismus." In *Homophobie und Devianz: Weibliche und männliche Homosexualität im* Nationalsozialismus, ed. Insa Eschebach, (Berlin: Metropol, 2012), 53–62.

[25] Laurie Marhoefer, "Lesbianism, Transvestitism, and the Nazi State: A Microhistory of a Gestapo Investigation, 1939–1943," *The American Historical Review* 121, no. 4 (2016): 1167–1195; Samuel Clowes Huneke, "Heterogeneous Persecution: Lesbianism and the Nazi State," *Central European History* 54 (2021): 297–325.

[26] Zavier Nunn, "Trans Liminality and the Nazi State," *Past & Present* 260, no. 1 (2023):123–157; "Transgender Experiences in Weimar and Nazi Germany, with Dr. Anna Hájková, Dr. Katie Sutton, Dr. Bodie A. Ashton, and Rabbi Marisa Elana James, Museum of Jewish Heritage—A Living Memorial to the Holocaust", accessed January 16, 2023, https://mjhnyc.org/events/transgender-experiences-in-weimar-and-nazi-germany/.

[27] As we will see, this is a main bone of contention in recent historiographical debates.

[28] Alexander Zinn, "Der Hang zu Opfererzählungen. Über Dramatisierung und selektive Wahrnehmung in Geschichtsschreibung und Erinnerungskultur zu Homosexuellen während der NS-Zeit," *Revue d'Allemagne et des pays de langue allemande* 53, no. 2 (2021): 331–346.

4 Queering gay history

A Badge of Injury not only looks at power asymmetries between communities, but also within one community. Taking the story of a historically gay symbol and deconstructing it enables an investigation of the Pink Triangle's potential to erase other identities. Exposing the hegemonic aspects of gay remains a fundamentally queer project; it nuances the idea that gay is a synonym for other non-heteronormative experiences. This book is correspondingly a contribution to queer theory, mapping the cultural construction of gay, demonstrating its formation outside of biology as a socio-cultural and fluid aspect of other structures of desires. It demonstrates the prevalence of gay power structures in queer circles and how the emphasis put on aspects of the triangle's journey contributed to the imposition of a gay framework on other experiences and realities.

Going beyond binaries of two sexes, two genders, and two possible structures of desires, this book understands queerness as a web where all aspects of desires and sexualities, including the hegemony that is heteronormativity, are interrelated to each other and are fluid. In this sense, the Pink Triangle as a symbol of queerness is entwined in the same web; it can appeal to many categories simultaneously in one context and exclude others in another moment. It is a fundamental queer symbol, but it is also in direct or indirect connection to the heteromatrix.[29]

If some have critically assessed the use of LGBTQIA+[30] as a broader umbrella of categories politically and historically put together, I maintain that its

---

[29] A term borrowed from Butler, it defines the norms and framing of heterosexuality as a natural constant, enclosing human relations, but portrayed, if named at all, outside given structures. In other words, everyone is deemed heteronormative until proven otherwise. For example, if I come out as gay, I am automatically put in relation with heterosexuality, and if I decide to hide, omit or refuse to mention my desire, I will be deemed heteronormative. See Judith Butler, *Gender Trouble: Feminism and the Subversion of Identity* (New York, NY: Routledge, 1990). The uses of the Pink Triangle by activists in the 1970s – as explored in section 1.4 – is another perfect example of this matrix.

[30] Meaning Lesbian, Gay, Bi, Trans*, Queer/Questioning, Inter* and Asexual / Aromantic. The + stands for other possibilities beyond the terms usually banded together. In the North American context, I would have added 2S for Two-spirit, a pan-indigenous term used to include indigenous conceptions of gender and sexuality beyond the spectrum of settler colonialism. As I am not focusing on indigenous struggles or activism, I have refrained from performatively including the 2S in the acronym. Readers are encouraged to read about the topic: Evelyn Blackwood, "Native American Genders and Sexualities: Beyond Anthropological Models and Misrepresentations." In *Two-Spirit People: Native American Gender Identity, Sexuality, and Spirituality*, ed. Sue-Ellen Jacobs, Wesley Thomas, and Sabine Lang, (Champaign, IL: University of Illinois Press, 2005), 284–296.

potential is still relevant and goes beyond a so-called alphabet soup.³¹ Indeed, the radical prospect of such an acronym allows us to visually interconnect the self-consciousness of diverse experiences. It is then possible to almost mathematically rearrange oneself inside a community in multiple possible manners, permanently constructing oneself as a subject along the way.³²

Following this idea of fluidity, the Q in LGBTQIA+ is tendentious; it becomes an in-between of both gender and sexuality.³³ Simply put, the Q is not another add-on to LGBTQIA+, but a reminder that identity as a concept is not static. Queer theory provocatively brings us in murky waters between the queering of history, and the historical recuperation of an insult. Queer is there to disrupt a glossy narrative of gay, lesbian, or homosexual history.

In her suggestion and project to queer German history, Jennifer Evans reminds us that queer history is not about bringing more people in, but about reviewing the constructivist aspect of identities.³⁴ Gay history enabled gay historians to find themselves in the past, but a queer approach understands the multifaceted potential of trying to re-imagine the past in the present and traces the processes and disruptions of identity construction. In other words, queerness allows an interpretation of primary sources in a time preceding the invention of given categories that are now in use to define the non-heteronormative. The idea is not to pin down who was gay, lesbian, homophile, homosexualist, pervert, sodomite, or heretic; nor is it to connect famous or infamous individuals from the past together. Queer opens the discussion on the non-heteronormative past, including heteronormative desires, and draws connections between histories of silence, persecutions, sex, identifications, labels, etc.

Consequently, *A Badge of Injury* uses queer as an analytical concept to identify non-heteronormative structures of desires and sexualities without having to pinpoint categories of analysis in the past and while trying to remain fluid. Throughout the book, I use 'gay' and 'lesbian' when quoting sources in their verbatim or when the political aspects of gay or lesbian has significance. This is also

---

31 The idea to drop all letters to adopt a "queer identity," erasing trans* or gender non-binary experiences, has its adepts outside of academia and outside of Germany. See Jonathan Rauch, "It's Time to Drop the 'LGBT' from 'LGBTQ' the Case for a New Term That Describes All Sexual Minorities," *The Atlantic* (January & February 2019).
32 For example, presenting oneself as 'gay' or 'queer' depending on the political context and fluctuation of one's statement about sexuality. For a discussion of the dangers of blurring the lines in a German and political context, see Christopher Ewing and Sébastien Tremblay, "Zündstoffe," *Siegessäule* (October 2019): 12.
33 The Q in LGBTQIA+ can also stand for questioning, not just queer. The idea of questioning one's own sexuality also reflects a fluid understanding of sexualities and desires.
34 Jennifer V. Evans, "Why Queer German History?," *German History* 34, no. 3 Special Issue: Queering German History (2016): 371–384.

a question of historical empathy and the limitations of the archives. For instance, I cannot be sure how the men branded by the pink triangle in the camps imagined or defined their sexualities. Bisexuality, homosexuality, or heterosexuality are all historical constructions and so are political identities such as gay or lesbian. Writing queer history, these concepts are useful to categorize and contextualize. Nevertheless, using analytical concepts allow historians to critically assess the past and semantically link experiences together. Embracing the fluidity of queerness, I am using queer to investigate the past without assigning artificial identities to the historical actors at the center of this study if they remained silent about their sexualities themselves or in the archive.[35] I also use it as a category beyond usages of the past.

As chapter one will show, this is beneficial for historical analysis when various queer individuals defined themselves differently – homophile or gay – but embraced similar conceptions in their experience of queerness. Using queer analytically throughout the book is thus the opposite of an anachronism. To put it differently, individuals attracted to and having sexual intercourse with the opposite sex 300 years ago had no concept of 'heterosexuality.' This of course does not mean that what we consider heterosexual sexual relationships did not take place. In other words, like queer, heterosexual sex predates the invention of the concept of heterosexuality, but it does not mean that people in the past cannot be studied and analyzed under the scope of heterosexuality.[36]

5 Provincializing queer history

This aim to queer gay history and expose the construction of the category also goes together with another one of this book's main leitmotifs: to provincialize Euro-American gay history.[37] Understanding global networks and the transfer of ideas can help scholars assess power asymmetries between various iterations of queerness across the world. For instance, in the second part of this book I show

---

35 Elisa Heinrich also uses *Intimacy*. I understand her use of the concept as a queer impetus for historians. By making the different components of relationships fluid, intimacy allows historians to examine connections between activists beyond fixed categories of analysis. *Elisa Heinrich, Intim und respektabel. Homosexualität und Freundinnenschaft in der deutschen Frauenbewegung um 1900* (Göttingen: Vandenhoeck & Ruprecht, 2022), 16.
36 Heiko Stoff, "Heterosexualität." In *Was ist Homosexualität?*, ed. Florian Mildenberger, Jennifer Evans, Martin Lücke, Rüdiger Lautmann and Jakob Pastötter, (Hamburg: Männerschwarm, 2014), 73–104.
37 Margrit Pernau, "Provincializing Concepts: The Language of Transnational History." *Comparative Studies of South Asia, Africa and the Middle East* 36, no. 3 (2016): 483–499.

how the adoption of the Pink Triangle is linked to the importance given to Euro-American narratives in the writing of queer history. By mainly centering queer origin stories in "the west," European and North American scholarship has so far reproduced a very Eurocentric understanding of queer history. I confront these narratives at face value, uncovering their construction in the Euro-American world. This focus is both an invitation to rethink Euro-American queer history as just one aspect of the global history of non-heteronormative sexualities and of queerness, but also a way to look at Euro-American queer stories horizontally, without essentializing their importance for the rest of the world. By historicizing the Pink Triangle and its importance for most Euro-American gay narratives, the book marks Euro-American gay history as one aspect among many, uncovering the power structures that make this history seem universal. Similarly, the whiteness of this Euro-American journey can only be understood as a simultaneous erasure or silencing of Black and other racialized narratives of queerness inside and outside the Euro-American world. To decentralize it, historians need to confront its hyperreal aspects, its construction. In this book, I underline one facet of this construction.

If queer history intrinsically needs to find its global turn, global history would benefit from the deconstructive prospective of queer scholarship. Indeed, scholars like Samuel Moyn and Andrew Sartori remind us that "unveiling the violence implicit in conceptions of the global requires an investigation of the theoretical foundations of historical discourse and the recovery of other forms of temporality."[38] This is why the disruptive potential of queer is so interesting for this project. By investigating queerness, it is possible to reinterpret the importance of victimhood in the creation of gay. By looking at a gay past of injury – in this case National Socialism – as it happened or as it was remembered by queer activists in the long postwar era, it is possible to appreciate how queer activists (re)interpreted their situation in a heteronormative world. Here I am mainly thinking of the HIV/AIDS crisis, which I analyze in chapter seven and where connections to National Socialism resurfaced on both sides of the Atlantic. The Euro-American space at the centre of this research was chosen because it is the most discursively powerful one, chiefly connected to imperialism, the gaygeoisie, and homonationalism; discourses I try to understand in my own present. In other words, the story at the core of *A Badge of Injury* goes beyond the commemoration of the Nazi persecutions of queerness. A global understanding of queer and a queer understanding of global history allow us to focus on this mainly cis white gay journey and fill up silences.

---

[38] Samuel Moyn and Andrew Sartori, "Approaches to Global Intellectual History." In *Global Intellectual History*, ed. Samuel Moyn and Andrew Sartori (New York, NY: Columbia University Press, 2013), 19.

6 Memory and victimhood

The following nine chapters focus on the construction of Euro-American queer cis white male historical awareness, the creation of a queer Euro-American white collective based in Nazi atrocities, and its potential to exclude other forms of queerness. As this book highlights, in many cases the importance of the Nazi past was not always only factual but was also often a fantasy of atrocities that were not committed in the ways that they were imagined. Indeed, queer non-Jewish men put forward narratives with the help of the Pink Triangle that reproduced a latent antisemitic resentment during the second part of the twentieth century. The idea that other victims of German fascism had stolen the spotlight in the marketplace of memory evolved out of the idea that gay history had been hidden by the state and by scholarship. Looking at this cultural trauma and employing concepts such as postmemory, virtual experience, and adopted memory, it is possible to expose the reasons behind the appeal of Homocaust narratives for queer liberation in the 1970s and 1980s and the universalization of one definition of queerness in North America. This memory eventually led to an identification process where the queer – often gay – subject reimagined themself as a victim of fascism even if they had not experienced the camps like the men forced to wear the pink triangle.

This book is not an ethical analysis of these recuperations or comparisons. Instead, by using the Pink Triangle as a prism and by looking at the entanglements of all these perspectives and discourses about presupposed Homocaust narratives, it analyses the interrelated aspects of the construction of gay and lesbian identities in the Euro-American world. In the case of lesbians, the erasure of most of their story of persecution by some gay historians and activists enabled the partial adoption of another symbol connected to National Socialism, the Black Triangle, and historicized contemporary dismissals of the scholarship on the persecution of non-male non-heteronormative individuals during the Nazi dictatorship.

7 Feeling the Pink Triangle

The Pink Triangle is an interesting case study from a semantics vantage point, as it has been symbolic, iconic, and indexical through its various uses since the 1930s, especially in the 1970s to 1990s in both the FRG and North America, but also in various other places in the world. It is sometimes worn as a symbol of memory directly recalling the experience of concentration camp prisoners; as a badge connecting a present situation to the fate of said prisoners; or even as an international emblem legitimizing queer narratives that sometimes have something to do with the Holocaust or sometimes not at all. In this regard, I argue in this book that the Pink Triangle is an idea, a traveling concept. I not only look at the textual sources analyzing its multiple meanings, but also go further by narrating here its history, how it traveled in a pictorial form, and as an image.

It is possible to look at reactions to the use of the Pink Triangle – or the use in itself – and to understand not only how images affect experiences and bodily practices, but also commemorations and interpretations of the politics, identity, and the everyday life of queer activists in the FRG and the east and west coasts of North America.[39] Inspired by a pictorial or iconic turn in the writing of history, this book confirms that our relation to objects "is a two-way street in which it is impossible to distinguish where the agency lies."[40]

I maintain that images not only have their role to play in our material interpretation of the world, but also that our practices and our memories of said practices are all entangled.[41] Through sensual encounters with the Pink Triangle – seeing or touching Pink Triangles – we trigger experiences or cultural memories shared in a community. Scholars have also shown that these memories do not have to be connected to real experiences shared by the community, noting the power of so-called virtual experiences.[42] The first part of the book will dive into these debates, demonstrating how postmemories and prosthetic memories can be transmitted through images and influence our conceptions of the world.[43]

---

39 Jennifer Milam and Alan Maddox, "Visual and Aural Intellectual Histories: An Introduction," *Intellectual History Review* 27, no. 3 (2017): 285–298.
40 Keith Moxey, "Visual Studies and the Iconic Turn," *Journal of Visual Culture* 7, no. 2 (2008): 134. For the Pictorial turn: Gottfried Boehm, *Wie Bilder Sinn erzeugen: Die Macht des Zeigens* (Berlin: Berlin University Press, 2008); Gottfried Boehm and Sebastian Egenhofer, *Was ist ein Bild?: Antworten in Bildern: Gottfried Boehm Zum 70. Geburtstag* (München: Wilhelm Fink, 2012). W. J. T Mitchell, *Picture Theory: Essays on Verbal and Visual Representation* (Chicago, IL: University of Chicago Press, 1994); W. J. T. Mitchell, *What Do Pictures Want?: The Lives and Loves of Images* (Chicago, IL: University of Chicago Press, 2005); *Image Science: Iconology, Visual Culture, and Media Aesthetics* (Chicago, IL: University of Chicago Press, 2015); Gerhard Paul, *Bilder einer Diktatur: Zur Visual History des "Dritten Reiches"* (Göttingen: Wallstein, 2020).
41 Jeffrey Escoffier offered an interesting queering of visual culture in 2017, demonstrating how an analysis of gay porn could offer different narratives on our understanding of the HIV/AIDS crisis. See Jeffrey Escoffier, "Sex in the Seventies: Gay Porn Cinema as an Archive for the History of American Sexuality," *Journal of the History of Sexuality* 26, no. 1 (2017): 88–113.
42 Dominick LaCapra, *History in Transit: Experience, Identity, Critical Theory* (Ithaca, NY: Cornell University Press, 2004).
43 Marianne Hirsch, *The Generation of Postmemory: Writing and Visual Culture after the Holocaust* (New York, NY: Columbia University Press, 2012); Craig Griffiths touches on this aspect in the fourth chapter of his book on West German gay liberation. See Craig Griffiths, *The Ambiva-*

Which experiences can then be conjured by the Pink Triangle? How can multiple experiences be invoked at the same time but for different members of the queer community, for activists in the 1970s or in the 2000s, in Germany or in the United States of America, for those who did not survive the death or concentration camps of the Nazi regime?

In his analysis of Aby Warburg, Georges Didi-Huberman maintains that the Hamburger art historian's idea of *Nachleben*, 'survival,' is crucial to understand the multiple layers of meanings existing within a particular image.[44] These surviving layers, haunting, waiting, floating around visuals, are themselves triggered depending on who is gazing at them and/or interacting with them.[45] Through this connection between our senses and visuals, it is then possible to confront different surviving aspects of the Triangle's journey at different points in time, synchronically with people sharing the same perspective, but diachronically from others. As a result of writing this book, my reaction to Pink Triangle memorabilia, monuments, or mention in historical sources is different from other queer activists. This is not saying that my understanding is better, but that my vision encompasses more surviving layers, interacting with more of them simultaneously.

Contemporary uses of the symbol in monuments conflate the symbol of the Pink Triangle with other icons, confusing layers of meaning together. The 2017 monument for queer victims of the Nazi regime in the Bavarian capital of Munich is a good example, ahistorically mixing various symbols together in an iconological smorgasbord, pretending to include all members of the queer community

---

lence of Gay Liberation: Male Homosexual Politics in 1970s West Germany (Oxford: Oxford University Press, 2021).

44 Georges Didi-Huberman, *L'image survivante: Histoire de l'art et temps des fantômes selon Aby Warburg* (Paris: Les Éditions de Minuit, 2002). See also his *Remontages du temps subi. L'Œil de l'histoire* (Paris: Les Éditions de Minuit, 2010). The idea to use Didi-Huberman comes from the work by Milam and Maddox (see ft. 36). Yet, works on iconology and the sedimentation on time coming from the University of Bielefeld inspired this hybrid of Warburg, Didi-Huberman and Koselleck. See Hubert Locher et al., *Reinhart Koselleck und die politische Ikonologie: [Anlässlich der Tagung "Reinhart Koselleck (1923–2006) – Politische Ikonologie"* (Berlin: Deutscher Kunstverlag, 2013). Bettina Brandt, "Politik im Bild? Überlegungen zum Verhältnis von Begriff und Bild." In *Politik: Situationen eines Wortgebrauchs im Europa der Neuzeit*, ed. Wilibald Steinmetz (Frankfurt [Main]: Campus, 2007). Bettina Brandt, Britta Hochkirchen, and Thomas Thiel, *Reinhart Koselleck und das Bild. Begleitung Broschüre* (Herzebrock-Clarholz: Heinrich Eusterhus, 2018); Cornelia Zumbusch, *Wissenschaft in Bildern. Symbol und dialektisches Bild in Aby Warburgs Mnemosyne-Atlas und Walter Benjamins Passagen-Werk*. (Berlin: Akademie-Verlag, 2004).

45 The idea of a haunted history or the haunting of images would also be an alternative to Didi-Huberman's framework. See also: Ethan Kleinberg, *Haunting History: For a Deconstructive Approach to the Past, Meridian: Crossing Aesthetics* (Stanford, CA: Stanford University Press, 2017); Margrit Pernau, *Emotions and Temporalities* (Cambridge: Cambridge University Press, 2021).

with a rainbow motif, a Black Triangle, and a Pink Triangle. This *mélange* is not the death of meaning, but the creation of others, as bystanders are seeing all these symbols in relation to each other.

To identify and analyze these different layers and focus almost exclusively on the Pink Triangle, I am following the steps of Martin Kemp and his work on iconic pop culture images. As a specialist of Da Vinci's work and an expert on the Mona Lisa, Kemp traced not only a visual history but also a conceptual history of iconic images – Che Guevara, the Cross, the Stars and Stripes, etc.[46] By doing so, he not only looked at the "life histories of each iconic image" but at "the origin and most notable and curious steps along the course of their ascent."[47] Furthermore, he defines – although half-heartedly – an iconic image "as one that has achieved wholly exceptional levels of widespread recognizability and has come to carry a rich series of varied associations for very large numbers of people across time and cultures, such that it has to a greater or lesser degree transgressed the parameters of its initial making, function, context, and meaning."[48] Both aspects of his research apply to the Pink Triangle. In this book, I trace the key moments of the triangle's Euro-American multiple lives and include them in the various surviving meanings of the symbol. Only then am I able to connect the ensemble of these various meanings to the use of the symbol as a marker of collective memory and identify ways in which these transfers took place between the 1970s and the 2000s.

Concordantly, *A Badge of Injury's* methodology takes feelings, bodily senses, and the potential of change offered by concepts (both visual and textual) into consideration.[49] This approach is especially interesting for global history, adding a new layer to debates about translation beyond language. Indeed, by looking at visual languages and the transmission of concepts beyond the textual it is possible to semantically link the feelings and interpretations of various social groups who would not have understood each other linguistically. However, it also enables an analysis of power because visuals as a language also operate within hierarchies. Beyond offering a critical examination of queer discourses regarding the Pink Triangle, collective memory, and collective identity, I show how contextual bodily

---

[46] Martin Kemp, *Christ to Coke: How an Image Becomes an Icon* (Oxford: Oxford University Press, 2011).
[47] Kemp, *Christ to Coke*, 2.
[48] Kemp, *Christ to Coke*, 3.
[49] For a link between conceptual history and memory studies going in the same direction, please refer to Margrit Pernau and Sébastien Tremblay, "Dealing with an Ocean of Meaninglessness: Reinhart Koselleck's Lava Memories and Conceptual History," *Contribution to the History of Concepts* 15, no. 2 (2020): 7–28.

encounters with Pink Triangles trigger cultural practices and how the symbol influenced both memory and the construction of the queer subject. I then focus on the direct power structures systematically affecting the queer subject when it encounters the symbol and reflects on history and memory. Sara Ahmed has already shown how the body and its sensual encounters are inescapable for the queer subject.[50]

Therefore, *A Badge of Injury* demonstrates how contextual bodily encounters with Pink Triangles – as a symbol, as a monument, as an image, etc. – trigger cultural practices and ponders on how the Pink Triangle influences both memory and the construction of the queer subject. The various chapters focus on the direct power structures shaping the queer subject when it sees, touches, feels or hear about the symbol and its history. Borrowing the metaphor from a speech by queer German historian Günter Grau, I see Pink Triangles as possible bridges between synchronic and diachronic temporalities, bodily encounters, collective memory, and the construction of the self. I name these links "Pink Triangle bridges." Grau stated the following in 1989:

> For us, offspring of a group persecuted by the Nazis, the continued stigmatization as criminals created forms of memories brought upon by historical consciousness. Homosexual identity was and is inextricably linked to the experience of discrimination and persecution in our century. [. . .] Remembering history is not just looking backwards but should also be understood as a bridge to the present. If this insight is not to become an empty phrase, we must ask: Isn't the fact that the Nazis wronged homosexuals a reason enough to rid men who were convicted under paragraph 175 of shame. To counter the fact that they were considered so-called criminals and allegedly sentenced fairly?[51]

Pink Triangle bridges are portals opening through sensual and contextual encounters of the queer subject with Pink Triangles. It is then possible to pass through these portals and walk toward an imagined queer past of injury or toward a political utopia. It is also possible for queer activists to connect their dreams and the future directly with victimhood in the past and therefore walk upon a bridge connecting past events with an open future, skipping present considerations. Relative to personal knowledge, these bridges can take multiple forms even if they share the same shores, the queer subject being plural and their own architects. *A Badge of Injury* still argues that these architects' plans re-

---

50 Sara Ahmed, "Happy Objects." In *The Affect Theory Reader*, ed. Melissa Gregg and Gregory J. Seigworth (Durham, NC: Duke University Press, 2010). Sara Ahmed, *Queer Phenomenology: Orientations, Objects, Others* (Durham, NC Duke University Press, 2006). Eve Kosofsky Sedgwick, *Touching Feeling: Affect, Pedagogy, Performativity* (Durham, NC: Duke University Press, 2006).
51 "Inauguration Speech by Günter Grau on the 28th of June 1989," Schwules Museum (Berlin). Box Nr 196. *Gedenkorte der Homosexuellen Verfolgung / Berlin Nollendorfplatz*.

main similar as the bridges are built from the same material, the same collective memory in the Euro-American world. Coming back to the anecdote opening this book and reflecting on the various layers of the symbol in the Euro-American world, I could not help but wonder if my fellow students in Dahlem were walking on different Pink Triangle bridges than me.

8 Searching for the Pink Triangle

Surprisingly, research on the Pink Triangle has so far been a rare sight despite its importance for the fields of gay, lesbian, and queer history. First, its appearance has been sporadically dismissed. In the late 1990s, scholarly papers even condemned its uses in moral and ethical terms.[52] At the end of the same decade, other writings on the commercialization of same-sex desires went in the same direction by portraying Pink Triangle memorabilia as a "slip to citified consumer fetish," mentioning its disappearance in favor of the rainbow flag, without mapping its journey nor trying to understand possible connections between the symbols' importance as factors and indicators of historical change.[53] In both cases, the Pink Triangle seems to be an anomaly undeserving of a proper historical inquiry. As the last chapter of this book will demonstrate, capitalism and Pink Triangle memorabilia played an important role in the transformation and transmission of queer memory.

As previously mentioned, Jennifer Evans redefined both German History and German Studies in 2016, forcefully arguing for the necessity of queering German history. Inviting scholars to approach heteronormative German history through queer methodologies and queer historians to investigate the potential of German history to illustrate empirically recent queer scholarship, she set the tone for new studies, inspiring numerous scholars to publish books tackling queer German history in the German-speaking world. Her call to action was heard and German queer history is now going through a very prolific phase to which *A Badge of Injury* is also part. Laurie Marhoefer's *Racism and the Making of Gay Rights,* or Ben Miller and Huw Lemmey's anthology, *Bad Gays* similarly offer a more critical turn, uncovering themes of racism and exclusion that have been missing from the literature until recently.[54] Evans's own *The Queer Art of History* tackles the

---
[52] R. Almy Elman, "Triangles and Tribulations," *Journal of Homosexuality* 30, no. 3 (1996): 1–11.
[53] Edward Ingebretsen, "Gone Shopping: The Commercialization of Same-Sex Desire," *International Journal of Sexuality and Gender Studies*, no. 4 (1999): 140.
[54] Huw Lemmey and Ben Miller, *Bad Gays: A Homosexual History* (London: Verso, 2022.); Laurie Marhoefer, *Racism and the Making of Gay Rights: A Sexologist, His Student, and the Empire of Queer Love.* (Toronto, ON: University of Toronto Press, 2022).

construction of German exclusions and their basis in *Vergangenheitsbewältigung*, 'the action of coming to term with the national socialist past,' a topic at the core of the second and third part of *A Badge of Injury*.[55] However, Marhoefer's examination ends in 1945 and Evans's study specifically focuses on respectability politics. This book follows Miller and Lemmey's invitation to look at uninviting moments of history, navigating the tumultuous waters of the queer past.[56]

This book is not a study of Nazi atrocities but is part of a conversation about the era. It is also a historical intervention on the scholarship of Nazi persecutions of queerness. It offers a necessary caveat to the dismissal of lesbian persecutions by some German historians, and it adds a transatlantic focus to a rich discussion on lesbian erasure, steered by the research of historians such as Anna Hájková in her research on queer Holocaust history.[57] What is more, several other monographs have appeared in recent years which are adjacent to this book in both geographic and temporal scope: Craig Griffiths's *The Ambivalence of Gay Liberation*, Samuel Huneke's *States of Liberation*, Benno Gammerl's *Anders Fühlen*, Andrea Rottmann's *Queer Lives Across the Wall*.[58] Consequently, this book is also not the first to place transnational analysis at the heart of the study of the Pink Triangle in the second half of the twentieth century. It is similar in topic to Jake W. Newsome's brilliant *Pink Triangle Legacies*, which also uncovers queer collective memories of National Socialism in the transatlantic world, thus writing about the recuperation

---

[55] Jennifer Evans, *The Queer Art of History: Queer Kinship after Fascism* (Durham, NC: Duke University Press, 2023).

[56] See also Heather Love's plea for an investigation of misfits and deviance. Heather Love, *Underdogs: Social Deviance and Queer Theory* (Chicago, IL: The University of Chicago Press, 2021). For a critique of lionization see also: Martin Duberman, *Has the Gay Movement Failed?* (Oakland, CA: University of California Press, 2018).

[57] Anna Hájková, *Menschen ohne Geschichte sind Staub: Homophobie und Holocaust* (Göttingen: Wallstein Verlag, 2021). See also: Joanna Ostrowska, Joanna Talewicz-Kwiatkowska, and Lutz van Dijk, *Erinnern in Auschwitz. Auch an sexuelle Minderheiten* (Berlin: Querverlag, 2020) or the transatlantic story uncovered by Jonathan Ned Katz: *Daring Life and Dangerous Times of Eve Adams* (Chicago, IL: Chicago Review Press, 2021).

[58] Samuel Clowes Huneke, *States of Liberation: Gay Men between Dictatorship and Democracy in Cold War Germany* (Toronto, ON: Toronto University Press, 2022); Benno Gammerl, *Anders fühlen: Queeres Leben in der Bundesrepublik. Eine Emotionsgeschichte*, (Munich: Hanser, 2021); Andrea Rottmann, *Queer Lives across the Wall: Desire and Danger in Divided Berlin, 1945–1970* (Toronto, ON: University of Toronto Press, 2023). Beyond these books, see also: Erik N. Jensen, "The Pink Triangle and Political Consciousness: Gays, Lesbians, and the Memory of Nazi Persecution." *Journal of the History of Sexuality* 11, no. 1 (2002): 319–349 and Régis Schlagdenhauffen, *Triangle Rose: La persécution nazie des homosexuels et sa mémoire* (Paris: Autrement, 2011).

of the Pink Triangle as a symbol of emancipation.[59] Yet, by underlining its significance as a historical concept while avoiding the lionization of historical queer movements thinking through forms of exclusion, this book is nonetheless a new contribution. Newsome writes in his introduction that his "is the first book to use a transnational approach to trace how personal and collective memories about the fate of queer communities in the Holocaust helped establish historical roots that nourished the formation of a modern, transatlantic gay identity."[60] *A Badge of Injury* pushes this focus on collective memory in another direction, highlighting how the Pink Triangle emblematizes the subjugation of many forms of queerness under one gay identity. Where Newsome's act of recovery convincingly recounts the construction of the Queer Atlantic based on memory, *A Badge of Injury* meticulously deconstructs this narrative by diachronically and synchronically studying power structures rooted in the uses of the symbol.

In fact, both *A Badge of Injury* and *Pink Triangle Legacies* should be read in parallel. Newsome and I both independently studied different moments of the triangle's cultural history while being aware of each other's work and corresponding at various junctures, and both books echo what Jennifer Evans has coined "queer kinship."[61] For Evans, queer kinship is more than the creation of solidarities, it is also a way to map queerness in the past without obscuring both the negative aspects of inclusion as well as the exclusions embedded in desires to belong. It is also a methodology, a call to queer memory beyond liberalism. In this book, I see my research of the Pink Triangle as a manifestation of queer kinship. On the one hand, I reflect on the importance of deconstructing and nuancing narratives of the queer past, without vindicating historical voices from the past. On another hand, I wrote this book not against my peers, but as another episode of the same narrative I aim to deconstruct. To put it differently, I do not think our writings live in a vacuum outside of the stories we uncover in the archives.

This book is based on broad archival research on both sides of the Atlantic. I have focused on the analysis of communication networks in the gay and lesbian communities of Canada, the United States of America, and Germany. With particular attention to the visual aspects of each periodical, I have examined various magazines and newspapers from the gay and lesbian press in Toronto, Vancouver, New York City, San Francisco, Boston, Washington DC, Munich, Cologne, and West Berlin. This study of editorials, articles, and reviews of cultural productions

---

59 Jake Newsome, *Pink Triangle Legacies: Coming out in the Shadow of the Holocaust* (Ithaca, NY: Cornell University Press, 2022.).
60 Newsome, *Pink Triangle Legacies*, 4.
61 Jennifer Evans, *The Queer Art of History: Queer Kinship after Fascism* (Durham: Duke University Press, 2023), 3–21.

has been limited to the period between the 1970s and the end of the 1990s. I have then paired this survey with various news articles from the mainstream press according to local context, for example pieces in *The New York Times* for the east coast of the USA or *Süddeutsche Zeitung*, 'South German Journal,' for the south of Germany. These investigations have been joined to empirical material of the private papers of cis gay US activists and German political groups, as well as the complete archives of mainly white queer organizations on both continents, including but not limited to correspondence, inner regulations, press communiqués, and minutes. Finally, I have been using zines, leaflets, and posters of prominent gay and lesbian campaigns from the second part of the twentieth century, online repositories of interviews conducted by other historians, and various memoirs and autobiographies written by queer activists and academics. All in all, these primary sources have allowed me to draw a convincing portrait of both the uses of and reflections on the Pink Triangle, keeping in mind the intersectional ties and diversity of the gay and lesbian communities.

9 Mapping the Pink Triangle's journey

This book is organized thematically and not chronologically, reflecting the many layers of a symbol and their synchronicity. If the reader is willing to forgive me a somewhat cheap metaphor, it is useful to imagine for a moment the Pink Triangle as a sort of aeroplane used for intercontinental flights. This aeroplane as a machine remains the same, but its pilot can change depending on the context, flying to both sides of the Atlantic back and forth. The plane was created for one purpose but has since been used for a variety of voyages, hosting different groups of people, and carrying luggage from one side of the world to the other. Some are too economically disadvantaged to even fly and do not get to board the plane, some are afraid of flying, and some enjoy premium memberships that give them access to privileges. *A Badge of Injury* is the story of such a passenger carrier. It follows the Pink Triangle at different moments in time, examining the way it flew to, from, and around both sides of the ocean, on domestic or international flights. Each chapter shows how different groups piloting this aircraft took it to different places, encountered turbulence, sometimes almost crashed, and opened new travel routes.

Attached on clothing, or printed on posters, the Pink Triangle became the insignia, the logo, the 'badge' of a Queer Atlantic; the symbol used by many queer organizations appealing to victimhood in their struggle for human rights. Each chapter of this book emphasizes one connection between the Pink Triangle and the queer subject, demonstrating the different ways it was metaphorically or concretely used as a badge – a portable visual concept of historical change. Thematically arranged, the book is also divided in three main parts. The first part looks at discourses, narratives, and memories attached to the symbol in the Euro-American world. The first chapter – *A Badge of Continuities* – focuses on the 1970s in the FRG. It investigates activists' recuperation of the Pink Triangle for political reasons, brandishing the symbol as a simultaneous affirmation of queerness and an attempt to historicize both their oppression by the state and their position in society at large. Underlining contestations inside queer printed media of the era and written communication networks as well as introducing many political organizations across the FRG – West Berlin, Cologne, Wuppertal, Brunswick, etc. – this chapter demonstrates how the Pink Triangle was already multilayered in the 1970s. Indeed, it was a reference to a perpetrator category, an appeal to the cohesive potential offered by victimhood narratives, and a badge of courage for dealing with day-to-day encounters with queerphobia.

The second chapter of the book – *A Badge of Narratives* – examines the influence of the Pink Triangle beyond the visual, focusing on its mention in written testimonies and cultural productions. It also underlines the significance of the symbol for the creation of a collective through the textual, for example through correspondence and scholarly monographs. The chapter introduces three transatlantic Pink Triangle brokers: James D. Steakley, Richard Plant, and Martin Sherman, whose writings propelled the international uses of the symbol. Looking at scholarly monographs, poetry, and theatre as transatlantic spaces of exchange, the chapter offers a genealogy of the Pink Triangle in gay writings of the 1970s and 1980s, mapping the creation of gay narratives referring to National Socialism and the establishment of a collective mythology. The chapter then contextualizes and debates the power asymmetries between gay and lesbian history, exposing how these narratives either erased lesbian experiences or pushed some lesbian activists in the Euro-American world to adapt to gay frameworks of victimhood.

The third chapter – *A Badge of Injury* – builds on the first two and discusses the consequences of the symbolic recuperation of victimhood and the construction of collective narratives in the Euro-American world. I expose how different uses of the Pink Triangle cemented certain definitions of queerness in the USA and the FRG. Going beyond a simple evaluation of multiple case studies, the chapter demonstrates how the integration of Nazi atrocities to global memory was central to the journey of the symbol and how the Pink Triangle's popularity can only be understood transregionally.

The second part of the book analyzes the effects of the narratives examined in the first part. The fourth chapter – *A Badge of Inclusion* – centres on conceptual history and memory studies, analysing the inclusive potential of the symbol throughout the second part of the twentieth century. It emphasises three moments of integration linked to the Pink Triangle: the integration of the queer community into German memory culture and the discourses of *Vergangenheitsbewältigung* connected to the case studies discussed in chapter one, the US musealization of a particular definition of queerness according to the narratives exposed in chapter two, and the inclusion of German queer history in world history.

Starting with the story of a Jewish congregation on the east coast of the USA, the fifth chapter – *A Badge of Exclusion* – begins with a reflection on groups who refrained from using the symbol even if some would have expected them to use it, in this case a group of Jewish queer men and their memorialization of both the Holocaust and the Nazi persecutions of male-male sexualities. A necessary historiographical intervention, the later parts of the chapter show how the emphasis on the Pink Triangle ironically silenced other commemorations of Nazi persecutions and structural oppression and erased other experiences, in this case, lesbian realities. The chapter shows the limits of Pink Triangle narratives, showing the discursive importance of political symbols and images for social movements and for cultural memory.

Following on the previous discussion on exclusion, the sixth chapter – *A Badge of Universalization* – analyses the ways in which the Pink Triangle universalized one definition of queerness beyond the Euro-American world. It begins by discussing different Pink Triangle monuments in Italy, the Netherlands, and Spain to identify Pink Triangle narratives beyond the USA and the FRG. It then examines the universalization of these narratives and of Euro-American queer memory to the rest of the world. By emphasizing the creation and symbolic language of the *International Lesbian, Gay, Bisexual, Trans and Intersex Association* and its discourse on human rights, I then emphasize international power asymmetries and hierarchies in the framing of queerness on the world stage, identifying possible reasons for the presence of the Pink Triangle outside of the Euro-American world.

The seventh chapter – *A Badge of Survival* – deals with the Pink Triangle and its aesthetic of survival. From its first recuperation in West Germany to the *AIDS Coalition to Unleash Power* (ACT UP), the symbol has been used as a political statement to mark the tenacity of a community outliving persecutions. This genealogy of survival, from National Socialism to the HIV/AIDS crisis, is intimately connected with transatlantic queer memory but also to the transmission of feelings and discourses through the power of images. This chapter examines the story of ACT UP and international AIDS activism, focusing on the multilayered aspects of the Pink Triangle as a referent to genocide. Once again using the symbol as a prism, this chapter introduces my notion of Pink Triangle bridges.

I consider the third and last part of the book as a treatise on the power of images and their role for memory studies. The first of these two essays, chapter eight – *A Badge of Temporality* – brings together my Pink Triangle bridges from the previous chapter and the discussion regarding universalization at the heart of chapter six. It shows how uses of the Pink Triangle have cemented a particular conception of European Time. Adding to a rich literature on queer temporalities, I show how the universalization of Euro-American queer memory is broadly used to frame European modernity in opposition to a so-called premodern non-European space. Coining the term *homosynchronism*, I discuss this amalgam of dystopia and political activism and I give contemporary examples linked to the history of the symbol, for example, protests in solidarity with queer individuals living in fear of violence in the Chechnyan Republic under the regime of Ramzan Kadyrov.

The final chapter of the book – *A Badge of Visibility* – underlines the affirmative aspects of the Pink Triangle in public spaces. Starting with the cases discussed in chapter one up to the discussion of AIDS activism in chapter seven, this concluding part reflects on the materiality of the triangle and the significance of capitalism for queer transfers of knowledge. Examining merchandizing and the branding of political groups using the symbol, I link Pink Triangle bridges with art, outreach campaigns, and a rich literature on visibility, analysing the triangle in tangible form as an object.

The concluding pages of *A Badge of Injury* highlight all the important aspects of the book, using memory studies to argue for a queer global history that appreciates the power of images to tackle other issues, for instance, issues of translation. In short, it insists on the significance of historical concepts beyond the textual.

1 A badge of continuities – Pink radical politics and identification with the Nazi past

Opening their mailboxes on March 3, 1977, paying members of the Gay Liberation Front in Cologne (GLF) found the schedule of the activities planned for March and April at the communal GLF community center.[1] In the program, members were invited by the *Arbeitsgemeinschaft homosexueller Emanzipationsgruppen in Westdeutschland,* 'Working Association of Homosexual Emancipation Groups in West Germany,' to the screening of a student film followed by a discussion panel. The film? *Rosa Winkel: das ist doch schon lange vorbei,* 'Pink triangle: that's so long ago,' a documentary by Peter Recht, Christiane Schmerl, and Detlef Stoffel, then-students of sociology at the University of Bielefeld. As the movie gained more and more recognition, screenings like the one in Cologne also took place across the Republic, namely in West Berlin, Wuppertal, Oberhausen, and Gießen.[2] The film introduced this symbol, created by Nazis to brand queer men in concentration camps, to a new audience and drew parallels between the persecution of queerness during the Adenauer era and the use of the Nazi version of §175 StGB against men in the Federal Republic of Germany (FRG) after 1969. The documentary was divided into three parts: the persecution of queer men during National Socialism; the oppression faced by non-heteronormative males in the long postwar era; the possible modes of action and glimpses of a possible gay emancipation.[3] The creators went to great lengths to explain how queer citizens would benefit from historical awareness and a recognition of victimhood, comparing the early democratic years of the FRG with the Nazi era regarding the persecution of queerness and underlining how all queer German men were united by a collective history. This communal past of injury had allegedly been erased by the state and historians, or at least hidden, and was in dire need of being (re)discovered.

---

1 Schwules Museum, Berlin. Sammlung Holy, Folder 027, *Gay Liberation Front Köln 1972–1977.*
2 Schwules Museum, Berlin. Sammlung Holy, Folder 054, *Übrige Gruppe, Kob-Wup.*
3 "Publicity for the Premiere of Rosa Winkel? Das ist lange schon vorbei . . .," *Emanzipation: Zeitschrift Homosexueller Gruppen* 5 (1976): 30.

Note: This chapter offers a more exhaustive version of the argument of an article previously published in 2019 – in German – in *Invertito-der Jahrbuch für die Geschichte Homosexualitäten.* See: Sébastien Tremblay, "'Ich Konnte Ihren Schmerz Körperlich Spüren': Die Historisierung der NS-Verfolgung und die Wiederaneignung des Rosa Winkels in der westdeutschen Schwulenbewegung der 1970er Jahre," *Invertito – Jahrbuch für die Geschichte der Homosexualitäten,* no. 21 Verfolgung homosexueller Männer und Frauen in der NS-Zeit & Erinnerungskultur (2019): 179–202.

Knowing about its origins, a burgeoning *Schwulenbewegung*, 'gay movement,' would then be able to fight for its own liberation.

Two years prior, West Berliners meandering down one of their city's most prestigious and famous streets on May 5, 1975, might have interrupted their shopping for a minute or two to pay attention to one of the men distributing flyers and wearing pink triangles. They might also have been surprised by the word plastered on the said pink geometrical form: *Schwul*, 'gay.'[4] Who were these men wearing an insult like a badge on *Kurfürstendamm* (Ku'Damm) on that afternoon in the mid-1970s? Inspired by hefty discussions in and out of their group's communication organ, members of *Homosexuelle Aktion Westberlin*, 'Homosexual Action West Berlin,' (HAW) publicly advocated for the use of the symbol and the idea that members of the *Schwulenbewegung* should brandish it to distance themselves from presupposed less-political factions of the city's queer activist circles and ally themselves around a new political awareness: *Schwulsein*, 'being gay.'[5] Other groups across the FRG picked up on this recuperation, adding their own spice to an already colourful mélange.[6]

These film projections or other flyer actions across the Republic had one thing in common, offering both inward and outward political impulses to queer men following the liberalization of §175 StGB at the end of the Adenauer era. Indeed, rhetorical uses of and references to the Nazi era conveyed to this burgeoning queer community that a past of injury united them and expressed broader unity. In other words, reclaiming public space through this narrative of victimhood and brandishing the Pink Triangle also confronted society at large while underlining the constitution of the social group.[7]

---

4 In this chapter, I use *Schwul* as noun and adjective in English and *Schwule* in plural. I do this to avoid confusing readers with *schwules*, *schwulen*, and other grammatical variations found in the German language. I have opted to use the term in German because it conveys its own history and is not a direct translation of the English 'gay.' Indeed, some organizations in Germany preferred to use the term 'gay' instead of *Schwul* for historical and linguistic purposes. See Maurice De Clare, "Voller Text des Teach-In und Begrüßung; erster öffentlicher Abend," 1971, in Schwules Museum, Berlin Sammlung Holy, Folder 027 *Gay Liberation Front Köln 1972–1977*.
5 Kris, "30 Jahre Danach: Warum tragen Homosexuelle wieder Rosa Winkel?," *HOBO Berliner Wochen Magazin* 5, no 25 (June 21–27, 1975): 25–26. The translation is again for clarity only. I would claim that *Schwulsein* and being gay are not completely historically interchangeable.
6 Craig Griffiths mentions an action by the group *RotZschwul* 'Red (Cell) Gay' in Frankfurt (Main) where men also used the Pink Triangle. The fourth issue of the short-lived Berliner magazine *Schwuchtel* 'Faggot' also advertised Pink Triangle badges sold for one DM in 1976. See Griffiths, *The Ambivalence*, 134.
7 Wendy Brown, "Wounded Attachments: Late Modern Oppositional Political Formations." In *The Identity in Question*, ed. John Rajchman (New York, NY: Routledge, 1995), 199–228.

This chapter focuses on queer men in the FRG in the 1970s. It investigates their recuperation of the Pink Triangle for political reasons, wielding the symbol simultaneously as an affirmation of queerness and an attempt to historicize their oppression by the state throughout the twentieth century. Underlining contestations inside queer printed media and written communication networks of the era as well as introducing many political organizations across the FRG – in West Berlin, Cologne, Wuppertal or Brunswick –, the chapter demonstrates the multiple layers of the Pink Triangle at the start of its transatlantic journey. It was already a reference to the apparent continuities of a category created by perpetrators of the past, an appeal to the cohesive potential offered by victimhood narratives, and a badge of courage for dealing with day-to-day encounters with queerphobia. This chapter is not just about the so-called *Schwulenbewegung*. I prefer to discuss queer men more generally, agglutinating various political manifestations of queerness in a broader semantic field where the *Schwulsein* of the HAW meets other aspects of German gay liberation. Recent literature on the era has shown the ambivalence of categories of analysis or the simple impossibility to separate different approaches to queer emancipation in the decades following World War Two.[8] For the sake of clarity, I borrow the label *rosa radikal* 'pink radical[s]' from Andreas Pretzel and Volker Weiß.[9] By using pink radical – as name or as adjective – I bring together various individuals who fought for the recognition of a queer past of injury and imagined a community born out of this historical awareness.[10] As part of the *Schwulenbewegung* or identifying themselves as "homophiles,"[11] these queer men historicized and legitimized their struggles through an appeal to the Pink Triangle. The following pages are contextualizing queer printed media published by the pink

---

8 See Gammerl, *Anders fühlen*, 25; Griffiths, *The Ambivalence*, 59.
9 Andreas Pretzel and Volker Weiß, "Die Schwulenbewegung der 1970er Jahre: Annäherungen an ein legendäres Jahrzehnt." In *Rosa Radikale: Die Schwulenbewegung der 1970er Jahre*, ed. Andreas Pretzel and Volker Weiß (Hamburg: Männerschwarm, 2012), 9–28.
10 Michael Holy, "Jenseits von Stonewall: Rückblicke auf die Schwulenbewegung in der BRD 1969–1980." In *Rosa Radikale: Die Schwulenbewegung der 1970er Jahre*, ed. Andreas Pretzel and Volker Weiß (Hamburg: Männerschwarm Verlag, 2012), 55.
11 On the ambivalence between the *Schwulenbewegung* and so-called homophiles, see Craig Griffiths, "Die Ambivalenz der Schwulenemanzipation der 1970er Jahre," *Invertito – Jahrbuch für die Geschichte der Homosexualitäten*, no. 23 (2021): 136–145. For a more regional example, see Julia Noah Munier, "Die Homophilenbewegung im deutschen Südwesten der 1950er und 1960er Jahre als Akteurin der Anerkennung," *Invertito – Jahrbuch für die Geschichte der Homosexualitäten*, no. 22 (2020): 77–112; Gottfried Lorenz, "Hamburg als Homosexuellenhauptstadt der 1950er Jahre – Die Homophilen-Szene und ihre Unterstützer für die Abschaffung des §175 StGB." In *Ohnmacht und Aufbegehren: Homosexuelle Männer in der Frühen Bundesrepublik*, ed. Andreas Pretzel and Volker Weiß (Hamburg: Männerschwarm 2010), 117–151.

radicals in the 1970s. Through their own readings of written communication networks, pink radicals indeed rediscovered queer suffering, namely the atrocities committed by the Nazis. Identifying with queer victims through acts of memory, they recuperated the Pink Triangle politically in numerous ways. The end of the chapter demonstrates how the power of images allowed multiple pink radical groups to unite under the banner of the Pink Triangle despite their differences.

1.1 Emancipation on paper

Although many local publications already existed, the publication of the magazine *Emanzipation* in 1975 created a distinct space for the evolution of the memory narratives at the heart of this chapter.[12] In its pages, the pink radicals made room for debates and findings. They could discuss local politics and create alliances, but more especially, they found a way to historicize their movement. In the first issue, the editorial team spelled out what this new national medium would mean for the exchange of information: a new and official platform for all West German leftist queer groups.[13] It is in its pages that the conversation started to shift from a critique of §175 StGB and a collectivization of day-to-day experiences of oppression, to the creation of a collective past linked to Nazi persecutions:

> Sure, the forms have changed, but oppression and discrimination continue to spread. This new tendency to pretend that things are changing clearly shows the danger that hypocritical tolerance can quickly turn back into active persecution. It is therefore important to recognize the beginning of a new push towards the right and to counter it. [. . .] We gays must never let ourselves be pushed into a ghetto, not even as a 'tolerated minority.' We have to get out of our hiding places and at least try to live our sexuality and drive freely and openly.[14]

Written by Alfred Heinlein of *Homosexuelle Aktion Nürnberg*, 'Homosexual Action Nuremberg,' this statement is one of the first to not only describe the persecutions of queerness under National Socialism, but to also conceptualize continuities and

---

12 Later known as *Homosexuelle Emanzipation*. For a survey of the queer media landscape during the the first decades of the FRG, see: Joachim Bartholomae, "Klappentexte: Verlage, Buchläden und Zeitschriften als Infrastruktur der Schwulenbewegung." In *Zwischen Autonomien und Integration schwule Politik und Schwulenbewegung der 1980er und 1990er Jahre*, ed. Andreas Pretzel and Volker Weiß, (Hamburg: Männerschwarm Verlag, 2013), 72–73.
13 With a focus on the *Schwulenbewegung*. See Erwin Mund (HIS Stuttgart) and Rainer Schilling (VSG München), "Gemeinsam die Stagnation überwinden: Süddeutsche Gruppen starten gemeinsames Info," *Emanzipation Zeitschrift Homosexueller Gruppen 1* (1975): 1–2.
14 Alfred Heinlein, "30 Jahre spatter..? Massenmord an Homos bis heute unaufgeklärt" *Emanzipation Zeitschrift Homosexueller Gruppen 3* (1975): 1–3.

link them to the present. Heinlein's essay not only quotes parts of another piece published by the HAW in the eighteenth issue of their *HAW-Info* at length, but also draws a lot of its material from the then-recent publication of Heinz Heger's *Die Männer mit dem Rosa Winkel*, 'The men with the pink triangle,' the life story of a queer male concentration camp prisoner. Heinz Heger was the pseudonym chosen by Austrian writer Johann Neumann and the story is based on interviews with concentration camp survivor Josef Kohout.[15] Its publication in 1972 sent a shockwave through the gay political circles and pushed many pink radicals to read and share the story of their perceived 'ancestors,' of those queers who had come before them.[16] They drew a direct connection between the fate of the men who had been murdered, tortured, and exploited by the Nazis and their own predicament. The *Homosexuelle Aktion Nürnberg* also tried to attract public attention by sending a letter to the daily newspaper *Nürnberger Nachrichten* 'News of Nuremberg' in 1975 just before the thirtieth anniversary of Liberation Day.[17] The editors dismissed their letter. However, *Emanzipation* reprinted it as supplement to Heinlein's piece:

> These days various media repeatedly refer to the surrender of the German Reich and the liberation from fascism [thirty] years ago. However, it remains largely unmentioned that this also opened the gates of the concentration camps for many thousands of homosexuals who had to endure unspeakable suffering for the sake of their sexual instinct. They, who had to wear the Pink Triangle in the concentration camps, were the lowest and most despised group. Tens of thousands of them died in the gas chambers. [. . .] While reparations were granted to political prisoners after liberation, they are still denied to the gays until today as they are still considered criminals. Though legal criminalization has largely been lifted, social taboo and discrimination against homosexuality continues unabated.[18]

In the following years, this newly created German pink radical press placed greater and greater importance on the horrors of National Socialism. This (re)dis-

---

15 Heinz Heger, *Die Männer mit dem Rosa Winkel*, 4. impr. ed. (London: GMP Publ., 2001).
16 In her critique of the historicist debate regarding queer temporalities, Laura Doan mentions a paradox. Queer historians are both trying to assert queerness in the past, on the lookout for 'ancestral genealogies,' while also trying to deconstruct categories of sexualities and gender identity in the present. See Laura Doan, "Queer History / Queer Memory: The Case of Alan Turing," *GLQ: A Journal of Lesbian and Gay Studies* 23, no. 1 (2017): 127.
17 Public mentions of May 8 as a day of Liberation happened much later in 1985 following a speech by then-Bundespräsident Richard von Weizsäcker. See Daniela Beljan and Mathias N. Lorenz, "Weizsäcker-Rede." In *Lexikon der 'Vergangenheitsbewältigung' in Deutschland: Debatten- und Diskursgeschichte des Nationalsozialismus nach 1945*, ed. Torben Fischer and Matthias N. Lorenz (Bielefeld: transcript Verlag, 2015), 253–256.
18 Homosexuelle Aktion Nürnberg, "Das Tabu besteht weiter" *Emanzipation Zeitschrift Homosexueller Gruppen 3* (1975): 3.

covery of the gay past under the Nazis became central to the formation of a newly created collective *Schwul* identity, of a *Schwulsein*.[19] Would-be queer historians explicitly started to reach out through the pages of *Emanzipation* to try and contact survivors, to construct the present by communicating with queer ancestors.[20] The objectives of abolishing §175 StGB and seeking reparations for the queer male victims of National Socialism were also merged together. Indeed, the pink radicals linked their crusade for state recognition of the Nazis crimes against queer men during the War to their own biographies, adopting the Pink Triangle as a symbol of unity, a badge of these continuities.

1.2 Wearing Pink Triangles, showing Pink Triangles

Let us go back to West Berlin in the spring of 1975. The flyer action on Ku'Damm consisted of two main recuperations: one symbolic and one linguistic. By wearing the Pink Triangle, members of the HAW were making a connection between themselves, concentration camps, and queer memory. Nevertheless, even if they were fighting for the rehabilitation of the men with a fate similar to the likes of Josef Kohout and therefore discussing the past, their use of the symbol on the streets of West Berlin was much more anchored into the present, at least rhetorically.[21]

The flyer begins with a statement on *Schwul* as a synonym for abnormality and ends up with the catchphrase "therefore we wear the pink triangle" capitalized over three political statements: – Rehabilitation for the gay concentration camp prisoners / away with §175! – Make your *Schwulsein* public! Wear the Pink Triangle! – *Schwule*, organize yourselves in the HAW![22] One can here observe a clear shift between a usual fight for the end of persecution, an appeal to victimhood conformed to the zeitgeist, and this blunt affront to the heterosexual mainstream. Beyond the recognition of a traumatizing collective past by the pink radicals, the triangle also marks a clear move between the private and the public, as queerness, in the form of *Schwulsein*, became a political public statement, a provocation

---

[19] Lutz van Dijk, "Die Folgen des Schweigens: Für unmittelbar Betroffene, die historische Forschung sowie jüngere Generationen von Schwulen und Lesben." In *Nationalsozialistischer Terror gegen Homosexuelle: Verdrängt und Ungesühnt*, ed. Burkhard Jellonek and Rüdiger Lautmann (Paderborn: Schoeningh, 2002), 392.
[20] Egmont Fassbinder, "Alter Schwule dringend gesucht" *Emanzipation Zeitschrift Homosexueller Gruppen* 3 (1975): 6.
[21] HAW, "Flyer 'Wir Sind Schwul,'" 17.05.1975, in Schwules Museum, Berlin, *Sammlung Holy*, Folder 045 *HAW*.
[22] HAW, "Flyer 'Wir Sind Schwul.'".

against an oppressing respectability. By recuperating this "mark of Cain"[23] and an insult, the pink radicals denounced what they considered to be a direct link between heteropatriarchy and National Socialism.

Condemning the mainstream discourse about queerness in the 1970s FRG, the HAW asked: "do you realize that these arguments were used to put gays in concentration camps under fascism? [. . .] they were murdered by the tens of thousands [. . .]. 'Pervert, abnormal' – These arguments are used to deprive gays of their right to recognition."[24] In the HAW's own words, this impulse to impose their queerness "*nach außen*," 'outward,' meant fighting against the alleged complacency of new parallel spaces created for the comfort of other pink radicals.[25] Inspired by the Black Power movement in the USA and by the women's liberation movement of the same era, they imposed their presence in public life, challenged the mainstream into dealing with their difference, confronting and opposing conceptions of normality of society at large.[26] On the one hand, pink radicals were addressing other queer men who were not necessarily attempting to gain more visibility and change society. According to groups such as the HAW, these other queer men evolved in a similar space but did not share the same political goals. Craig Griffiths highlights this space, the homosexual arena, as a counter-public inside alternative milieu of the 1970s.[27] Outside of this counter-public lies another mainstream, the heteronormative world of the dominant parts of German society.[28] Through their activism and faced with a social order where heterosexual parts of society remained either unaware of their own dominance or convinced of their normality, pink radicals spoke to a counter-public in the homosexual arena and also to society at large. They were disrupting two different mainstreams.

---

[23] Michael Föster, "VVN liess schwulen Flugblatt nicht zu: Rosa Winkel noch immer Kainszeichen?," *Emanzipation* 4 (July–August 1979): 9.

[24] HAW, "Flyer 'Wir Sind Schwul'", 17.05.1975, in Schwules Museum, Berlin, *Sammlung Holy*, Folder 045 *HAW*. See also another flyer by the group: HAW, "Schwule – Was wollen die denn hier?", October 1975,in Schwules Museum, Berlin, *Sammlung Holy*, Folder 045 *HAW*; Ina and Funny, "Die Männer mit dem Rosa Winkel," *HAW-Infos* 18 (1975): 3–8; Reinhard, "Rosa für Schwule," *HAW-Infos* 18 (1975): 9–15.

[25] Activists from the HAW considered such spaces a form of fluffy ghettos. See Kris, "30 Jahre Danach," 25–26.

[26] HAW, "Die Homosexualität in uns – Vorgelegt auf dem Plenum von 07.07.1974," in Schwules Museum, Berlin, *Sammlung Holy*, Folder 045 *HAW*.

[27] Griffiths, *The Ambivalence*, 51. He is referring to Christopher Bollas, "Cruising in the Homosexual Arena." In *Being a Character Psychoanalysis and Self Experience*, ed. Christopher Bollas (London: Routledge, 1992), 144–164.

[28] Birgit Rommelspacher, *Dominanzkultur: Texte zu Fremdheit und Macht* (Berlin: Orlanda Frauenverlag, 1995).

However, this appropriation of space and of language, common to many social movements emanating from the margins of society and constructing their own narrative of emancipation, was not necessarily anchored in collective memory, a feeling of injustice, or what Wendy Brown names "wounded attachment."[29] Groups such as the HAW have a rich history of debates, squabbles, and political conflicts and one can easily be confused by the variety of positions defended by the group after their first call to wield the Pink Triangle as a sword in their fight toward emancipation and liberation.

One of these discussions was a reaction to the so-called *Feministenpapier*, 'Feminist memoranda.' In this position paper, some members of the HAW vehemently denounced a sort of *Scheinheterosexualität*, 'façade of heterosexuality,' among their ranks.[30] They were drawing attention to the privilege held by some of the more normatively masculine gay activists in everyday life and the double oppression of *Tunten* 'sissies/queens' inside the movement. They pointed at everyday discrimination faced by effeminate men dealing with the accusatory heterosexual gaze both outside but also inside queer circles.[31] The *Feministenpapier*, a discussion about the inner problems of the HAW, is important to understand the recuperation of the triangle. In June 1975, some HAW members appealed to other leftist organizations and strongly condemned those who imagined that the Pink Triangle was used to gain their pity or empathy.[32] According to the authors, "comrades" of the Communist Party had to reflect on their own machismo.[33]

By confronting other leftists with the Pink Triangle, the HAW criticized the New Left for its oppressive behavior toward alternative forms of sexualities. These HAW members were not pleading acceptance in the New Left but disrupting what it meant to be a woman or a man, contesting reactionary enforced gender binaries.[34] This has led some scholars to incorrectly label and understand

---

29 Wendy Brown, "Wounded Attachments," 214.
30 Erik N. Jensen, "The Pink Triangle and Political Consciousness," 326–327.
31 For a reaction and a reflection on the conflict, see Claire Egmont, "Glanz und Elend des Feministenpapiers," *HAW-Infos* 9 (1975): 15–21. See also Craig Griffiths, "Konkurrierende Pfade der Emanzipation: Der Tuntenstreit (1973–1975) und die Frage des "respektablen Auftretens." In *Rosa Radikale: Die Schwulenbewegung der 1970er Jahre*, ed. Andreas Pretzel and Volker Weiß (Hamburg: Männerschwarm Verlag, 2012), 143–159.
32 "Zum Rosa Winkel 1. Teil," *Info BUG (Berliner Undogmatischer Gruppen)* 62 (June 1975): 4–5.
33 By using the image of the reactionary communist comrade from the *Kommunistische Partei Deutschlands* 'Communist Party of Germany,' activists of the HAW criticized what they perceived as a problem of orthodox Marxism in the 1970s, the machismo and heteropatriarchy inside the so-called "dogmatic Left."
34 "Zum Rosa Winkel 1. Teil," 4–5.

these cis-queer activists as trans* activists.[35] By wearing pink triangles, HAW activists were standing "against general sexual repression and against the reactionary division into what a man has to be and what a woman has to be!"[36] This battle against gender norms highlights how the association was fighting simultaneously on two different fronts: referring to the national past, but also disrupting gender expression in the public space. An article in the Berlin biweekly HOBO illustrates this double fight. Insisting that the Pink Triangle was a mark of recognition for other like-minded activists, HAW members maintained that the symbol was primarily a reminder of the injustice and torment caused by §175 StGB in the long postwar era and recalling the atrocities committed by the Nazi regime.[37]

This dual use of the Pink Triangle by the HAW also nuances known tropes of queer liberation about overcoming shame and finding emancipation through a form of pride. The recuperation of the symbol, associated with National Socialism and negativity, can be seen as a traditional gay narrative of pride; the movement spread its wings and flew away from the darkness of the past. However, HAW activists were expressing their disdain for this narrative; they were assessing their own queerness, refusing the pity of the heteronormative bourgeoisie, insisting that their main reason for using the triangle was to make themselves known in the present.[38]

A look at the literature on queer shame helps to understand how the use of the symbol was not only about overcoming shame.[39] Indeed, the rhetoric of victimization at the root of identity-based scholarship – eager to academically perform a scholarship of pride – needs to be examined under the scope of the political transfer of emotions – like shame – inside of social movements.[40] In her

---

35 Rosa Hamilton categorized *Tunten* of the HAW as trans* activists. I consider these assumptions to be false, as members of the HAW played with their gender identity but sporadically and as a sort of drag activism. See: Rosa Hamilton, "The Very Quintessence of Persecution. Queer Anti-Fascism in 1970s Western Europe," *Radical History Review*, no. 138 (2020): 60–81. Following criticism, Hamilton explained her analysis. See: Rosa Hamilton, "A Clarification," *Radical History Review*, no. 141 (2021): 221–223. It is very important to decentralize and provincialize white cis-gay history. Nevertheless, without dismissing trans* activism in the FRG, pretending that trans* women were the first ones to recuperate the Pink Triangle is factually incorrect.
36 "Zum Rosa Winkel 2. Teil," *Info BUG (Berliner Undogmatischer Gruppen)* 64 (June 1975): 11–13.
37 Kris, "30 Jahre Danach," 25–26.
38 On the surface, this seems to contradict the point claimed by the HAW that the primary purpose of the Pink Triangle was to remember the past.
39 Sally Munt, *Queer Attachments: The Cultural Politics of Shame*, Queer Interventions (Aldershot: Ashgate, 2008).
40 See the work of Sara Ahmed on the stickiness of this transfer. Sara Ahmed, *The Cultural Politics of Emotion* (Edinburgh: Edinburgh University Press, 2004).

2007 book, *Queer Attachment,* Sally Munt connects the habitus of shame with queer emancipation and shows how embodiments of shame can be the basis for emancipation by itself.[41] In her analysis of the stickiness of the word "queer" to non-heteronormative and trans experiences, Munt follows a similar path to my understanding of the recuperation of *Schwul* and the pink triangle by the pink radicals. She points to the potential for shame to trigger a lack of empathy inside a community, but also at the connection between agency and shame.[42] Similarly, she bases her work on Wendy Brown's critique that "identity politics may be partly configured by a peculiarly shaped and peculiarly disguised form of class resentment, a resentment that is displaced onto discourses of injustice other than class, but a resentment [. . .] that retains the real or imagined holdings of its reviled subject as objects of desire."[43]

Based on Munt, it is possible to see that, in the burgeoning years of German queer liberation, the HAW and other pink radicals anchored their politics in a habitus of shame and a resentment against the bourgeoisie. This resentment is apparent in their lack of solidarity with other forms of queer activism.[44] The recuperation of a negative symbol and a negative appellation were emancipatory but tied to their participation in 'the struggle.' The pride was in the political fight *per se* and not in the identity. A HAW *Tunte*, Helene, explained in 1975 that "with the Pink Triangle I not only show solidarity with the thousands who had to wear this sign in a concentration camp, but I also show solidarity with the *Schwule* who make their *Schwulsein* public nowadays."[45] Looking at a past of injury only made sense when mixed with the appeal of a revolutionary future devoid of oppression, with an emancipation found at the frontline of queerness. For instance, another HAW *Tunte*, Anna, specifies that

> [m]akeup is great and *feminisieren* 'to make oneself looks feminine' is great as a collective action toward showing *Schwulsein*. The Pink Triangle on the other hand is a unified sign that I can only make known together with you. [. . .] When I heard *Schwul* [four of five] years ago, I got goosebumps (horror). Today I use it all the time when I talk about myself and about other sisters, as a matter of course. [. . .] The straight public needs to learn the value reversal of the word as well. This is exactly how we must use the triangle, this is how we are most likely to do justice to the victims of fascism.[46]

---

41 Munt, *Queer Attachments*, 16.
42 Munt, *Queer Attachments*, 26.
43 Brown, *Wounded Attachments*, 206–207.
44 Notably against homophiles. See Griffiths, *The Ambivalence*, 58.
45 Helene, "Diskussionsbeiträge des Rosa Winkel Kollektivs: Warum tragen wir den Rosa Winkel???????????", *Der Rosa Winkel* 1 (July 1975): 28–29.
46 Anna, "Diskussionsbeiträge des Rosa Winkel Kollektivs": 27–28.

Anna's statement once again demonstrates how activists expressed solidarity in the present while being conscious of the necessity to commemorate the past, to seek justice but also to rescue the queer past from the heritage of National Socialism. To put it differently, the past of injury was a trigger for action, a battle cry. Some other groups, such as the *Homosexuelle Aktion München*, 'Homosexual Action Munich,' in the Free State of Bavaria considered the society in which they lived to be more than reminiscent of a queer cultural trauma. They stated: "Today we wear it [the Pink Triangle] again to show that we feel that this society is a new concentration camp not only for *Schwule* but for all who want to be free."[47]

Here it is necessary to highlight the ambivalence of the HAW's recuperation of the Pink Triangle. Brown's "wounded attachments" is not originally about an opposition to bourgeoisie, but a desire for liberal inclusion. By using injuries and stigmata of the past to define themselves, members of the HAW were not asking for inclusion into society at large, they were defining themselves in opposition to sexual norms. Yet the HAW was also aiming for state recognition of the queer men persecuted under National Socialism. As I will now demonstrate, they felt a connection to and identified with these men. The group's uses of the triangle are therefore not only a rejection of norms, but a longing to belong in national narratives, tying pink radical politics to *Vergangenheitsbewältigung* and to the importance of victimhood for the creation of the political subject in late twentieth century Germany.[48] Other symbols, such as the rainbow flag, are intrinsically tied to narratives of inclusion and institutionalization, asking for state recognition, acceptance, or even tolerance as an endgame. The Pink Triangle is more ambivalent. It is indeed based on historical injury and violence, asking for justice as well as the possibility to exist beyond societal norms. Yet it is also entwined in narratives of victimhood and national belongings, as well as a longing for historical justice, ultimately only marking difference if the injury has not been repaired or as long as justice has not been obtained. As I show later in this book – particularly section 8.1 – this can have dire consequences if a part of a social movement based on historical trauma considers the battle won and its goals achieved.

So how did other groups pick up on the call of the HAW to recuperate the triangle? Did they anchor their plea totally in the past and tried to fight for a queer future entirely dependent on the fate of the men forced to wear the pink

---

[47] HAM, "Wir Tragen den Rosa Winkel: Die HAM ist auferstanden" *Der Rosa Winkel* 1 (July 1975): 16.
[48] Manuela Bauche, Patricia Piberger, Sébastien Tremblay, and Hannah Tzuberi, "From Opferkonkurrenz to Solidarity: A Round Table," *Bulletin of the German Historical Institute London* 44, no. 2 – Special Issue Memory Culture 2.0: From Opferkonkurrenz to Solidarity (2022): 32–85.

triangle? Did they advocate for an emancipation using the Pink Triangle as a mark of solidarity in the present? The answer goes both ways.

1.3 Remembering the men with the pink triangle

To understand the recuperation of the pink triangle and its performative effects on collective memory, it is vital to examine the various steps leading to the pink radicals' association between the queer past and their queer present. It would be too simple to brush away this possible instrumentalization of past atrocities as a rhetorical device to end discrimination in the 1970s. It would be overlooking decades of research on the transmission of trauma through cultural memory. By identifying themselves with queer men who had suffered the horrors of National Socialism, activists strengthened their own definition of queerness. For example, Almut, a HAW member, explained in 1975 why he started to wear the Pink Triangle as a symbol:

> One of the reasons I wear the Pink Triangle is because I read the book: "The Men with the Pink Triangle," which is clearly showing the Nazi's torture of gays in concentration camps and the oppression of the gays by other camp inmates. For the first time in my life, I felt personally affected by the story. I could fully identify with the gays in the camp; I could feel their pain physically.[49]

By reading about Kohout's fate in *The Men with the Pink Triangle*, others like Almut realized that not only were queer men, people like them, victims of the Nazi murder apparatus, but that they could also feel a direct connection between the past and the present: "I could fully identify with the gays in the concentration camp, could physically feel their pain."[50] They unveiled a history that had been hidden away; an archival aspect of cultural memory had been rediscovered.[51]

Context is also of primary importance. Almut related to these queer victims in a country where he could still identify continuities with the regime of the perpetrators; he could be criminalized by a similar paragraph of the FRG penal code. The integration of traumatizing events of the past in the politics of the pink radicals confirmed this understanding of cultural memory. By bearing witness, the

---

49 Almut, "Diskussionsbeiträge des Rosa Winkel Kollektivs": 29–30.
50 Almut, "Diskussionsbeiträge des Rosa Winkel Kollektivs": 29–30.
51 On archival forms of cultural memory see Aleida Assmann, "Re-Framing Memory: Between Individual and Collective Forms of Constructing the Past." In *Performing the Past: Memory, History, and Identity in Modern Europe*, ed. Jay Winter, Karin Tilmans, and Frank van Vree (Amsterdam: Amsterdam University Press, 2010), 35–50.

few queer male survivors confirmed and historicized the persecution of queerness. Like an act of speech, the act of memory allowed the transmission of a story across time.[52] It embedded the experience in what Leo Spitzer characterizes as a "retrospective mirage."[53] In other words, confronted with memories that are social and collective – in this case, the memory of other men whom people like Almut could identify with – pink radicals could connect the "world of yesterday" with the "world of here-and-now," drawing continuities between their individuality and a collective identity.[54] The traumatic experiences of oppression in the 1970s were historicized and connected to the traumatic horrors of experiences that preceded them.

Readings of West German pink radical newspapers in the 1970s demonstrate much more than a constellation of "preserved knowledge" about the queer past however.[55] Not only did pink radicals feel a connection with queer men in concentration camps, but they also seem to have indirectly felt the traumatic effects of the event; they considered themselves victims as well. In other words, they were fighting for the recognition of a victim status for people like Josef Kohout to subsequently reappropriate this status for themselves, thereby putting an end to their own traumatic and oppressive present.

Experiences are not only necessarily something that people have. Feminist scholars have shown the triggering effect of hearing about traumatic events like rape when someone recalls their experience. Indigenous scholars have also written about the transmissible trauma of colonialism and genocide and psychologists have written about the transmissible importance of memory in the case of Jewish families and the Holocaust.[56] Yet most of what Ernst van Alpen has called the "dis-

---

[52] Mieke Bal, "Introduction." In *Acts of Memory: Cultural Recall in the Present*, ed. Mieke Bal, Jonathan V. Crewe, and Leo Spitzer (Hanover, NH: University Press of New England, 1999), vii–xvii.

[53] Leo Spitzer, "Back through the Future: Nostalgic Memory and Critical Memory in a Refuge from Nazism." In *Acts of Memory: Cultural Recall in the Present*, ed. Mieke Bal, Jonathan V. Crewe, and Leo Spitzer (Hanover, NH: University Press of New England, 1999), 92.

[54] Spitzer, "Back through the Future," 92.

[55] Here I borrow the concept of preserved knowledge used by Anna Reading. See Anna Reading, *The Social Inheritance of the Holocaust: Gender, Culture and Memory* (Houndmills: Palgrave Macmillan, 2002).

[56] Menakem, Resma, *My Grandmother's Hands: The Bloodline of Racialized Trauma and the Mending of Our Bodies and Hearts: Racialized Trauma and the Pathway to Mending Our Hearts and Bodies* (Buffalo, NY: Central Recovery Press, 2017.) For information on the subject, see also Carolyn Quadrio, "Family Therapy with Families of Holocaust Survivors," *Journal of Aggression, Maltreatment & Trauma* 25, no. 6 (2016): 618–634; Pierre Fossion et al., "Transgenerational Transmission of Trauma in Families of Holocaust Survivors: The Consequences of Extreme Family

cursive effects of experience," the way one's experience affects others, is usually subsumed to the sphere of the family or intimacy.[57] Experience is not only dependent on the event that historically happened, but also on its discursive effects, on the way that those on the receiving end of an act of sharing conceptualize the moment of exchange.

This is where notions of collective trauma and postmemory help us understand this shift toward a collective queer memory. Based on her own experience with the traumatic past of her Jewish family, Marianne Hirsch coined the term postmemory at the end of the 1990s. Analysing her family archives, her work considers her relation to photographs taken of and by her relatives. Following the pictorial turn and the zeitgeist of the turn of the millennium, she writes of the possibility of an image-text and the picture as a "double-coded system of mental storage and retrieval."[58] Marianne Hirsch's reflection on postmemory has potential for queer history if we expand it to a non-Jewish context.[59] According to Hirsch, postmemories are memories that were not necessarily experienced directly – experiences that have not been 'had' by the people under examination – but were still transmitted through discursive effects to others, that is, "not through recollection, but through an imaginative investment and creation."[60] These conveyed experiences are dominated by narratives with deferred stories of the traumatic past, of tales told by a previous generation, affirming the past while leaving enough holes for their receivers to relate through present-day experiences.[61]

Hirsch's postmemories are strongly connected to transgenerational memory and, like Aleida and Jan Assmann's various levels of social and cultural memories, strongly oriented toward a heteronormative schema of family narratives and memories.[62] According to Jan Assmann, and reminiscent of Maurice Halbwachs,

---

Functioning on Resilience, Sense of Coherence, Anxiety and Depression," *Journal of Affective Disorders* 171 (2015): 48–53.

[57] Ernst van Alpen, "Symptoms of Discursivity: Experience, Memory, and Trauma." In *Acts of Memory: Cultural Recall in the Present*, ed. Mieke Bal, Jonathan V. Crewe, and Leo Spitzer (Hanover, NH: University Press of New England, 1999), 24.

[58] Here Hirsch quotes W.J.T Mitchell. Marianne Hirsch, *Family Frames: Photography, Narrative, and Postmemory* (Cambridge, MA: Harvard University Press, 1997): 22.

[59] Craig Griffiths and I agree on this topic. See the fourth chapter of his book. Griffiths, *The Ambivalence*, 160.

[60] Marianne Hirsch, *Family Frames*, 22.

[61] Hirsch, *Family Frames*, 23. For her more recent take on the same matter see also *The Generation of Postmemory: Writing and Visual Culture after the Holocaust* (New York, NY: Columbia University Press, 2012), 36–40.

[62] Aleida Assmann, *Erinnerungsräume: Formen und Wandlungen des kulturellen Gedächtnisses* (München: Beck, 2006).

individual acts of recollection are embedded in 'the social;' they are formed in daily social interactions within the realm of the family and daily social life in the community. These acts of recollection are synchronically framed by 'the cultural' through state-sanctioned commemoration and rituals. Societies then reproduce their mnemonic culture through "a system of culture as it is stored in texts, images, rituals."[63] Assmann bases the construction of culture on socially transmitted experiences that have been had by some and transferred to others. Hirsch's addition to the model argues that cultural transfers through objects and visuals not only allow identification throughout the sphere of the family or the nation, but that individuals can indirectly identify with events – and their possible traumatic effects – as if they had experienced them directly.[64] Hirsch's model is also distinct from Kaja Silverman's widely discussed "heterophatic memory." In her work, Silverman explores the possibility for the self and the other to share similar memories if they share the same space – for example, two West Germans born around the same year. Hirsch goes further and makes the connection between the self and the other connected by a closer bond, like family or group relation.[65]

It is possible to conjugate Hirsch's postmemories with collective memories even if no direct transmission took place by focusing on the intimacy of pink radical circles.[66] For queer men, remembering National Socialism meant searching for queer clues in an "opaque and haunting past" to make sense of the present.[67] There are two moments of identification here: an identification of queerness in the past and an identification with the queerness in the past. Having uncovered what had happened, queer West Germans highlighted similarities and adopted the experiences of others to make sense of their own.

---

[63] For a discussion on the subject, see Silke Horstkotte, "Recollective Processes and the 'Topography of Forgetting' in W.G. Sebald's Austerlitz." In *Diaspora and Memory: Figures of Displacement in Contemporary Literature, Arts and Politics*, ed. Marie-Aude Baronian, Stephan Besser, and Yolande Jansen (Amsterdam: Brill, 2016), 193.
[64] Pascale R. Bos, "Adopted Memory: The Holocaust, Postmemory, and Jewish Identity in America." In *Diaspora and Memory: Figures of Displacement in Contemporary Literature, Arts and Politics*, ed. Marie-Aude Baronian, Stephan Besser, and Yolande Jansen (Amsterdam: Brill, 2016), 97.
[65] Marianne Hirsch, "Projected Memory: Holocaust Photographs in Personal and Public Fantasy." In *Acts of Memory: Cultural Recall in the Present*, ed. Mieke Bal, Jonathan V. Crewe, and Leo Spitzer (Hanover, NH: University Press of New England, 1999), 9.
[66] Here I understand intimacy similarly to Elisa Heinrich. See Elisa Heinrich, *Intim und Respektabel. Homosexualität und Freundinnenschaft in der deutschen Frauenbewegung um 1900* (Göttingen: Vandenhoeck & Ruprecht, 2022), 16.
[67] Marianne Hirsch and Leo Spitzer, "Testimonial Objects Memory, Gender and Transmission." In *Diaspora and Memory: Figures of Displacement in Contemporary Literature, Arts and Politics*, ed. Marie-Aude Baronian, Stephan Besser, and Yolande Jansen (Amsterdam: Brill, 2016), 138.

Coming back to the case of Almut, how can we understand his connection to the traumatic events of the past based on his lecture of Josef Kohout's memoirs? In her analysis of Jewish memories centred on Jews in America with no direct family connection to the Holocaust, Pascale R Bos examines the way postmemories could work among peers of the same minority group if the 'diasporic discourse' was centred enough on the traumatic past.[68] In doing so, she analyses the way US Jewish lives changed from "a culture in which adaptation had been the main cultural norm to one in which 'survival' became the primary virtue, making it particularly receptive to the events of the Holocaust."[69] Her "adoptive memories" help our readings of the pink radicals in the 1970s. Joining both a projected memory of oppression with a present historicized by lectures on testimonies, pink radicals adopted the traumatic memory of the men with the pink triangle, appropriating their trauma. It is these adoptive memories that allowed them to sing during a demo organized by the *Vereinigung der Verfolgten des Naziregimes*, 'Union of the Persecutees of the Nazi Regime' (VVN):

> Do you hear the voices of the reaction
> They insult us gays as sick and perverse
> The division of the people is their tone
> But we have had enough of it now
> So we fight together against the reaction
> Rise up against the laws of the state
> That regulate oppression
> Gays on the pink front
> [. . .]
> Do you hear the voices of the reaction
> The fascists threaten us with annihilation
> They strive for the final solution in the camp
> Boldly prevent that from happening[70]

The trade in information concerning the fate of the men with the pink triangle, the narrative accounts of the tortures they had endured, and the 1970s struggles for the recognition of said atrocities are all linked through transfers of experience. By writing a genealogy of queerness through references to the past, but also by embodying it through bodily practices like demonstrations, pink radicals reinforced this link between the past and the present, constantly referring to experiences in the past to make sense of contemporary discriminations. Queer memory activism in the period was therefore more than simply commemoration, a sense

---

68 Bos, "Adopted Memory," 101.
69 Bos, "Adopted Memory," 101.
70 Schwules Museum, Berlin, Sammlung Holy, Folder 028, *Schwule Aktion Köln*.

of solidarity with the past, or a quest for recognition. It was also a transfer of experience. This recollection of a collective memory became a unifying factor for pink radicals, offering personal as well as cultural meanings for a (re)creation of the queer self in the 1970s. To put it another way, queer men gave political importance to their sexuality in the present by reading traumatic experiences of the past and then relating these readings to their own lives. In doing so, they constructed a historical queer subject; they created meaning through social phenomena and acts of memory.[71]

These transfers of experience were also transfers of historical trauma. Scholars have been researching this way of adopting and appropriating a transmitted form of trauma, naming it "cultural trauma."[72] By constructing a form of cultural memory based on trauma, social groups – as well as national imagined communities – cognitively project their suffering into the suffering of the past, creating a collective sentiment of belonging based on the shared projected experience.[73] In the case of the Holocaust, Dominick LaCapra has demonstrated the importance of this form of virtual experience to understand how whole social groups have been affected by the tragic events of genocide.[74] As they identify with the cause of trauma, "members of collectives define their solidary relationships in ways that, in principle, allow them to share the suffering of others."[75]

For Cathy Caruth, trauma is not only a violent event in someone's past, but is also the unassimilated nature of the event that comes back later to haunt the survivor, even if the traumatic instance of the event had been unknown to them.[76] Additionally, traumata can metaphorically be considered like an act of speech.[77] Navigating the waters of the public sphere, social groups can persuasively project their suffering into the past and demonstrate the particularity of the historical

---

[71] On the constructivist uses of trauma, see Susan Brillon, "Trauma Narratives and the Remaking of the Self." In *Acts of Memory: Cultural Recall in the Present*, ed. Mieke Bal, Jonathan V. Crewe, and Leo Spitzer (Hanover, NH: University Press of New England, 1999), 41.
[72] Jeffrey C. Alexander, "Toward a Theory of Cultural Trauma." In *Cultural Trauma and Collective Identity*, ed. Alexander Jeffrey, Ron Eyerman, and Bernard Giesen (Berkeley: University of California Press, 2004), 1–30.
[73] Alexander, "Toward a Theory of Cultural Trauma," 1–30. See also Ernst van Alpen, "Symptoms of Discursivity," 34.
[74] See Dominick LaCapra, *History in Transit: Experience, Identity, Critical Theory* (Ithaca, NY: Cornell University Press, 2004); Dominick LaCapra, *Representing the Holocaust* (Ithaca, NY: Cornell University Press, 1996).
[75] Alexander, *Toward a Theory*, 1.
[76] For a better introduction on what constitutes trauma, see Cathy Caruth, *Unclaimed Experience: Trauma, Narrative, and History* (Baltimore: Johns Hopkins University Press, 1996).
[77] Alexander, *Toward a Theory*, 12.

situation. These processes are primarily noticeable inside a given community, convincing the close collective of its own trauma before opening the discourse to members of a broader society.[78]

Once again, an overview of the West German gay press in the 1970s shows a particular interest in the excavation of memorial treasures from the past, rescuing the experience from oblivion, and sharing a sort of queer cultural trauma. In 1977, *Emanzipation* republished a rare testimony of the 1950s, the 1954 story of LD Classen von Neudegg and his experiences in the concentration camp of Sachsenhausen.[79] The magazine printed the story alongside various reviews of *Rosa Winkel*, the student film mentioned in the introduction to this chapter. Most of these reviews drew a clear connection between the past and the present.[80] In the same issue, Peter Hedenström of the newly formed *Rosa Winkel Verlag*, 'Pink Triangle Press,' advocated for the creation of an edited volume on *Schwul* history and persecution under National Socialism. *Emanzipation* also printed a speech given in the West Berlin's Hasenheide park at an event denouncing discrimination in the job market. The speakers, members of the HAW, stated the following:

> We know the line of persecuted minorities from which our persecution stems from: women as 'witches' in the Middle Ages. N [*] as 'animals' in the colonial states (UK, US, FR). Jews as 'subhumans' from the nineteenth century until their systematic extermination in the concentration camps of German fascism, *exactly* like the 90,000 gays branded as 'pigs' by the Pink Triangle. [emphasis in original].[81]

Later in this issue, a written add-on flanked a news excerpt from the *Deutscher Depeschendienst*, 'German Dispatch Service,' about the murder of legendary filmmaker Pier Paolo Pasolini in Italy. This addendum made a direct connection between Pasolini's queerness and the act of murder by commenting: "A typical *Schwul* fate."[82]

---

78 Alexander, *Toward a Theory*, 12–15.
79 L.D Classen von Neudegg, "Die Dornenkrone: Ein Bericht aus dem KZ Sachsenhausen,"*Emanzipation: Zeitschrift Homosexueller Gruppen* 2 (1977): 26–28. The testimony first appeared as L.D Classen von Neudegg, "Die Dornenkrone: Ein Bericht aus dem KZ Sachsenhausen," *Humanitas* 2 (1954): 58–60.
80 During a projection in Munich, the discussion apparently turned sour as a woman in the audience started to scream at homosexual activists that they were, in fact, the 'real' oppressors and should go back to Dachau. See Florian Mildenberger, *Schwulenbewegung in München 1969 bis 1996. Materialien zur Geschichte der Homosexuellen in München und Bayern* (Munich: Forum Homosexualität und Geschichte München e.V., 2000), 15.
81 "Vorschlag für einen HAW-Redebeitrag zum Tribunal gegen Berufsverbote am 14.11.75 in der Hasenheide" *HAW-Info 20* (1975): 12–14. The N* word appears in its entirety in the original.
82 *HAW-Info 20* (1975): 30.

These examples are telling. They are all written in a proselytizing tone about the necessity to awaken, to act, to change. They are warning readers or listeners about a dangerous potential or already occurring repetition of the past in the present. In his ground-breaking work on memory paradigm shifts in the European eighteenth and nineteenth centuries, Peter Fritzsche mentions the importance of the ritual aspects of these kinds of warning for proto-historicized collectives: "[T]hey [survivors of the past and witnesses of the past stranded in the present] are not only shared by readers but, by providing events with explanation, motive, and judgement, place individual catastrophes into an embracing collective narrative."[83]

In the context of pink radical communication networks of the 1970s, the nature of the victim is superposed by the nature of the pain. Indeed, for queer men in the 1970s, not only were the men wearing pink triangles victims of the Nazis, but their exclusion from the official status of 'victim of fascism' was a retraumatization. The Pink Triangle became the symbol of acting out.[84] By acting out to effectively gain representation, pink radicals in the 1970s were trying to come through with the queer traumatic past.[85] As recent research shows, this representation of cultural trauma could ultimately be transferred to a North American audience and broadcast across social groups if the collective trauma or genocide was cross-referenced sufficiently.[86]

Overall, by connecting with and adopting the memory of queer men who were traumatized or murdered by the Nazi regime, pink radicals in the 1970s identified with a traumatic experience and found cohesion in acting out this newly discovered queer past of suffering. Thus, they historicized their own discrimination. They collectivized queerness into a shared postmemory of suffering. They oriented their emancipation towards a future devoid of discrimination but rooted in the negative experience of people like Josef Kohout. In other words, pink radicals were not instrumentalizing the murder of queer men they had just (re)discovered; they identified with their fate and shared a collective cultural trauma. Following trends seen in other social movements based on collective forms of belonging, they used this cultural trauma as a call-to-arms for the fu-

---

83 Peter Fritzsche, *Stranded in the Present: Modern Time and the Melancholy of History* (Cambridge, Mass.: Harvard University Press, 2004), 208.
84 Dominick LaCapra proposes a "sociocultural Lamarckianism involving the 'inheritance' of acquired characteristics through interacting processes of acting out – or compulsively repeating – posttraumatic symptoms and working through them, including educational and critical processes." LaCapra, *History in Transit*, 11.
85 LaCapra, *History in Transit*, 55–57.
86 LaCapra, *History in Transit*, 57. See also Jake Newsome, *Pink Triangle Legacies: Coming out in the Shadow of the Holocaust* (Ithaca, NY: Cornell University Press, 2022.)

ture.[87] In this sense, the HAW recuperation of the Pink Triangle in 1975 is linked to this sentiment of collective awakening. Echoing the importance of this collective moment, the *Tunte*, Anna, wrote in 1975: "[T]he Pink Triangle shows that I stand in solidarity with the gays. I want to do something with you, the Pink Triangle can only be the sign of what we want to change, and in that sense, I think the triangle is quite good."[88]

1.4 Collectivizing the triangle

How did other pink radicals relate to the HAW and its recuperation of the triangle? In the city of Brunswick in Lower-Saxony, the *Arbeitsgruppe Homosexualität Braunschweig*, 'Working Group Homosexuality Brunswick,' (AHB) invited queer men to a discussion evening in the summer of 1975. On July 15, the group not only produced material with basic information about their triweekly meetings, but also echoed the pink radical zeitgeist of the mid-1970s. One of the group's posters is a perfect example of wounded attachment linked to recuperation of the triangle. Minimalist in pink and white with combative rhetoric, the poster is flanked by a big Pink Triangle facing downwards, taking up half of the page. The text reads: "400,000 gays died in concentration camps! [. . .] Homosexuals in Brunswick think they have good reason to fear persecution again . . . could you be a persecutor?"[89] Next to the Pink Triangle, a small interstice explains how the symbol forced on queer men is like the red triangles worn by political prisoners or the "yellow ones" for Jews.[90]

The poster can be understood as an outreach tactic simultaneously targeting both fellow pink radicals and heteronormative society in Brunswick. The text invites heterosexual readers to reflect on their own position – "Could you also be a persecutor?" – but to also identify queerphobic oppression and the importance of solidarity across structures of desires – "This situation can only be eliminated by

---

[87] For a connection to identity politics, see Lory Britt and David Heise, "From Shame to Pride in Identity Politics." In *Self, Identity, and Social Movements*, ed. Sheldon Stryker, Timothy J. Owens, and Robert W. White (Minneapolis, MN: University of Minnesota Press, 2000), 252–268. For a connection to feelings of frustration and social movements in Germany, see Joachim C. Häberlen and Jake P. Smith, "Struggling for Feelings: The Politics of Emotions in the Radical New Left in West Germany, C.1968–84," *Contemporary European History* 23, no. 4 (2014): 615–637.
[88] Anna, "Diskussionsbeiträge des Rosa Winkel Kollektivs": 27–28.
[89] *"400 000 Schwule kamen in Konzentrationslagern um!,"* Schwules Museum, Berlin, *Sammlung Holy*, Folder 006, *AHB*.
[90] This is, of course, incorrect. Jewish deportees in Nazi concentration camps were not wearing Yellow Triangles.

the commitment of each individual."[91] The artwork hints at a different understanding of emancipation on the side of the AHB. The text mentions *Schwulen* like in the material by the HAW but is more closely connected to cultural trauma. Contrary to the HAW, the discourse is oriented toward change and toward an alliance with possible heterosexual allies.

Still, the AHB was not a group fighting for a mere acceptance of queerness – here *Schwulsein* – by a presupposed heterosexual core in German society. In their *AHB-Info* of March 1977, the group strongly condemned the longing for tolerance of other queer groups and expressed its contempt for the naiveté of such a discourse, tolerance never excluding a possibility for further persecution.[92] Like the HAW and other pink radicals, the AHB used the Pink Triangle as a symbol for their emancipation. Even if the aim was different, the group advocated for a recuperation of the symbol and plastered parts of the city with their poster. The *Braunschweiger Zeitung*, 'Brunswick Newspaper,' reported on the event on the same day, explaining the meaning of the triangle to its readership.[93] If the AHB and the HAW were using the symbol, other groups went further and included the Pink Triangle not only on their material and logo, but also in their name. For instance, the group *Rosa Winkel Wuppertal*, 'Pink Triangle Wuppertal,' explained the significance of its name in the pages of *Emanzipation*.[94] The connection with the triangle was meant as both a reminder that queer male victims of National Socialism were still awaiting justice and that West German society in the 1970s was still the heir to this past.[95] However, like a hybrid between the HAW and the AHB, the *Rosa Winkel Wuppertal* understood itself both as an emancipatory group seeking alliance with other progressive forces and other social movements on the left.[96] Thorough archival research confirms that the *Rosa Winkel Wuppertal* stance on the symbol was also widely spread across the Federal Republic at the time.[97]

---

91 Schwules Museum, Berlin, Sammlung Holy, Folder 006, *AHB*.
92 "Toleranz nur aus der Distanz," *AHB-Infos*, (March 1976): 3.
93 HH, "Ein 'rosa Winkel' als Symbol der Emanzipation: Aktion der 'ahb' – 400 000 Homosexuelle starben im KZ," *Braunschweiger Zeitung* (July 15, 1975).
94 Rosa Winkel Wuppertal, "Die Gruppe Rosa Winkel Wuppertal stellt sich vor," *Emanzipation Zeitschrift homosexueller* Aktionsgruppen 2 (1978): 35–36.
95 Rosa Winkel Wuppertal, "Die Gruppe Rosa Winkel Wuppertal stellt sich vor": 35–36.
96 Rosa Winkel Wuppertal, "Die Gruppe Rosa Winkel Wuppertal stellt sich vor": 35–36.
97 Another example would be *Aktionsgruppe Homosexualität Osnabrück* 'Action Group Homosexuality Osnabrück' in North Rhine-Westphalia. The group produced extensive material on the Pink Triangle and why they were using it. See Schwules Museum, Berlin, Sammlung Holy, Folder 054 *Gruppe KOB–WUP*.

Most of the pink radicals continued to use the Pink Triangle in the second half of the 1970s but – contrary to the HAW – kept the cultural trauma of National Socialism in the foreground, appealing to the victimhood narratives of the concentration camps, and reimagining their position in society based on a collective association with the past. Sometimes the link between the past and the present was far more concrete than a mere recall of past persecution. For instance, groups in North Rhine-Westphalia who suffered attacks by neo-Nazis were quick to make the connection with the virtual experience of their imagined community.[98]

However, one should be wary of a homogeneous portrayal of the Pink Triangle's recuperation. Some pink radicals were still against the use of the symbol for any other reasons beyond the commemoration of the queer men who had actually been prisoners of the Nazis or the memory of the deaths in Dachau, Sachsenhausen, Buchenwald, and other crime scenes of the murderous and genocidal Nazi program.

One such example is an action organized by a coalition of queer political groups in Cologne in 1976. In a joint plenum to discuss the funding of an action in the center of the city, discordant voices started to argue against the use of the symbol.[99] Activists had planned to organize an information stand on *Schildergasse* like the one by the HAW on Ku'Damm. They intended to distribute leaflets emblazoned with the Pink Triangle. Two opposite positions are traceable in the archive. On one side, proponents of the triangle reiterated their discourse on work-based discrimination, attacks by the Church, and what they considered continuities between life in the FRG and under National Socialism.[100] For them, it was a question of self-consciousness, an adopted memory, and queer trauma. On the other side, opponents of the triangle considered the use of the symbol "arrogant" and "cynical," refusing to link the events during and before the War. They were afraid that the use of the symbol would reactivate the fears of survivors.[101] The minutes of the plenum do not clearly indicate if they meant pedestrians passing by or if the groups had members who survived the camps and would feel forced to wear the triangle again.

---

98 The neo-Nazi group *Aktion Scharfes Messer* 'Action Sharp Knife' attacked the meeting space of the *Aktionsgruppe Homosexualität Osnabrück* at the end of the decade. The *Aktionsgruppe Homosexualität Osnabrück* published the letter accompanying the event and released a communiqué on the matter. See Schwules Museum, Berlin, Sammlung Holy, Folder 054 *Gruppe KOB–WUP*.
99 The action was called the *Rosa Winkel-Aktion* 'Action Pink Triangle.' See Schwules Museum, Berlin, Sammlung Holy, Folder 027 *GLF Köln 1978–1980* and Folder 028 *SAK*.
100 Schwules Museum, Berlin, Sammlung Holy, Folder 028 *SAK*.
101 Schwules Museum, Berlin, Sammlung Holy, Folder 028 *SAK*.

Faced with these critiques, the GLF recused itself from the event, but the *Schwule Aktion Köln*, '*Schwule*/Gay Action Cologne,' (SAK) went along with the project. In its essence, this conflict proves that ideas of cultural trauma did not seem to have permeated the whole movement. The archive offers a caveat as many students – some heterosexual? – took part in the plenum for financial purposes that evening.[102] The minutes are unclear about who voiced these critiques. Yet the recusal of the GLF could be taken as evidence that at least some of the criticism came from other queer men. Nonetheless, most pink radicals ended up using the Pink Triangle as a symbol. The SAK was one of them.[103]

1.5 The power of images

This new form of cohesion is not only a result of the wounded attachment expressed by the pink radicals and the symbol itself; the powers of the triangle as an image was eventually responsible for the creation of a collective memory across the Republic. The discursive effects of images also played an important role in the development of this collective identity. A brief stop in Munich exemplifies the possibility to share multiple discourses using one image, the Pink Triangle.

The *Verein für sexuelle Gleichberechtigung e. V.*, 'Association for Sexual Equal Rights,' (VSG) in the Bavarian capital adopted the symbol in its fight for recognition of the queer men murdered by the Nazis or having survived Dachau. The association would then make this fight its warhorse for most of the 1990s, and chapter four discusses its struggle and collaboration with the Munich chapter of the *Ökumenische Arbeitsgruppe Homosexuelle und Kirche e.V.*, 'Ecumenical Working Group Homosexuals and the Church e.V.,' (HuK) and the evangelical *Versöhnungskirche*, 'Reconciliation Church,' on the grounds of the Dachau memorial museum. Together, all three organizations pushed for the recognition and official memory of queer male victims. The VSG and the *Homosexuelle Aktion München*, 'Homosexual Action Munich,' were already pushing for stronger commemoration of queer victims in the 1970s, repeatedly demanding permission to lay a wreath of flowers during official ceremonies.[104] Apart from an iconic use of the triangle, the VSG was not prompted to use the symbol in its official material. By iconic, I understand here a use of the Pink Triangle as a direct representation of the one

---

102 This means that the issues brought during the meeting could have been voiced by heterosexual voices or by participants not necessarily connected to the *Schwulenbewegung*. The minutes of the meeting are not precise enough. Schwules Museum, Berlin, Sammlung Holy, Folder 028 *SAK*.
103 Schwules Museum, Berlin, Sammlung Holy, Folder 028 *SAK*.
104 Mildenberger, *Schwulenbewegung in München*, 14–16.

worn in the camps and in clear reference to a struggle associated for justice for the survivors and those who were killed.

Resonant with Didi-Hubermann's understanding of Warburg and his idea of survival, it is possible to reconcile both the use of the VSG and the uses by the HAW and other groups in West Germany. The survival of one of the triangle's significations, an iconic one for a group connected to a local fight nearby to Dachau, did not exclude a more symbolic and indexical form by the HAW. The triangles used by the HAW in West Berlin and the VSG could coexist simultaneously in the pages of the pink radical press without cancelling each other out. In fact, this coexistence reinforced the pink radical collective. By enabling various individuals or groups with different understandings or uses of the triangle to associate the Pink Triangle with queerness, the image became more important than the discourse. To put it differently, a Pink Triangle effectively meant pink radical. No matter if it meant Marxism, a fight for the victims of Dachau, or the sentiment that queer men were an oppressed minority, the triangle became the vector of a multitude of discourses related to queerness.

Indeed, the symbol influenced a plurality of readers by visually conveying multiple discourses simultaneously. For instance, a queer man from the AHB reading *Emanzipation* was in contact with material of the VSG or the HAW. He would then associate the Pink Triangles illustrating these pieces with AHB discourses, his own political context, but eventually also assimilate the interpretations given to the symbol by the other groups. In doing so, our hypothetical queer activist from Brunswick would simultaneously understand that all these Pink Triangles were connected to his understanding of queerness. Seeing one triangle, he was experiencing many triangles: the one from the Nazis, the historicization of the AHB, the disruption of heterosexuality of the HAW, etc. Local magazines played similar roles. The VSG slowly started to use the Pink Triangle as logo for its *Rosa Telefon*, 'pink telephone,' its queer support service line in the region.[105] This usage was not comparable to the badge of the HAW, but an activist in Berlin reading the *Kellerjournal*, 'Cellar Journal,' printed in Munich would have understood that the symbol of this hotline targeted him as well. Simply put, multiple Pink Triangles co-existed across the Republic, but they all referred to queerness and the pink radicals – they united queer activists.

By recuperating the symbol, pink radicals also influenced the way that their contemporaries perceived and read images, and Pink Triangles ended up shaping

---

[105] Verein für sexuelle Gleichberechtigung, "Rosa Telefon," Forum Queeres Archiv München e.V., Folder *VSG 1974–1980* and Forum Queeres Archiv München e.V., Folder *VSG Kellerjournal 70er*.

queer identity. In his essays on photographs, Roland Barthes demonstrates that reading photographs and images is divided into two distinct actions: the *studium*, or the action of looking and recognizing faces, events, and memories; and the *punctum*, the moment of reading associated with one or more details piercing the mind and the image.[106] The punctum brings distinct memories from the studium and can change a received narrative.[107] It could also be influenced by postmemories and cultural trauma.

An anecdote in Lower-Saxony illustrates the importance of both punctum and studium. In an undated dispatch, the AHB mentions that their "indispensable" Pink Triangle stickers were a must-have for every mobilization table, but that a "heterosexual employee" had produced them the wrong way up – the triangle facing up – mistaking the command for an order regarding traffic signals.[108] For 2.50 DM, activists could usually buy the sticker with the statement: "[T]o be gay means to defend oneself! Position yourself in the gay struggle!"[109] Here, one sees the importance of the triangle not as the mere image of a triangle, but as a representation of the symbol created by the Nazis: a triangle facing down. Influenced by other key moments – see chapter seven – the importance of this orientation would eventually fade, but it confirms that reading the image politically invites an interpretation of both studium and punctum. To trigger an association to cultural trauma and have an effective logo, West German emancipatory groups had to use a Pink Triangle facing down.

The chromatic punctum only seems to have been important according to context. An unfilled black and white triangle facing down on a pamphlet seems to have been read as pink if the pamphlet concerned queerness. In the same vein, a black and white triangle facing down next to a memorandum by the *Comité International de Dachau*, 'International Dachau Committee' (CID), seems to have been read as red.

A pamphlet by the *Rosa Winkel Verlag* is here particularly relevant. Would-be buyers reading the brochure and browsing through merchandise ended up on a double page. On one side, the publisher advertised queer novels and used the Pink Triangle. On the other side of the page, a red triangle topped the list of books about

---

106 Roland Barthes, *La chambre claire: Note sur la photographie* (Paris: Gallimard, 1980). For more on Barthe's understanding of photography see Michael Fried, "Barthes's Punctum," *Critical Inquiry* 31, no. 3 (2005): 539–574; Elena Oxman, "Sensing the Image: Roland Barthes and the Affect of the Visual," SubStance 39, no. 2 (2010): 71–90. See also Gottfried Boehm, *Wie Bilder Sinn erzeugen: Die Macht des Zeigens* (Berlin: Berlin University Press, 2008).
107 Hirsch, *Family Frames*, 4.
108 Schwules Museum, Berlin, Sammlung Holy, Folder 006, *AHB*.
109 Schwules Museum, Berlin, Sammlung Holy, Folder 006, *AHB*.

"Homosexuality and fascism." This is the only red triangle in the whole pamphlet.[110] The publisher may have chosen a red triangle on this page for political reasons. During this period, queerness and fascism were often put in the same basket by some members of the New Left. By selecting a red triangle, the creators of the pamphlet legitimized the claim of victimhood. The men with the pink triangles were like the men with red triangles; they deserved a history, they deserved a memory, and they deserved books about them. Additionally, the use of red instead of pink paired with an image denouncing the queerphobia of the premier of Bavaria on the same page, sent a clear message: this has happened, it is still happening, and it is in a way connected to the plea to be regarded as victims of fascism.[111] This clash between pink and red triangles is not restrained to this one pamphlet. It is part of a much grander conjunction between queer men and the heterosexual men persecuted for political reasons during the Nazi era. This conflict played a significant role in the creation of an emancipatory movement among queer men and clearly defined a new opponent.

Five queer activists from Berlin made their way to Stuttgart at the end of April 1979. Through contacts with the *Allgemeine Homosexuelle Arbeitsgemeinschaft e.V* 'General Working Group for the Homosexual Community' (AHA), they were able to find a *pied-à-terre* and stay the night. The state capital was the first stop on their way to an important antifascist demonstration in Strasbourg. Indeed, at the end of the decade, *Verjährungsdebatte*, 'debates about the limitation period for crimes committed by the Nazis,' were raging and the VVN organized a pan European campaign to publicly express its outrage.[112] About 10,000 protesters gathered at the *Place de l'Étoile* at the centre of the Alsatian city and the five activists reported on the event in the pages of *Emanzipation* that summer. Their account is interesting, for it illustrates a variety of topics at the core of this chapter.

---

110 National Archive of Lesbian, Gay, Bisexual and Transgender History, Collection 84 "Jonathan Ned Katz Papers," Box 1, Folder 40: *Rosa Winkel Verlag*.
111 The image denounces the queerphobia of then-Bavarian premier Franz Josef Strauß, linking his queerphobia in the second part of the twentieth century with the persecution of queer men during National Socialism. It is a reproduction of a poster by the Anti-Strauß committee. For more information on the Anti-Strauß committee, see Sébastien Tremblay, "Visual Collective Memories of National Socialism: Transatlantic HIV/AIDS Activism and Discourses of Persecutions," *German History* 40, no. 4 (2022): 563–582.
112 Discussions about temporal limitations for the prosecution of former Nazi criminals were particularly present at the end of the 1960s and the end of the 1970s. For the case in the 1960s, see Caroline Sharples, "In Pursuit of Justice: Debating the Statute of Limitations for Nazi War Crimes in Britain and West Germany During the 1960s," *Holocaust Studies: A Journal of Culture and History* 20, no. 3 (2015): 81–108.

Already on their way to France, the five men were apparently anxious about their participation in the protest. One of them, Harry Böhlke, recalled that: "My fears: hopefully there are other gay groups so that the five of us are not alone; how will the other demonstrators react. Furthermore, this is the first demonstration for which I hold a sign to say to thousands of people: I am *Schwul*! The cramp I had in the stomach still lingers today."[113] Harry feared the backlash expected by queer men speaking out in the 1970s. First, he was scared to affirm queerness in a public manner among other members of the New Left. He was afraid that his emancipation, his act of speech, would be met with violence. Second, he was also acting memory, reminding his fellow protesters of a queer past of injury, of their antifascist bond, of the link between queerness and victimhood anchored in Nazi persecution. In his reminiscence of the events, Harry recalls the moment where he and his comrades unrolled a banner that they had brought with them. In front of the passing train of demonstrators, their banner drop called for a collective understanding of the fate of the men with the Pink Triangle: "*Schwule* in concentration camps, never again!"[114] As soon as they unrolled their political statement, Harry writes that two members of the demonstration's organizing team in long greyish blue raincoats fell on them "like cops" and expulsed them violently from the demonstration.[115] He remarks that his peers were shaken by the lack of solidarity of the other protesters and were left with the bitter taste of being outsiders, a feeling of not belonging in the New Left and in society at large.[116] Still, Harry and his peers once again unrolled the banner that day and received a mixture of reaction from applause to laughter.[117]

Next to Harry's report, *Emanzipation* printed another piece on the VVN in the same issue. With the evocative title "VVN Didn't Approve Gay Leaflet: Pink Triangle Still a Mark of Cain," the authors related an anecdote from a federal VVN Congress in Dortmund, when members of the board had apparently refused to read or acknowledge the plight of queer men. According to the members of the political organization, the story of queer male victims in concentration camps was a "special" story that fell beyond their significant political work and was too marginal to be taken seriously.[118] For the authors in *Emanzipation*, this was yet more proof that queer men were still discriminated against; they linked their virtual

---

113 Harry Böhlke, "Schwule und die Antifaschismus-Demo am 21. April in Straßburg – Eine Fahrtbeschreibung," *Emanzipation* 4 (July–August 1979): 8–9.
114 Böhlke, "Schwule und die Antifaschismus-Demo am 21. April in Straßburg": 8–9.
115 Böhlke, "Schwule und die Antifaschismus-Demo am 21. April in Straßburg": 8–9.
116 Böhlke, "Schwule und die Antifaschismus-Demo am 21. April in Straßburg": 8–9.
117 Böhlke, "Schwule und die Antifaschismus-Demo am 21. April in Straßburg": 8–9.
118 Föster, "VVN liess schwulen Flugblatt nicht zu," 9.

and adopted experience of the concentration camp to a collective oppression of queer men in the 1970s.

Overall, these events are a good illustration of the context at the end of the 1970s and at the centre of this chapter. One decade after the liberalization of §175 StGB, pink radicals had succeeded in creating both concrete and epistemological spaces in which they could speak out and emancipate themselves. Throughout the decade, they were able to collectivize their experience of the present by searching for answers in the past. By adopting a certain memory of National Socialism through communication networks and scarce testimonies, they identified with a virtual experience of persecution that they disseminated throughout their community. In doing so, they were both assessing themselves and pleading to a broader audience. A fight for justice for queer survivors and a denunciation of persecutions in the long postwar era slipped into a larger struggle for an end to oppression based on the torments experienced by queer men during German fascism.

Their (re)discovery of this queer past and its appropriation allowed groups like the HAW to recuperate the Pink Triangle and to enlarge its meaning. The symbol of the persecutor was expanded to become a medal of emancipation. Going beyond a traditional narrative transmuting shame into pride, this recuperation of the Pink Triangle also cemented the cohesion of an imagined queer community. Through communication networks, the textual references to and the visual uses of the symbol transcended the local divides of the movement. The triangle became a badge of continuities, a tribute to the past, and a warning for the future. It simultaneously assessed queerness in the present, as pink radicals used the symbol to make their sexuality public. To put it differently, different discourses on emancipation did coexist across the Republic, but the recuperation of the symbol by the pink radicals allowed a form of cohesion, a sentiment of collective belonging, of queer kinship.[119] Yet the Pink Triangle's journey had only begun. In the mid-1970s, the symbol flew over the Atlantic and evolved in its own way in North America. The outreach of the pink radicals and their identification with Josef Kohout branded the imaginary of queer men fighting for their own liberation in the United States of America.

---

119 Jennifer Evans, *The Queer Art of History: Queer Kinship after Fascism* (Durham, NC: Duke University Press, 2023), 3–21.

2 A badge of narratives – Pink Triangles, written communication networks, and the Queer Atlantic

In 1981, Jewish German scholar and journalist Richard Plant concluded a review of the English translation of Heger's *The Men with the Pink Triangle* for the magazine *Christopher Street* (a sort of gay equivalent to *The New Yorker*) with a condemnation of what he considered the "pinnacle of gay historical ignorance" of a younger generation of queer men living in New York. Having exiled himself to the east coast of the United States following the seizure of power in Germany by the Nazis, he did not understand the lack of interest displayed by US American queer men in what had happened in his home country and was appalled by the erotization of some aspects of the violence committed by the Nazi regime. In his words,

> [j]ust as I was beginning to go over the English version, I was taken by friends to visit a well-to-do, college-educated gay stockbroker who had recently acquired his first condominium, a handsome, four-room, well-appointed place. Yet, he complained, the color scheme bothered him and the thermostat did not function well. He knew I was working on a study of gays under Hitler. As we left, he took me aside and said, 'Now listen, you lucky guy. You were there with these tough, black-shirted SS men when they played their S-M games. Tell me about it, in hunky details.' I now have the perfect housewarming gift for him: *The Men with the Pink Triangle*.[1]

As he was writing these lines, Plant had already assembled four interviews with queer male survivors of the Nazis and, following short trips to the Federal Republic of Germany, was writing one of the first books in English on the fate of the men wearing pink triangles in concentration camps. Half memoir and half history lesson, his 1986 *The Pink Triangle: The Nazi War Against Homosexuals* is an interesting piece of work that resonated for decades after its publication.[2] Plant did not write the book alone. He remained in contact with West German scholars and activists and *The Pink Triangle* is embedded in this transatlantic correspondence. The writings of this adopted New Yorker are one of three sets of works at the core of this chapter.

---

1 Richard Plant, "Think Triangles," *Christopher Street* (February 1981): 54.
2 MS Richard Plants Papers: Series I Correspondence 1948–1998 Box 1, Folder 21. *Letters from Students*, New York Public Library. For a small biography see: Andreas Sternweiler, *Frankfurt, Basel, New York: Richard Plant* (Berlin: Verlag Rosa Winkel, 1996). Plant's book became the anglophone go-to on this topic until Jake Newsome published his *Pink Triangle Legacies* in 2022.

Analyzing the importance of narratives for the collective memory of persecution of male-male sexualities by the Nazi regime, it centers on ways the Pink Triangle, as a textual concept, influenced the creation of a transatlantic collective identity and historicized queerness in Germany, Canada, and the United States of America. It follows the journey of the symbol in its textual iteration, a written icon of memory, as well as a marker and indicator of historical change on the page. In other words, it demonstrates how classical readings of the Pink Triangle were constitutive for a transregional transfer of ideas. Sometimes juxtaposed to other forms of visual readings, for instance, the combination of written texts and pictorial representations, but sometimes only present as a word, the Pink Triangle remained a marker of knowledge for the queer Atlantic.

The following pages first explore the oeuvre of three gay men: James D. Steakley, at this point an activist and future Germanist waltzing between North America and West Germany; Martin Sherman, a Jewish US American gay playwriter; and Richard Plant. All three wrote different types of texts with the Pink Triangle at their center. Using their writings as a prism to map the production and circulation of knowledge on both side of the Atlantic, this chapter illustrates how the Pink Triangle was not only an important visual concept of queer history, but how writing about the symbol and discussions regarding images in textual forms also influenced the creation of a transnational gay community. Writing the image into plays, theater booklets, monographs, and magazine articles, the story of these three gay men shows how queerness is based on exchanges or kinship and how textual intimacies created a web across the Atlantic. Through their testimonies, these three 'Pink Triangle brokers' not only produced knowledge about a past of injury but also propagated myths about the persecutions of queer men and set the table for invisibility, erasure, and resentment. As our three main protagonists are all gay men, their writings are also a good space to analyse the prevalence of male homosexuality in queer memory culture. Beyond the cohesive and constitutive aspect of their writings for a gay collective memory across the northern Atlantic, their writings also need to be read with consideration for power asymmetries. Reading their work against the grain, I close this chapter by examining how encountering the Pink Triangle on paper confirmed the dominance of gay narratives in both Germany and North America.

This story is also a personal one. Every summer in the Canadian city where I was born, a myriad of political collectives come together to organize the biggest anarchist bookfair in North America. Thousands of people from across the continent gather in the southwest of Montréal to exchange about leftist politics. As a 15-year-old still-closeted queer boy with a passion for history, this is where I learned about HIV/AIDS activism, and the Stonewall and Compton's Cafeteria riots. This is also where, in 2004, I first got my hands on *Bent*, the play by Martin

Sherman and one of the central components of this chapter. Lingering at the queer table (there was only one back then), I read it from cover to cover, thinking that history was full of examples of queer men like me who had been tortured, persecuted, and killed. As we have seen in chapter one, these kinds of discoveries can evoke virtual experiences of suffering. Far from being paralyzing, these mediated encounters with the past can also trigger political self-realization and generate collective action. Beyond the effect of reading about suffering, this chapter investigates and focuses on the circulation of the knowledge hidden between a book's cover.

Five years later, I unearthed a 1981 French copy of Sherman's play in a pile of second-hand books at the queer radical bookfair *Queer Between the Covers*. Knowing that the play was a part of my journey as a now openly queer political activist, I bought it. The name of this then-new fair was far from innocent; it evoked a sexuality as both a discourse and a praxis, encountering queerness on the page and in the bedroom. By then, having learned German and started studying history, I knew that these writings linked my journey not only to the Pink Triangle, but also to specific narratives and collective memories of queer injury of the past. On paper and 'between the covers,' the Pink Triangle traveled as a written concept. Let us now follow the inspiration of three men who made it happen.

2.1 Pink Triangles over the Atlantic: Narrating victimhood in the press

During a particularly warm autumn in 1975, Richard Plant opened his mailbox in New York City to find a letter addressed to him from West Berlin. The letter had been penned by a certain James D. Steakley. The two men had started corresponding earlier in the year, exchanging notes about this and that, sharing their thoughts on German history, and especially about the fate of the men forced to wear the pink triangle in concentration camps. Coming back from a visit in the East Berlin *Museum für Deutsche Geschichte*, 'Museum for German History,'[3] on November 11, 1975, Steakley shared his astonishment with Plant. He explained how he had seen the uniforms of concentration camps detainees, some of them with the infamous pink triangle. He recalled his surprise emotionally – "Amazing . . . I nearly fainted when I saw it, I'll be taking photos of that too" – as well as being intrigued to find

---

3 Situated in the *Zeughaus* and opened in 1952, the collection of this GDR Museum was incorporated in today's *Deutsches Historisches Museum*.

that the triangles were smaller than he had previously imagined.[4] He wrote further, "in West Berlin, too, various people I know have talked to *Rosa Winkel* [in German in the original]. They sell *Rosa Winkel* at the gay booksellers here, enamelled metal – they all wear them at the demos."[5]

By reading further letters, it becomes clear that Steakley was in contact with many activists from the *Homosexuelle Aktion Westberlin* (HAW) as the group started to recuperate the symbol in the mid-1970s.[6] As chapter one made clear, the assertion that everyone was wearing Pink Triangles at demonstrations is an exaggeration. However, this confirms that Plant was aware of the recuperation of the Triangle a couple of years before he started his research on the same topic. In the subsequent months, Steakley became Plant's eyes in West Berlin and encouraged him to write to gay German publishers to acquire some sources for his writings. He also confirmed that he could send him some paperbacks himself: "In any case, the two fellows who run and operate the *Verlag Rosa Winkel* are good friends of mine; they put up a table every Tuesday and Thursday in the TU Mensa[7] over in West Berlin and sell the titles I've indicated."[8] Steakley also pointed out that back in New York, Greenwich Village was also a good source for material:

> For your work on the Nazi period, you should be sure – BE SURE– that you rush out and get the periodical *Gay News*, which is printed in London but is on sale at the Oscar Wilde Bookstore on Chris Street. Issue No. 82 has a long article on the Nazi period by Rictor Norton, who's one of the best writers the gay movement has produced thus far – essayists, I mean.[9]

The symbol landed in the pages of the North American gay press almost simultaneously with its appropriation by the pink radicals in West Germany. However, its North American journey did not begin near the Hudson River, nor on the east coast of the United States, but commenced on the coast of Lake Ontario, in Tor-

---

[4] "Letter November, 1975," MS Richard Plants Papers: Series I Correspondence 1948–1998 Box 3, Folder 12. *James/Jim Steakley 1975–1982*, New York Public Library. The myth that pink triangles were somewhat bigger than other concentration camp symbols is still pervasive in some queer narratives of National Socialism.

[5] "Letter November, 1975," MS Richard Plants Papers: Series I Correspondence 1948–1998 Box 3, Folder 12. *James/Jim Steakley 1975–1982*, New York Public Library.

[6] Steakley was doing his PhD in East Berlin while being close to the HAW in West Berlin.

[7] The *Technische Universität Berlin* 'Technical University of Berlin' in the Western parts of the city. A *Mensa*, from the Latin *mensa academica*, refers to the refectory of an institution of higher education.

[8] "Letter December, 1975," MS Richard Plants Papers: Series I Correspondence 1948–1998 Box 3, Folder 12. *James/Jim Steakley 1975–1982*, New York Public Library.

[9] "Letter November, 1975," MS Richard Plants Papers: Series I Correspondence 1948–1998 Box 3, Folder 12. *James/Jim Steakley 1975–1982*, New York Public Library. Emphasis in original.

onto. In 1971, a collective emanating from the underground gay and lesbian scene of the Queen City decided to band together, releasing a magazine in November of the same year that would end up being one of the most important organs of the gay and lesbian – and eventually LGBTQIA+ – press in Canada: *The Body Politic* (TBP). The collective would subsequently change its name to *Pink Triangle Press* and was also responsible for many other publications until 2015. It also funded the Canadian Lesbian and Gay Archives in 1973, known since 2018 as the ArQuives. At its zenith, *Pink Triangle Press* estimated the TBP readership at around 3,000 people.[10] Ultimately, *Pink Triangle Press* would stop publishing the magazine after its 135th issue in 1987, citing financial difficulties, and switched focus instead to *Xtra*, its cultural supplement on Canadian subcultures.[11] Nevertheless, TBP was responsible for many societal debates both in and outside of Ontario, was one of the first queer publications to receive a governmental grant, and extensively covered the events surrounding Operation Soap in 1981, a bar raid widely known as the 'Canadian Stonewall.'[12] In February 1974, TBP published the third part of James Steakley's series on homosexuality and the German State.[13] After two previous pieces on gay and lesbian history during both Wilhelmine era and the Weimar Republic, Steakley offered a deep dive into the horrors of National Socialism.[14] He had previously covered every classic pivotal point of German gay history, from the infamous Eulenburg affairs to the creation of Magnus Hirschfeld's institute in Berlin.[15] International coverage of gay affairs in TBP was not new and Steakley also covered the liberalization of §175 StGB in the Federal

---

10 Ashy Mann, "What was The Body Politic anyway?," *Xtra*, accessed April 4, 2021, https://www.dailyxtra.com/what-was-the-body-politic-anyway-71206. For more information on the creation and some of the debates surrounding TBP see Julia Pyryeskina, "'A Remarkable Dense Historical and Political Juncture,' Anita Bryant, the Body Politics, and the Canadian Gay and Lesbian Community in January 1978," *Canadian Journal of History / Annales canadiennes d'histoire* 53, no. 1 (2018): 58–85.
11 For the complete history of *Pink Triangle Press*, see Edward Jackson and Stan Persky, *Flaunting It!: A Decade of Gay Journalism from the Body Politic: An Anthology* (Vancouver, Toronto: Pink Triangle Press, 1982).
12 For more on Operation Soap, see Tom Hooper, "'Enough Is Enough': The Right to Privacy Committee and Bathhouse Raids in Toronto, 1978–83" (York University, 2016).
13 Jim Steakley, "Homosexuals & the Third Reich," *The Body Politic* 11 (1974): 1, 20–21.
14 Jim Steakley, "The Gay Movement in Germany 1860–1910: Part One" *The Body Politic* 9 (1973): 12–16; and Jim Steakley, "The Gay Movement in Germany 1910–1933: Part Two," *The Body Politic* 9 (1973): 14–18.
15 Norman Domeier, *Der Eulenburg-Skandal. Eine politische Kulturgeschichte des Kaiserreichs* (Frankfurt (Main): Campus Verlag, 2010).

Republic of Germany.[16] Still, if TBP had shown empathy and solidarity with contemporary issues abroad, Steakley's third piece stirred up the idea that a whole chapter of gay history, of a gay past starting in Germany, had been hidden from the contemporary world. It also advocated for the necessity of gay historical research, a scholarship which would save "hundreds of thousands" of gay victims of Nazi terror from oblivion.[17]

Browsing through the magazine, readers were probably hit by the power of the first page's layout. Almost completely printed in black and framed with a red border, the text surrounded the infamously iconic Nazi flag with central swastika. Topping the page, just underneath a title stylized in a pretense of Gothic script: one big Pink Triangle facing downward, taking a major portion of the page. It is widely accepted that this triangle, this otherwise anodyne pink geometrical form, was the first time a North American audience laid eyes on the future symbol of emancipation in a widely circulated publication.[18] Yet at the time, readers were still unaccustomed to the symbol created by their persecutors, or at least, the persecutors of other non-heteronormative men living on the other side of the Atlantic. In other words, the mere view of the symbol was not yet enough to conjure the horrors of the camps. The triangle first had to gather meanings through the essay with which it was juxtaposed.

As in the previous two parts of his series, Steakley focused on key moments from the traditional German narrative of the time: the 'Night of the Long Knives,' Himmler's witch-hunt, the destruction of the bar scene in Germany, and a focus on the concentration camps of Sachsenhausen, Buchenwald, and Dachau. He additionally shared some of the myths – or at least deformations of the actual facts – constituting a narrative that could be called the 'Homocaust myth.'[19] Important aspects of this mythology would eventually include but are not limited to:

---

[16] Jim Steakley, "The Gay Movement in Germany Today." *The Body Politic* 13 (1974): 14–15, 21–23. See also the comparison made by the magazine between Nazi Germany and police repression in the 1980s in Canada. Michael Lynch, "Bent: Martin Sherman's Play, parallels Between Toronto in 1981 & Germany in 1934," *The Body Politic* 72 (1981): 28–29.

[17] Steakley, "Homosexuals & the Third Reich": 1. On the importance of ancestral genealogies for queer history, see again Doan, "Queer History / Queer Memory": 113–136.

[18] Similar to Erik Jensen, I could also not find other sources except one demonstration by activist David Thorstad two months later in August 1974. Jensen, "The Pink Triangle and Political Consciousness": 329.

[19] As mentioned in the introduction, Massimo Consoli coined the term in 1981 in an article for *Gay Journal*, which was also read by people in Germany. The 1990s saw broader uses of the term to describe narratives and tropes already existing in the 1970s. Here, the term 'Homocaust' is therefore not an actor-based concept but a term of analysis. Regarding the uses of the term 'Homocaust,' see the banner of a gay group on the cover of the Basel gay magazine *Anzeiger* 23

grossly over-assessed and exaggerated numbers of non-heteronormative men killed in concentration camps from hundreds of thousands to millions; the idea that non-heteronormative non-Jewish or non-Romani men were at the bottom of the hierarchy in concentration camps, the implicit accusation being that the story of these men had been lost by focusing 'too much' on Jewish victims; and the idea that the persecutions of these men were similar to that of the industrial killings of European Jews. The most exaggerated numbers of victims did not emanate from the pink radicals in West Germany, but from the pages of US publications. Access to corrected numbers provided by scholars such as Rüdiger Lautmann did not reach US soil until the publication of subsequent research, born from a dialectical engagement with gay history by gay Jewish men such as Richard Plant. It is thus no surprise that Steakley propagated information available to him at the time.

His tendency to use Pink Triangles as a metonymy for queer male victims of the national socialists is however a habit that still permeates both literature and activist pamphlets nowadays.[20] German literature also often used the term '175er,' people accused and condemned under §175 StGB. Since the 1970s, Steakley has been vocal about his own writings, harshly criticizing ways in which narratives of a Homocaust expanded in the 1970s and 1980s.[21] However, while historians have fortunately corrected the faux pas of the past, the focus on non-heteronormative male victims of the Nazis (even in their most inflated numbers) and the inclination to refer to queer victims as "the pink triangles" emphasized the symbol and associated Nazi oppression with one form of queerness, that is, the persecution of male-male sexualities. From the get-go, a transatlantic memory of what had happened in Germany focused on the legal persecutions under §175 StGB and on those wearing a pink triangle. This would have repercussions for the acknowledgment of other victims of Nazi queerphobia in the second part of the twentieth century.[22]

(1979). The banner says: "Homocaust – Holocaust" and is flanked with a triangle facing downward. One can imagine that this triangle was pink. The photo is in black and white.

20 Steakley, "Homosexuals & the Third Reich": 1, 20–21.

21 James D. Steakley, "Selbstkritische Gedanken zur Mythologisierung der Homosexuellenverfolgung im Dritten Reich." In *Nationalsozialistischer Terror gegen Homosexuelle: Verdrängt und Ungesühnt*, ed. Burkhard Jellonek and Rüdiger Lautmann (Padeborn: Verlag Ferdinand Schöningh, 2002): 55–68. He also did so in the 1990s during conferences, for instance in 1995 in Vancouver. See Miodrag Kojadinovic, "Holocaust < L < G neut. < holos whole + kaustos burned" ANGLES, (January 1995): 17.

22 Anna Hájková, "Das verspätete Gedenken an lesbische NS-Opfer," *Der Tagesspiegel* (April 30, 2022); Martin Lücke, "Die Verfolgung lesbischer Frauen im Nationalsozialismus: Forschungsdebatten zu Gedenkinitiativen am Beispiel des Frauen-Konzentrationslagers Ravensbrück," *Zeitschrift für Geschichtswissenschaft* 79, no 5 (2022): 422–440.

Steakley eventually published his findings in a monograph: *The Homosexual Emancipation Movement in Germany*.[23] In one of the early issues of *Christopher Street*, the book made the editors' list of essential readings to understand gay liberation. According to the magazine, knowledge "about the gay past" was a cornerstone of gay liberation. For *Christopher Street*, books such as Steakley's were the perfect opportunity to "understand and appreciate what Gays are fighting for" and a "vital study, which document[ed] and recount[ed] the growth of the German homosexual rights movement from its early beginnings in the nineteenth century to its almost complete annihilation by the Nazis."[24] These words are significant, as they differentiate between the German character of the non-heteronormative men oppressed by the Nazis and the presupposed North American character constituting the backbone of *Christopher Street*'s readership. As time would tell, this was about to change. Following the growing attention given to the memory of National Socialism, the idea of a transatlantic gay community began to emerge.

In the year following Steakley's contribution in TBP, the Pink Triangle also left the pages of the Canadian gay press to appear in *The New York Times*. Ira Glasser, then executive director of the NY branch of the American Civil Liberties Union, wrote a piece about the Pink Triangle and its hinted similarities with the odious yellow star used to humiliate and brand Jews during the so-called Third Reich. In his segment *The Yellow Star and the Pink Triangle*, Glasser mentions "the killing of a quarter million homosexuals" and questions what he considered to be a selective moral revulsion about the Holocaust.[25] Stating that federal and local laws had outlawed and "discouraged" religious discrimination, he added that similar laws were still dismissed and voted down by various echelons of government concerning homosexuality.[26] Pushing the comparison further, he added that "just as the Jews of Europe had to hide or perish, so many homosexuals today must hide in New York City to avoid the penalties of 'coming out' in the open: loss of job, harassment and abuse, even rejection by family and friends."[27] He concluded with a plea to support a new bill, Intro. 554, to combat discrimina-

---

23 James D. Steakley, *The Homosexual Emancipation Movement in Germany* (New York, NY: Arno Press, 1975).
24 "8 Basic Books on Gay Liberation," *Christopher Street* (September 1976): 1.
25 Ira Glasser, "The Yellow Star and the Pink Triangle," *The New York Times*, September 10 (1975). Mentioned in Erik N. Jensen, "The Pink Triangle and Political Consciousness: Gays, Lesbians, and the Memory of Nazi Persecution." *Journal of the History of Sexuality* 11, no. 1 (2002): 319–349.
26 He doesn't mention antisemitism by name.
27 Jensen, "The Pink Triangle and Political Consciousness": 319–349.

tion against gay and lesbians and invited his readers to demonstrate in front of the city council, brandishing Pink Triangles.[28]

This piece confirmed a broader zeitgeist at the time and, similar to Steakley's original article in TBP, furthered elements of the Homocaust myth. First of all, it traces a bridge between the persecutions of non-heteronormative men in Germany and the oppression or discrimination of gay men in North America, all while putting aside transnational forms of antisemitism. While not ignoring the dire situation in which queer individuals found themselves in New York in the 1970s, the two contexts were evidently different. A burgeoning post-Stonewall political queer community by the Hudson River was not the same as living under Nazi torture and murders, regardless of whether one used real or extrapolated numbers of victims. Yet, narrating the killings of the men wearing a pink triangle had entered the North American psyche. The effect of the Pink Triangle as a badge of narratives is thus similar to the badge of continuities discussed in the first chapter – see section 1.4; victimhood was a new mortar for the community and linking a common past to German National Socialism, the iconic evil of the twentieth century, had a cohesive potential.

Magazines and newspapers were on the front line of constructing an imagined gay collective past in the United States; they drew upon an activist tradition of explaining discrimination in the present by looking at the past. They were also cultural agents of memory, mapping transatlantic connections with Germany in the process. As chapter three will show, this was also linked to the importance of the Holocaust in US life. Still, queer communication networks went beyond journalism. Pink Triangle narratives and writings by the likes of Steakley inspired works of fiction. As we will now see, the significance of the Pink Triangle continued to accrue when it entered the world of theater.

2.2 Writing a play, sharing a myth: *Bent* and collective memory

Bent, a play by Jewish US American Martin Sherman, opened in May 1979 at the Royal Theatre in London with Ian McKellen in one of the leading roles. After the first performances, the production was transferred to the Criterion near Piccadilly Circus where it enjoyed mixed success. Michael Billington commended the play in *The Guardian*, but the *Daily Mail*, *Daily Telegraph* and *Sunday Telegraph* tore the production apart as a "sadist's feast, an orgy of violence conducted to no

---

28 Jensen, "The Pink Triangle and Political Consciousness": 319–349.

purpose and with inartistic ends in mind."[29] The polarization of his work in the British capital surprised Sherman, as he had chosen to open his new production in London because audiences were, in his words, usually more responsive to his work.[30] During its run in the British capital, the play continued to polarize critics, in both the mainstream and the gay press. If *The Guardian* had praised the play as a "parable about the way selfish survival gives way under pressure" and if tabloids had butchered Sherman's artistic aspirations, others like Peter Jenkins in *The Spectator* were appalled by the fact that the US playwright seemed to enlist the horrors of Dachau to the service of queer liberation.[31] Simultaneously, London's *Gay News* first published a deadly negative review, then ran an editorial attacking their own critique, and finally ended up sending another reporter who acclaimed the piece as the "best gay play ever written."[32]

Moving beyond London, *Bent* crossed the Atlantic and opened on Broadway almost a year later. I shall first focus on the play's influence and reception in North America and the way it strengthened both the Homocaust myth on which it was based, as well as the idea of a transatlantic collective gay identity. Second, I examine the reception of *Bent* once it made its way back to Europe and premiered in West German theaters. Sherman's work illustrates how theatre was an important vector of queerness in the 1980s, that is, how stage productions created a sense of belonging for a burgeoning queer community, specifically for gay men. At the core of this cohesion, the Pink Triangle once more played a central role. The story of *Bent* and of a nascent transatlantic gay identity was entangled twice over. Narratives associated with the Homocaust myth circulated in the USA and made their way back to the Federal Republic of Germany (FRG), inspiring new politics of belonging in the gay scenes of cities such as Berlin and Cologne. Here, I emphasize the fact of return to Germany, as these US tropes had their origins on European grounds. What is more, the circulation of knowledge highlights overlapping aspects of Euro-American gay communication networks in the 1980s.

---

29 Schwules Museum Berlin E Deutschland: Bundesrepublik Deutschland 1945- Heute, Box Nr 18b *Schauspielkritiken (M. Sherman "Bent" bis Okt. 1981)*. This section is based on my readings of hundreds of international reviews of the play, most of them compiled in the archives of the Schwules Museum in Berlin. In the following, I refer to the exact reviews whenever possible. I refer to the archival folders when the newspaper clips were not identified properly and when I could not trace the originals.
30 Quoted in Charles Ortleb, "Sharing the Holocaust," *Christopher Street* (January 1980): 13.
31 Schwules Museum Berlin E Deutschland: Bundesrepublik Deutschland 1945- Heute, Box Nr 18b *Schauspielkritiken (M. Sherman "Bent" bis Okt. 1981)*.
32 Schwules Museum Berlin E Deutschland: Bundesrepublik Deutschland 1945- Heute, Box Nr 18b *Schauspielkritiken (M. Sherman "Bent" bis Okt. 1981)*.

Bent follows the story of Max and Rudy, two gay men inhabiting the world of Weimar Berlin's cabarets on the eve of the so-called Night of the Long Knives. After Max's affair with a young *Sturmabteilung* 'the Nazi Storm Detachment' (SA) member is discovered, he is captured by the Gestapo and deported. Forced to see Rudy tortured and killed during their transportation, Max successfully hides his homosexuality and meets another man wearing the Pink Triangle, Horst, who is condemned for having signed a petition against §175 StGB. On the way to Dachau, Max successfully exchanges his pink triangle for a yellow star, telling his new companion that he intends to survive by pretending to be a Jew, having heard that men wearing pink triangles were automatically sent to their death. Both men end up in the same command where they are forced to endlessly carry white granite blocks under the supervision of the guards. Taking advantage of moments of reprieve, they develop a relationship with each other. At the end of the second act, Horst is forced to retrieve his cap thrown on the electrified fence. Following Horst's death at the hands of these sadistic games played by their guards, Max picks up his lover's body, switches his yellow star for the dead man's pink triangle and commits suicide.

The play is significant for many reasons, not least because it reproduces many tropes of the Homocaust myth. In the last scene of the first act, before arriving in Dachau, Max tells Horst that he "made a deal" by exchanging his pink triangle for a yellow star. Max further tells his companion that as a result he will not be at the bottom of the camp hierarchy and will be able to survive.[33] This scene is interesting as it relativizes the industrial death of millions of Jews in the German camps and the chance of survival of some non-Jewish non-heteronormative men sent to their death through slave labor.[34] Nevertheless, the inclusion of this scene is not surprising if one knows how Sherman anchored his work in the Homocaust myth, coming from readings of the work of James Steakley in TBP. However, social scientists such as Rüdiger Lautmann in Bremen had by then dived into the statistics and the history of the persecutions and debunked this mythology. The estimated number of murdered non-heteronormative men dropped from almost three million to about 15,000 and Lautmann's work inspired countless others to expose a much more nuanced version of reality.[35]

---

33 Martin Sherman, *Bent* (New York, N.Y.: Avon Books, 1980).
34 If it has been shown that some commandos reserved for queer men were particularly harsh, Jewish prisoners – queer or not – were often automatically sent to their death with no chance of survival.
35 Rüdiger Lautmann, Winfried Grikschat, and Egbert Schmidt. "Der rosa Winkel in den nationalsozialistischen Konzentrationslagern." In *Seminar: Gesellschaft und Homosexualität*, ed. Rüdiger Lautmann (Frankfurt (Main), 1977), 325–365.

However, this scholarship was not available to a non-German-speaking public. Before identifying the key moments of the Pink Triangle, it is therefore crucial to pause an instant and engage with the transatlantic story of Sherman's work. *Bent* became the vector of an imagined collective identity; it convinced gay activists in North America that the fate of the men with the pink triangle was not only connected to their own community's imagined past, but it also created the basis of a new sense of belonging for an international brotherhood of gay men. The German past, artistically rearticulated by Sherman, united with North American gay liberation and gave birth to the hybrid child of virtual experiences, victimhood, and collective identity formation.

In 1980, when *Bent* opened on Broadway with Richard Gere in one of its leading roles, the play had already benefited from an active word-of-mouth campaign. *Christopher Street* had already published excerpts and a dithyrambic piece on the production, stating on its cover that *Bent* was the play that "could change the 80s!"[36] In the same issue, the editorial team stated that: "[W]e at CS view Bent as one of the most important political and cultural events of the last few years. It is not to be missed."[37] Although the play garnered massive success and introduced many younger generations of North American activists to the persecution of male-male sexualities by the Nazi regime, the scene where Max exchanges his triangle also caused uproar in North America. Sherman had to fight uphill battles on two fronts. First, he refused to see his play reduced to a universal story of survival to make it more palatable to the general public. For him, it was first foremost, an unapologetic queer story. Second, he had to answer harsh critiques emanating from various Jewish communities who accused him of relativizing the Holocaust. Sherman answered in 1980 that he "wrote the play every bit as much as a Jew as as a gay man. My next play will be very Jewish," asserting that, like the fate of homosexual men in concentration camps, "there are areas of the Jewish past that are rarely written about."[38]

If some journalists like Richard Goldstein from *The Village Voice* denounced and criticized *Bent* for its historical inaccuracy, and some intellectuals attacked Sherman in open letters, the play nonetheless became a touchstone for many younger gay activists.[39] *The New York Times,* in particular, praised Sherman's

---

[36] Cover, *Christopher Street* (January 1980).
[37] Ortleb, "Sharing the Holocaust": 12.
[38] Ortleb, "Sharing the Holocaust": 11.
[39] Richard Goldstein, "Whose Holocaust? Review of Bent by Martin Sherman," *Village Voice* (December 10, 1979).

courage and the way he "exposed" another side of the Nazi terror in Germany.[40] Throughout its successive runs in North America and subsequent productions, *Bent* and the story of the so-called 'forgotten homosexual victims' began to take on certain sheen of acceptance.[41]

On the other hand, some journalists received letters from Holocaust survivors who were infuriated that their memory was being tarnished by pretending that homosexuals were victims of the Nazi death apparatus. In some of these letters, survivors stated that there had been no such thing as inmates wearing pink triangles and how all perpetrators were in fact homosexuals.[42] Yet, despite these complaints, journalists and critics mostly agreed that "the slaughter of homosexuals is something few of us associate with the Holocaust, and *Bent* does a service to draw this to the world's attention."[43] At the end of the decade, Sherman's work premiered in the Bay Area, staged by a gay theatre company in the Castro district. It was announced as a "vivid portrayal of the anti-homosexual persecutions of the Nazi-era."[44] By this time, the play had transitioned from a never-before-seen story about a hidden past, to a sort of ritual, a re-enactment of known historical facts (or narratives perceived as facts) for educational purposes.

The same thing can be said about the play's trajectory elsewhere in the northern transatlantic world. Belgian literary critic Robert Kanters wrote for the Parisian *L'Express* in 1981 that *Bent* presented in "a terribly boring prose," the fate of people who were persecuted for what they were and what/who they had loved, and not for what they had done.[45] In this way, the actors on stage reminded the audience that they could either find male-male sexualities repulsive and take the side of the executioner, or refuse to judge the "psychophysiology" of the protagonists. Kanters concluded that the audience was confronted with a choice: siding with the Nazis or accepting male-male sexualities.[46] While he refused to consider non-heteronormative men as martyrs of the Second World War, the Belgian critic had nonetheless put forward a new trope connecting the fate of queer men in

---

40 For example: Tom Buckley, "'Bent' to Dramatize Little-Told Nazi Horror," *The New York Times* (November 15, 1979.); Ellen Schiff, "Play About the Holocaust – Ashes into Art," *The New York Times* (December 2, 1979).
41 Schiff, "Play About the Holocaust."
42 Schwules Museum Berlin E Deutschland : Bundesrepublik Deutschland 1945- Heute, Box Nr 18b *Schauspielkritiken (M. Sherman "Bent" bis Okt. 1981)*.
43 Clive Barnes, "'Bent' Reveals One More Nazi Horror," *New York Post* (December 3, 1979).
44 MS International Gay Information Center Archives – Ephemera – Individuals, Box 15, Folder: *Martin Sherman*, New York Public Library.
45 Robert Kanters, "Peste Brune Et Triangle Rose," *L'Express* (October 22, 1981).
46 Kanters, "Peste Brune Et Triangle Rose."

Nazi Germany to the acceptance of queerness in French society, bourgeois Paris specifically.

The kind of relationship between the past and the present expressed by Kanters took another, possibly even stronger, form in West Germany. Mere months after the premiere on the east coast of the United States, *Bent* opened in the South German town of Mannheim, on the National Theater's smaller stage. Sherman himself stated that he "wouldn't have missed it for the world!"[47] Mainstream newspapers across the republic also focused on the 'hidden history' of the Holocaust. As the play was eventually renamed *Rosa Winkel* in German by its two translators, its promotion in the German press introduced the symbol to a national audience, way beyond the pink radicals who recuperated the triangle in the 1970s. More than ever before, it became associated with the experience of the non-heteronormative men persecuted during the so-called Third Reich. The *Frankfurter Allgemeine Zeitung* had already reported on this "Auschwitz Drama" during the play's original London run, showing interest for what the newspaper considered a "bizarre homosexual comedy."[48] At first, the play did not attract the same attention as it had in the United States but through the support of gay activists and intense scrutiny by the mainstream press, the play slowly travelled across West Germany to West Berlin during the early 1980s.

More than a hundred articles, reviews, and editorials about the play have been collected and preserved in the archives of the *Schwules Museum*, 'Gay Museum,' in Berlin. This repository mainly consists of small local newspaper coverage of regional productions, but also debates about the meaning of the play and its importance for memory culture in Germany. An extensive review of German reporting of Sherman's work across the decade allows the identification of three dimensions.

First, *Bent* included gay men in the discourse of the past and the societal discussions about National Socialism. Largely absent from public discourse in the long postwar period, gay men were now included in the conversation about *Vergangenheitsbewältigung*, 'the struggle of coming to term with the negative aspects of the past.' For example, in a critique of the Hamburg production, the *Holsteinischer Courier* from Neumünster asked in October 1981 if such a theater production, which dealt with the discrimination and persecution of minorities by the Nazi regime, should even be criticized at all in Germany.[49] By asking this question, the review

---

[47] Ortleb, "Sharing the Holocaust": 13.
[48] *Frankfurter Allgemeine Zeitung* in Schwules Museum Berlin E Box Nr 18b *Schauspielkritiken (M. Sherman "Bent" bis Okt 1981)*.
[49] "'Ecce Homo' — Drama der Homosexuellen: 'Bent von Martin Sherman im Theater im Zimmer," *Holsteinischer Courier* (October 15, 1981).

conflated the representation of the persecution of non-heteronormative men during National Socialism with the historical and political treatment of queerness in the Federal Republic's society at large. To put it another way, by centring queer memory production in the 1980s, the play also admitted gay men into broader societal debates. By naming queerness and sharing queer voices in the context of an ongoing broader processing of the Nazi dictatorship, the play had repercussions for the formation of a gay – and eventually queer – community in Germany. In this regard, the Nazi aspect only played an indirect role, but it did center queerness in contemporary debates.

Second, a plurality of reviewers pointed out to their readers that by attending a performance of *Rosa Winkel*, they were forced to reflect on the myriad continuities between the persecutions of queerness in Nazi Germany and the ongoing climate of queerphobia in the FRG. For example, a review of *Bent* in the biweekly Berlin magazine *TIP* in 1981 emphasized the complicity of the Church and the role of religious authorities in the persecution of queer men.[50]

Third, Sherman's version of the Homocaust myth had a much longer lasting symbolic effect. Renamed *Rosa Winkel*, it disseminated the Pink Triangle as a symbol to a larger audience in the Federal Republic. In almost every critique of the first German runs, journalists devoted extended paragraphs to the nature of the symbol. Through uses of terms such as "homosexual yellow star," the "perverse mark" and the "hidden triangle," various newspapers launched the Pink Triangle into prominence on a level never expected by groups like the HAW during the prior decade. The same news outlets even ventured the idea that, by talking "too much" about the Shoah, a "homosexual Holocaust" had been overlooked or even hidden.[51]

Going beyond yet another example of a certain antisemitic resentment in some gay circles, these reviews also display canonical and archival forms of cul-

---

50 Matthias Matussek, "Die Liebe in der Todeszone: Bent' in der Berliner Schillertheater-Werkstatt," *TIP* (September 1981).
51 See Josef Heumann, "Das Brandmal des Rosa Winkels," *Augsburger Allgemeine* (July 3, 1982); Werner Rolf Thielo, "Holocaust der Rosa Winkel: Martin Shermans 'Bent' im Münchner Theater an der Briennerstraße," *Hofer Anzeiger* (March 11, 1982); Rainer Hartmann, "Der Rosa Winkel auf der Lagerkleidung: Jürgen Bosse inszenierte in Mannheim Martin Shermans Stück über Homosexuelle im KZ," *Nürnberger Zeitung* (April 23, 1980); Krämer-Badoni, "Verhängnis im Zeichen des Rosa Winkels," *Die Welt*, 2 (April 4, 1980); Otto Beer, "Männer mit Rosa Winkel: Shermans 'Bent' im Wiener Schauspielhaus," *Süddeutsche Zeitung* (December 22, 1980); "'Die Männer mit dem 'Rosa Winkel': 'Bent' von Martin Shermann in der Werkstatt des Schiller-Theater," *Die Tageszeitung* (March 6, 1981).

tural memory.⁵² By bringing to the fore that which had been hidden, *Bent* brought collective memories from the archives of the gay movement to the cultural columns of the mainstream media. In other words, Steakley, a US-based activist, writing for the Canadian gay press in the 1970s, inspired Sherman, the gay son of an east coast Jewish émigré family to write a play about the persecution of male-male sexualities by the Nazis, which finally allowed a later generation of German gays and lesbians to fight openly for their rights using *Bent* as a springboard for their claim to victimhood.

Additionally, the play had a domestic impact for the queer community, especially in Germany, as it confronted gay men with their own perception of cultural memory.⁵³ Paradoxically, a play based on and spreading Homocaust narratives also kickstarted a scholarly inquiry that brought most of the historical inaccuracies to an end. Henceforth, the falsehoods and fallacies at the core of the play lost their grip as historians coming from the ranks of the gay community debunked them. Still, the educational aspects of the play had substantial outreach. Activist groups bought tickets in great numbers and organized salons and panels on the topic at the centre of Sherman's work.

A brief overview of the official *Bent* playbills for the productions in Mannheim, Ulm, Munich, Cologne, and West Berlin identifies informative and educational aspects of the stage. Each playbill contains research on the fate of the men discussed and represented in the play, as well as scholarly works by famous precursors in the field. For instance, writing a text introducing the play, Rüdiger Lautmann confronted readers with a text on the false link between homosexuality and fascism and another piece on his studies on the numbers of men persecuted during the so-called Third Reich. Each of the four booklets also contained an excerpt from the book *The Men with the Pink Triangle*.⁵⁴

The program for the German premiere at the National Theater in Mannheim is of particular interest. Images of happy homosexual couples were juxtaposed with pictures of prisoners who had committed suicide in Dachau; texts about the then already mythologized gay subculture in the Weimar Republic were juxtaposed

---

52 See Aleida Assmann, "Re-Framing Memory: Between Individual and Collective Forms of Constructing the Past." In *Performing the Past: Memory, History, and Identity in Modern Europe*, ed. Jay Winter, Karin Tilmans, and Frank van Vree (Amsterdam: Amsterdam University Press, 2010), 35–50.
53 Michael Holy, "Der entliehene Rosa Winkel," in *Der Frankfurter Engel, Mahnmal Homosexuellenverfolgung: Ein Lesebuch*, ed. Initiative Mahnmal Homosexuellenverfolgung (Frankfurt (Main): Eichborn, 1997): 74–87.
54 The library at the Schwules Museum in Berlin has the booklets from West Berlin, Cologne, Mannheim, Munich, and Ulm.

with an exposé on the long struggle against §175 StGB in the FRG. The Mannheim playbill goes on to publish interviews and testimonies with queer survivors.[55] In going to the theater, spectators could therefore find information on the tropes and narratives they were about to witness on stage. By reading material about the context of the play and other pieces about contemporary problems like §175 StGB in the FRG, people in the audience may have been able to identify with the protagonists. They also may have drawn the conclusion that their life echoed what was happening on stage or similar to the life of the others sitting next to them, united by history, part of a similar community represented by the Pink Triangle.

In this sense, even though the play propagated a somewhat dubious portrayal of historical facts, the theatre itself became a space of exchange and of circulation of knowledge. This exchange reached yet another level, crossing the Atlantic once again and influencing academia in the United States, when a gay German-Jewish émigré from the generation before Sherman decided to expand the ongoing discourse in another way.

2.3 A man with a mission: Richard Plant and transatlantic gay historiography

Born in 1910 in Frankfurt (Main), Richard Plaut earned a PhD in German literature at the University of Basel in 1935. After a brief career as a journalist and the publication of a novel for children in the 1930s, he fled the Nazi terror and migrated to the United States. He later changed his surname to Plant and settled in New York City. After contributing to the war effort as a translator, Plant ended up making ends meet with small gigs as a freelance author, a career that eventually led him back to journalism. He ultimately became a professor in German Studies at the City University of New York and at the New School for Social Research. While much beloved as a professor by faculty members and students alike, Plant's real time to shine came after his retirement from the university, when he finally researched, wrote, and published his ground-breaking work already mentioned in the introduction to this chapter.

Plant's personal involvement in his writings was twofold: he tried to make sense of his own experience as a gay Jewish émigré while also trying to share his testimony with others. He considered testimonies a useful tool – indeed, almost a weapon – to combat the erasure of marginalized voices from canonical narratives in history. His 1986 opus is therefore simultaneously an important work on the

---

55 *Bent Rosa Winkel von Martin Sherman* (Mannheim: Nationaltheater Mannheim, 1980).

Nazi persecutions of male-male sexualities and a very personal memorial essay about the era. By encountering testimonies, readers or listeners can be enlightened about the horrors of history, learn who they are, and where they come from; they can, by now almost a cliché, learn from history. An investigation of Plant's papers confirms this stance, as he quasi-religiously made a point of retelling his story in almost all his written pieces on the era. It is necessary to note that Plant was already in Basel when the repression and persecutions of queer men intensified in the 1930s. Yet his writings (especially his final monograph) conflate his personal memories, his interviews with first account witnesses, and historical facts that he only later learned following his move to New York.

Like Martin Sherman's play, Plant's 1986 monograph is a good example of how both factual information and misleading claims about the persecution of queer men paved the way for a transatlantic gay collective memory and helped create cohesion for a presupposed international homosexual experience or identity. Sherman had written his play in a North American context and had drawn inspiration from transatlantic communication networks. Plant, a gay Jewish exile, had also direct connections to the genocide of the European Jewry. During his time as a reviewer and writer for *The New Yorker*, *The Saturday Review*, and *The Nation*, Plant had already touched and reflected on the fate of the men wearing a pink triangle in Nazi concentration camps. Writing an unpublished review of *Bent* during the play's first run on Broadway, he reflected on the symbolism of the Pink Triangle as both a Jew and a non-heteronormative émigré.[56] Inspired by what he felt, Plant decided to dedicate the rest of his life to writing an extensive overview of the fate of the queer men persecuted by the regime.[57] Plant had lost his lover to the horrors of Sachsenhausen and Sherman's work sparked his endeavour into writing and researching these events. Writing to his publisher in the late 1970s, he recalled that seeing the fate of Max and Horst on stage had an enduring effect on him throughout the rest of his life.[58] Little did he know then that his mission would eventually shake up the discourse in both the USA and in the FRG.

Reading his early publications in the US gay press reveals how Plant bestowed importance on the memory of the men with the pink triangle and to the symbol itself. *Christopher Street* published "What the Nazis did to gays," in 1977. It

---

[56] MS Richard Plants Papers: Series II Writings 1926–1996 Box 13, Folder 9. *Theater Reviews 1970s 1980s*, New York Public Library.
[57] MS Richard Plants Papers: Series II Writings 1926–1996 Box 13, Folder 9. *Theater Reviews 1970s 1980s*, New York Public Library.
[58] MS Richard Plants Papers: Series I Correspondence 1948–1998 Box 3, Folder 4. *Letters to New Republic Books*, New York Public Library.

is one of his early pieces and one of the first articles in English about the fate of these men after the articles by Steakley. In another piece, "Nazis and gays," Plant sprinkled his article with personal anecdotes, employing a diaristic tone that would eventually become his trademark style when tackling the Nazi persecutions of the men with the pink triangle. "Nazi and gays" was a recollection of his return to Frankfurt (Main) in 1954, especially his interviews with survivors. Confronted with the silence forced upon them by §175 StGB, he wrote: "I had already learned that most survivors had isolated their experiences in some time-proof capsule and were loath to bring back the past."[59]

These testimonies, mixed with his own, became central to his subsequent writing in the 1980s before the publication of his book in the second half of the decade. Plant had by then become passionate about the possible death of an archive, a hiatus in the transgenerational social memory of the gay community. For this reason, he became a fervent advocate of the preservation of gay memories of National Socialism from his position as both an eyewitness and a gay Jewish scholar.[60] In 1977, he wrote that "the Eichmann trial, thoroughly explored by Hannah Arendt, alerted even the larger segments of the American public to the fate of the European Jews. But the gay minority has no Hannah Arendt. The books, the documents we have, most of them written in German, are sparse, and no film exists of the sufferings inflicted upon those men with the pink triangle."[61]

Plant started his enterprise by doing as much research as possible on the topic. Shocked by the numbers of victims being discussed in the 1970s, he reached out to Steakley who had, in the meantime, become a professor at the University of Michigan and had already started to retract some of his claims about millions of murdered homosexual men. Both men exchanged letters for years on various topics ranging from the gossipy to the scholarly and developed what seems to have been a long-lasting friendship.[62] It is Steakley who eventually introduced Plant to Rüdiger Lautmann's work and to others such as Egmont Fassbender, a German activist and eventual chairman of the gay publishing house *Verlag Rosa Winkel*, Pink Triangle Publishers.' Lautmann had already heard of Plant, his attention having been attracted to one of his pieces in *Christopher Street*. Plant likewise subscribed to *Homosexuelle Emanzipation*, in which he learned about Lautmann's work.[63]

---

[59] Richard Plant, "The Men with the Pink Triangles," *Christopher Street* (February 1977): 9.
[60] Plant, "The Men with the Pink Triangles": 40.
[61] Plant, "The Men with the Pink Triangles": 5.
[62] MS Richard Plants Papers: Series I Correspondence 1948–1998 Box 3, Folder 12. *James/Jim Steakley 1975–1982*, New York Public Library.
[63] MS Richard Plants Papers: Series I Correspondence 1948–1998 Box 3, Folder 10 *E. Fassbender 1975–1976*, New York Public Library.

Both men finally met in Germany and exchanged ideas on the importance of gay history years before the publication of *The Pink Triangle*.

Looking at the first versions of Plant's manuscript, the revisions he made after this meeting are telling: updates of statistics, new nuances in the comparison between Jewish and [non-Jewish] persecutions, as well as the addition of many more primary sources to complement Plants reflections.[64] As the correspondence and exchange with Lautmann and Steakley became friendships and spaces of reflection, Plant's mission became plural. He would bring light to the fate of the men with the pink triangle but would also fight the ignorance across communities: the heterosexual world's denial of the status of victimhood to gay men, and the obscene exaggeration of this status by activists wearing the Pink Triangle as a new 'badge of honour.' Still, Plant never stopped believing and propagating the idea that non-heteronormative men received the harshest treatments in the camps.[65] In this regard, Plant's work can be seen as a historicization and professionalization of the legacy of *Bent*. Plant did indeed refer to Sherman's work in order to attract the attention of the homosexual community, commenting that "those who have seen or read Martin Sherman's *Bent* will recognize some of the games that the SS men invented for the 'queer scum.'"[66]

In March 1976, Plant sent a letter to Lautmann in Bremen asking him for material and stating how challenging it was to obtain works on the subject in the United States. In so doing, he made his goals clear: "I really want to write a book about it. Because people here still believe 'that all Nazis were gay,' it's a given for them."[67] Following this first letter, the two men began an ongoing correspondence that would continue for years. From the formal tone of the early exchanges to the trivial information about each other's lives and relationships in the later stages of their friendship, their exchange of letters traces a joint transatlantic effort to correct factual errors in popular narratives on the east coast of the United States and in West German academia. Throughout the years, Lautmann introduced Plant to other scholars from the Federal Republic and Plant shared West German literature around New York and New England.

From the beginning, Lautmann made it clear that his own research, done with the help of his students, had shown how the first estimations of hundreds of thou-

---

64 MS Richard Plants Papers: Series II Writings 1926–1996 Box 11, Folder 7–8. *The Pink Triangle Typescript circa 1996*, New York Public Library.
65 MS Richard Plants Papers: Series I Correspondence 1948–1998 Box 3, Folder 20 *R. Lautmann 1976–1981*, New York Public Library.
66 Plant, "Think Triangles": 53.
67 MS Richard Plants Papers: Series I Correspondence 1948–1998 Box 3, Folder 20 *R. Lautmann 1976–1981*, New York Public Library.

sands of homosexual victims were grossly exaggerated.[68] Meanwhile, Plant was coming back from an emotional stay in the archives of the International Tracing Service at Bad Arolsen in Hessen, where he spent countless hours trying to meditate on his own involvement with the past. Going through a small bout of sadness in the archives, Plant also realized that the numbers of non-heteronormative men murdered by the Nazi regime were much lower that he had expected.[69] Even if the statistics might have countered some of the exaggerated numbers put forward by gay activists, the publication of Lautmann's major work still emphasized how a lower number of deaths did not mean that these victims should be acknowledged any less. This is a point he had to defend many times in the mainstream media before the awakening brought by *Bent* in the FRG.[70]

Coming back home to the USA, Plant found solace in the necessity of writing his book and Lautmann reminded him in another letter about the imperative of publishing on the topic in English. All in all, Plant's correspondence with Steakley, Lautmann, and other German intellectuals and activists allowed him to navigate in the space between the autobiographical aspects and the historiographical contribution of his final product. These quotidian intellectuals – simultaneously writers, activists and academics – left their mark through their scholarship and public interventions in printed media.[71]

The Pink Triangle, published in 1986, became a massive success in the USA. In his book, Plant succeeded in simultaneously drawing a portrayal of the horrors of National Socialism, giving a chilling account of his own experience, and shedding light on Himmler's involvement in the persecution of homosexuals. By using primary sources that had never been analysed at such great lengths in the English-speaking world, he demonstrated how the persecution of queer men was orchestrated from the top of the Nazi regime.[72] Praise came from all sides. For instance, Professor Wayne Dylon of Hunter College in New York City commended his work for its perspective of an "intellectual historian interested in Nazi ideology" and

---

68 "Letter August 1976" MS Richard Plants Papers: Series I Correspondence 1948–1998 Box 3, Folder 20 *R. Lautmann 1976–1981*, New York Public Library.
69 Ibid. "Letter July 1976" MS Richard Plants Papers: Series I Correspondence 1948–1998 Box 3, Folder 20 *R. Lautmann 1976–1981*, New York Public Library.
70 *Frankfurter Allgemeine Zeitung* in SM E Box Nr 18b *Schauspielkritiken (M. Sherman "Bent" bis Okt 1981)*.
71 For a brilliant use of the term quotidian intellectuals in a transatlantic perspective, see Tiffany N. Florvil, *Mobilizing Black Germany: Afro-German Women and the Making of a Transatlantic Movement*, (Champaign, IL: University of Illinois Press, 2020).
72 Richard Plant, *The Pink Triangle: The Nazi War against Homosexuals* (New York City, NY: Henry Holt and Company, 1988).

Eric Marcus tried to obtain an interview for what would become his famous *Making History: The Struggle for Gay and Lesbian Equal Rights, 1945 to 1990*.[73]

Going through Plant's papers, one can spend hours reading all the fan mail he received between 1986 and 1992. Most of these express highly emotional reactions following the reading and discovery of such persecutions. Furthermore, people writing to Plant thanked him for publishing a "much-needed" survey of the story in the English-speaking world, praising him for the accessibility and usefulness of such a book for the movement and for the understanding of gay history.[74] For months, this man on a mission traveled the United States, giving talks and lectures at universities, at the headquarters of gay and lesbian organizations, and in the FRG.[75] At the culmination of an extensive and successful tour, Plant spoke at the newly created Gay Community Center in New York City, now the LGBT Community Center.[76] The room was packed, people apparently had to stand on chairs to be able to see, and Plant seemingly had to stay longer than expected, remaining to answer many questions hours after the event had officially ended.[77]

This fame also followed him outside of North America. The book, being written in English, became the go-to source for international gay activists. For instance, a young gay man in then-Yugoslavia wrote to Plant to ask for permission to translate the book into Slovenian for the Eastern bloc. The young activist wanted to combine the translation of the book – which was eventually published – with an exhibit in Ljubljana about 'Homosexuality and Fascism.'[78] Enthusiastic readers from Australia and Belarus also contacted him to tell him that his book had changed their lives.[79] Yet, not all critiques were positive. In 1989, a professor of Holocaust Studies at the Hebrew University of Jerusalem praised aspects

---

[73] MS Richard Plants Papers: Series I Correspondence 1948–1998 Box 1, Folder 9. *Fan letters for the Pink Triangle, 1986–1992*, New York Public Library.

[74] MS Richard Plants Papers: Series I Correspondence 1948–1998 Box 1, Folder 9. *Fan letters for the Pink Triangle, 1986–1992*, New York Public Library.

[75] MS Richard Plants Papers: Series III Lectures and Speeches 1949–1991 Box 16, Folder 8. *The Pink Triangle Speeches*, New York Public Library.

[76] MS International Gay Information Center Archives – Ephemera – Organizations, Box 10, Folder 6, *Jewish Lesbian Daughters of Holocaust Survivors*, New York Public Library.

[77] MS Richard Plants Papers: Series I Correspondence 1948–1998 Box 3, Folder 14, *Lutz van Dijk 1990–1992*, New York Public Library.

[78] Dr. Bogdan Lešnik, e-mail messages to author, April & May, 2018.

[79] MS Richard Plants Papers: Series I Correspondence 1948–1998 Box 1, Folder 9. *Fan letters for the Pink Triangle, 1986–1992*, New York Public Library.

of the book, while pointing out that Plant's talks about a shared agony of non-Jewish homosexuals and Jews was a terrible exaggeration.[80]

At the end of the decade, Plant's contacts in Germany put him in touch with the author Günther Grau who agreed to help him publish a translation of the book in German. After the publication, Plant was scandalized to receive a colder reception of his writings in the Federal Republic. He seems to have felt personally betrayed by now well-known gay German-Dutch historian, Lutz van Dijk, who had pressured him into publishing in Germany. In a review for the German gay magazine *Magnus*, van Dijk questioned some of the assertions in the volume, stating how *The Pink Triangle* would have benefited from the work of other historians and that the mixture of memoirs and historical research made the book an uneven yet important read.[81] Van Dijk also argued that the equivalence between the Nazi "final solution" and the murder of non-heteronormative men could not and should not be put on the same level.[82] Plant penned his reply in a letter clearly written in a burst of fury.[83]

This exchange and the reception go beyond Plant's at times difficult temperament.[84] It is a good representation of the asymmetry in gay history at the end of the 1980s, as well as a tendency in North American scholarship, to still conflate the Holocaust with other atrocities, employing Holocaust as an umbrella term for all murders committed by the Nazis.[85] In this context, Plant was an in-between, an intellectual, but also a witness of the horrors of National Socialism, a memory activist. If Plant's work was still met with mainstream success in German libraries, the public also had access to other books in German. Lautmann recalls, for example, that people commended Plant's analysis of Himmler's role in the perse-

---

80 "Letter by Jona M. Machover, professor of Holocaust Studies at the Hebrew University in Jerusalem December 23, 1989," MS Richard Plants Papers: Series I Correspondence 1948–1998 Box 1, Folder 9. *Fan letters for the Pink Triangle, 1986–1992*, New York Public Library.
81 MS Richard Plants Papers: Series II Writings, 1926–1996 Box 11, Folder 6 *The Pink Triangle – reviews and news clippings, 1980s–1990s*, New York Public Library.
82 MS Richard Plants Papers: Series II Writings, 1926–1996 Box 11, Folder 6 *The Pink Triangle – reviews and news clippings, 1980s–1990s*, New York Public Library.
83 MS Richard Plants Papers: Series I Correspondence 1948–1998 Box 3, Folder 14 *Lutz van Dijk 1990–1992*, New York Public Library.
84 For example, Richard Plant had the tendency to write letters to his critics. He wrote a particularly intransigent letter to the *Lambda Book Review* to complain about his exclusion from the "Best of the Year" section at the end of the 1980s. MS Richard Plants Papers: Series I Correspondence 1948–1998 Box 1, Folder 19 *Lambda Book Report 1991*, New York Public Library.
85 Jake W. Newsome, *Pink Triangle Legacies: Coming Out in the Shadow of the Holocaust* (Ithaca, NY: Cornell University Press, 2022).

cutions but were left aghast by the oversimplifications of his book.[86] These critiques notwithstanding, Plant's work became the go-to book for many activists due to international power structures and the prevalence of the English language. The dialectical transfer of knowledge across the Atlantic underlines the underestimated importance of entanglements in the already existing historiography on the Pink Triangle.[87] Reactions to Plant's book further show that the transatlantic conversation could not escape local national contexts of memory.

Through the title of his book, but also by continuing a tradition from Hans Neumann of referring to these men as the ones 'with the pink triangle,' the symbol gained traction in the transatlantic world. Named, listed, and referred to, a visual historical concept was also influential in its textual form. Discourses on the Pink Triangle shaped by the pink radicals in the FRG in the 1970s were brought to Canadian queer communication networks by a US writer – Steakley –, then picked up by a non-survivor gay Jewish writer in North America – Sherman –, then translated and shared by gay groups across West Germany, who themselves inspired German historians – radical gay activists who had seen *Bent* –, who corresponded with a gay Jewish survivor of the Nazi era – Plant –, who brought it back to international attention in an English publication. Only after this back and forth did activists in North America really pick up on the imagery of the Pink Triangle, an image more associated with the 1970s in Europe. This travel over and across the Atlantic in notebooks, letters, plays, memoirs, and newspapers is an integral part of the story of the symbol. From a direct indexical connection to the fate of the men with the pink triangle, the symbol became the go-to icon representing both queerphobia and the struggle against queerphobia. By using the Pink Triangle, pressure groups, militant organizations, and gay and lesbian rights activists were able to historicize the suffering of gay men and construct an international identity based on victimhood. Chapters three and six show the reasons behind and the impacts of this universalization, but this reference to the triangle and to 'the men with the pink triangle' also had repercussions for lesbian memory culture and politics from the start.

---

86 Dr. Rüdiger Lautmann, e-mail messages to author, June, 2018.
87 If historians like Newsome and Jansen have mapped these transfers, they seem to leave them uncommented on.

2.4 Pink Triangles against the grain: Lesbian symbolism and memory

Let us travel back to the beginning of January 1987 to a commemorative event in the former concentration camp of Bergen-Belsen. Next to the gay members of the *Ökumenische Arbeitsgruppe Homosexuelle und Kirche* (HuK) and the *Vereinigung der Verfolgten des Naziregimes* (VVN), lesbians were also present through the ranks of the *Lesbenring*, 'Lesbian Ring,' a national organization defending the rights of lesbian women since 1982.

During the ceremony, Bea Trampenau came forward in front of about 300 individuals, snow up to her ankles, to take the floor in the name of the women who had been persecuted by the Nazi regime. Her intervention hinted in three directions.[88] First, she mentioned debates surrounding the 'catastrophic historical research' [*katastrophale Geschichtsaufarbeitung*] of the fate of thousands of lesbian women during the dictatorship, a discussion which is central to the fifth chapter of this book. She compared the silence on lesbian persecutions and the confusion surrounding sources to the hidden history of gay persecutions in the 1960s and 1970s. How many lesbians had been branded with the Pink Triangle? With the Black Triangle? Was the perpetrators' category of *Asozialität*, 'anti-social behavior,' represented by a black triangle, a good prism through which to uncover the truth about these women?

Second, she referenced the debates concerning the claim that women were persecuted in the same way as men for their sexualities during this period. Going beyond simple comparison or statistics, she invited her audience to reflect on the 'divide and conquer' strategies of the federal government, in her words the real opponent in the quest for justice for non-heteronormative men and women. Trampenau was clear; by "separating hetero and homosexual victims," women against men, gays against lesbians, the politicians in Bonn were denying their responsibilities toward all victims of German fascism.

Finally, she reminded the men present that day that lesbian women were still discriminated against, asking them to show solidarity against patriarchy. In her words, the fight went beyond §175 StGB; it was a question of justice, of feminist solidarity with the systemic and structural erasure of women from homosexual liberation.[89] Ending her poignant plea against lesbian erasure, Trampenau recited a poem by Gerda Bierwagen. Bierwagen was a lesbian activist who had already

---

88 Helke Mews, "Entschädigung – 'ein Menschenrecht,'" *Dorn Rosa Zeitung der Demokratischen Lesben- und Schwuleninitiative* 5 (1987): 9.
89 Mews, "Entschädigung – 'ein Menschenrecht'": 9.

denounced the male-exclusive focus on gay victims. In the pages of the lesbian magazine *Unsere kleine Zeitung*, 'Our Small Newspaper,' she had written a strong essay against what she considered to be male chauvinism. According to her and other contributors to *Unsere kleine Zeitung*, lesbian women had to reflect upon what had been done to 'them' in concentration camps and investigate the fate of women sent to their death.[90] Trampenau's speech was also reprinted in *Unsere kleine Zeitung* and Bierwagen was an active proponent of the idea that women had worn a pink triangle in the concentration camp.[91] In her poem, "For Jenny Schermann," she writes:

> I saw the photo of a beautiful
> woman with questioning eyes.
> Of a woman
> With the number of a prisoner
> And the PINK TRIANGLE,
> Which meant for her the death sentence.
> Doctor Mennecke
> The Euthanasia doctor of Ravensbrück,
> Who gave the diagnosis
> "Libidinous Lesbian,"
> Considered your life unworthy.
> (. . .)
> But you should know:
> I, who mourns for you,
> Am one of the descendants,
> Who dug up the PINK TRIANGLE
> Back from the ruins of History
> And wear it today with pride.[92]

These lines are fascinating as a condensed version of West German lesbian struggles in the 1970s and 1980s, almost a mirror of the gay narratives. First, Bierwagen uncovers the hidden history of lesbian women in concentration camps. Second,

---

[90] "Verfolgung lesbischer Frauen im Nationalsozialismus" *Unsere kleine Zeitung* (January 1989): 3. Cited in Erik N. Jensen, "The Pink Triangle and Political Consciousness: Gay, Lesbians, and the Memory of Nazi Persecution." In *Sexuality and German Fascism*, ed. Dagmar Herzog (New York, NY: Berghahn, 2004), 334.

[91] "Eine Rede des Lesbenrings zur Gedenk- und Protestveranstaltung für vergessene KZ-Opfergruppen am 11.01.1987 in Dachau," *Unsere kleine Zeitung* (February 1987): 44; Gerda Bierwagen, "Lesben im Nationalsozialismus," *Unsere kleine Zeitung* (May 1985): 10.

[92] Mews, "Entschädigung – 'ein Menschenrecht,'" 9. The poem is reprinted next to the article and the page is flanked by an assemblage of both a Star of David and a Black (or Pink printed in Black) Triangle on which one can read "LESBE." The poem seems to have been popular, as I stumbled upon reproductions in multiple 'zines' in different archives.

she considers herself in direct connection with this lesbian past (*eine von den Nachgeborenen*, 'one of those later-born.') Third, she pushes the idea that the Pink Triangle meant an automatic death sentence, and fourth, she reclaims the Pink Triangle for herself. As Erik N. Jensen demonstrated in his research, this parallel also came with a lesbian resentment toward homopatriarchy. If non-Jewish gay men were accusing Jews of "stealing the spotlight," lesbians considered the silence of gay men on the issue as another proof of the reproduction of patriarchy among the gay community.[93] Even if not all women reclaimed the Pink Triangle the same way than Bierwagen did, the trope of being 'silenced victims' remained. For instance, a reader of the magazine *Emma* wrote a letter in 1999 expressing her outrage that the magazine had omitted lesbian victims in an earlier article on the Nazi atrocities.[94] In that narrative, if the Pink Triangle was the lowest of the low, the Black Triangle was the lowest of the lowest. Lesbians in North America indeed oscillated between a use of the Pink Triangle and the Black Triangle as a symbol of both lesbian survival to persecution and a symbol of pride.[95] Bisexual activists, regardless of their gender identity, had also pushed for two triangles, one blue and one violet, for their fight against Bi-erasure in the twentieth century.[96] Women's organizations of the children of Holocaust survivors and lesbian activists in the United States also mirrored the historical pretenses of queer men.[97]

However, the divide was clear. On one side, gay men were saying that their 'forefathers' had been murdered and silenced, and on the other, lesbian women pointed out the hypocrisy of removing lesbians from the equation. This split has been denounced by gay scholars and activists as both a dubious instrumentalization of the suffering of gay men and falsehoods propagated by lesbians to harness gay men's struggle for recognition to their own cause. These deceptive accusations were still floating around inside and outside of academia when the memori-

---

[93] Jensen, "The Pink Triangle and Political Consciousness," 334–335.
[94] Jensen, "The Pink Triangle and Political Consciousness," 335.
[95] Terri Couch, "An American in West Germany or . . . Did Lesbians Wear the Pink Triangles?" *Off our Backs* (March 1991): 23. Naina Ayya, "Scholars Disagree Who Were Marked by Black Triangles," *Washington Blade* (March 9, 1990): 7. Arie Schwartz, "What Color Is Your Triangle?" *Womyn's Words* (1993).
[96] "Brochure by Visibility in Pride New Jersey." Lesbian Herstory Archives: Subject Files: Part 6: Spinsters-Youth Folder No.: 14120. Gale, "Archives of Sexuality & Gender," accessed February 19, 2018, http://tinyurl.galegroup.com/tinyurl/5ybus5.
[97] MS International Gay Information Center Archives – Ephemera – Organizations, Box 10, Folder 6, *Jewish Lesbian Daughters of Holocaust Survivors*, New York Public Library.

alization of queer political memory was carved into stone in the early 2000s.[98] It still bleeds through into new publications and recent memorial debates.[99]

In the 1970s, radical feminists and proponents of lesbian separatism also found symbols to represent their own experience of hetero-patriarchy and the oppression they faced in homosexual communities. The Labrys, the double-axe of the Amazon, was used on necklaces and buttons, presented as an empowering emblem of independence and warrior-like strength. At the time, many DIY circulating publications, zines and pamphlets established three narratives about this ancient war weapon. First, they stressed how far its usage extended in the past. By pointing out how women warriors of mythical and immemorial times used the weapon, they also mythologized lesbianism into history, like Sappho's paradise on Lesbos, hence connecting their present to an ancient past, significantly empowering their struggle against the 'normality' of patriarchal societies. Second, they essentialized their struggle through spiritual connections with the "power of womanhood." Numerous contemporary publications go to great lengths in describing the power of "the Goddess" and her retribution for years of "enslavement to men."[100] Wearing the Labrys meant channeling the power of the Divine to fight back against the oppression of women. Third, in the Labrys, lesbian feminists laid claim to a possible life without men, between women, fighting for women, like the mythical Amazons of ancient Greek legend.[101] The Labrys was also *en vogue* in West Germany.[102]

---

98 Jennifer Evans. "Harmless kisses and infinite loops. Making space for queer place in twenty-first century Berlin." In *Queer Cities, Queer Cultures Europe since 1945*, ed. Jennifer Evans and Matt Cook (London: Bloomsbury Academic, 2014), 75–94; Corinna Tomberger, "Das Berliner Homosexuellen-Denkmal: Ein Denkmal für Schwule und Lesben?" In *Homophobie und Devianz. Weibliche und männliche Homosexualität im Nationalsozialismus*, ed. Insa Eschebach (Berlin: Metropol 2012), 187–207. Stefanie Endlich, "Das Berliner Homosexuellen-Denkmal: Kontext, Erwartungen und die Debatte um den Videofilm." In *Homophobie und Devianz. Weibliche und männliche Homosexualität im Nationalsozialismus*, ed. Insa Eschebach (Berlin: Metropol 2012), 167–186.
99 Insa Eschebach, "Queere Gedächtnisräume: Zivilgesellschaftliches Engagement und Erinnerungskonkurrenzen im Kontext der Gedenkstätte Ravensbrück," *Invertito – Jahrbuch für die Geschichte der Homosexualitäten* 21 Verfolgung homosexueller Männer und Frauen in der NS-Zeit & Erinnerungskultur (2019): 62.
100 "The Double-Axe is the Sign of the Goddess," Lesbian Herstory Archives: Subject Files: Part 3: Feminism-International Lesbian Movement Folder No.: 06450. Gale, "Archives of Sexuality & Gender," accessed June 24, 2022, http://tinyurl.galegroup.com/tinyurl/62aCDX.
101 "The Amazons Roots of a Lesbian Symbol," Lesbian Herstory Archives: Subject Files: Part 3: Feminism-International Lesbian Movement Folder No.: 06450. Gale, "Archives of Sexuality & Gender," accessed June 24, 2022, http://tinyurl.galegroup.com/tinyurl/62aCDX.
102 Beate Schappach, "Geballte Faust, Doppelaxt, Rosa Winkel: Gruppenkonstituierende Symbole der Frauen-, Lesben- und Schwulenbewegung." In *Linksalternative Milieus und Neue Soziale*

2.4 Pink Triangles against the grain: Lesbian symbolism and memory — 83

Nonetheless, the Black Triangle, a symbol related to the Pink Triangle through historical events and collective memory, became one of the foremost symbols of lesbianism throughout the second part of the twentieth century. For many lesbians, separatist or not, the focus on the Pink Triangle erased the particularity of the sexist subjugation of women even while raising awareness of the persecution of both male and female homosexuals. Throughout the years, the Black Triangle, which had been used to brand many different people including women who refused to conform to the hetero-patriarchal norms of the Nazi regime, became pervasive as a synonym for lesbian persecution in North America.[103] Some started to vehemently suggest using both triangles, pink and black, while discussing the past.[104] This recuperation is much more anchored in US tradition, but existing cases can be traced in Germany up to the present.[105]

The historiographical dismissal of lesbian oppression under National Socialism has finally been corrected due to the efforts of queer feminist historians and activists fighting for the acknowledgment and recognition of decades old empirical research that began in the 1990s.[106] However, the struggle for recognition is not new – as gay narratives of National Socialism became central to a collective memory of Nazi queerphobia, lesbians interjected in attempts to gain visibility. By reading Bierwagen's poem in Bergen-Belsen, Trampenau not only made a plea for the recognition of lesbian persecution, but completely incorporated the Pink Triangle as a possible symbol of lesbian identities. Numerous images of demonstrations on both continents show how lesbians waved the symbol, just as their male counterparts did.[107] This is especially true of Jewish lesbian groups in the United States, who were inclined to make a clear connection between their les-

---

Bewegungen in den 1970er Jahren, ed. Cordia Baumann, Sebastian Gehrig, and Nicolas Büchse (Heidelberg: Universitätsverlag Heidelberg, 2011), 259–283.
103 "Visibility in Pride New Jersey," Lesbian Herstory Archives: Subject Files: Part 3: Feminism-International Lesbian Movement Folder No.: 06450. Gale, "Archives of Sexuality & Gender," accessed June 24, 2022, http://tinyurl.galegroup.com/tinyurl/62aCDX.
104 Schwartz, Arie, "What Color Is Your Triangle?" 4.
105 "Nie Wieder! Das Motto Cologne Pride 2017," Blog Cologne Pride, accessed April 4, 2020, https://www.colognepride.de/de/2017/06/08/unser-motto-2017/.
106 Aktivistinnen des lesbischen Gedenkens, "Anna Hájková und Birgit Bosold im Gespräch mit Ulrike Janz, Irmes Schwager und Lisa Steiniger," *Invertito – Jahrbuch für die Geschichte der Homosexualitäten*, 21 Verfolgung homosexueller Männer und Frauen in der NS-Zeit & Erinnerungskultur (2019): 86.
107 For example, lesbian activist Rachel Lurie went to a pride march on June 30, 1991, dressed as a giant Pink Triangle mascot. Lesbian Herstory Archives: Subject Files: Part 3: Feminism-International Lesbian Movement Folder No.: 06450. Gale, "Archives of Sexuality & Gender," accessed June 19, 2022, http://tinyurl.galegroup.com/tinyurl/62aCDX.

bian and Jewish identity.[108] Lesbians have simultaneously built their movement in gay memory culture and integrated lesbian politics into gay symbolism. This is a paradox. It disrupts the gay narrative by forcing gay men to mention lesbian memory, and to include lesbian suffering to their story but it concurrently erases the differences of a lesbian 'herstory' of National Socialism, subsuming lesbian narratives into one all-encompassing homosexual narrative of the era. In other words, it amalgamated lesbian identity with a broader tale, anchoring it in a gay story.

2.5 From narratives to the streets

Gathered in Paris for an international gay and lesbian conference in 1992, a group of activists held a symbolic action and demonstration in the city, renaming a street of the 16ᵉ Arrondissement. The street – named after Alexis Carrel, a known eugenicist and national socialist supporter – was rebaptized *Rue du Triangle Rose*, 'Pink Triangle Street,' amid a minute of silence and speeches by various local organizations. In the words of the protesters, this toponymical intervention commemorated the "gay brothers and sisters" who had died during the Nazi dictatorship. The action was also a call for the protection of human rights against the background of the rise of the far-right in France.[109]

Once again, by naming, listing, and referring to the Pink Triangle, not as an image or symbol but as a written concept, activists in the Euro-American world were building on a memory of National Socialism to legitimize and historicize their militantism. Like the encounters with the symbol through newspapers of the gay and mainstream press, works of fiction, or scholarly monographs, the mention of the symbol accompanied a narrative of victimhood connecting queer belonging to the Nazi era.

Born from communication networks, a gay republic of letters, and from the meeting of art and historical narratives, the symbol had united activists and intellectuals on both sides of the Atlantic. As the action in Paris epitomizes, the iconography associated with these gay narratives had by then also subsumed

---

108 MS International Gay Information Center Archives – Ephemera – Organizations, Box 10, Folder 6, *Jewish Lesbian Daughters of Holocaust Survivors*, New York Public Library.
109 "Parisian Action Flyer," National Archive of Lesbian, Gay, Bisexual and Transgender History, Collection #121 "Dr. Harold Kooden Papers," Box 1, Folder 11: *ILGA Conference – 1992*. The name of the street has officially been changed in May 2002 in memory of the antifascist and *Résistant* Jean Pierre Bloch. See M.C, "La rue Alexis-Carrel sera débaptisée," *Le Parisien* (March 12, 2002).

lesbian experiences of oppression under one historical concept: the Pink Triangle. As the next chapter will demonstrate, the recuperations of this concept beyond the textual also had transregional repercussions, as visual uses of the Pink Triangle fixed definitions of queerness in the transatlantic world. In this case, the integration of Nazi atrocities to global memory was central to the journey of the symbol.

3 A badge of memory – Defining and remembering victimhood in the queer Atlantic

Shortly before passing away in the mid-1990s, Paul Monette, the acclaimed writer, poet, and queer rights activist from Massachusetts wrote about the impact of death in his community in his 1988 *Borrowed Time: An AIDS Memoir*. In his vibrant testimony, Monette describes the ostracization, exclusion, and the pain of accompanying the love of his life through his final moments, all against the backdrop of a national backlash that used the sexual freedom of the 1970s as a stooge and scapegoat.[1] In this context, Monette contemplates the loss of a generation of queer men in lyrical terms, often comparing the HIV/AIDS crisis with examples of past atrocities, namely the Holocaust. These comparisons are anchored in the poet's own metaphorical language: "I suppose I felt there was something innately shameful about dying of a venereal disease. All the self-hating years in the closet were not so far behind me. And any brand of shame lays one open to the smug triage of the moralists, whose vision of AIDS as a final closet is clean and efficient as Buchenwald."[2]

Yet Monette's most fascinating comparisons are the meta links he draws between the reaction to the disease and the genocide of the European Jewry. Other queer men were considering political inaction and repression regarding HIV/AIDS as a possible genocide against queer men and comparing the epidemic with the persecutions of queerness during National Socialism.[3] Monette instead linked what he considered to be a certain North American predisposition to inflate the Holocaust in public and private discourses with heterosexuals' incomprehension of the HIV/AIDS crisis. He was paradoxically taking part in the same memorial practice by evoking this tendency. In his memoirs, going to his doctor to seek advice about having a lover living with the virus, he is confronted with both the crudeness of the doctor's response – "burn the blankets" – and the accompanying attempt to sympathize with his suffering – "his brother had died in a car crash while he was still in med school."[4] Monette then meditates on the stinging pain of

---

[1] John Petrus, "Discussing the Undiscussable: Reflecting on the 'End' of Aids," *GLQ: A Journal of Lesbian and Gay Studies* 25, no. 1 (2019): 68.
[2] Paul Monette, *Borrowed Time: An Aids Memoir* (San Diego: Harcourt Brace Jovanovich, 1988), 32.
[3] Larry Kramer, *Reports from the Holocaust: The Story of an Aids Activist*, Updated and Expanded. ed. (New York, NY: St. Martin's Press, 1994), 229.
[4] Monette, *Borrowed Time*, 85.

https://doi.org/10.1515/9783111067711-004

this exchange in the following lines. He asks himself, "[i]s this how a Jew feels when he hears 'holocaust' [sic] appropriated to some other calamity? Yet I was still so wounded by the news itself, desperate for allies, that I didn't have the wit to slam out of his office."[5]

His words are reminiscent of a question asked in 1981 by another prominent queer Jewish writer asking about the presence of Anne Frank's diary in the US school curriculum while pondering on the absence of queer authors.[6] Instead of dismissing this kind of resentment as a form of 'oppression Olympics,' this chapter examines the evolution of this discourse in North America, especially in the context of the long quest of queer liberation in the United States.

Considering words by the likes of Monette, it deals with comparisons and cross-referential memories of the Holocaust and other Nazi atrocities and extends the story of the last two chapters in the Euro-American world, shedding light on the recuperation of the Pink Triangle in a North American context. It first displays forms of global and North American Holocaust memories and explores the potential of multidirectional, cross-referential, and competitive forms of cultural memory. Indeed, the ways that Nazi crimes against humanity were remembered in North America is intrinsically connected to the tendencies by queer men to focus on victimhood while historicizing their experience of queerness during the second half of the twentieth century.

Simply put, this chapter discusses the consequences of the symbolic recuperation of victimhood and the construction of collective narratives in the transatlantic world. In doing so, I expose how different uses of the Pink Triangle cemented certain definitions of queerness in the USA and in the Federal Republic of Germany (FRG). Going beyond a simple evaluation of multiple case studies, I argue that the integration of Nazi atrocities to global memory was central to the journey of the symbol. Concordantly, the Pink Triangle's popularity can only be understood transregionally.

Discourses on a multidirectional memory of the Holocaust in a US context are the entry point to the second part of this chapter. I focus on the Pink Triangle's first steps in the Euro-American world, the discovery of an imaginary queer collective past, its importance for North American queers in the 1970s, and the invented collectivization of gay and lesbian identities in the USA following the recuperation of the symbol, a formative moment reminiscent of the pink radicals in the FRG.

---

5 Monette, *Borrowed Time*, 85.
6 Gore Vidal, "Some Jews & the Gays," *Christopher Street* (December 1981): 37.

Projecting their own identity across the Atlantic toward Europe, these North American activists based their contemporary experiences (their present) and their specific domestic experience of oppression on two imported foreign narratives: The destruction of a queer emancipation movement by the Nazis, and the idea that the Nazi persecution of queerness had been hidden from everyone. These assertions were at the base of a broader discourse on the Pink Triangle that lingers to this day and is at the core of queer politics in North America. It also serves as a basis for a conflation of the Nazi persecutions of queerness and the Holocaust, as well as a continuation of the Homocaust myth. In other words, queer activists, particularly gay men, used the connection they had built to the 'sacred evil' of history to find a place in a heteropatriarchal society that could despise their existence, but could not ignore a connection to the genocide at the centre of American cultural memory.[7]

3.1 Americanizing and globalizing the Holocaust

One does not need to dig deep into the layers of history to find the first glimpses of a universalization of Nazi atrocities. A good example is the de-Jewishization of the diary of the young Anne Frank before her murder at the hands of the Nazis in the camp of Bergen-Belsen. In North America, the *Diary of Anne Frank* is one of the most read documents about the Holocaust. In her introduction to her volume on the Americanization of the Holocaust, Hilene Flanzbaum specifies that what she calls the "unfailingly optimistic" interpretation of the text in popular culture has obscured other culturally significant names: Eichmann, the Warsaw Ghetto or Dachau.[8] Flanzbaum does not refute the importance of the young girl's testimony, but condemns the construction made from it via new editions, television series, and theatre plays. She sides with other scholars in their criticism of the final 1994 edition's popularity in North America.

Indeed, Lawrence Langer and Alvin Rosenfeld claim that the "sugar-coating of gruesome subject matter" and the "little horror in the stage version" and in the diary itself permit "the imagination to cope with the idea of the Holocaust without

---

[7] Peter Novick, *The Holocaust in American Life* (Boston, MA: Houghton Mifflin, 1999); Jeffrey C Alexander, "On the Social Construction of Moral Universals: The 'Holocaust' from War Crime to Trauma Drama," *European Journal of Social Theory* 5, no. 1 (2002): 5–85.
[8] Hilene Flanzbaum, "Introduction: The Americanization of the Holocaust." In *The Americanization of the Holocaust*, ed. Hilene Flanzbaum (Baltimore, MD: Johns Hopkins University Press, 1999): 1.

forcing a confrontation with its grim details."⁹ The theater versions of the *Diary* also usually gloss over (or even get rid of) the journal's Jewish aspects: "Anne's nightmare, the Hanukkah celebration, Van Daan's stealing bread, and the security police hammering on the door at the end."¹⁰ Flanzbaum concludes that the US-version of Anne Frank "downplay[s] or den[ies] the dark and brutal sides of life and [. . .] place[s] a preponderant emphasis on the saving power of individual moral conduct."¹¹ She illustrates this by pointing out how the *New York Times* considered that "Anne is not a victim, but a survivor. Because of her diary, she triumphed over her death at Bergen-Belsen."¹²

This framing raises eyebrows but is also reminiscent of other political instrumentalizations of the young Jewish girl. In the 1960s, laying a wreath of flowers at Anne Frank's House in Amsterdam, then US Secretary of Labor Arthur Goldberg delivered a message from President John F. Kennedy that Anne's words, "written in the face of a monstrous tyranny, have significant meaning today as millions who read them live in the shadow [. . .] of another such tyranny."¹³ This presidential backing effectively made the Jewish girl killed by the Nazis a warrior for freedom in the United States' Cold War propaganda.

So how did the Americanization of the Holocaust lead to this genocide becoming the embodiment of evil in US and international politics? Via the nature of its representation, a traumatic event's ontological evil is conceived as something unique, something insurmountable, coded by people identifying with it into a lesson for the rest of history.¹⁴ Here, the Americanization of the Holocaust holds primacy, as the coding of the genocide comes from the forces co-responsible for liberation from and the fall of the Nazi regime. It is no surprise that the sacred evil, the possible universalization of one story of suffering, concerned the Holocaust in North America and not for instance, the 500 years of colonialism and continuing murders of Indigenous people. The Americanized Holocaust – and its importance in a cultural memorial context – is not necessarily a Jewish story. It is a Jewish-inspired trope for a political and future-oriented memory of genocide to make sense of the present without questioning one's own flawed past. This North

---

9 Flanzbaum, "Introduction," 3.
10 Lawrence Graver, *An Obsession with Anne Frank: Meyer Levin and the Diary* (Berkeley: University of California Press, 1995), 85.
11 Alvin Rosenfeld quoted in Flanzbaum, "Introduction," 4.
12 Flanzbaum, "Introduction," 4.
13 "Kennedy, Praising Anne Frank, Warns of New Nazi-like Peril," *The New York Times* (20 September 1961) quoted in Novick, *The Holocaust*, 127.
14 Jeffrey C. Alexander, "Toward a Theory of Cultural Trauma." In *Cultural Trauma and Collective Identity*, ed. Alexander Jeffrey, Ron Eyerman and Bernard Giesen (Berkeley, CA: University of California Press, 2004), 11.

American de-Jewishization of the Holocaust and other Nazi antisemitic crimes had consequences for a global discourse on genocide and for a comparative use of the genocide by non-Jewish queer activists up to today.

In its reaction to the November pogroms of 1938, the non-Jewish press in North America was horrified by the crimes committed by the Nazis. The attacks on Jewish property and places of worship were the most covered European events during the war before D-Day. However, most of the uproar surrounding the coverage did not refer to the Jewishness of the pogrom's victims.[15] The horror of antisemitism in Europe had not suddenly moved the hearts of Christians, who had for centuries accused Jews of the assassination of their lord and savior. Yet National Socialism was symbolically associated with the enemy of universalism as presented by the USA and the Jews were the proclaimed enemies of the regime.[16] The events, deprived of their antisemitic focus, offered new discourses of suffering and catharsis of identification with the victims. Framed as a sacred evil, the murder of the European Jewry became an event outside of the borders of history and 'out of time'; an archetype for evil experiences whatever the credo, whatever the oppression, whatever the perpetrator or the victim.[17] Some grassroot organizations or social groups have also dangerously waltzed with controversial views, somehow accusing 'the Jew' of having stolen memorial spotlights or implying the urgency of looking at "real American–based problems."[18] In other words, discourses on the singularity of the Holocaust sometimes hides a double-talk about the Shoah being worse than other genocides, while other memorial ac-

---

15 They were instead referred to as "defenceless and innocent people" as "others" or "defenceless people"; see: Novick, *The Holocaust*, 15. On the US intervention and antisemitism, see: Susan L. Carruthers, *The Good Occupation: American Soldiers and the Hazards of Peace* (Cambridge, MA: Harvard University Press, 2016).
16 Novick, *The Holocaust*, 15.
17 Novick, *The Holocaust*, 30.
18 At the turn of the century, an assemblyman from Queens sponsored a law that was eventually passed by the state legislature in Albany. The man, Joseph Crowley, held a seat in a largely Irish part of the borough and the law in question mandated the New York City's school curriculum to include the nineteenth-century Irish potato famine, as well as the resulting mass migration. When Crowley was met with a vocal opposition against laws forcing schools to teach particular subjects, the New Yorker counterattacked on the National Public Radio: "Shouldn't Irish-American students be given the opportunity to learn about their heritage? After all, African American students learned about Slavery and Jewish American students got to talk about the Holocaust." In her recounting of this episode, Hilene Flanzbaum points out how Crowley's comments pre-supposed that learning about one's own heritage and identity entails engaging with the history of either suffering or persecution and that denying Irish- Americans or other citizens with hyphenated identities access to their ancestral pain would block a form of presupposed empowerment through the collectivization of victimhood. See Flanzbaum, "Introduction," 14.

tors have sometimes expressed and projected misplaced antisemitic resentment against European and North American Jews.[19]

Michael Rothberg has offered an intriguing and useful critique of what he calls competitive memory in debates about cultural memory. His contribution is a very useful conceptual approach for understanding the importance of the Holocaust in the Euro-American world that eventually led to a branding of every liberation struggle as a fight against a new Holocaust. These frameworks of competitive memory are leading social groups and memory actors astray. They shift the focus away from the productive aspects of cross-references and metaphors in the public sphere. This is what Rothberg calls multidirectional memory, the "interaction of different historical memories" illustrating "productive, intercultural dynamics."[20] The memory of colonialism as linked to Holocaust memory is a great example of this cross-referential approach to cultural trauma.[21] Rothberg states how,

---

[19] This tension has been at the center of many German debates regarding genocides and memories during the last decade. Michael Rothberg, *Multidirectional Memory: Remembering the Holocaust in the Age of Decolonization* (Stanford, CA: Stanford University Press, 2009); Michael Rothberg and Yasmin Yildiz, "Memory Citizenship. Migrant Archives of Holocaust Remembrance in Contemporary Germany," *Parallax* 17, no. 4 (2011): 32–48; Steffen Klävers, "Kollektive Erinnerung: Ein kompetitives Nullsummenspiel? Michael Rothbergs Theorie multidirektionaler Erinnerung im Spannungsfeld von Holocaust und postcolonial Studies." In *Decolonizing Auschwitz? Komparativ-Postkoloniale Ansätze in der Holocaustforschung*, ed. Steffen Klävers (Oldenbourg: De Gruyter Oldenbourg, 2019), 133–137; Jonathon Catlin, "'A New German Historians' Debate? A Conversation with Sultan Doughan, A. Dirk Moses, and Michael Rothberg," *Journal of the History of Ideas Blog* (2022). For a great summary of the so-called Historian Quarrel 2.0, see Mirjam Sarah Brusius, "Introduction," *Bulletin of the German Historical Institute London* 44, no. 2 – Special Issue Memory cultures 2.0: From Opferkonkurrenz to Solidarity (2022): 3–20.

[20] Rothberg, *Multidirectional Memory*, 3. The 2020 reception of the book in Germany unleashed its own debate. Paired with a highly discussed blog entry by historian Dirk Moses on the Swiss blog *Geschichte der Gegenwart*, discussions of Rothberg's decade-old work on memory, proved the delay of some transatlantic conversations. See Michael Rothberg and Mirjam Sarah Brusius, "'Victimhood Is a Tricky Terrain to Negotiate': Michael Rothberg in Conversation with Mirjam Sarah Brusius," *Bulletin of the German Historical Institute London* 44, no. 2 – Special Issue Memory cultures 2.0: From Opferkonkurrenz to Solidarity (2022): 22. See also Michael Rothberg, "Multidirektionale Erinnerung: Missverständnisse und gezielte Verschleierungen," *Frankfurter Rundschau* (February 14, 2022). As for Dirk Moses' text, the blog *New Fascism Syllabus* curated a scholarly debate in the summer of 2021 with fascinating interventions –among others– by Zoe Samudzi, Paula Villa Braslavsky, Johannes von Moltke, Alon Confino, Tiffany Florvil, Mirjam Sarah Brusius. I participated myself in the debate. See "The Catechism Debate", *New Fascism Syllabus* (2021), accessed January 16, 2022, http://newfascismsyllabus.com/news-and-announcements/the-catechism-debate/.

[21] See Maha El Hissy, "Die Erinnerung an den Holocaust gehört nicht einer weißen, deutschen Mehrheit," *Berliner Zeitung* (May 7, 2022): 12–13; Zoe Samudzi. "In Absentia of Black Study," *New Fascism Syllabus* (May 31, 2021), accessed January 16, 2022, https://newfascismsyllabus.com/opin

far from blocking other historical memories from view in a competitive struggle for recognition, the emergence of Holocaust memory on a global scale has contributed to the articulation of other histories (some of them predating the Nazi genocide, such as Slavery) [. . .]. Because of the Holocaust's salience to the relationship of collective memory, group identity, and violence, an exploration of its ongoing public evocation in multiple national contexts stands as the central example of [. . .] multidirectional memory.[22]

The memory of Nazi atrocities in Europe and its Americanization have marked later discussions about race, religion, and nationalism. These connections should be seen as many memorial nodes through a broader semantic net of collective memories relating to genocides and persecutions.[23] By appealing to the Holocaust, minority groups are in other words using a sort of lingua franca of persecution where the Holocaust is the hyper-coded paroxysm of suffering. It is the ultimate atrocity that no group wishes upon itself while constantly linking it to its own pain.[24] In the case of the USA, social groups are additionally using this trope according to the Americanization of the Holocaust; they are focusing on a culture of testimony, identification with a culture of victimization, and ultimately, a future-oriented lesson of history's darkest hours.

In this context, the Holocaust may be the climax of a new language of suffering, but certainly not an exception to cultural memory. Theaters of memory[25] may be analyzed in less competitive ways, but they are still battlefields on which contested pasts are brought back to life and pitched against each other. The fight for recollections of the past connects the individual to the group, the past with an awareness of the present, and the imaginative collective past to future expectations.[26] In other words, collective memories forge the heart of contemporary po-

---

ions/in-absentia-of-black-study/. See also: Zoe Samudzi, "Paradox of Recognition: Genocide and Colonialism," *Postmodern Culture* 31, no. 1–2 (2020).
22 Rothberg, *Multidirectional Memory*, 22.
23 Dirk Moses, *The Problems of Genocide: Permanent Security and the Language of Transgression* (Cambridge: Cambridge University Press, 2021). See also the effects of such a semantic net in contemporary Germany regarding antisemitism and Jewish life: Hannah Tzuberi, "'Reforesting' Jews: The German State and the Construction of New German Judaism,"*Jewish Studies Quarterly* 27, no. 3 (2020): 199–224.
24 Charlotte Wiedemann, *Den Schmerz der Anderen begreifen: Über Erinnerung und Solidarität – Ein Plädoyer für eine empathische Erinnerungskultur* (Berlin: Ullstein, 2022).
25 I borrow this term from Samuel's classic. Raphael Samuel, *Theatres of Memory: Past and Present in Contemporary Culture* (London: Verso, 2012).
26 Vita Fortunati and Elena Lamberti, "Cultural Memory: A European Perspective." In *Cultural Memory Studies: An International and Interdisciplinary Handbook*, ed. Astrid Erll, Ansgar Nünning, and Sara B. Young (Berlin: De Gruyter, 2008), 129. For an understanding of the media quality of remembrance and the systems of recollection see Siegfried J. Schmidt, "Memory and Remembrance: A Constructivist Approach." In *Cultural Memory Studies*, 198.

litical and social life. By doing so, they solidify allegiances to the group and enable an understanding of the collective present and contemporary struggles.[27] Paired with wounded attachments, such as the ones mentioned in chapter one in the case of the pink radicals – see section 1.2 –, these allegiances are legitimized for the group, which in turn tries to gain legitimization outside of its bounds.

The first chapter illustrated the struggle of queer men in Germany to make sense of their cultural trauma and their fight for a better acceptance in or for a new society. The Americanization of the Holocaust eventually led to the same results for queer men in North America. This appropriation of a memory that was not – what Alison Landsberg calls "prosthetic memories" – came about through the unexpected availability of group-specific memories via mass culture, thus opening them to people of different backgrounds for their own struggles.[28] Landsberg is right, but this appropriation was only possible through a theatre of memory free of national boundaries. The transatlantic and eventually transnational resonance of the Americanization of the Holocaust and its paradigm shifts ultimately extended the trope on a global scale. To put it another way, the Americanization of the Holocaust is not merely a part of the globalization of Holocaust memory. It also formed an assemblage within Holocaust political memory across the Euro-American world, influencing local memorial practices beyond North America. This is not to say that local memorial contexts did not play a role. For instance, comparison with the Holocaust in the German Left is still mostly taboo.[29] Nonetheless, other aspects of the Americanization of the Holocaust have reached Europe beyond Germany: A focus on survivorship, the idea of a sacred evil, and its framing as a warning from the angels of history.[30]

Approaching these issues from a global perspective, Aleida Assmann and Sebastian Conrad raise the idea that the alteration of global conditions through global mobility have also affected memory debates. Both pushed for an interdisciplinary approach to global history and memory studies, inviting scholars to reflect on memory actors' networks beyond the nation-state.[31] In so doing, they

---

27 Jeffrey K. Olick, "From Collective Memory to the Sociology of Mnemonic Practices and Products." In *Cultural Memory Studies*, 152.
28 Alison Landsberg, *Prosthetic Memory: The Transformation of American Remembrance in the Age of Mass Culture* (New York, NY: Columbia University Press, 2004), 10–11.
29 On the transnational aspect of local memory debates and international entanglements see Sa'ed Atshan and Katharina Galor, "Introduction." In *The Moral Triangle: Germans, Israelis, Palestinians*, ed. Sa'ed Atshan and Katharina Galor (Durham, NC: Duke University Press, 2020), 1–10.
30 Alexander, "On the Social Construction of Moral Universals," 30–34.
31 Aleida Assmann and Sebastian Conrad, "Introduction." In *Memory in a Global Age: Discourses, Practices and Trajectories*, ed. Aleida Assmann and Sebastian Conrad (Basingstoke: Palgrave Macmillan, 2010), 1–16.

asked two very important questions: "Are transnational connections prone to level national differences or does memory serve to foster an identarian particularism in the face of the challenge of globalization? Is memory in a global age equivalent to global memory?"[32] In order to answer these questions, Conrad and Assmann focus on Holocaust memory as a "referential core," taken out of space and out of time and presented as a universal memory.[33] Simultaneously, they remind us that the global is anchored in the local and that global structures subsequently reinforce local forms of memories.[34]

They are not the only ones to have engaged in this endeavor. Daniel Levy and Natan Sznaider laid the table for an understanding of cosmopolitan memory in 2002, examining how supranational understandings of the Holocaust affect individual memories at the local level. They refer to this as a process of "internal globalization" of memory.[35] All in all, a global memory of the Holocaust evolved through the predicament of the genocide's Americanization in the long postwar era and during the 1970s and 1980s.[36] The 2000 Stockholm Declaration canonized the genocide as the ultimate evil when a plurality of state leaders co-signed a plea to keep the memory of the Holocaust alive in order to fight the atrocities of tomorrow, a clear reminiscence of the lessons of history offered by the Americanization of the Holocaust.[37]

Even if fragmented, global memory icons such as the Holocaust retain a certain "affective quality for which it is used and re-mediated in ever-new contexts."[38] This is why queer men's interest in and identification with the Holocaust

---

32 Assmann and Conrad, "Introduction," 7.
33 Assmann and Conrad, "Introduction," 8.
34 Assmann and Conrad, "Introduction," 9.
35 Daniel C. Levy and Natan Sznaider, "Memory Unbound: The Holocaust and the Formation of Cosmopolitan Memory," *European Journal of Social Theory* 5, no. 1 (2002): 88. They deepened their understanding of cosmopolitan memory in Daniel Levy and Natan Sznaider, *The Holocaust and Memory in the Global Age* (Philadelphia, PA: Temple University Press, 2006). Sznaider has also taken a position in more recent debates regarding a postcolonial reading of Germany's *Vergangenheitsbewältigung* showing a peculiar understanding of postcolonial theory. See: Natan Sznaider, *Fluchtpunkte der Erinnerung: Über die Gegenwart von Holocaust und Kolonialismus* (Munich: Hanser, 2022).
36 Aleida Assmann, "The Holocaust: A Global Memory? Extensions and Limits of a New Memory Community." In *Memory in a Global Age*, 97–117.
37 For a conversation on European Holocaust memory in the context of multidirectional memory, see: Edward Kissi, Tom Lawson, Ulrike Lindner, and Mirjam Zadoff, "A European *Vergangenheitsbewältigung*? New Entanglements of Holocaust and Colonial Histories." In *Colonial Paradigms of Violence: Comparative Analysis of the Holocaust, Genocide, and Mass Killing*, ed. Michelle Gordon and Rachel O'Sullivan (Göttingen: Wallstein, 2002), 217–242.
38 Kissi, Lawson, Lindner, and Zadoff, "A European *Vergangenheitsbewältigung*?," 108–109.

in 1970s US America is central to understanding the key moments of the Pink Triangle and mapping the construction of a queer cultural memory in the Euro-American world. It is also significant because it offers the first steps of the symbolic and cultural construction of the Holocaust as a global icon.[39] Using multidirectional memory, it is possible to understand the social, cultural, and historical factors behind the desire of queer US Americans to focus on the suffering of non-heteronormative German men under National Socialism.[40] Beyond the Holocaust, the omnipresence of National Socialism in the North American psyche meant that a connection to its other crimes and to victimhood was seen as a possible method of legitimation for political struggles.

3.2 Remembering the injury

In August of 1974, picketers were demonstrating in front of a synagogue with armbands emblazoned with a Pink Triangle. under the hot sun of a summer afternoon in Manhattan. Their leader, the later-controversial activist David Thorstad, denounced the opposition of an Orthodox Jewish group to a City Council bill and appealed to their memories of Nazi atrocities, underlining how queer men had *also* been victims.[41] Thorstad was not the only one trying to prove his point by linking the oppression of queerness in the United States – in this case, the oppression of gay men – and the suffering of Jews under National Socialism. Echoing the pink radicals in the FRG, he drew parallels between the queer male victims of the Nazis and his present reality, even though the historical comparison had now travelled both through time and through space. Like his West German contemporaries, he emphasized alleged continuities between the persecution of queerness by the Nazis and his time in order to legitimize his own battle toward a world devoid of homophobia. Thorstad was also a pioneer of gay history, having co-written a volume

---

39 Kissi, Lawson, Lindner, and Zadoff, "A European *Vergangenheitsbewältigung?*," 110–112. Assmann traces four principal steps in the social construction of a global memory icon: Decontextualization, symbolic extension, emotional identification, and analogy, convincingly demonstrating her claim by using the Holocaust as her object of study.
40 Hirsch also states that comparison is productive to open archives of memory. See the last two chapters of Marianne Hirsch, *The Generation of Postmemory: Writing and Visual Culture after the Holocaust.* (New York, NY: Columbia University Press, 2012).
41 David Thorstad, "AOL Post" in Lesbian Herstory Archives: Subject Files: Part 6: Spinsters-Youth Folder No.: 14120. Gale, "Archives of Sexuality & Gender," accessed January 19, 2023, http://tinyurl.galegroup.com/tinyurl/5ybus5. Thorstad was and remains a controversial figure linked to pedosexuality. Erik Jensen mentions the demonstration in his 2002 article. See Jensen, "The Pink Triangle," 329.

about the emancipation movement of Magnus Hirschfeld in the year prior to this demonstration.[42] Framing and anchoring his fight in a transatlantic community united under the yoke of a similar oppression, and embracing a victimhood narrative intertwined with the violence that this community had been subject to, Thorstad was able to make demands about the future.[43] In this case, identity was not only connected to memory. It was imported and transformed throughout its transatlantic voyage.[44]

Queer North American men were not only using multidirectional practices of memory by referencing the Holocaust and other Nazi atrocities. They were also fighting for their community to be recognized as victims of fascism, even though the crimes had been committed thousands of kilometres away. West German pink radicals had a dual mission to fight against Nazi legacies and for a recognition of victimhood in the FRG. They drew a direct connection between queerphobic crimes in the German past and possible ways to change and influence the future for the better. Queer North American men were adding a new level to this narrative by collectivizing their own experience across the Atlantic and including cultural memory from Europe. In other words, North American queer postmemories of National Socialism were intrinsically transnational. This was only possible in the context of the Americanization and then emerging globalization of the Holocaust and representation of National Socialism as ultimate sacred evil. But how did these men learn about what happened during the so-called Third Reich, if the situation was already 'hidden from history' in the Federal Republic? How did the Pink Triangle of the pink radicals end up on posters in demonstrations in New York City and San Francisco?

The gay press is and was both a vector for historicizing the past, but also the gravedigger of canonical memory.[45] Indeed, media tend to gravitate toward simplistic narratives and a "minimization of nuance and the grey areas of a phenom-

---

[42] David Thorstad and John Lauritsen, *The Homosexual Rights Movement* (1864–1935) (Washington, NJ: Times Change Press, 1973).
[43] From this kind of connection to the Holocaust or culture of victimization in a global age, see Jie-Hyun Lim, "Victimhood Nationalism in Contested Memories: National Mourning and Global Accountability." In *Memory in a Global Age*, 138–162.
[44] For another example of memory and identity mixed in a transatlantic perspective, see Paul Gilroy, *The Black Atlantic: Modernity and Double Consciousness* (Cambridge, MA: Harvard University Press, 1994). For another more provocative take on identity and reflections on collectivization and culture, see Gilroy's *Against Race: Imagining Political Culture Beyond the Color Line* (Cambridge, MA: Belknap Press of Harvard University Press, 2000).
[45] In her essay about canonical and archival memory, Aleida Assmann describes how acts of remembrance and forgetting can shift discourses in cultural memory. Aleida Assmann, "Canon and Archive." In *Cultural Memory Studies*, 99.

enon."⁴⁶ Yet these journalistic accounts are also written for the archive as coverage in the present eventually becomes a repository of data, the past analysed by historians of the future.⁴⁷ In the context of the gay press, the already fine line between a journalistic construction of collective memory and historiography was blurred. Most known queer scholars of the first generation of queer historians were wearing multiple hats at the same time, being simultaneously grassroots activists, contributor to the gay press, and intellectuals.⁴⁸ Gay and then lesbian history was based on these predicaments, on an amalgam of cultural memory and transition to history writing. It is therefore the task of queer history to not only untangle these threads, but also to identify the important moments of juncture. Here, by looking at the import of the Pink Triangle throughout the pages of the gay press in the 1970s and 1980s in North America, I am not only tracing the constructivist approach of queer memory through a transatlantic story, but I am examining the factors underlying such a construction: the border zones between gay cultural memory and gay history.

Throughout its decades of existence, *Christopher Street*'s pages have provided space for aspiring gay writers trying to land a book deal. The magazine was also the node of a mainly gay political scene trying to frame an imagined community and trying to memorialize its struggles, its dystopias, and its utopias.⁴⁹ Numerous contributors therefore covered political demonstrations, defined the main enemies of their imagined community, and gathered support for numerous causes, seeking unity. Browsing through two decades of issues, it is apparent that the memory of the queer past in Germany, the cultural trauma referred to by the pink radicals, remained present in the collective imagination of the *Chistopher Street* editors, and therefore its readership. The Homocaust narrative hung like a

---

46 Barbie Jelizer, "Journalism's Memory Work." In *Cultural Memory Studies*, 379–388.
47 Sometimes a depository for historians as well. This includes, for example, the databases by institutions like the *Times* and *The New York Times* and their own archives.
48 Here the concept of quotidian intellectual is particularly useful. Tiffany Florvil uses the concept in her analysis of Black feminism and Black solidarity in Germany in the fourth and fifth chapters of her *Mobilizing Black Germany: Afro-German Women and the Making of a Transnational Movement* (Champaign, IL: University of Illinois Press, 2020.) See also Tiffany N. Florvil and Sina Speit. "Intellektuelle des Alltags. Die Afro-Deutsche Frauenbewegung – Ein Gespräch." In *Geschichte der Gegenwart*.
49 What is a gay imagined community? Is it possible to be queer and male without being part of "gay culture"? Is being gay an entry point to a community if one does not adhere to certain cultural parameters? See David M. Halperin, *How to Be Gay* (Cambridge, MA: Harvard University Press, 2012). Contributors to *Christopher Street* were already engaged in these discussions during the 1970s, especially when brainstorming about the goals of what they considered to be their movement and their community.

sword of Damocles over every piece, over every item of news, over every piece of fiction. If a Christian rally took place in the country's capital, it was a clear sign of the impending Homocaust.[50] If progress was made, gay Jewish intellectuals reminded readers that tolerance was an illusion leading to the naive acceptance of oppression and eventually fascism.[51]

Renowned gay icon Gore Vidal, in a discussion on identity, refuted the idea of a gay community, refusing to consider himself a 'gay man' based on heteronormative conceptions of sexuality. He advocated for the term "homosexualist," anchoring his sense of belonging in a community that had been decimated by the horrors of fascism, a community of victims.[52] Up to the HIV/AIDS crisis, *Christopher Street*'s intelligentsia constantly reminded its readers to be ready, to never be complacent, and to remember that they were a minority group, a group of victims like the Jews. In 1983, summarizing all these aspects in one lengthy piece, Seymour Kleinberg concluded that,

> [t]he history of the persecution of Jews is well documented, carefully observed everywhere it occurred, both by Jews and by their oppressors. But the history of the persecution of homosexual men and women is obscure, tenuous and euphemistic. The Jew was condemned for his belief, the homosexual for what he did. Jews were hated "simply" because of an accident of birth; homosexuals were hated because of their nature. Jews appeared to earn their fate in the eyes of their enemy because they clung so stubbornly to their faith, rejecting the proffered safety of conversion – though that safety hardly meant acceptance. Homosexuals, because they appeared to be heterosexual, were accepted until they revealed themselves as sodomites. They then betrayed the society in which they hid, and the wrath that fell upon them was partly revenge [. . .]. In the last two decades, the position of homosexual men and women in America has begun to resemble the condition of Jews in Europe before the rise of fascism.[53]

According to Kleinberg – himself Jewish – not only were queer victims of the Nazis implicitly deserving of rights, but he also underlined a contemporary emergency. According to him, queer men were on the verge of a genocide; they were the new Jews. This central tenet of the Homocaust, the idea of the persecuted (non-Jewish) queer male as a Jew, is important for understanding the recuperation of the Pink Triangle in North America. After years of cultural memory debates surrounding National Socialism and the establishment of a gay imagined community in the gay press, queer men had found a new symbol to raise awareness for their cause, a link to the historical roots of their struggle: the Pink Trian-

---

50 "Fundamentally Fascist," *Christopher Street* (April 1980): 4.
51 Martin Duberman, "Hunting Sex Perverts," *Christopher Street* (January 1982): 43.
52 Gore Vidal, "Some Jews & the Gays," *Christopher Street* (December 1981): 30.
53 Seymour Kleinberg, "The Homosexual as Jew," *Christopher Street* (July 1983): 35.

gle. Like the rainbow flag, which represented the idea of cohesion in difference, the Pink Triangle eventually entered the hall of fame of queer symbols.[54] Feminist newspapers used it throughout the 1980s and queer organizations propagated the symbol through countless brochures explaining the benefits of having an emblem based on history that was at the same time a secret sign for the community.[55]

Even if they were based on an interpretation of German history, these pamphlets stood in complete opposition to the recuperation by the HAW in the FRG.[56] Indeed, the Pink Triangle in these leaflets lacked the outward impulse of the HAW. They made the Pink Triangle a secret symbol of cohesion, miles away from the triangle used by the Berliners to disrupt heteronormativity. If some of these pamphlets name famous German researchers such as Ilsa Kokula, they were also loaded with inaccuracies, for example, that queer victims had to wear pink triangles outside of concentration camps.[57] Many publications also started to include Pink Triangles in their logos and in their names. This narrative is identifiable throughout the English-speaking world beyond Euro-American spaces. A major organ of the gay press in New Zealand, on the other side of the world, was even named *Pink Triangle*.[58] The triangle also gained traction in Australia.

Just as in Europe, the publication of Kohout's (now translated) life story proved to be a key moment in the transmission of the Pink Triangle, helping it move from one continent to the other. The possibility to gain access to mediated autobiographical memories from a member of the imagined community meant that queers in North America could also come into contact with descriptions of trauma, projecting their own experience of oppression onto them. In a review of the English translation in 1980, Helen Pausacker of *Gay Community News* in Chicago summarized the lessons learned from the book: "It is a gruesome tale, certainly not bedtime reading [. . .] as I forced myself to turn the pages, I was constantly asking myself why I was doing so [yet], by the time I finished reading, I knew what I had gained from the book. I feel the book is a lesson in survival."[59]

---

54 For example, historian and activist Jonathan Ned Katz mentions the Pink Triangle in his piece on canonical symbols of the queer community in: Jonathan Ned Katz, "Signs of the Times: The Making of Liberation Logos," *The Advocate* (October 10, 1989): 49.
55 For example: "This Logo Is a Reminder of the Pink Triangle Gays Were Forced to Wear in Nazi Concentration Camps." *Women's Press* 10, no. 5 (November & December 1980): 20.
56 "Brochure by Visibility in Pride New Jersey," Lesbian Herstory Archives: Subject Files: Part 6: Spinsters-Youth Folder No.: 14120. Gale, "Archives of Sexuality & Gender," accessed January 19, 2023, http://tinyurl.galegroup.com/tinyurl/5ybus5.
57 "Brochure by Visibility in Pride New Jersey."
58 "Gay Pride Week," *Pink Triangle* (May 25, 1979): 1.
59 Helen Pausacker, "'The Men with the Pink Triangle,'" *Gay Community News* 2, no. 10 (December 1980–January 1981): 31.

Pausacker hinted at these lessons again further in the review, stating that queer men would benefit from a comparison between Kohout's story and contemporary realities in the United States, focusing on their survival and fighting against a complacent view of activism.[60]

On the other side of the country in Sacramento, John Hilgert wrote in 1986 that the book was an important read to commemorate the thousands of "immortal martyrs" of the community, but also that "the tragedy of this young man's story [. . .] is an indictment of the 'normal' and 'just' world which not only continues the discrimination against gays, but also perpetuates the crimes of silence regarding those with pink triangles who died in the concentration camps."[61] In a couple of years, pushed by Homocaust narratives and by a certain marketing buzz regarding the possibility to read a true memoir of injury, the book eventually became a literary pilgrimage for queer men.[62] Interestingly, after Kohout's death in 1994 in Vienna, his partner bequeathed some of the man's belongings to the United States Holocaust Memorial Museum (USHMM), including, among other things, the famous pink triangle badge of his late lover.[63]

All in all, following the memorialization of persecutions in Germany by the gay press and by their contact with sources such as the *Men with the Pink Triangle*, queer men interacted with the Pink Triangle as an emblem for their imagined mutual history, as a symbol of collective memory, and of a collective injury, slowly becoming an image of collective identity. North American queer women also began to use the symbol, another transatlantic story entangled in historiographical debates at the core of chapter five. Already in 1978, *Gay Awareness Iowa Nebraska* was mentioning that "the pink triangle is becoming a popular symbol worn by gay men and women," stipulating that, like many other symbols in the community, its origin could be found in the persecution of non-heteronormative individuals.[64] The organization continued: "We wear it also as a symbol of all gays who have lost their lives, jobs, their families, their friends, and who have suffered in so many other ways for being homosexuals."[65] Back in New York, the Christopher Street Liberation Day Committee at Columbia University incorporated the symbol as one of

---

60 Pausacker, "'The Men with the Pink Triangle'": 31.
61 John Hilgert, "Nazi Terrorism – Gay Victims," *Mom Guess What* (July 1986): 15.
62 *The Advocate* declared it its book of the year in 1983. See also "Good Reading for You from Alyson Publications," *Christopher Street* (November 1983): 3–4.
63 David W. Dunlap, "Personalizing Nazis' Homosexual Victims," *The New York Times* (June 26, 1995).
64 Robert Darst, "The History of the Pink Triangle," *The Northbound Companion* (December 1978): 10.
65 Darst, "The History of the Pink Triangle," 10.

gay *and* lesbian oppression in their 1982 Stonewall commemorations, underlining that, because of revolts like the ones in the bar on Christopher Street in 1969, "this will never happen to us again."[66] All across the continent – even in literature – the Pink Triangle became a synonym for queer memory, for queer injury, for the fight for a better queer future, and for a retrieval of the queer past.[67]

Ultimately, the Pink Triangle facilitated a transition between collective memory and collective identity, as many gay and lesbian activists across North America started to use it not only to compare the past to their present, but also to weaponize its symbolism. Looping back to the shores of Lake Ontario, a strange Canadian tradition is the perfect illustration of such a switch toward a celebration of gay and lesbian identity. Reunited in 1979 in Ottawa for a national congress, Canadian queer organizations decided to proclaim February 14 the annual day in honor of Pink Triangle Press, which had just won a case in courts in Ontario.[68] Proposed by the Gay and Lesbian Association of Nova Scotia – then Gay Alliance for Equality – the resolution to name February 14 'Pink Triangle Day' stated:

> We propose a yearly celebration to mark the day. We realize that this date, February 14, has traditionally been celebrated as St. Valentine's Day and dedicated to the expression of heterosexual affection. We take this opportunity to challenge what Christopher Isherwood has called "the heterosexual dictatorship" by affirming, for ourselves and the world, the existence, the strength, and the beauty of gay love. [. . .] We intend to make this day a celebration of the liberation of Eros, both as a reality in our personal lives since coming out, and as a common political goal to be achieved. We therefore proclaim February 14 as an annual Canadian gay holiday to be known as Pink Triangle Day.[69]

This peculiar celebration is still observed throughout Canada by various organizations.[70] The unofficial holiday also has its own web presence, inviting everyone to share queer love by exchanging dubious postcards with Pink Triangle designs

---

66 Lesbian Herstory Archives: Subject Files: Part 3: Feminism-International Lesbian Movement Folder No.: 06450. Gale, "Archives of Sexuality & Gender," accessed January 19, 2023, http://tinyurl.galegroup.com/tinyurl/62aCDX.
67 For instance, in erotica. There is a bar in Berlin-Schöneberg named the Pink Triangle on Martin Luther Str. cited in Andrew Holleran, "Cinderella Defects or Lust on Leninplatz," *Christopher Street* (July 1984): 10.
68 Ontario had sued Pink Triangle Press after the publication of an article talking explicitly about pedophilia. This case is a pivotal moment in Canadian queer history.
69 Posters from the Canadian Lesbian and Gay Archives 1237; 1994–070/08. Gale, "Archives of Sexuality & Gender," accessed February 19, 2018, http://tinyurl.galegroup.com/tinyurl/62YdD3.
70 For Ontario see AMAPCEO, "Pink Triangle Day 2017," accessed March 20, 2019, https://amapceo.on.ca/pink-triangle-day-2017.

and proclaiming a "Happy Pink Triangle Day" to their loved ones.[71] One queer university organization in the Queen City has also moved its yearly pride celebration from the heat of summer months to the chills of mid-February. At Toronto Metropolitan University, students are celebrating pride in winter and hold a yearly vigil on "Pink Triangle Day," in commemoration of "LGBT victims of the Holocaust & victims of gay-bashing."[72] Similarly, students at the University of Guelph organized a "Pink Triangle Dance" around 14 February.[73] These events may seem random or even offensive to some, but they are the logic of years and years of collective memory and of the cohesion factor of Homocaust narratives.

In the 1990s, a gay group from Nova Scotia explained the significance of both the Pink and the Black triangles on a poster explaining the nature of the festivities. I already discussed the Black Triangle in chapter two – see section 2.4 –, but here I would like to highlight the explanation behind the pink one: "pink triangle[s] [. . .] were used by the Nazis to identify and persecute people because of their sexual orientation; just as a yellow star (two triangles – one inverted) was used to identify Jews."[74] The assertion that the yellow Star of David used as a mark of disgrace by the Nazi regime is made of "two triangles" is particularly telling. It insists on the similarities between the genocide of the European Jewry and the murder of thousands of queer men in concentration camps. In Canada, the Right to Privacy Committee, a multilayered and politically diverse group created in the aftermath of Operation Soap in Ontario, not only fought against infamous US Christian fundamentalist Anita Bryant's rhetoric north of the forty-ninth parallel, but also connected one of her queerphobic campaigns to Nazi persecutions.[75] On a poster in 1982, the group reminded the viewer that the Pink Triangle "remains as a symbol of the history that others have tried to obliterate. It is a reminder of our history

---

71 Pink Triangle Day, "February 14 2020 Happy 41st Anniversary," accessed April 3, 2020, http://www.pinktriangleday.com/.
72 The Toronto Metropolitan University was then known as Ryerson University, named after a white settler colonist. Here, "LGBT Holocaust victims" does not mean Jewish queer victims. Holocaust is used as an all-encompassing concept for Nazi atrocities. Posters from the Canadian Lesbian and Gay Archives 3281;2006–017/029N. Gale, "Archives of Sexuality & Gender," accessed February 19, 2018, http://tinyurl.galegroup.com/tinyurl/62Yqi1.
73 Posters from the Canadian Lesbian and Gay Archives 2034;2006–108/14. Gale, "Archives of Sexuality & Gender," accessed February 19, 2018, http://tinyurl.galegroup.com/tinyurl/5ybuS4.
74 Posters from the Canadian Lesbian and Gay Archives 1237; 1994–070/08. Gale, "Archives of Sexuality & Gender," accessed February 24, 2018, http://tinyurl.galegroup.com/tinyurl/62YdD3.
75 On Bryant see Stacy Braukman, "Epilogue: Anita Bryant and Florida's Culture Wars." In *Communists and Perverts under the Palms: The Johns Committee in Florida 1956–1965*, ed. Stacy Braukman (Gainesville, Tallahassee, FL: University Press of Florida, 2013), 193–208.

which we must recover, and a ghost of where oppression can lead if gay people ignore the active struggle for their rights."[76] The fight against Bryant's prejudice and other Christian fundamentalisms proves the significance of the Pink Triangle as a symbol of connection, of injury, of a struggle.

3.3 Pink Triangle injuries, Pink Triangle warnings

Some other actors of the period had harsher words and more dire warnings for their contemporaries. Martin Duberman, activist and ultimately one of the leading gay scholars of his generation, wrote in *Christopher Street* in 1982 that complacent gay men and lesbian women should think twice about their position in society and the hate facing them:

> But I keep hearing those Jewish voices in Germany in the thirties: 'We're too well-integrated into society, too powerful in our influence, to worry unduly about the frothing of the lunatic fringe.' Knowing the fate of the Jews, we're denied the comfort they took, the faith they placed in conventional safeguards –or in human 'reason' and 'compassion.' Still, the ostriches among us have a fallback position: all that took place in Germany. This, after all, is the United States. It couldn't happen here. Wrong. It already has –not merely repression, but genocide. Ask Native Americans. Ask Blacks.[77]

Duberman's quote is substantial. It shows how cross-referential collective memories of the Holocaust or of other Nazi persecutions legitimized calls to action. It voices a sense of urgency, fear of an impending doom, the necessity of the struggle, and the lessons of history.[78] Through the uses of the Pink Triangle, persecutions were not a distant gay past; they were always present, ready to be turned to again by conservative forces. Investigating a campaign against Anita Bryant's queerphobia in Dade County in 1977, one is struck by other examples of these warnings. *Christopher Street* interviewed Ethan Geto in 1977 for his role in the Dade County Coalition for Human Rights. Geto, knowing that a major part of the electorate in the county was Jewish, purposefully used Holocaust memory for his

---

76 "The Pink Triangle 1982," Posters from the Canadian Lesbian and Gay Archives 458;1989–570 Gale, "Archives of Sexuality & Gender," accessed February 24, 2018, http://tinyurl.galegroup.com/tinyurl/62Ybf0.
77 Martin Duberman, "Hunting Sex Perverts," *Christopher Street* (January 1982): 43.
78 Historians have often debated the uses of History. What is the role of history? Are historians supposed to teach these "lessons of history"? For a critical reflection on the matter see: Pernau, Margrit, "Aus der Geschichte lernen? Die Rolle der Historiker:innen in der Krise," *Geschichte und Gesellschaft*, no. 46 (2020): 563–574.

campaign in the *Miami Herald,* trying to shame conservative Jewish voices in the region. He also tried to appeal to heteronormative gentiles by drawing connections to National Socialism.[79]

Two ads are particularly striking in this regard. Both were partially censored by the *Miami Herald* at the time. On one – mentioning the ever-exploitable Anne Frank – Geto's campaign ran: "A message from people of Holland . . . We in the land of Anne Frank, know what prejudice and discrimination can lead to."[80] Another one read, "Prejudice and discrimination are serious matters. They stem from fear and hate. And sometimes, they have terrible consequences. Let's stop bigotry raising its head in Dade County." This tirade was flanked by a 1936 decree by Himmler.[81] If the strategy was far from subtle, Geto asserted in the same interview that his goal was merely to show how dictatorships started slowly by taking away minorities' rights. His aggressive and affirmative campaign made complete sense at the time. It fit with the Americanization of the Holocaust and with discourses on queer injury. In the words of Reverend Robert Darst writing for *Gay Awareness Iowa Nebraska:*

> The death of all these gay men and women must not be forgotten because all people have to be reminded of the evil which human beings can do to one another whenever tolerance for others is replaced by a fanaticism that insists on a single norm for all. It has happened in Germany but hatred, intolerance and evil know no national boundaries. I wear my pink triangle not only in memory of what happened in Germany, but as a vow that I will not allow the Anita Bryants of this country to let it happen here.[82]

This "never again" discourse shows how the persecution of queerness under National Socialism had permeated queer collective memory in North America, interrelating domestic and international stories of struggle. By following the journey of the Pink Triangle in North America, it is possible to investigate ways in which multidirectional memories of National Socialism were central to the formation of queer cultural memory. If this chapter has shown how local or national contexts are still relevant to the interpretation of discourses and symbols, it has also highlighted how these national contexts cannot be isolated. Especially while writ-

---

[79] "I made analogies with the Jews in Germany and the black experience. Those were the tenets of the campaign." Charles Ortleb, "Ethan Geto: Interview," *Christopher Street* (August 1977): 27.
[80] Ortleb, "Ethan Geto: Interview": 27.
[81] Ortleb, "Ethan Geto: Interview": 26.
[82] Lesbian Herstory Archives: Subject Files: Part 3: Feminism-International Lesbian Movement Folder No.: 06450. Gale, "Archives of Sexuality & Gender," accessed February 24, 2018, http://tinyurl.galegroup.com/tinyurl/62aCDX.

ing a queer history establishing the fluidity of identity and memory, it is necessary to go beyond the nation-state and look at broader communication networks. This chapter highlights how difficult it is to disentangle the Pink Triangle from its transatlantic journey. The story of the symbol also underlines how queer history and social movements need to be understood in a transregional perspective.

4 A badge of inclusion – Carving Pink Triangles into stone and shaping the queer subject

In the summer of 1995, the Lambda book award recipient and gay Jewish American writer David Bergman published an extensive piece in a New York men's fashion magazine, in which he reflected on antisemitism, queerphobia, and his life as an openly queer Jew.[1] In his essay, Bergman writes about the intersection of oppressions, the anxiety of being part of two minorities, and his confrontation with both the murder of the European Jewry and the erasure of the Nazi persecutions of queerness in official political memory. For him, the fear of never fully being accepted was intrinsically linked to his belonging to these two minority groups. Saddened by what he considered to be a false binary between being Jewish and being gay, he appealed for the memory of both the Holocaust and the persecution of queerness by the Nazis, a dialogue between victims of the "evils of history."[2]

In order to do so, Bergman offers his readers a personal anecdote to illustrate his disarray. As he visited the then newly inaugurated US Holocaust Memorial Museum in Washington DC (USHMM), Bergman remembers being surrounded by children and non-Jewish visitors, strolling through the museum to learn "the lessons of history." As he reached the part of the exhibit mentioning the other groups of victims targeted by the Nazi, he remembers stopping in front of a five-minute video explaining the fate of political dissidents, Roma and Sinti, Jehovah Witnesses, and queer men. He bitterly noted that the crowd surrounding him started to disperse as the video switched to the fate of the men with the pink triangle, remembering that: "I continued to stand there [. . .] I was alone, feeling very self-conscious, feeling that I was the only gay man in the entire museum. Then I noticed a second man standing at a distance [. . .]. Together we watched the loop once more as school kids and their parents walked away."[3]

His story at the USHMM is an interesting tale of representation. By entering some official spaces of Holocaust memory, like the USHMM, queer claims to victimhood were finally inscribed in political memory. However, Bergman also concludes that being visible is not always synonymous with being seen. His story is interesting because it touches many facets of the debates surrounding the push by queer political organizations to enter official memory in the 1980s and 1990s

---

1 David Bergman, "Final Thoughts," *Men's Style* (July & August 1995): 100–106.
2 Bergman, "Final Thoughts": 100–106.
3 Bergman, "Final Thoughts": 106.

regarding Nazi atrocities. In Europe, as in North America, one can observe a synchronicity in this fight for political visibility and the inscription of queer memory in official political memory. This is a complicated story and one difficult to disentangle.

As the persecutions of queer men under National Socialism became more and more recognized during these decades, the form of commemoration became a source of increasing discord. This chapter shows the necessity of unravelling the various aspects of these debates in order to focus on the constructivist aspects of queer memory and the Pink Triangle. Bergman warns us against the siren call of binary analysis. If it is true that many Holocaust survivors expressed homophobic sentiments when discussing or dismissing the inclusion of queer memory in memorials, then one needs to dig deeper beyond the bigotry. Past the discriminatory rhetoric, these critiques are also echoed in the incessant demands by queer scholars of the time to once and for all stop referring to the Nazi persecution of queerness as 'a Holocaust.'[4] Surely, these queer scholars who paved the way for the inclusion of gay history in academia were not queerphobic themselves! At the same time, queer Jewish men seemed to be left behind, as many gay activists expressed antisemitic resentment in response to their alleged exclusion from German *Vergangenheitsbewältigung* or the transatlantic remembrance of National Socialism.

This chapter analyses the inclusive potential of the Pink Triangle as a symbol throughout the second part of the twentieth century, beyond the construction of narratives of victimhood and an identification to a past of injury. With the help of conceptual history and memory studies, I emphasize three moments of queer integration anchored in the prevalent uses of the Pink Triangle: Integration of the queer community into German memory culture and discourses of *Vergangenheitsbewältigung* through Pink Triangle monuments; the US musealization of a particular definition of queerness linked to the triangle; the inclusion of German queer history in world history through the symbol's transatlantic journey. The chapter is divided in two parts. The first deals with German-speaking queer activists seeking justice for Nazi persecutions on the perpetrators' ground, and their fight to gain official commemoration and memorialization in the *Gedenkstätte* 'memorial sites'[5] of the former Nazi concentration camps. Through various case studies (namely Dachau, Mauthausen, and Sachsenhausen), I highlight the strug-

---

4 Lloyd Nicholson, "The Past is Not So Distant," *ANGLES* 13, no. 1 (1995): 6.
5 In this chapter, I use the German word *Gedenkstätte* to differentiate concentration camps during the Nazi era and memorials inaugurated on the grounds of former concentration and extermination camps. I decided against the use of the official translation 'memorial site' to avoid confusion with a part of the Anglophone literature focusing on Pierre Nora's *'lieux de mémoire.'*

gles of queer activists in their fight with or against other victims of the regime and the connection between Pink Triangle memorials and the search for solidarity. The second part expands this 'this happened to us here' to a 'this happened to us as a community' and deals with the memorialization of fascism in both Germany and North America, its entry into museums, and its carving into stone outside of concentration camp memorials. It tackles the link between the Pink Triangle as a symbol of commemoration and the international collective memory of injury mentioned in chapter three. It brings us to the Berlin boroughs of Schöneberg and Mitte and eventually to the shores of North America and the USHMM.

4.1 Of triangles and reliefs

On September 8, 1968, military dignitaries from France, the United Kingdom, Belgium, and the USA inaugurated a new international monument on the ground of the former Nazi concentration camp in Dachau, Bavaria. Student protests against a military presence on former fascist grounds cast something of a cloud over the character of the event organized by the *Comité International de Dachau* (CID). However, the inauguration of the so-called *Internationales Mahnmal*,[6] 'international monument,' marked the first steps of official antifascist memorialization in Dachau and foreshadowed the various memorial clashes between the CID – a committee based in Brussels and consisting chiefly of past political prisoners who had been branded with the red triangle – and various other memory activists.[7]

In this case, the monument by artist Nandor Glid and a relief sculpted by Yugoslavian artist Ana Bešlić are of main interest [Figure 1]. This so-called *Winkelrelief*, 'triangle relief,' is one of the early examples of the CID dismissal of some of the Nazis' victims. Arranged on three equally sized shackles of a figurative chain casted in metal and fixed to a stone parapet on the former *Appellplatz*, 'roll call place,'[8] the relief features numerous enamelled triangles of various colours facing

---

[6] The German word *Mahnmal* connotes a warning.
[7] Lukas Schretter, "Anmerkungen zum Winkelrelief im internationalen Mahnmal der KZ-Gedenkstätte Dachau." In *Der Rosa-Winkel-Gedenkstein*, ed. Albert Knoll (Munich: Forum Homosexualität und Geschichte e.V., 2015), 35. I am grateful for Dr. Knoll's generosity as he provided me direct access to his personal collection during my research in the archives of the *Gedenkstätte* Dachau in 2018. He also provided me with the corpus of sources he used for his study of queer memory activism in Dachau.
[8] The place in a concentration or extermination camp on which prisoners were forced to stand every morning and every evening during roll call. Prisoners were sometimes forced to stand up for hours in all sorts of weather, and for as long as the SS wanted. Many died of exhaustion during these calls.

downward and superposing each other across the chain. These triangles are red, blue, violet, respectively representing political prisoners, *émigrés*, and Jehovah witnesses. Some of them are emblazoned with a second yellow triangle, creating a Star of David, the well-known symbol also used by the Nazis in their antisemitic policies and murder campaigns to mark Jewish victims. To the acute eye, three colours are missing from the *Winkelrelief*: green, black, and pink, the green being for so-called *Berufverbrecher*, 'career criminals,' a category meaning nothing and everything.[9] As the reading of the minutes of a CID general assembly at the end of May 1963 confirms, this omission is no accident.

During the assembly, the general secretary and member of the Belgian delegation, Georges Walraeve, brought up the topic of the *Winkerelief*, then in its conceptual phase. He mentioned that the sculptor planned, to commemorate all victim categories, to include the three triangles that eventually did not make the cut. Walraeve concluded that the monument should honour the victims of the Nazi atrocities and not people imprisoned for being queer, "antisocial" or "criminals." The German Democratic Republic (GDR) delegate also dismissed the architect's idea or any compromises, expressing his concern of being commemorated side by side with "these kinds of people," stating that it would be a travesty for people to visit the memorial and think that "green triangles" had similarly been victims as well. Indeed, he falsely declared that most of the individuals associated with the black, pink and green triangles were part of the killing apparatus of the Nazis.[10] As for the black triangle, another member of the CID presidency concluded that it had been worn by individuals who were "beating up their wives and abandoning their children."[11] Without further consideration, and without even mentioning the fate

---

9 The category "Green Triangles" is sometimes misunderstood as a classification for murderers, rapist, burglars, etc. or remembered by survivors as being the triangle worn by so-called *Kapos* in their barracks. The story is more complicated. For instance, the *Gedenkstätte* Ravensbrück's main exhibit exposes the tools used by one woman who facilitated clandestine abortions during the 1930s. She was arrested and sent to the concentration camp as a 'career criminal.' Furthermore, political saboteurs were sometimes also branded with a green triangle. This is, of course, not to imply that murderers or people we would still brand as criminals today should have been worked to death in concentration camps.
10 "The green triangles were worn by people who exterminated us in the camps at Buchenwald, Mauthausen and other places, it would be beyond imagination" ("*Les triangles verts ont été portés par des gens qui nous ont exterminés dans les camps de Buchenwald, Mauthausen et d'autres lieux, cela dépasserait l'imagination*"). DaA 42263, III. Comité International de Dachau, Procès-verbal intégral d'assemblée générale des 24/25/26 mai 1963 à Munich, 14–15.
11 "*Le triangle noir était porté par des gens qui maltraitaient leurs épouses, qui abandonnaient leurs enfants, c'étaient les raisons pour lesquelles ils étaient asociaux.*" DaA 42263, III. Comité International de Dachau, Procès-verbal intégral d'assemblée générale des 24/25/26 mai 1963 à Munich, 15.

Figure 1: The so-called 'Triangle Relief' on the grounds of the former concentration camp of Dachau in 2018. Photo taken by the author.

of queer men wearing the pink triangle, the assembly decided to dismiss the inclusion of green, black and pink triangles from the *Winkelrelief* and closed the discussion.[12]

This early episode of commemoration in former concentration camps in Germany is not an isolated case. It relates the stories of forgotten or demonized victims in the first years of the postwar era. Indeed, many individual stories nuance the all-encompassing pretences of liberation. For example, Georg Tauber was imprisoned in the final phase of persecution, which accompanied the start of the Second World War. The son of a master brewer, he was born in 1901 and later committed to the Sachsenhausen concentration camp in the beginning of January 1940, before being transferred to Dachau two months later. Georg Tauber survived the camps, but 1945 was not synonymous with his liberation. Today, some of his watercolour paintings are displayed in the *Gedenkstätte* in Bavaria, the memorial museum honouring him with a special exhibit in 2016. However, Tauber fought for most of the rest of his life, through his art and writing, to seek justice for the thousands of sur-

---

[12] DaA 42263, III. Comité International de Dachau, Procès-verbal intégral d'assemblée générale des 24/25/26 mai 1963 à Munich, 15.

vivors for whom, like him, 1945 did not mean liberation. Georg Tauber was a so-called antisocial element in the Dachau concentration camp. In 1946, he wrote a heart-breaking open letter to political prisoners' associations and co-created the journal *Die Vergessenen*, 'The Forgotten,' in which he invited, Green, Black (and Pink) Triangles to express their grievances. The journal ceased to exist mere months after its creation – it was banned – but it is a testimony of the difficult entanglements between victimhood, liberation, and memory. Georg Tauber, engulfed in bitterness, died in poverty of tuberculosis on October 21, 1950, aged 49. Tauber's fate is reminiscent of the fate of queer survivors in the long postwar era.[13]

It is likewise difficult to talk about the fate of so-called political prisoners as a monolithic block. Many had a solidarity network in the concentration camps, but one should not forget that solidarity in these camps was limited and did not necessarily improve one's existence. Moreover, many political prisoners were also persecuted after the war, as browsing through the records of the *Vereinigung der Verfolgten des Naziregimes* (VVN) can confirm. Once again, it is easy to show how categories chosen by the perpetrators only give a limited perspective on genocide, on persecutions, and on their aftermath, even as they are recuperated for empowerment and identity purposes like the famous Pink Triangle. No category expresses it better then so-called *asoziale* who were forced to wear a black triangle. From sex workers to long term bachelorettes, from teenage delinquents to swing kids, from lesbian women to homeless men, many people were forced into a category still considered not worthy enough for commemoration today. Nonetheless, focusing on perpetrator's categories allows us to also analyse the various forms taken by Nazi violence. Without falling into hierarchies of victimhood, it allows scholars to differentiate, for example, between Nazi antisemitism, anti-Roma racism,[14] or queerphobia.

---

13 Andrea Riedle, "Georg Tauber: An 'Asocial' Prisoner in the Dachau Concentration Camp and His Futile Struggle for Recognition as a Nazi Victim." In *Catalogue of the Special Exhibition: Evidence for Posterity. The Drawings of the Dachau Survivor Georg Tauber*, ed. Stefanie Pilzweger-Steine and Andrea Riedle (Berlin: Metropol, 2016), 13–35. See also Albert Knoll, "'Die Vergessenen' und die 'ausgeschlossenen Opfer' – Spurensuche nach homosexuellen Überlebenden des Konzentrationslagers Dachau." In *Ohnmacht und Aufbegehren: Homosexuelle Männer in der frühen Bundesrepublik*, ed. Andreas Pretzel and Volker Weiß (Hamburg: Männerschwarm Verlag, 2010), 39–61.
14 Sebastian Lotto-Kusche, *Der Völkermord an den Sinti und Roma und die Bundesrepublik: Der lange Weg zur Anerkennung 1949–1990* (Oldenbourg: De Gruyter, 2022); Gabi Meyer, *Offizielles Erinnern und die Situation der Sinti und Roma in Deutschland: Der nationalsozialistische Völkermord in den parlamentarischen Debatten des Deutschen Bundestages* (Wiesbaden: Springer VS, 2013).

In the mid-1970s, German queer activists shifted their identification with the past – see section 1.3 – and began to seek justice for the past in a contemporary struggle for their inclusion in official memory on the perpetrators' grounds, namely in various *Gedenkstätte* across Germany and Austria. They were acting out on the cultural trauma at the core of the Pink Triangle.[15] First, they had unveiled a history a persecution – sometimes exaggerating it – to connect it to their understanding of their own oppression. Second, they had clashed with other groups of victims, trying to convince both their own community and a broader collective of survivors of their own status as such. Here, it is necessary to repeat that these queer activists had not survived the camps themselves. By inserting their own memory activism into the space where the crimes against others were committed, they were carving into stone narratives anchored in the recuperation of the Pink Triangle. In other words, they were historicizing queer suffering and legitimating their fight to end queerphobia.

It would be short-sighted to denounce this contemporary collectivization of past injuries as an instrumentalization by queer initiatives.[16] The identification processes of the 1970s blurred the connection between the past and the present in such a manner that queer men were convinced that, by fighting for an older queer generation, they were salvaging their own past as well. They perceived themselves as second-generation survivors. For example, in a preface to Lutz van Dijk's 1992 study on Nazi persecutions, Germanist Wolfgang Popp – himself queer – wrote that his generation was connected to the previous ones, especially through the symbolic of the Pink Triangle:

> In the death notice for my partner W.G. who died in 1989 I wrote: "The Nazi Pink Triangle branded us too." That scandalized some, including friends, gays and others. Yes, my partner and I belong to a generation that was no longer exposed to this reality of annihilation: that is true. But didn't the Pink Triangle brand us anyway? In 1969, with the effort and enormous democratic determination of homosexuals, the fascist §175 was at least defused [. . .]. Yet, little has changed in the public stigmatization of our presence in the broader society.[17]

The re-localization of queer memory struggles in former concentration camps was gradual and reached its climax in the 1980s. At the dawn of a new decade, queer

---

15 Dominick LaCapra, *History in Transit: Experience, Identity, Critical Theory* (Ithaca, NY: Cornell University Press, 2004), 107.
16 For that argument please refer to "les usages stratégiques du nous," in Regis Schlagdenhauffen, *Triangle Rose: La persécution nazie des homosexuels et sa Mémoire* (Paris: Autrement, 2011), 247–249.
17 Wolfgang Popp, "Auf den Spuren einer schwulen Identität: Vorbemerkungen zu Lutz Van Dijk ,Ein erfülltes Leben . . .'" In *"Ein erfülltes Leben Trotzdem": Erinnerungen Homosexueller 1933–1945*, ed. Lutz van Dijk, (Hamburg: Rowohlt, 1992), I.

initiatives in Munich were already organizing Masses on the ground of the *Gedenkstätte* Dachau, and sending invitation letters to combine these events of worship with a call of reparation for queer men.[18] Likewise, funerals were organized for former queer inmates in the *Versöhnungskirche*, 'reconciliation church,'[19] with an explicit mention of the postwar persecutions, sometimes implying that the shock of postwar re-criminalization was the main reason of a person's demise.[20] By the end of the 1980s and beginning of the 1990s, these symbolic events had evolved into official protests organized by queer initiatives, sometimes supported and sometimes opposed by other groups of victims. In January 1987, 300 men and women protested in Bergen-Belsen and 120 showed up in Dachau, demanding "human rights and reparations" for queer victims. The *Zentralrat Deutscher Roma und Sinti*, 'central council of German Roma and Sinti' and the VVN united their voices with those present.[21]

At the time of the demonstrations, queer organizations in Bavaria were fighting for the inclusion of a *Gedenkstein*, 'memorial stone,' on the official terrain of the *Gedenkstätte* Dachau and for a similar memorialization in Sachsenhausen. In these former places of terror, the relations between the various memory actors were not always as tranquil. Indeed, the blurring of identification and subjectification entangled within the symbol of the Pink Triangle was not always perceived as appropriate by other victims of the Nazi regime. Undeniably, the attitude of some activists was also partly responsible for the heated reaction to their complaints. For instance, the organizing team of some demonstrations were quite clear about the possible triggering effects of the infamous triangles during events where survivors would be present, especially when worn by queer men who were not themselves imprisoned during the times of terror. The *Bundesverband Homosexualität*, 'Federal Union Homosexuality,' and the *Schwulenverband in der DDR*, 'Gay Union in the German Democratic Republic' – now the *Lesben- und Schwulenverband in Deutschland*, 'Lesbian and Gay Federation in Germany' – warned protesters in advance to leave their Pink Triangle buttons and effigies at home and opt instead to bring pink roses.[22] This did not discourage known promi-

---

18 Guido Vael, "Letter to the press 13.06.1980, Vorstand Verein für sexuelle Gleichberechtigung e. V," *Kellerjournal Informations-Blatt des VSG* 1, no. 1 (1980): 3.
19 The evangelical church on the grounds of the former concentration camp in Dachau. It was built in the 1960s.
20 See obituary of Hermann Rieger "Ansprache zu Beerdigung von Herman Rieger am 4 September 1981 auf dem Neuen Südfriedhot in München" *KellerJournal Informations-Blatt des VSG* 2, no. 9 (October 1981): 4–5.
21 Heike Mew, "Entschädigung ein 'Menschenrecht' 11. Januar 1987 Bergen-Belsen und Dachau," *Dorn Rosa Zeitung der Demokratischen Lesben- und Schwuleninitiative* 5 (1987): 7–10.
22 "Totgeschlagen aber nicht mehr totgeschwiegen," in Schwules Museum Berlin C Box Nr. 66 *Gedenken an die Homosexuellen Häftlinge in Sachsenhausen*.

nent queer activists like Egmont Fassbender of the *Rosa Winkel Verlag* from wearing his Pink Triangle in the *Gedenkstätte* Sachsenhausen.[23] In the same vein, queer activists finally allowed to participate in official commemorative ceremonies in Dachau in 1988 came to the event not only wearing Pink Triangles as badges, but also unfolding banners connecting the CID's obtuse rebuke of their demands to the crimes committed by the Nazis – "Whoever conceal crimes against homosexuals actually endorses them in the end".[24] These banners further fractured positions between communities, impeding inclusion of queer victims in the official memory of *Gedenkstätten*.[25]

4.2 Seeking justice for the community: Working out trauma at the site of injury

To contextualize the events leading to the inclusion of Pink Triangle monuments in Sachsenhausen and Dachau, we need to head south of Bavaria some years earlier, to another site of Nazi atrocities near the Austrian city of Linz, the former concentration camp of Mauthausen. On December 9, 1984, around 150 individuals passed the front gate of Mauthausen, braving the winter cold and assembling near the so-called *Klagemauer* 'wailing wall' where former prisoners had been forced to stand in the cold, face to the wall, to await their fate after their arrival in the camp. The hundred or so people who gathered this time came for a more festive, yet still sombre, occasion organized by the *Homosexual Initiative Wien*, 'Homosexual Initiative Vienna,' (HOSI Wien): the unveiling of a 120 cm equilateral Pink Triangle carved from Scandinavian granite, the first memorial stone worldwide in memory of queer men who had been murdered in the camp.[26]

Since its unveiling, sister organization HOSI Linz has laid wreath of flowers annually on December 10 to celebrate the International Day of Human Rights.[27] Indeed, the stone has evolved into one of Austria's central queer memorial sites,

---

23 Micha Schulze, "Eklat beim Gedenken: Schwule durften nicht nach Sachsenhausen," in *Pink Power Berlins Schwules Stadtmagazine*. Schwules Museum (Berlin) C Box Nr. 66 *Gedenken an die Homosexuellen Häftlinge in Sachsenhausen*.
24 Jürgen Zarusky, "Tafel für homosexuelle Opfer reißt alter Wunden wieder auf: Komitee berichtet nach Ablehnung von Protesten und Beschimpfungen" reprinted in *Rosa Info* 7 (June–July 1988), 5.
25 "Lettre du VSG et HuK au CID 30.05.1986" and "Lettre de G. Walraeve et A. Guerisse aux administrateurs du CID 09.04.1986" in DaA Sammlung Homosexuelle u. Gedenktafel Folder: *VSG-Schwule Gruppe*.
26 *LAMBDA-Nachrichten* 7, no. 1 (1985): 6.
27 Kurt Krickler. "Gedenken und demonstrieren" *LAMBDA-Nachrichten* 23, no. 6 (2001): 62.

and part of HOSI Wien's branding. While the Viennese organization already used the Pink Triangle as an official symbol in the 1970s, it re-centred its identity around the stone in the following decades,[28] making sure to plan pilgrimages to the memorial site in 1989 and 1998 when queer activists organized international conferences in the country, respectively in Vienna and Linz.[29] The inscription on the stone commemorates not only the torture experienced by the victims, but also the deadly silence that had plagued the long postwar period: "*Totgeschlagen Totgeschwiegen – Den Homosexuellen Opfern des Nationalsozialismus*," 'Beaten to death, silenced to death – To the homosexual victims of National Socialism.' [Figure 2]

By literally carving queer visibility into stone on the grounds where the traumatic experience took place, Austrian queer organizations spoke up for the past, and issued a warning for the future: they would not be silent anymore. The *Klagemauer* is not alien to other commemorative acts imbued with a similar subjective identification process. A brief tour around the wall today offers visitors a condensed version of the Cold War and the end of the twentieth century. For example, a plaque for Yugoslav victims is now flanked by one from Serbia, then Montenegro, and then Kosovo. Simply put, the commemoration of victims by national group seems to legitimize the nation-state as national victimhood connected to National Socialism becomes part of the *roman national*. In an especially telling example, standing in front of the Catalonian plaque on the *Klagemauer* in 2019, Catalan representatives drew a comparison between the national fight for independence of Catalonia and the Republican fighters deported by Franco who were murdered in Mauthausen.[30] On the other hand, the position of a group's memorial stone also seems to be influenced by struggles between victim communities or bigotry. In fact, HOSI Wien is inclined to relate the following anecdote: when Albanian representatives were invited to adorn the wall with their own commemorative plaque, they made sure to leave a gap between theirs and the Pink Triangle, a breach that was only filled much later.[31]

Yet this was not the only case of prejudice following the unveiling of the monument in the late mid-1980s. Mere months after the inauguration, in May 1985, 25,000 people gathered in Mauthausen for the fortieth anniversary of Liberation. Queer activists were present as well, unfolding two new banners for the occasion: *1,000e homosexuelle KZ-Opfer warten auf Rehabilitierung*, '1000 homosexual victims of the concentration camps are waiting for rehabilitation,' and *40 Jahre 2.*

---

28 *LAMBDA-Nachrichten* 27, no. 1 (2005): 2–11.
29 Kurt Krickler, "Gedenken und demonstrieren": 62.
30 Ana Carbajosa, "Catalan official uses Mauthausen victim tribute to defend jailed separatists," *El País*, (May 6, 2019).
31 Krickler, "Gedenken und demonstrieren": 62.

Figure 2: The Pink Triangle memorial stone on the so-called 'Wailing Wall' of the former concentration camp of Mauthausen in 2019. Photo taken by the author.

Republik – 40 Jahre Schwulen- und Lesbenunterdrückung, '40 Years, second Republic – 40 years of gay and lesbian oppression.'[32] These demands and linkage of the past to the present were far from pleasing for many other attendees. Heated debates and altercations exploded between factions, with some participants allegedly telling queer activists that the furnaces of Mauthausen should still be open for them.[33] Even if HOSI groups mention how other survivors supported them, commending their courage, the confrontations affected and branded memory beyond the Austrian borders.[34] One commentator of the Bavarian gay press warned

---

[32] Krickler, "Gedenken und demonstrieren": 62.
[33] Krickler, "Entschädigung: Bis heute kein Rechtsanspruch": 53–56.
[34] Krickler, "Gedenken und demonstrieren": 62.

his contemporaries with reference to Homocaust narratives, stating that: "Even if we have fought for freedom today, even if the social climate has become a little more tolerant and we have founded our own advocacy groups, we should not deceive ourselves, believing something like that could not happen again."[35]

Many other queer organizations were inspired by the endeavours of the Austrians. For instance, the *Unabhängige Homosexuelle Alternative*, 'Independent Homosexual Alternative' in the Hanseatic city of Hamburg inaugurated a plaque in 1985 at the former concentration camp of Neuengamme for queer male victims killed in the camps nearby.[36] Yet the year also marked the debut of a new drama surrounding a memorial in Bavaria, which blew up to international proportions over the following decade – a drama in which HOSI Wien also played a role. This episode unfolded in the former concentration camp of Dachau, starring actors that we encountered before in the previous chapters, namely multiple groups from Munich – such as the *Verein für sexuelle Gleichberechtigung e.V.* (VSG) – and their struggle with the CID.

In response to calls emerging from Munich[37] and from across Western Europe during the next decade,[38] executive board members of HOSI Wien contacted the CID in June 1985, reminding its members that denying "homosexual victims the respect they deserve" in the *Gedenkstätte* would go against the official spirit of the CID and be a direct affront to fellow victims of the Nazi regime.[39] Most of the letters landing on the CID desk during these years reference two distinct events that had just happened the same year: the aforementioned unveiling and Liberation ceremonies in Mauthausen,[40] and the then still fresh words by German Federal President, Richard von Weizsäcker, who had mentioned the fate of

---

[35] C.R, "Gedenktafel in Mauthausen," *Kellerjournal* 1 (1985): 8.
[36] MGC, "Die Geschichte des Magnus Hirschfeld Centrum," accessed May 24, 2019, https://www.mhc-hh.de/%C3%BCber-uns-1/historie/.
[37] Correspondence between the HuK, HOSI Wien and the CID in DaA Sammlung Homosexuelle u. Gedenktafel, Folder: *VSG-Schwule Gruppe*.
[38] For example, see "Dachau: ne jetez pas les gays à la poubelle!" *Gai Pied Hebdo* 252 (January 1987): 11.
[39] *"Nous sommes convaincus que vous, les membres du Comité, avez sans aucun doute pris conscience du fait qu'une décision négative constituerait un fort affront envers les victimes homosexuelles. Dans l'espoir que le Comité International de Dachau prendra une décision digne du vrai esprit humaniste, anti-fasciste et anti-discriminatoire qui, sûrement, anime votre Comité."* In "Correspondence between HOSI Wien and the CID 14.06.1985" in DaA Sammlung Homosexuelle u. Gedenktafel, Folder: *VSG–Schwule Gruppe*.
[40] "Letter by Casimir Elsen of the Federatie Werkgroepen Homofilie on the 30.07.1985 (Antwerp)" in DaA Sammlung Homosexuelle u. Gedenktafel, Folder: *VSG-Schwule Gruppe*.

"homosexuals" for the first time in an official speech on May 8, 1945.[41] Most of the furore focused on the irony that the committee responsible for the official memory of a former place of torture seemed to condone bigotry against one of the victim groups in the present, or seemed to simply ignore the suffering of one group of victims. This of course shows how effective the Munich campaign, the influence of the gay press, and the existence of an international network of European queer organizations had become in the 1980s throughout the 1990s.[42] The CID seemed to confirm the idea that liberation had not been fully realized for queer survivors. So how did this affair start? What was at the roots of this difficult relationship between the committee of former political prisoners based in Brussels and the Bavarian queer initiatives?

The VSG had already amassed donations in the 1970s to lay wreaths of flowers in the *Gedenkstätte*.[43] In February 1985, inspired by the events in Mauthausen to take commemoration a step further, the regional Munich division of the *Ökumenische Arbeitsgruppe Homosexuelle und Kirche e. V.* (HuK)[44] forwarded an official demand for a formal inclusion of queer victims in the *Gedenkstätte*. It addressed its petition to Albert Guérisse – then president of the CID in Brussels – indicating that Munich activists wished to inaugurate a similar plaque for the fortieth anniversary of Liberation, in the same pink and triangular format, with the same inscription – *Totgeschlagen Totgeschwiegen – Den homosexuellen Opfern des Nationalsozialismus*.[45] After multiple inquiries on the side of the German queer community, the CID finally answered that the organization's director board was in no position to make a decision, and that the general assembly in early 1986 would have to settle the matter. Restless, queer activists sent a petition with 1,300 names to Brussels, asking the CID if the real issues at hand were homophobia and bigotry, implying that the CID considered homosexual victims to be of second-class importance. In

---

41 "Letter by Otto Schily (Grüne MdB) 25.09.1985 (Bonn)" in DaA Sammlung Homosexuelle u. Gedenktafel, Folder: *VSG–Schwule Gruppe*.
42 Most of the Viennese and Bavarian initiatives were members of the *International Gay and Lesbian Association*.
43 What follows is the summary of a complicated story. Please refer to Albert Knoll's work for an extensive almost month per month chronology of the events: Albert Knoll and Burghard Richter, "Initiative zu dem Rosa-Winkel-Gedenkstein." In *Der Rosa-Winkel-Gedenkstein: Die Erinnerung an die Homosexuellen Im KZ Dachau*, ed. Albert Knoll (Munich: Forum Homosexualität München e.V., 2015), 39–55.
44 Founded by Christian members of the *Allgemeine Homosexuelle Arbeitsgemeinschaft* 'General Homosexual Working Group' in Berlin in 1977. See "Eine kleine Geschichte der HuK" *HuK Info* 40 –Sonderinfo zum 20. Deutschen Ev. Kirchentag Hannover (1983): 22.
45 "Letter HuK to CID February 1985" in DaA Sammlung Homosexuelle u. Gedenktafel, Folder: *VSG–Schwule Gruppe*.

April 1986, after further queries by both the VSG and the HuK, the CID informed both parties that the general assembly would not convene, and that the *Conseil d'Administration,* 'Board of Directors,' would meet to settle the matter. This decision would unfortunately happen after the forty-first liberation ceremonies. Without informing queer activists, the CID board eventually unanimously rejected their demand. Barbara Distel – then head of the *Gedenkstätte* – was informed later via telephone, but neither Distel nor the VSG/HuK alliance were given a reason for the rejection.[46]

During these exchanges, activists implied more than once that the CID echoed an attitude similar to the Nazi regime. Likewise, the appellation "homosexual victims" was often synonymous for both queer men in the 1980s and queers persecuted under National Socialism.[47] Until the official inauguration of the plaque in 1995, this struggle became a crusade for both the VSG and the HuK. The press organs of both organizations published updates almost every month for ten years onward with titles like *Der Stein,* 'The Stone,' *Der Gedenkstein muss sein,* 'The Memorial Stone needs to happen,' *Der stein kommt,* 'The Stone is underway,' *Der Stein muß endgültig sein,* 'The Stone definitely needs to happen,' or *Dachau um kein Ende,* 'Still no end in sight in Dachau.'[48] Each of these pieces suggests that a group of survivors was responsible for the injustice. If a group of victims of the Nazis were acting so contemptuously toward queers in the present, then according to activists surely this meant that queer men were worse victims of sorts, confirming Homocaust narratives. Not only were they denied reparations by the government and shunned by society at large but they were apparently also discriminated against yet again by other survivors of the Nazi atrocities.[49]

The fight for the pink triangular stone eventually made it to the *Gedenkstätte* itself, on the grounds of the evangelical *Versöhnungskirche*. Queer activists had associated with various clubs inside the church for years before, organizing an exhibition in 1984 inside its walls on the history of queer discriminations.[50] That

---

46 Knoll and Richter, "Initiative zu dem Rosa-Winkel-Gedenkstein": 47.
47 "Petition and Letter to CID 10.10.1985" in DaA Sammlung Homosexuelle u. Gedenktafel, Folder: *VSG-Schwule Gruppe*.
48 See for example: Claus, "Der Stein muß endgültig sein" *Rosa info* 6 (April & May 1988): 3; Hans Jürgen, "Dachau-und kein Ende," *Rosa Info* 7 (June & July 1988): 3–5.
49 The CID also rebuked Barbara Distel multiple times when she was taking position in the media or when she was not considered harsh enough in her position toward queer activists and associations. See for example "Letters between Barbara Distel and CID 22.08.1988 and 14.01.1987" in DaA Sammlung Homosexuelle u. Gedenktafel, Folder: *VSG–Schwule Gruppe*.
50 Axel Kay, "Freiwilliger der Aktion Sühnezeichen Friedensdienste e.V. in der Evangelischen Versöhnungskirche KZ-Gedenkstätte Dachau" *Kellerjournal – München Schwul* 5 (1984): 15.

is to say, the church's community already had a standing tradition of showing solidarity when it eventually allowed a pink *Gedenkstein* to be erected on its private grounds. The HuK had communicated with the *Versöhnungskirche*'s curatorial committee, answering directly to the evangelical and Lutheran regional churches as well as to the Evangelical German Church. As a result, it did not need the permission of the CID and in May of that year, the stone finally saw the light of day. Covered both in the Bavarian press and in the gay press, the matter greatly irritated the CID.[51] Numerous queer activists took part in personal and collective events during the week.[52] The matter also reached the *Bundestag* and the *Bundeskabinett* 'Federal cabinet,' but the rift between the CID and the Munich activists remained for years.[53] Queer groups received permission to attend official commemoration ceremonies in the 1990s, and some of their actions – as mentioned above – created *éclat*. After the *Versöhnungskirche* provided *Gastrecht*, 'official hospitality,' to the stone in 1994,[54] the CID finally gave its consent[55] and a new stone was transferred to Dachau in June 1995, just in time for the Munich Pride event.[56] It was installed in the official commemoration room of the museum part of the *Gedenkstätte*, where it still stands today. [Figure 3]

The Pink Triangle stone in Dachau, like the one in Mauthausen, became a symbol of queer affirmation in the past and a parallel struggle for inclusion in the present. The case in Dachau particularly nationalized the struggle as the mainstream press took part in the debates. While some newspapers took the side of the activists, many also used the story to spew more bigotry: were homosexuals really victims if they were raping people in concentration camps? Were homosexuals pushing too much for tolerance? Were homosexuals obscenely attacking other victims of fascism? Wasn't that fascist? Were they not all dying of AIDS anyway? These accusations were not solely coming from the Right side of the political spectrum.[57] In all these cases, the attacks on queer activism and the idea that queers were once again the lowest of the low in concentration camps fuelled a

---

51 "Letter between CID and Barbara Distel 22.08.1988" in DaA Sammlung Homosexuelle u. Gedenktafel, Folder: *VSG–Schwule Gruppe*.
52 Jürgen, "Dachau-und kein Ende": 5.
53 "Letter on 2007.1988 sent by CID to Dr. Hans-Jochen Vogel, leader of the SPD parliamentary group in the Bundestag" in DaA Sammlung Homosexuelle u. Gedenktafel, Folder: *VSG–Schwule Gruppe*.
54 Jürgen. "Dachau-und kein Ende": 3.
55 Knoll and Richter, "Initiative zu dem Rosa-Winkel-Gedenkstein": 52–55.
56 The original had been damaged by hazardous weather.
57 See for example: Günter Amendt. "Homosexuelle Suchtkultur" *Konkret* 4 (1985): 58–60.

Figure 3: The Pink Triangle memorial stone in the museum of the former concentration camps of Dachau in 2018. Photo taken by the author.

sense of collective identity in the gay press. The Pink Triangle, as a stone and a symbol, became synonymous with the community, with resilience, and with survival.

It would take another episode in Brandenburg to anchor this symbolism into myth, and to help the Pink Triangle to transition into the post-unification years. By 1985, Berlin gay groups had already organized trips to the former concentration camp of Sachsenhausen, despite the difficulties in crossing the border. For the fortieth anniversary of Liberation, *Treffen Berliner Schwulengruppen*, 'The coalition of gay groups in Berlin,' had declared the commemoration of queer male victims to be its focal topic of the year.[58] The planned visit included a ceremony with a wreath of flowers and small political and historical speeches about the fate of the men with the pink triangle.[59]

During the visit, a sort of pilgrimage for the Berliners present at the event, prominent activists explained that their presence on these grounds spoke to two obvious facts: the discrimination and persecution of queer men had not ceased since National Socialism, and that Sachsenhausen was the "Auschwitz of Homosexuals."[60] This provocative statement had roots in the Homocaust narrative of the 1970s and the need for queer men to geographically anchor their victimhood. Most of this "Homoschwitz" rhetoric came from two sources: the known fact that the clay and brick factory of the former concentration camp was a death trap, and the proof that queer men were deliberately assigned to this duty more than once throughout the years. Historians have indeed uncovered specific and orchestrated murder commandos where men with pink triangles were assigned to their untimely death because of their queerness or alleged queerness.[61]

The second source of this narrative brings us back to Joseph Kohout's fate and the book, *The Men with the Pink Triangle*. In their reports on the events, Neumann/Kohout relate how Sachsenhausen was particularly full of homosexual men, and that these men were treated the worst out of all groups in the camp. Rüdiger Lautmann debunked this idea as early as 1981, mentioning that Dachau, Buchenwald, and Neuengamme had seen more murder commandos specifically targeting queer men than Sachsenhausen, and always in relatively "low" numbers.[62] Still, activists in the gay press focused on Sachsenhausen as a place of gay terror and the reason behind a missing generation of gay men – "*diese Männer*

---

58 "Letter by TBS to Pädagogische Abteilung of the Nationale Mahn- und Gedenkstätte Sachsenhausen on the 15.04.1985" Schwules Museum Berlin C Box Nr. 66 *Gedenken an die homosexuellen Häftlinge in Sachsenhausen*.
59 "Letter by Hans-Joachim Müller to the direction of the Nationale Mahn- und Gedenkstätte Sachsenhausen on the 15.06.1985" in Schwules Museum Berlin C Box Nr. 66 *Gedenken an die homosexuellen Häftlinge in Sachsenhausen*.
60 "Joachim Müller's Speech (Begleitende Worte zur Kranzniederlegung des Treffens der Berliner Schwulengruppen on the 27.06.1985 at Nationalen Mahn- und Gedenkstätte Sachsenhausen, Oranienburg)" Schwules Museum Berlin C Box Nr. 66 *Gedenken an die homosexuellen Häftlinge in Sachsenhausen*. Queer women in the German Democratic Republic were also organizing actions and events in the grounds of former concentration camps. See Maria Bühner, "Die Kontinuität des Schweigens. Das Gedenken der Ost-Berliner Gruppe Lesben in der Kirche in Ravensbrück" *Österreichische Zeitschrift für Geschichtswissenschaften* 29, no. 2 (2019): 111–131.
61 Joachim Müller, "Unnatürliche Todesfälle: Vorfälle in den Außenbereichen Klinkerwerk, Schießplatz und Tongrube." In *Homosexuelle Männer im KZ Sachsenhausen*, ed. Joachim Müller, Schwules Museum (Berlin) and Andreas Sternweiler (Berlin: Verlag rosa Winkel, 2000), 216–263.
62 Rüdiger Lautmann, "Die mit dem 'Rosa Winkel'" *Frankfurter Rundschau* (June 16, 1981).

fehlen uns als schwule Generation," 'We are missing these men as a gay generation.'[63] However, at the time, the goal behind these pilgrimages in the German Democratic Republic (GDR) had less to do with unravelling facts about the atrocities, and more with honouring those that had been murdered for being queer and "that were still dying."[64]

Inspired by what was happening in Austria and in Bavaria, activists considered that the time had come to also unveil a memorial stone in Sachsenhausen. In a press release soon after unification, the Berlin chapter of the HuK explained that, while groups in the GDR had been actively commemorating queer victims at Sachsenhausen, these events had been heavily surveilled by the *Staatssicherheitsdienst*, 'Ministry for State Security,' – the infamous Stasi –, and that most of the crowns of flowers were destroyed after each ceremony.[65] The HuK and the gay association inside the newly formed *Partei des Demokratischen Sozialismus*, 'Party of Democratic Socialism,' (PDS)[66] pushed for an official mention of queer male victims in the former concentration camp.[67] In early July 1992, after a call for action by the official gay group in the PDS, activists unveiled a Pink Triangle stone with the popular epitaph *"Totgeschlagen Totgeschwiegen"* with a particular addition: *"Den schwulen Opfern von Sachsenhausen,"* 'To the gay victims of Sachsenhausen.' A provisional Black Triangle with the inscription *"Totgeschlagen Totgeschwiegen – den lesbischen Opfern des Nationalsozialismus,"* 'Beaten to Death. Silenced to Death – to the lesbian victims of National Socialism,' was supposed to stand side by side with the pink triangular stone, but conflict and heated discussions among activists buried the idea.[68]

---

[63] Joachim Müller, "Ehrung im Ex-KZ" *Siegessäule* (June 1985): 10.
[64] "Joachim Müller's Speech (Begleitende Worte zur Kranzniederlegung des Treffens der Berliner Schwulengruppen on the 27.06.1985 at Nationalen Mahn- und Gedenkstätte Sachsenhausen, Oranienburg)" Schwules Museum Berlin C Box Nr. 66 *Gedenken an die homosexuellen Häftlinge in Sachsenhausen*.
[65] "HuK Press release Berlin 15.11.1992" Schwules Museum Berlin C Box Nr. 66 *Gedenken an die homosexuellen Häftlinge in Sachsenhausen*.
[66] From the ashes of the East German *Sozialistische Einheitspartei Deutschland* 'Socialist Unity Party of Germany,' the PDS was eventually a partner and merged with the *Arbeit & soziale Grechtigkeit – Die Wahlalternative* 'Labour and Social Justice – The Electoral Alternative' to create today's *Die Linke* 'The Left.'
[67] The PDS Schwule Gruppe also contributed to the donations for the stone: "Der schwule Dachverband Bundesverband Homosexualität e.V. 'übersicht Spenden "Gedenktafel Sachsenhausen""' Schwules Museum Berlin C Box Nr. 66 *Gedenken an die Homosexuellen Häftlinge in Sachsenhausen*.
[68] "PDS Press release on the 1st of July 1992 for the action on the 4th of July 1992" Schwules Museum Berlin C Box Nr. 66 *Gedenken an die homosexuellen Häftlinge in Sachsenhausen*. See section 5.3 in this book.

The local press reported that in response to the disagreement, the *Gedenkstätte* and activists were trying to come up with a solution.[69] In November of the same year, a plaque "against oblivion" was unveiled in front of hundreds of activists and dignitaries. The *Freie Demokratische Partei*, 'Free Democratic Party,' (FDP) and the PDS attended the ceremony. Both parties laid wreaths of flowers, with the other political forces of the republic remaining silent on the issue.[70]

Although the episode at Sachsenhausen did not take the dramatic proportions of the affair in Bavaria, and although politicians and victim groups like the VVN were willing to show solidarity with the endeavour, queer activists were quick to remind the community that there was still much to be done. For instance, the official program of a 1995 seminar on homosexuality and Sachsenhausen in Berlin organized by queer organizations stated that discrimination against queerness still existed, that neo-Nazis were on the rise, and that the lessons of Sachsenhausen were a constant reminder of the oppression they were facing in the Federal Republic of Germany (FRG).[71] Several incidents of the previous years confirmed these fears. Indeed, according to the Berlin gay press, the provincial police of Brandenburg had violently blocked activists' visit to Sachsenhausen for official ceremonies that same year, following orders to arrest potential "peace-breakers."[72] All in all, although the final memorial stone in Sachsenhausen ended up being different from the ones in Dachau and Mauthausen, the results remain similar. Through pilgrimage to the places of trauma, through a connection between the present and the past, and through the creation of myths and places of memory, queer activists in Berlin and Brandenburg managed to include and canonize their narrative in the official political memory of the FRG.

These episodes in southern and northern Germany, as well as the original episode in Austria, ritualized queer narratives and attracted the attention of both the mainstream press and the foreign gay press. By working through the cultural trauma and reinforcing their narrative of victimhood vis-à-vis other victim groups, queer activists managed to collectivize their identity through both the symbolism of the Pink Triangle, and through their insistence that the places of demise for the

---

69 "Rosa Winkel gegen Vergessen: Mahnmal erinnert an Schwule Opfer in Sachsenhausen," *Oranienburger Generalanzeiger* (July 6, 1992).
70 "Totgeschlagen- totgeschwiegen," *TAZ* (November 24, 1992).
71 "'Schwule in Sachsenhausen' a seminar for gay men organized by the group Bildungswerk für Demokratie und Umweltschutz 'Education for Democracy and Environmental Protection' in April 1995." *Schwules Museum* Berlin C Box Nr. 66 *Gedenken an die homosexuellen Häftlinge in Sachsenhausen*.
72 Micha Schulze, "Eklat beim Gedenken: Schwule durften nicht nach Sachsenhausen," *Pink Power Berlins Schwules Stadtmagazine*, Schwules Museum Berlin C Box Nr. 66 *Gedenken an die homosexuellen Häftlinge in Sachsenhausen*.

men forced to wear pink triangles were places of collective queer injury. As the Pink Triangle became the representation of these struggles, it also became the catalyst of its memorialization. Confronted incessantly with debates about Pink Triangle stones, Pink Triangle banners, and Pink Triangle symbolism, activists were assessing themselves in the present but reframing their use of the symbol as an icon for memory, for history, and for inclusion. This icon also became the ambassador of German political struggles abroad, where other organizations felt a deeper connection between German *Vergangenheitsbewältigung* and other historical experiences of queerness. The table was set for an international debate on the place of queers in official memory beyond the walls of former concentration camps – a debate where the Pink Triangle would also play an important role. This journey starts in Germany but also takes us to the shores of North America.

4.3 Getting a seat at the table: Transatlantic official Holocaust memory and queer activism

To commemorate the Nazi seizure of power the Social Democrat parliamentary group in Berlin's House of Representatives introduced a motion in March 1982 to erect a memorial for the victims of the Nazi dictatorship in the divided city. According to the project, this memorial would contain a research centre and exhibit area focusing on the victims of the regime's antisemitic atrocities.[73] The Social Democrats settled on the Prinz-Albrecht Palais, former headquarters of the infamous Gestapo. If members on the far-right denounced such a memorial project as an attack by Jews, queers, Roma, and Sinti against the "fallen heroes of the Fatherland,"[74] civic society generally accepted the venture as a long overdue enterprise,[75] supporting what today's visitors to Berlin may know as *Topographie des*

---

[73] "Antrag der Fraktion der SPD über Errichtung eines Mahnmals für die Opfer der nationalsozialistischen Gewaltherrschaft March 5 (1982)," Schwules Museum Berlin C, Box Nr. 178 *Denkmal Debatte NS-Zeit*.
[74] See Uwe Detlevsen, "Dann besser kein Denkmal: Unsere Helden leben in unseren Herzen," *Deutsche National Zeitung* (June 9, 1985). This kind of discourse is reminiscent of the more recent paroles by fascist politician Björn Höcke of the so-called *Alternative für Deutschland* calling the resulting monument "a monument of shame for Germany." See excerpts of his antisemitic speech on German memory culture: dpa-Newskanal, "Die Höcke-Rede von Dresden in Wortlaut-Auszügen," *Süddeutsche Zeitung*, accessed April 14, 2020, https://www.sueddeutsche.de/politik/parteien-die-hoecke-rede-von-dresden-in-wortlaut-auszuegen-dpa.urn-newsml-dpa-com-20090101-170118-99-928143.
[75] P. Theodor Hoffmann, "Wie gehen wir den mit unserer Vergangenheit um? Nationalsozialismus und Weltkrieg in Denkmalen von 1945 bis 1985" *Hamburger Abendblatt* (November 22, 1985).

Terrors, 'Topography of Terror.'[76] Indeed, proponents of the project at the time denounced the somewhat scandalous realization that Washington DC and Jerusalem had created research centres, but that the land of the perpetrators had no central commemorative grounds for one of the worst genocides in history in the columns of countless newspapers.[77]

It is along these lines of thought that an initiative formed by German scholars and activists started to push the idea of an official federal monument for the murdered Jews of Europa in the 1990s, the one now situated near *Pariser Platz*, at the centre of post-unification Berlin.[78] It is this focus on the main and biggest group of victims of the Nazi regime that eventually turned into the biggest bone of contention in a complicated and difficult memory conflict between various actors of the post unified German civic society. At the heart of this struggle lay the importance of victimhood and the Holocaust for German national identity politics,' the definition of the Holocaust, and the awakening of antisemitic resentment. Queer organizations were at the centre of this episode.[79]

Before long, debates surrounding the creation of a new Holocaust memorial into the public sphere crystallized into two fronts: proponents of a monument for the Jewish victims, and organizations denouncing the perceived injustice of being allegedly once again erased from history. In this second group, queer organizations specified that "their suffering" had too long been silenced and that an official monument without mention of the men with pink triangles would be another example of postwar German queerphobia. At this point, the German *Bundestag* had not offered any form of apology nor reparations to queer men or women persecuted under National Socialism. This would come much later at the turn of the millennium for queer male victims. Still, as many historians emphasized during the years surrounding these debates, queer persecutions were not based on the same grounds as the antisemitic policies of the regime. The atrocities were also far from similar in numbers. However, it was – and still is today – difficult to argue along these lines without falling into emotional conversations about hierar-

---

76 For the official website: https://www.topographie.de/.
77 Eberhard Jäckel, "–Aufruf einer Bürgerinitiative– An alle und jeden erinnern?," *Die Zeit* (April 7, 1989).
78 Claus Leggewie and Erik Meyer, *"Ein Ort, an den man gerne geht": Das Holocaust-Mahnmal und die Geschichtspolitik nach 1989* (Munich: Carl Hanser Verlag, 2005).
79 Much has been written about the debates surrounding German memory politics and *Vergangenheitsbewältigung*. Here I mainly focus on queer discord, alliances, and the idea of casting multiple possible histories in stone. See Manuela Bauche, Patricia Piberger, Sébastien Tremblay, and Hannah Tzuberi, "From Opferkonkurrenz to Solidarity: A Round Table," *Bulletin of the German Historical Institute London* 44, no. 2 – Special Issue Memory Culture 2.0: From Opferkonkurrenz to Solidarity (2022): 32–85.

chies of victimhood and resentment against the place given to Jewish victims of the Nazis.[80] This has much more to do with the importance of Nazi atrocities as a vector for legitimacy in Germany, and less with the presupposed myth that Jewish memory in Germany had always been supported by the federal government.[81]

Similar to their use of the Pink Triangle, queer organizations linked Nazi queerphobia with contemporary political struggle. Reinhard Naumann of the *Berliner Schwusos,* 'gay interest group in the Berlin branch of the Social Democratic Party of Germany,' (*Sozialdemokratisches Partei Deutschland,* SPD) signed a press communiqué at the time, stating that it was "extremely strange that the concerned politicians and the Central Council of Jews in Germany have refused to accept all reasonable arguments for a common, central, and, in each case, differentiated memorial for the individual victim groups."[82] His statement illustrates a tension between the readiness to consider differences between the queerphobic, racist, ableist, and – of course – antisemitic horrors committed by the Nazis, while doggedly insisting on a horizontal commemoration of victimhood. Simultaneously, proponents of a memorial for only the murdered Jews of Europe maintained the uniqueness of the fate of the European Jewry.[83]

The debates soured even further as queer activists allied themselves with other so-called forgotten victims,[84] allying themselves with the *Zentralrat der*

---

[80] Jean-Michel Chaumont, *La Concurrence des victimes: Génocide, identité, reconnaissance* (Paris: Éditions la Découverte, 1997); Aleida Assmann. *Das neue Unbehagen an der Erinnerungskultur: Eine Intervention* (Munich: C. H. Beck, 2013): 142–180.

[81] Frank Stern, *Im Anfang war Auschwitz: Antisemitismus und Philosemitismus im deutschen Nachkrieg* (Gerlingen: Bleicher Verlag, 1991); Peter Reichel, Harald Schmid, and Peter Steinbach, "Die 'zweite Geschichte' der Hitler-Diktatur." In *Der Nationalsozialismus – Die Zweite Geschichte,* ed. Peter Reichel, Harald Schmid and Peter Steinbach (Munich: C. H. Beck, 2009), 7–21.

[82] SPD Schwusos, "Presseerklärung: Vorentscheidung für ausschließlich jüdisches Mahnmal an Pariser Platz gegen Sinti/Roma und andere Opfergruppe," Schwules Museum Berlin. C, Box Nr. 178 *Denkmal Debatte NS-Zeit.*

[83] For different points of view and perspectives see: Ute Frings, "Nationales Holocaust-Denkmal – für wen?," *Der Freitag* (July 10, 1992); "Der geteilte Holocaust: ein Denkmal-Streit," *TAZ* (July 8, 1992); Christine Richter, "Erschreckend," *Berliner Zeitung* (July 7, 1992); Christine Richter, "Holocaust Denkmal bleibt umstritten," *Berliner Zeitung,* (March 11, 1992); Horst Seferens, "Holocaust-Gedenken an einer grausigen Stätte," *Jüdische Wochenzeitung,* (July 16, 1992); Rudolf Kraft, "In trennendem Gedenken," *Die Zeit,* (24 July 1992); "Eins an jeder Ecke," *Der Spiegel,* (March 20, 1996): 11–13; Dick Schümer, "Erlebnisraum Holocaust – Wider die Inflation der Mahnmäler und Gedenkstätten –," *Frankfurter Allgemeine Zeitung,* (11 November 1994); "Historiker wirft Sinti und Roma falsches Geschichtsbild vor," in *Tagblatt* (Traunstein); "Die Schlacht um Berlin," *Ha'aretz* –original in Hebrew– (October 15, 1993): 7. Olivera Stevanovic, "Fatal, daß die Opfer sich streiten," *TAZ* (December 2, 1992); Eberhard Jäckel, "Wider zwei Legenden über den Holocaust," *Das Ostpreußenblatt* (July 15, 2000).

[84] Queer Jews are never mentioned in these discussions, nor did I find newspaper articles written from a queer Jewish perspective on the matter.

Roma und Sinti with whom they wrote open letters and expressed indignation.[85] As the *Zentralrat* argued, centuries old anti-Roma racism was and still is rampant across the European space, Germany included. Following this stream of thought, the exclusion of Romani suffering from the official memorial would only legitimize the pursuit of racism in the FRG and the erasure of Romani presence in Germany.[86] As the *Bundestag* confirmed and ratified the creation of the memorial, a debate about inclusion did not in any case lead to a more nuanced discussion.

On one side, those underscoring the singularity of the Holocaust attacked Romani memorial activists in the press, stating, for example, that their businesses had never been boycotted nor destroyed as they were during antisemitic pogroms.[87] Concurrently, historians backing the project of a memorial uniquely for Jewish victims also refused to discuss the possibility of creating other subsequent monuments for other victims, denouncing a presupposed relativization of the Holocaust. As this discourse took off,[88] queer and Romani organizations' fear of era-

---

[85] "Letter from Vorstand des Zentralrats Deutscher Sinti und Roma 'Ein gemeinsames Nationales Holocaust-Mahnmal in Berlin – Aufruf-'" *Tagesspiegel* (September 14, 1992).

[86] "Letter from Vorstand des Zentralrats Deutscher Sinti und Roma." See also Albert Eckert, "Antrag der Fraktion Bündnis 90/Grüne (AL)/UFV über kulturelle und stadträumliche Auseinandersetzung mit der NS-Geschichte," September 7, 1992. Schwules Museum Berlin Box Nr 178 *Denkmal Debatte NS-Zeit*. As previously mentioned, it would be inaccurate to pretend that Jewish voices were automatically heard in Germany and that a monument to the Jewish victims of the Holocaust did not meet fierce nationalist and revisionist opposition in the press from the 1980s up to the 2000s. It is also true that other victims of the Nazis were ignored for decades. This book has so far demonstrated the hurdles awaiting queer memory activists. For various reasons – racism is also here playing a key factor – Roma and Sinti were also ignored and silenced, even though around 500,000 people from the community died in a concerted effort at extermination on behalf of the regime. Still, in the 2000s, the antisemitic and racist physician – and self-appointed '*Z*geunerexperte*' – Hermann Arnold could write in a national newspaper that the *Porajmos* had never taken place. See Hermann Arnold, "Falsche Gleichsetzung," *Frankfurter Allgemeine Zeitung* (December 28, 2004). Things are slowly changing. For example, the *NS-Dokumentationszentrum* in the city of Cologne presented an exhibit in late 2017 focusing on the life of Roma and Sinti survivors after the war and their struggle to gain recognition as victims of fascism. One room also shed light on the movement fighting anti-Roma racism in contemporary Germany from a Roma and Sinti perspective.

[87] Rudolf Kraft, "In trennendem Gedenken," *Die Zeit* (July 24, 1992).

[88] "Eins an jeder Ecke" in *Der Spiegel* (March 20, 1996). The satirical magazine *Titanic* also published bigoted caricatures ridiculing the debate, imagining what "other" memorials for victims of fascism would look like. The artists drew a huge bar of soap for queer men (toying with the idea of prison rape as a punchline – "don't drop the soap") and a huge car park surrounded by barbed wire, reproducing the racist idea that Roma and Sinti are thieves. See "Male für Alle" *Titanic* (August 1999): 34–35.

sure increased,[89] denouncing the canonization of only one type of victimhood in official narratives.[90] The tone of such discussions was rarely denuded of highly problematic rhetoric. If queers were not innocent of engaging in troubling antisemitic resentment, instigators of the monument also talked about "the legends" [sic] of the *Porajmos*, the Romani genocide, sometimes also denying victim status to the men with the pink triangle.[91]

This inflation of discourses had long lasting impacts. On one hand, as it ratified the creation of the foundation associated with the monument, the *Bundestag* also ratified the eventual creation of other forms of remembrance in the middle of the city. Political parties in Germany even settled for an official monument for homosexuals in their charters and statutes.[92] Each of these monuments also brought their own debates and controversies.[93] As for the scandals surrounding the Holocaust memorial near *Pariser Platz*, they shifted to nonetheless passionate architectural and artistic deliberations before its inauguration in 2005. On the other hand, the discursive aspects of these conjunctures marked discourses on victimhood and National Socialism for decades to come. By entering the political arena to be included in the carving into stone of marginalized narrative regard-

---

89 They were not the only ones. During a discussion evening at the Martin-Gropius-Bau in the Fall of 1992, panellists from the queer community highlighted this fear of erasure. Albert Eckert illustrated his point by mentioning the suggestion by the (then-) governing mayor of Berlin to inaugurate a monument for Roma and Sinti victims on the outskirts of Berlin – in the borough of Marzahn – where Nazis had opened a special camp. No member of the Roma and Sinti community were on stage that night, although the organizers invited activist Otto Rosenberg. See: Humanistische Union, "Pressemitteilung –Podiumsdiskussion 'Ein Denkmal für die europäischen Juden' in Berlin: Wie gedenken wir der anderen Opfer" (probably October 1992) and "Einladung zur Podiumsteilnahme 30.11.92" October 14, 1992. Schwules Museum Berlin. Box Nr 178 *Denkmal Debatte NS-Zeit*. For a summary of the event and Eckert's mention of the "Marzahn dilemma," see: Olivera Stevanovic, "Fatal, daß die Opfer sich streiten," *TAZ* (December 2, 1992). Rosenberg's name has been given to the place in Marzahn where a small monument was inaugurated in the 2000s.
90 A monument for the Roma and Sinti victims of the Nazi regime has by now seen the light of day following the artistic vision of Israeli artist Dani Karavan. The then-*Bundespräsident* Joachim Gauck and Angela Merkel inaugurated it in 2012 in a small area of Tiergarten south of the Reichstag and near the Brandenburg Gate.
91 Eberhard Jäckel, "Wider zwei Legenden über den Holocaust," *Das Ostpreußenblatt* (July 15, 2000)."Eins an jeder Ecke," *Der Spiegel* (March 20, 1996): 11–13.
92 See "Koalitionsvereinbarung zwischen PD und PDS 2001–2006 §17 Gleichgeschlechtliche Lebensweisen." Schwules Museum Berlin C, Box Nr 178 *Denkmal Debatte NS-Zeit*.
93 Jennifer Evans, "Harmless Kisses and Infinite Loops. Making Space for Queer Place in Twenty-First Century Berlin." In *Queer Cities, Queer Cultures Europe since 1945*, ed. Jennifer Evans and Matt Cook, (London: Bloomsbury Academic, 2014), 75–94.

ing the atrocities committed by the regime, queer organizations also pushed for an integration to German *Vergangenheitsbewältigung*.

These debates were not necessarily queerphobic. Contemporary historians have shown how the fate of non-Jewish queer victims was different from the industrial murder of Jews across Europe. Without saying that it should be less commemorated, nor that it is of lesser importance, it should nonetheless be memorialized differently.[94] It would also be an exaggeration to consider the story of the Holocaust memorial as a pure instrumentalization on behalf of a queer agenda. These stories are part of the coming of age of queer history in Germany as Homocaust narratives were slowly dissolving by the end of the twentieth century. The appeal to victimhood, however, did not necessarily fade away.

Queer men made sense of queer suffering throughout the twentieth century and of their struggles at the turn of the millennium through the connection to the past offered by the Pink Triangle. Writing for a gay regional magazine in the mid-1990s, a man named Robert offered his thoughts on the Pink Triangle and the persecution of queerness under National Socialism. He first relates his visit to a synagogue in Aachen, pointing out to a US American Jewish friend that if he had been alive at the time, "he too" would probably have ended up in a concentration camp "just like her." Robert linked this awareness to his position within German national history. He writes: "for me, the Pink Triangle is not only a sign of my identity, but also a warning that something like this must never happen again."[95] In Robert's writings, the Pink Triangle once again opens a bridge between the past and the present.

Through the integration of queer memory into German *Vergangenheitsbewältigung*, queer activist reassessed some aspects of earlier Homocaust narratives. Many German activists continued to brandish enamelled Pink Triangles and cross Pink Triangle bridges during the 1990s while fighting for the creation of a distinct monument for the queer victims of the Nazis. At the same time, reconsidering Homocaust narratives did not mean that queer German men stopped linking their present with the past and identifying with victims of the Nazi dictatorship.

Yet, the monument inaugurated in the twenty-first century in the Berlin *Tiergarten* park does not refer to the Pink Triangle.[96] Could it be that the Pink Triangle was too closely linked to pink radicals' narratives and was not considered

---

94 Neil Miller, "Controversy: Our Holocaust – Legends and propaganda flourish in the absence of well-documented history concerning the fate of gays in the Third Reich," *The Advocate* (April 2, 1996): 35–38.
95 Robert, "Gedanken zum Rosa Winkel," *Anstoß die regionale Trierer Schwulenzeitschrift*, (January 23, 1995): 17.
96 Tomberger, "Das Berliner Homosexuellen-Denkmal," 187–207.

appropriate for a monument in the early 2000s? Was there a possible reconciliation between Robert's Triangle, the Holocaust memorial near *Pariser Platz*, and a new monument with a distinct narrative based on the same symbol? This is maybe due to the loaded aspect of the triangle's history. Symbols and images often work as a two-way street influencing discourses while being influenced by context. They are also multilayered and evoke the survival of the past. Thus, the Pink Triangle is a fascinating and nuanced contribution to the critique of monuments. It illustrates how the carving into stone of one narrative in official political memory does not necessarily void other accounts in the public sphere. However, the solidification of one perspective may in turn influence the discourses of another narrative. The Pink Triangle and the story of queer integration to German official memory contradict the warnings of historians on the limits of monuments.[97] They both show that it is possible to carve one fragment of memory into stone and yet how that immutable act can cement another narrative. In other words, the official definition of queer suffering and historical queer injuries as 'not a Homocaust' through the canonization of queer memory redefined the narrative of the Pink Triangle; it also reinforced the importance of the symbol for the community. Consequently, when Robert writes his piece, he can confirm that "the Pink Triangle, for me, has a lot to do with Germany and to do with my relation to this country, a relation *cum ira et studio*."[98]

The episode of the Holocaust memorial in Berlin demonstrates how queer activists have tried to integrate German *Vergangenheitsbewältigung* by suggesting a horizontal way of looking at victimhood. This was based on their experience of creating their own memory of victimhood on concentration camp sites. If the creation of Pink Triangle monuments in *Gedenkstätte* had reinforced Holocaust narratives and opened old wounds, the debates in Berlin also debunked them. As queer memory entered a new era following the inauguration of official monuments, the Pink Triangle remained the bridge between a past of injury during National Socialism, the memory of the initial clashes of the first episodes in *Gedenkstätte*, and the link between victimhood and identity.

This is still far from just a German story. Let us now travel across the Atlantic to North America to identify episodes that demonstrate similar tensions between the canonization of queer memory and activism, between non-Jewish queers and non-queer Jewish communities. As we will discover, these tensions were syn-

---

[97] Margrit Pernau and Sébastien Tremblay, "Dealing with an Ocean of Meaninglessness: Reinhart Koselleck's Lava Memories and Conceptual History," *Contribution to the History of Concepts* 15, no. 2 (2020): 7–28.
[98] Robert, "Gedanken zum Rosa Winkel," 17.

chronically manifested with and echoed some of the debates in Germany, even if the contexts were not necessarily the same.

4.4 Same triangles, different triangles: Transatlantic inclusions

In the mid-late 1990s, Rick Landman, the founder of the *International Association of Lesbian and Gay children of Holocaust Survivors*, wrote a letter to *The Advocate*,[99] one of the leading organs of the US gay press, to commend a previously published piece[100] on some of the Jewish opposition to the inclusion of "the Nazi persecutions of homosexuals" in the newly created Museum of Jewish Heritage in the south of Manhattan. In his letter, he congratulates the magazine for covering the "latest attempt to obscure part of our history."[101] Landman was known for his various comparisons of the governmental reaction to the HIV/AIDS crisis with the Holocaust.[102] Other readers also conveyed their opinions on the apparently popular piece. Some blatantly compared the racist and antisemitic politics of extermination by the Nazis with the persecution of queerness,[103] some obscenely drew parallels between the rhetoric of the rabbis quoted in the piece and the vitriolic hatred of Adolf Hitler,[104] while some surprisingly took the opportunity to draw racist parallels with an alleged oppression of gay and lesbians by African Americans, claiming one identity would be mutually exclusive of the other.[105] These letters offer a window into the importance of identity politics at the end of the last century in the USA.

The story went a little bit like this: non-queer Jewish Americans were so focused on antisemitism that they were apparently denying queers the right to be commemorated in official US memory of National Socialism. Browsing through the debates of the time, these claims echo the antisemitic resentment expressed in the FRG. The

---

99 Rick Landman, "Whose Holocaust? Letters to the Editors," *The Advocate* (January 20, 1998): 6.
100 Robert L. Pela, "Taking the Triangle Out of the Star: An Attempt by Orthodox Rabbis to Keep Gays out of a Holocaust Memorial is Fueling a Debate Among Jews," *The Advocate* (December 9, 1997): 45–46.
101 Rick Landman. "Whose Holocaust?": 6.
102 Pamela Druckerman, "Jews join N.Y. Gay-rights March," *The Jewish Journal* 19 (July 1, 1994): 18.
103 Bryan Bridges, "Whose Holocaust? Letters to the Editors" *The Advocate*, (January 20, 1998): 6.
104 Michelle Criscuolo Brunelle, "Whose Holocaust? Letters to the Editors" *The Advocate*, (January 20, 1998): 6.
105 Simone Toulon, "Black-and-white Rainbow: Letters to the Editors," *The Advocate* (January 20, 1998): 6.

reality was different. Rabbis marching on Washington DC during the March for Lesbian and Gay Rights had already expressed their desire to talk about the persecutions of queerness under National Socialism during the 1993 World Jewish Congress, stating they knew "what a minority feels like."[106] Yet for non-Jewish queer readers of *The Advocate*, especially those conflating the Holocaust and the Nazi persecutions of queer men and women, queerphobia was "as bad" as racism and "as bad" as antisemitism. Men like Landman, themselves Jewish, also tried to pitch queerphobia against antisemitism – Was he not oppressed by both? – His attitude toward the New York rabbis underscored his own affirmation as a gay Jewish man and not necessarily a criticism of Judaism. In 1994, joining a parade for the twenty-fifth anniversary of the Stonewall uprising, he cheered at the realization that he was now able to be out and proud as both a Jew and a gay man.[107] Vocal queer Jewish congregations in North America also argued for the inclusion of the Nazi persecution of queer men and women in Holocaust memory, highlighting cases where victims had been both Jewish and queer or simply fighting for the recognition of queer victims.[108] In North America, Jewish queer organizations such as *Yakhdav*, 'Symbolism,' in Montréal organized an international gay and lesbian Jewish conference and put pressure on the city's own Holocaust memorial center to include an acknowledgment of queer men as victims of the Nazis.[109]

However, this inclusion in the lists of "other victims," did not necessarily mean that queerness was centered in the queer memory of the National Socialism. There is a clear distinction in the acknowledgment of persecutions of political prisoners, queers, Jehovah Witnesses, etc. and the idea that queer men were victims "of the Holocaust" or had it worse in concentration camps. Historian Klaus Müller was quick to denounce the uses of phantasms and big numbers in activist circles and prioritized the fact-based approach of a research centre, like the one in the USHMM. In a 1996 interview with *The Advocate*, he repeats that the "goal of the Nazi antigay campaign was not the extermination of homosexual men, but rather some brutal form of 're-education.'"[110] Müller was at the heart of the USHMM's mission to include artefacts and stories of queer victims in the permanent exhibition

---

[106] Deborah Kalb, "Jews March For Gay Rights," *The Jewish Journal* (April 30, 1993): 18.
[107] Druckerman, "Jews join N.Y. Gay-rights March," 18.
[108] This layer was less present in Germany, probably for historical reasons. Laurence Duchaine-Guillon, *La vie Juive à Berlin après 1945* (Paris: CNRS Editions, 2011). See also Anna Hájková, *Menschen ohne Geschichte sind Staub: Homophobie und Holocaust* (Götingen: Wallstein, 2021).
[109] Janice Arnold, "Gay and Lesbian Jews to Hold Montreal Conference," *Canadian Jewish News* (30 June 1994): 18.
[110] Neil Miller, "Controversy: Our Holocaust – Legends and propaganda flourish in the absence of well-documented history concerning the fate of gays in the Third Reich," *The Advocate* (April 2, 1996): 35–38.

and in the research done on site. He also advocated for a better dialogue and for the mingling of queer activism and historical research. This fusion of both aspects of the community would eventually lead to the re-questioning of the uses of the Pink Triangle as a symbol for homosexual civil rights movement.[111] For Müller, by focusing on the present and the emotional appeal of a projection in the past – like Robert in Germany or various activist groups in the United States – the same people supposedly brandishing what was presented as knowledge of queer history were in fact obfuscating research about the past.[112]

Still, this perspective ignores the multilayered aspects of the symbol and the possibility of co-existing significations of the Pink Triangle. This tension is at the core of the inclusion of Pink Triangle memories in the transatlantic world. On one hand, queer stories of persecutions were being integrated into museums and memorials. This is the case in Berlin or in the USHMM. On the other hand, this inclusion forced a source- or fact-based approach to the inclusion of these narratives to official memory. Shying away from the emotional impulses of the identification processes of early pink radical politics, the recognition of the men with the pink triangles also seemed to disavow the use of the symbol, to denounce its provocation, its inflammatory rhetoric linked to Homocaust narratives.

The opening of the USHMM in April 1993 tells another story, showing the possible co-existence of many Pink Triangles that survived the inclusion of Pink Triangle narratives to the official memory of National Socialism. The inauguration of the museum, one day after the March for Lesbian and Gay Rights in DC, convinced many queers to prolong their stay in the capital and attend the ceremony wearing the same Pink Triangle they had worn during the demonstration.[113] An article for *The Advocate* recalls how those present were excited to finally be included in official discourses and to finally be able to see artefacts connected to the oppression of queerness by the Nazis.[114] The presence of these queer activists also made national news and the museum was criticized for not including "enough" material on these

---

111 Sara Hart, "A Dark Past Brought to Light: The Most Silent Victims of the Holocaust Were the Third Reich's Homosexual Targets. Historian Klaus Müller Uncovers Their Story," *10 Percent* (Winter 1993): 74.
112 Private Discussion with Dr. Klaus Müller, July 2019. We both agreed on the tension between referring to history while obscuring historical facts. I would like to thank Dr. Müller for having taken the time to discuss with me and share his insight on queer oral history in the United States of America. I still see things differently. Sébastien Tremblay, "Der Rosa Winkel: Vielschichtige Symbolik und Erinnerung in der Schwulenbewegung beiderseits des Atlantiks / The Pink Triangle: Multilayered Symbolism and Memory in the Queer Atlantic." In *Queer Lives 1900–1950*, ed. Karolina Kühn and Mirjam Zadoff (Munich: Hirmer Verlag, 2023), 328–341.
113 The symbol of the March also included a Pink Triangle.
114 Rick Rose, "Museum of Pain," *The Advocate* (October 19, 1993): 40.

persecutions.¹¹⁵ Officials retorted that some of the identification cards were following the lives of queer victims¹¹⁶ and that the museum was still one of the only ones presenting such material to its visitors.¹¹⁷

Famously, Josef Kohout's pink triangle made its way to the museum from the bottom of a shoebox bequeathed by his partner, Wilhem Kroepfl. It is one of the only original pink triangles preserved in a museum and reconstructing an individual story.¹¹⁸ Side by side with other victims, queers were now part of the official memory of Nazi atrocities. The pink triangle in the museum's possession and the Pink Triangle held by protesters in April 1993 were not the same Pink Triangle, but they were indeed the same symbol. Entangled, they only make sense when appraised together. The triangle in the museum's vault is the fruit of decades of political struggles such as the one in Bavaria and on the street of West Berlin. It was simultaneously a symbol of queer postmemory and a tangible artefact of suffering created during the war. The Pink Triangle held by protesters or printed on t-shirt was the result of transatlantic narratives of the real persecutions of queer men forced to wear pink triangles such as the one now in the museum's possession.

4.5 The cohesive potential of the triangle

Following the inclusion of the Pink Triangle in official memories of National Socialism, this chapter explains how the fight for the recognition of victimhood was a multilayered transatlantic saga and how the reception, as well as the use of the Pink Triangle as a symbol, opened new wounds between communities while reinforcing the cohesion potential of the Pink Triangle as a symbol of queer identity. By focusing on different memorials, I have shed light on the solidarity and opposition shown by other victims of National Socialism. Through all these episodes,

---

115 David M. Fetterman, "The U.S. Holocaust Memorial Museum Dedication: Standing in the Presence of History," *San Francisco Bay Times* (September 9, 1993): 10.
116 All 600 identification cards can be found online at the United States Holocaust Memorial and Museum, "Holocaust Encyclopaedia: identification Cards," accessed February 23, 2019, https://encyclopedia.ushmm.org/landing/en/id-cards. See for example the cards for Willem Arondeus, Gad Beck, Karl Lange, and Henny (Jenny) Schermann.
117 Rose, "Museum of Pain," 42.
118 See the short film on the USHMM starring Klaus Müller, explaining the story behind the acquisition of Kohout's triangle. USHMM, "Documenting Nazi Persecution of Gays: The Josef Kohout/Wilhelm Kroepfl Collection," Curators Corner, accessed April 12, 2020, https://www.ushmm.org/collections/the-museums-collections/curators-corner/documenting-nazi-persecution-of-gays-the-josef-kohout-wilhelm-kroepfl-collection.

the Pink Triangle as a symbol thrived and absorbed many new meanings, narratives, and tropes. Some scholars have denounced the uses of the symbol as dangerous, as a way to erase the original story of the men with the pink triangles.[119] The tension between the use of the past and historical instrumentalization is definitely present in this story, but these key moments also highlight how symbolic Pink Triangle bridges toward the past strengthened queer cultural memory and identity. To put it differently, it intensified the need for the past, a desire to understand what happened under National Socialism. Ironically, this does not mean that this past was not, in the words of Klaus Müller, "a fantasized past."[120]

---

[119] See Klaus Müller's words in Hart, "A Dark Past Brought to Light," 74.
[120] Hart, "A Dark Past Brought to Light," 74.

5 A badge of exclusion – Pink Triangle frameworks and the limits of collective memory

Joachim Müller, future member of the advisory council of the *Stiftung Brandenburgische Gedenkstätten*, 'Brandenburg Memorial Foundation,' and researcher at the *Schwules Museum* in Berlin, published a piece in the gay magazine *Magnus* in June 1992, discussing his findings regarding the murders of hundreds of queer men in the concentration camp of Sachsenhausen and putting forward the idea of a monument for the men forced to wear pink triangles.¹ Müller eventually made a career of commemorating the gay victims of the camps, published a book on the subject, and became one of the most fervent opponents of commemoration side by side with lesbian victims of the Nazi era.² During the same year, Müller took part in the newly formed *Initiative Schwulendenkmal*, 'Initiative Gay Monument.' Between 1992 and 1995, in parallel with multiple activities commemorating the murders in Sachsenhausen, the Initiative irritated some with its dismissal of one of the seminal works on the oppression of lesbians under National Socialism by historian Claudia Schoppmann and for repeatedly emphasizing that only male victims were referred to as *'homosexuals'* in Nazi documents.³

In April 1995, the *Nürnberger Schwulenpost*, 'Nuremberg Gay Post,' announced an informative evening with pioneer historian Ilse Kokula on the fate of both lesbians and gays during the era: "The time of fascism was a time of persecution for lesbians and gays. The Nazis [. . .] suffocated lesbians and gays with a multitude of decrees and ordinances and [. . .] tightened §175, battered and murdered lesbians and gays in concentration camps and prisons."⁴ In the same month, days before Holocaust Remembrance Day, a piece in the *Die Tageszeitung* connected the impor-

---

1 Joachim Müller, "An Flucht war nicht zu denken" *Magnus* 4, no. 6 (June 1992): 34–37.
2 Joachim Müller, "Vergleichbarkeit der Lebenssituation lesbischer Frauen mit der Lebenssituation schwuler Männer im Nationalsozialismus (und nach 1945) – lesbische Frauen, schwule Männer, zum ‹Mahnmalsstreit› in Berlin 2006/2007 um Kuss-Symbole, Widmung, Zielsetzung", 2007: 49–60.
3 Claudia Schoppmann is widely recognized as the instigator of research on lesbian suffering and oppression during National Socialism. She published her dissertation in the 1990s. Claudia Schoppmann, *Zeit der Maskierung: Lebensgeschichten lesbischer Frauen im "Dritten Reich"* (Berlin: Orlanda, 1993). Particularly noteworthy is her micro history analysis of lesbian oppression: Claudia Schoppmann, "Elsa Conrad – Margarete Rosenberg – Mary Pünjer – Henny Schermann: Vier Porträts." In *Homophobie und Devianz. Weibliche und männliche Homosexualität im Nationalsozialismus*, ed. Insa Eschebach (Berlin: Metropol, 2012), 97–111.
4 "Lesben und Schwule im Dritten Reich – Vortrag und Diskussion mit Prof Dr. Ilse Kokula," *Nürnberger Schwulenpost* (April 1995): 13.

tance of both Sachsenhausen and Ravensbrück for gays and lesbians, mentioning how a "coalition of lesbians" invited women to lay down a wreath of flowers for lesbian victims in the former concentration camp.[5] The author, feminist and sociologist Ulrike Helwerth, alleged that female sexuality had not been included in the 1935 version of §175 StGB "because female homosexuality was considered by the Nazis to be a comparatively low danger for the 'people's body' – from a moral as well as from a population-political point of view."[6] She continued, "although there is little evidence that 'lesbian love' was decisive for imprisonment, lesbian women were not spared from persecution and concentration camps. Many were admitted as 'antisocial elements' often on charges of prostitution and marked with a black triangle. As a result, they inevitably belonged to the lowest classes within the camp society." Others echoed Helwerth's allegations. The Austrian gay magazine *Info HOSI Linz* provocatively asked: "How many lesbians were still alive in the camp brothels at the end? [. . .] And how many of those who survived all this will now survive the ignorance of the Austrian parties?"[7]

During the summer of the same year, the '*Initiative Schwulendenkmal*' organized a podium discussion with, among others, Kokula and Rüdiger Lautmann. Present during the events, Müller caused uproar by denouncing the idea of lesbian persecution under National Socialism as fantasy. His microphone was allegedly cut.[8] Clashes like this were common. In autumn of 1996, the *Initiative Schwulendenkmal* – then newly renamed *Initiative HOMO Monument* – invited scholars for a two-day symposium on memory culture and homosexualities. Müller was scheduled to offer a tour of the memorial at Sachsenhausen. Irritated by what he considered an "active-positive position" of the event on lesbian persecutions, he cancelled his presence via an open letter to the organizers.[9] These events were not only scrutinized by the German press but also by international media. For instance, the *New York Times* covered Müller's *éclat* at the symposium.[10] Both the German and international press already separated the burgeoning quarrel on two fronts. On one side, some activists

---

5 Ulrike Helwerth, "Lesbisch waren nur die Asozialen," *TAZ* (April 21, 1995): 5.
6 For a good survey of the problem regarding rebutting lesbian suffering based on these kinds of conclusions: Sylvia Köchl, "Real Talk: Lesbisch, Verfolgt, Vergessen," *Missy Magazine* (April/May 2017): 45; Huneke, "Heterogeneous Persecution." and by the same author: "The Duplicity of Tolerance: Lesbian Experiences in Nazi Berlin," *Journal of Contemporary History* 54, no. 1 (2019): 297–325.
7 "1000e Lesben und Schwule warten auf Wiedergutmachung," *Info HOSI Linz* (June 26, 1995): 15.
8 Müller, "Vergleichbarkeit der Lebenssituation," 53.
9 "Open letter by Joachim Müller, October 19 1996," reprinted in Heinrich-Böll-Stiftung, *Der homosexuellen NS-Opfer gedenken* (Berlin: Heinrich Böll Stiftung, 1999), 120–121.
10 Alan Cowell, "Memorial to Gay Pain of Nazi Era Stirs Debate," *The New York Times* (December 29, 1996).

argued for a broader understanding of power structures and oppression during National Socialism. On the other side, some proponents of the monument advocated for an exclusion of lesbian experiences from the project, underlining the absence of women wearing pink triangles in the camps or highlighting the gendered specificities of §175 StGB.[11]

An intersectional analysis of queer memory culture in the second part of the twentieth century unveils ways in which the Pink Triangle influenced discourses and collectives in absentia. If the postwar and contemporary history of the symbol is inherently connected to integration, it is also coupled with processes of silencing and exclusions. Starting with the story of a gay Jewish congregation on the East Coast of the United States, this chapter begins with a reflection on groups who refrained from using the symbol even if some would have expected them to do so; in this case, a group of gay Jewish men and their memorialization of both the Holocaust and the Nazi persecution of male-male sexualities. The chapter then sheds light on tensions and exclusions perceptible through an intersectional approach to Pink Triangle bridges. The chapter finally highlights how an emphasis on the Pink Triangle ironically silenced other commemorations of Nazi persecutions and structural oppression, erasing other experiences of the era, namely trans*, inter*, and lesbian realities.[12] I focus here on lesbian suffering and a plea for a historiographical paradigm shift in our understanding of persecutions. A necessary historiographical and conceptual intervention, this chapter highlights the limits of Pink Triangle narratives, showing how considering visual sources and protest symbols is essential for research on social movements and for our understanding of cultural memory.

5.1 The men without the Pink Triangle

On Friday, August 8, 1975, the Congregation Beth Simchat Torah (CBST) wrote a letter to the Episcopal Church of the Holy Apostles, thanking the church for letting them use the space in the past year and a half.[13] By then, this new and unique

---

11 Heinrich-Böll-Stiftung, *Der homosexuellen NS-Opfer gedenken*, 148.
12 Zavier Nunn, "Trans Liminality and the Nazi State," *Past & Present* 260, no. 1 (2023):123–157.; Aktivistinnen des lesbischen Gedenkens, "Anna Hájková und Birgit Bosold im Gespräch mit Ulrike Janz, Irmes Schwager und Lisa Steininger," *Invertito – Jahrbuch für die Geschichte der Homosexualitäten* 21 (2019). See also the very interesting panel discussion between Bodie A. Ashton, Anna Hájková and Katie Sutton organized by the Museum of Jewish Heritage, accessed January 19, 2023, https://mjhnyc.org/blog/transgender-experiences-in-weimar-and-nazi-germany/.
13 National Archive of Lesbian, Gay, Bisexual and Transgender History, Collection #65 "Congregation Beth Simchat Torah Records," Box 1, Folder 10: *Board of Trustees Minutes, 06/1975–08/1975*.

queer Jewish congregation had about 150 queer members, men and women.[14] It paved the way for other queer Jewish congregations in Montréal, Boston, Chicago and down-under in Sydney, Australia.[15] Paring strong spiritual Jewish values with community-based activities, CBST is still a thriving and vibrant part of life in New York City and a space where Jews and gentiles, heteronormative or not, can meet and partake in many social and cultural events.[16]

In the mid-late 1970s, CBST opened its doors in Greenwich Village for sociopolitical Oneg Shabbats, manned a yearly sauerkraut stand at the Christopher Street festival in June, and took part in Pride marches across the city. It managed to spark reflections on queer Jewish identity in New York and beyond, even as far away as the pages of Israeli newspapers.[17] One of the early flyers of the congregation, a simple do-it-yourself invitation for Rosh Hashanah covered with Lambda symbols and Stars of David, asked the question at the core of CBST's mission: "Why a separate synagogue for gays? There are probably as many reasons as there are people in attendance. Whatever the reason, though, undoubtedly the greatest attraction of all is the opportunity to enjoy openly one's Jewishness and one's gayness."[18] Throughout the years, the community met for services and discussed important issues about the difficulties and joys of reconciling both queerness and their Jewishness, although the former was not necessarily defined as an identity.[19] While many of these discussions appealed to the experience of both antisemitism and queerphobia, none of them drew direct comparisons with or appealed to Nazi atrocities as a sort of legitimization for the respect and dignity of queer Jews.

Every month, CBST published a newsletter, *Congregation Beth Simchat Torah Gay Community News*. A browse through the small publication's back catalogue is a window into detailed reports of the events at the synagogue, the strong religious sentiments of its members, and debates inside the queer and Jewish communities of New York City. By analyzing CBST *Gay Synagogue News* between 1975 and 1994, I was also able to follow the synagogue's view of the main trends and discourses

---

14 Women only became a major presence at CBST at the end of the 1970s. In a testimony in 1989, Regina Linder remembers how she was the only lesbian woman for years after its creation in 1974. See *Gay Synagogue News* (June 1989).
15 *Gay Synagogue News* (April 1977).
16 See CBST's website: Congregation Beth Simchat Torah, "Mission," accessed April 5, 2020, https://cbst.org/content/about.
17 National Archive of Lesbian, Gay, Bisexual and Transgender History, Collection #65 "Congregation Beth Simchat Torah Records," Box 1, Folder 11: *Board of Trustees Minutes, 09/1975–12/1975*.
18 National Archive of Lesbian, Gay, Bisexual and Transgender History, Collection #65 "Congregation Beth Simchat Torah Records," Box 1, Folder 10: *Board of Trustees Minutes, 06/1975–08/1975*.
19 For example, see *Gay Synagogue News* (June–July 1982).

examined in the previous chapters: cultural productions that were discussed in the gay press, the circulation of knowledge about a queer past of injury, and other major events in the northern Atlantic world relevant for queer history. Every April or May, CBST published a text for *Yom Ha-Shoah* and a reflection on the memory of the Holocaust. Every June or July, it would publish a small report on Pride, elaborating on new demands and subjects of interest regarding the various parts forming New York City's queer community.[20]

However, neither the *Gay Synagogue News* nor the other official CBST documents (flyers, press releases, posters) make use of the Pink Triangle as a symbol. The CBST preferred a combination of the Star of David and the Lambda to the triangle. The Greek letter, a symbol still in use by many queer organizations across the world, was already a known symbol used by the *Gay Activist Alliance* in New York. Member Tom Doerr famously said that he had chosen the letter for its representation as "a complete exchange of energy" referring to what he called the "absolutism of gay energy."[21] Other Jewish queer groups on the East Coast used a mixture of known community symbols paired with the Star of David. For instance, the Boston-based solidarity group *Jewish Lesbian Daughters of Holocaust Survivors* – for daughters of former concentration camp prisoners who survived the horrors of Nazism – opted for the Labrys, a doubled-blade battle-axe, with a Star of David at its centre.[22] This raises several questions: were these Jewish groups consciously ignoring the use of the Pink Triangle? Moreover, did they know the extent of the Nazi persecution of queerness?

A look in CBST documents confirm that both the board of trustees and members attending events at the synagogue knew about the fate of the men wearing pink triangles in the German camps. Naturally, *Yom Ha-Shoah* commemorations were emotional and important annual events. Throughout the years, the focus on the Jewish victims of Nazism evolved into a double focus on both Jewish and queer victims:

> As each of six candles was lit, various members of the congregation recalled the pain of the past through readings from eyewitness account of the violations of dignity and the horrible deaths suffered by our Jewish and gay brothers and sisters during the Nazi regime. (1981)[23]

---

[20] All of them between 1974 and 1999. National Archive of Lesbian, Gay, Bisexual and Transgender History, Collection #65, "Congregation Beth Simchat Torah Records," Box 4 and Box 5.
[21] "Statement and letter of the GAA to CBST," National Archive of Lesbian, Gay, Bisexual and Transgender History, Collection #65, "Congregation Beth Simchat Torah Records," Box 1, Folder 23: *Board of Trustees Minutes, 01/1980–03/1980*.
[22] MS International Gay Information Center Archives – Ephemera – Organizations, Box 10, Folder 6 *Jewish Lesbian Daughters of Holocaust Survivors*, New York Public Library.
[23] *Gay Synagogue News* (June–July, 1981).

> The Hebrew word Shoah means devastation and ruin. On Yom Ha-Shoah, the day of remembrance of devastation, Jews throughout the world will be gathering to recall the destruction of our people in the European holocaust. Our congregation has a special obligation, not only to the six million Jews who perished at the hands of the Nazi tyrants, but also to the multitude of gay martyrs who were part of our spiritual family – we are their Kaddish. (1982)[24]

> On May 6 Tuesday evening, Yom Ha-Shoah/Holocaust Memorial Day was commemorated at CBST. About 30 members and friends gathered at the Synagogue to pay homage to the memory of six millions martyrs of the Jewish people and to also bear witness to the many thousands of Gays and Lesbians who were exterminated by the Nazi Scourge. (1986)[25]

> Jews were sent to concentration camps. Until then, concentration camps were reserved for political dissidents, criminals and any kind of social "deviant", which of course included homosexuals. The world stood silent to their plight, just as it would stand silent to the plight of the Jews. (1988)[26]

This transition to a focus on both the persecution of gays and lesbians alongside Jews and other victims of the Nazis is telling. CBST knew about non-Jewish victims and commemorated them. Moreover, they invited queer male survivors to share their experiences at public events.[27] Regarding one 1982 issue of *Gay Synagogue News*, the editing team recalls how an audience hungry to learn more about the fate of queer Jews and non-Jewish queers during the war reacted with gratitude to the testimony of two men, Wolfgang and Yossel. The small piece concludes that an event like this one illustrated the "tragic realities for Jews and gays that are portrayed in such recent works as Martin Sherman's drama *Bent* and Josef Kohout's memoirs *The Men with Pink Triangle*."[28] Sherman's play was also analyzed by one of the CBST members, Edward Paolella, a teacher of English literature at Brooklyn College. In May 1981, he led a discussion on the "moral and cultural themes found in *Bent*."[29] Paperback editions of the play were also available at the synagogue for purchase, "so that those interested in participating in the discussion may be prepared."[30]

Finally, through its ties with the World Congress of Gay and Lesbian Jewish Organizations and through its contacts with other gay organizations like the Gay Activist Alliance, CBST members definitely came into contact with members of international queer organizations using the Pink Triangle as we shall see in the

---

24 *Gay Synagogue News* (April 1982).
25 *Gay Synagogue News* (June–July 1986).
26 "Commemoration of the events of the so-called *Kristallnacht*," *Gay Synagogue News* (June 1988).
27 *Gay Synagogue News* (June 1981).
28 *Gay Synagogue News* (June 1981).
29 *Gay Synagogue News* (May 1981).
30 *Gay Synagogue News* (May 1981).

next chapter. These organizations also petitioned the congregation to support their efforts to include gay victims at the United States Holocaust Memorial Museum (USHMM), a campaign that attracted the attention of the CBST board of trustees.[31]

Knowing all this, it might be surprising that the CBST and other Jewish organizations like the Jewish Lesbian Daughters of Holocaust Survivors, both fully aware of its existence, passed on using the Pink Triangle as a symbol. Even a famous Jewish queer attorney defence league in New York City, the Lambda Legal Defence and Education Fund, which was created in the 1970s and was responsible for countless advances in civil rights in the United States, toyed with sometimes using the Lambda in combination with the Pink Triangle.[32] Yet the fact that the CBST did not is unsurprising. Other North American groups had always focused on a collective gay or lesbian identity connected to Nazi atrocities to make a point about history and legitimate their struggle. The triangle was seen as a symbol of the world's ongoing queerphobia throughout history. At least, it was a call to unite queer groups under the yoke of their oppression and use a queer past of suffering as a basis for their dreams and utopias, a world devoid of oppression. As seen in the first part of this book – see section 2.3 – Richard Plant drew from his own experience of queerness for his research. His writings focused on a "gay Holocaust." Similarly, Sherman's work was supposed to bring light to a forgotten history. By contrast, a Jewish organization like CBST, one already remembering the death of millions of their ancestors, and one conscious of being part of a traumatized community might not have needed a symbolic coagulant like the triangle. The addition of gays to the plurality of victims seems to have been important enough to commemorate them alongside the murder of most of the European Jewry, but a thorough examination of CBST outreach documents and minutes does not show an attempt to claim an international gay identity based on the Holocaust or collectivize a queer memory of National Socialism in the Euro-American world. Maybe the layers of meaning of a symbol created by the Nazis held too many negative connotations for a Jewish organization as well.

The story of the CBST leads to two other conclusions. First, cultural productions and the circulation of knowledge in the Queer Atlantic permeated a large range of organizations. Second, an intersectional approach enables a focus on the artificial aspects of the queer collective memory pushed by mostly non-Jewish

---

31 "Statement and letter of the GAA to CBST," National Archive of Lesbian, Gay, Bisexual and Transgender History, Collection #65, "Congregation Beth Simchat Torah Records," Box 1, Folder 23: *Board of Trustees Minutes, 01/1980–03/1980*.
32 National Archive of Lesbian, Gay, Bisexual and Transgender History, Collection #121 "Dr. Harold Kooden Papers," Box 1, Folder 11: *ILGA Conference – 1992*.

groups at the end of the 1970s and during the 1980s. If some organizations were pushing for a queer story universally connected to and by the Pink Triangle, other factors, in this case one's Jewishness, played a role in the adoption of the symbol. All in all, that Jewish organizations did not need to be reminded of the Holocaust to make a point about National Socialism and other persecutions is also not unexpected.

Looking for the Pink Triangle against the grain and analyzing its journey intersectionally makes it possible to map its absence and recognize how some queer organizations avoided using the symbol. In the case of queer Jewish associations or religious congregations, other cultural trauma and postmemories might have precluded a walk on Pink Triangle bridges. They did not necessarily exclude themselves from a broader queer collective memory but integrated a commemoration of the men with the pink triangle with another narrative, namely remembrance of the Holocaust. Yet although the Pink Triangle was not necessarily a badge of self-exclusion, it was also linked to the marginalization of queer voices. Searching for the Pink Triangle enables us to unveil and consider tensions inside queer Jewish life.

5.2 The men not just wearing the Pink Triangle

Haunting the history of the second part of twentieth century, the categories as defined by the perpetrators are still affecting ways in which people discuss the atrocities committed by the Nazis. In the case of queer Jewish victims and queer Jewish survivors, this *longue durée* led to difficult clashes in different communities. This is not to say that queer Jewish stories have not been told. The autobiography of resistance fighter Gad Beck is one famous example.[33] However, by recuperating the Pink Triangle, non-Jewish queer activists perpetuated fictitious divides that originated in the camps. Of course, the memory of the Holocaust and Nazi persecutions have often followed categories created by the perpetrators or national boundaries. This has allowed a better understanding of parallel persecutions and a better analysis of the different aspects relating, for example, to the regime's racism and antisemitism.[34] However, attempting or wanting to trans-

---

[33] Gad Beck, *An Underground Life: Memoirs of a Gay Jew in Nazi Berlin* (Madison, WI: The University of Wisconsin Press, 2000); see also Anna Hájková, "Queere Geschichte und der Holocaust," *Aus Politik und Zeitgeschichte* (2018): 42–47.
[34] Eugen Kogon already touched on this directly after the war. Eugen Kogon, *Der SS-Staat: Das System der deutschen Konzentrationslager* (München: Heyne, 1946). See also Albert Knoll, "'Die Vergessenen' und die 'Ausgeschlossenen Opfer' – Spurensuche nach homosexuellen Überleben-

form the Pink Triangle from a symbol of Nazi queerphobia to a badge for their struggle, many queer activists dug deeper trenches between these categories.

Recent research on sexuality and the queer history of the Holocaust has started to correct this gap, investigating queer suffering and Nazi antisemitism intersectionally.[35] Still, by brandishing a Pink Triangle and talking about a hidden history, a so-called Homocaust, non-Jewish queer activists imagined a social group of victims in opposition to others, all the while pretending to be muzzled by Jewish survivors and former political prisoners. In doing so, they silenced those whose existence went beyond fixed categories created by the Nazis. Hence, by killing solidarity in the camps through categorization, the oppressors and murderers set the later agenda for the conversation on justice, emancipation, and reparation.

Queer Jewish organizations tried to make place for the inclusion of other victims between the walls of their institutions. Nevertheless, things were not always that simple. If non-Jewish queer activists fell prey to a certain antisemitic resentment, some of the rebuttal they faced was indeed anchored in queerphobia. At the end of the 1990s, a group of sixteenth Orthodox rabbis filed a lawsuit to block the opening of the New York Museum of Jewish Heritage. In the words of Rabbi Yehuda it was simply "outrageous" to "use something as sacred as the Holocaust as a mean of achieving the political goals of the militant homosexual community."[36] Quoted in the gay press, he continued: "We certainly don't want to harm homosexuals or any group we disagree with, but we also don't want to see homosexuality elevated to the martyred status of six million Jews who perished in the Holocaust. To do that is to kosher the homosexual lifestyle on the backs of victims of the concentration camps, and that isn't right."[37] This bigotry was denounced by

---

den des Konzentrationslagers Dachau." In *Ohnmacht und Aufbegehren. Homosexuelle Männer in der frühen Bundesrepublik*, ed. Andreas Pretzel and Volker Weiß (Hamburg: Männerschwarm Verlag, 2010), 39–61; Andreas Pretzel, "Wiedergutmachung unter Vorbehalt und mit neuer Perspektive – Was homosexuellen NS-Opfern verweigert wurde und was wir noch tun können." In *Ohnmacht und Aufbegehren. Homosexuelle Männer in der frühen Bundesrepublik*, ed. Andreas Pretzel and Volker Weiß (Hamburg: Männerschwarm, 2010), 91–113.

35 Anna Hájková, "Den Holocaust queer erzählen," *Sexualitäten Jahrbuch*, ed. Janin Afken, Jan Feddersen, Benno Gammerl, Rainer Nicolaysen and Benedikt Wolf (Göttingen: Wallstein, 2018), 86–110. See also Hájková's special issue on the topic for *German History*: Anna Hájková, "Introduction: Sexuality, Holocaust, Stigma," *German History* 39 – Special issue 'Sexuality, Holocaust, Stigma,' no. 1 (2021): 1–14; Anna Hájková, "Between Love and Coercion: Queer Desire, Sexual Barter, and the Holocaust," *German History* 39 – Special issue 'Sexuality, Holocaust, Stigma,' no 1 (2021): 112–133.

36 Robert L. Pela, "Taking the Triangle Out of the Star: An Attempt by Orthodox Rabbis to Keep Gays out of a Holocaust Memorial is Fueling a Debate Among Jews," *The Advocate* (December 9, 1997): 45.

37 Pela, "Taking the Triangle Out of the Star": 46.

others, for instance Rabbi Sharon Kleinbaum, board member on the Gay and Lesbian Project of the United States Holocaust Memorial Museum (USHMM) and CBST: "He's a hatemonger and he's using the museum as an excuse to express his homophobia. I'm deeply sad that a rabbi should express such malice. I want to remind him that such hatred was what led to the Holocaust and that that kind of hatred knows no boundaries. It destroys everything in its path."[38] Roberta Bennett, chair of the Gay and Lesbian Project of the USHMM emphasized that "the Holocaust is something that happened to humanity [...] not something that happened more to one group than another. We're not promoting homosexuality by researching the missing history of homosexuals in the Holocaust. It's important to remember that they were victims of this nightmare too."[39]

Another story connected to David Bergman with whom we opened the last chapter goes in a similar direction and demonstrates how visibility and representation can also come with a broader cultural backlash.[40] During his time on the faculty at Towson State University in Maryland, Bergman was invited to read a poem by the Jewish Student Association at a Holocaust memorial service where another professor, Aaron Seigman, himself Holocaust survivor, would deliver a speech. The ceremony was co-sponsored by the Diverse Sexual Orientation Coalition, a group for which Bergman was faculty advisor. Seigman cancelled his presence after learning that a queer organization was co-sponsoring the event.[41] The Jewish Student Association eventually found another survivor to attend the memorial, denouncing Seigman's decision as bigotry, and making a parallel between Nazi prejudices and any form of persecutions in the present.[42] Seigman would later tell *The Baltimore Jewish Times* that he was strongly against the take-over of Holocaust memory for "homosexual propaganda."[43]

Yet behind his queerphobia lies the historical fact that the persecution of non-Jewish queer men and women during National Socialism was distinct from the Holocaust. The intent was different. This nuance does not mean that queer oppression was irrelevant, nor does it trivialize the murder of thousands. Indeed, this episode underlines the complexity of the situation at the end of the 1990s in North America. On one side, some conservative and queerphobic forces were trying to obscure the story of the men who had worn pink triangles in concentration

---

[38] Pela, "Taking the Triangle Out of the Star": 46.
[39] Pela, "Taking the Triangle Out of the Star": 46.
[40] Yener Bayramoğlu, *Queere (Un-)Sichtbarkeiten: Die Geschichte der queeren Repräsentationen in der türkischen und deutschen Boulevardpresse* (Bielefeld: transcript, 2018).
[41] Pela, "Taking the Triangle Out of the Star": 105.
[42] Pela, "Taking the Triangle Out of the Star": 105.
[43] Pela, "Taking the Triangle Out of the Star": 106.

camps. On the other, focusing on this bigotry allowed an inflation of the opposition of some to a degree where non-Jewish queer activists wrongly made Judaism responsible for the exclusion or dismissal of queer experiences of National Socialism from official memory. Rallying under Pink Triangle banners, queer activists who were not themselves survivors accentuated these divides while referring to the camps. Once again, queer Jews were the ones most penalized.

The queer press in North America was very interested in events happening in Israel during the same years. For instance, members of Israel's principal queer organizations went to *Yad Vashem* in 1994 during the World Congress of Gay and Lesbian Jewish Organizations in Jerusalem. They were met with physical threats. Nineteenth rabbis in the *Jerusalem Post* had denounced their action the week prior.[44] Images of crying gay Jews reciting the Kaddish while being intimidated within the walls of a Holocaust memorial made international news.[45] The coverage especially highlighted both the queerness of the Jewish victims but also the Jewishness of the bullies. What is more, queer activists were effectively confronted with right-wing propaganda trying to depict them as Nazis. The aforementioned debate in the *Jerusalem Post* includes one particular open letter by a Jewish survivor stating that he had indeed met queer men in concentration camps, but that they were Nazi accomplices, that they had raped Jewish children and that they were all capos.[46] Similarly, anti-gay activist Scott Lively published in 1995, *The Pink Swastika: Homosexuality in the Nazi Party*, a bestseller propagating the conspiracy theory that most members of the Nazi Party were non-heteronormative men fetishizing virility and that persecutions of the era were only targeted at ephebes and feminine men.[47] Identifying these queerphobic tropes allows us to understand the context in which non-Jewish activists focused on the bigotry of some Jewish groups to feed their own antisemitic resentment. Yet, as demonstrated above, this is certainly also due to the clash of different discourses competing for official recognition.

Overall, the uses and recuperations of the Pink Triangle by queer activists during the second part of the twentieth century have cemented fixed categories of analysis and strengthened communal divides. Many queer Jewish groups such as CBST seem to have refrained from using the symbol themselves, proving the importance of reading the Pink Triangle's story against the grain, the significance of its absence. Anchored in the symbol's journey is a complexed web of grievances by non-Jewish associations accusing Jewish victims of actively having hidden

---

44 Macy Gordon, "'Gay' Jews who are proud of Sin," *The Jerusalem Post* (June 3, 1994).
45 Dvorah Getzler, "Gays Under Fire at Yad Vashem," *The Jewish Journal* (June 3, 1994): 27.
46 Jack P. Eisner, "Nazi Gays – Letters to the Editors," *The Jerusalem Post*, (June 14, 1994).
47 Scott Lively and Kevin Abrams, *The Pink Swastika Homosexuality in the Nazi Party* (Keiser, OR: Founders Publisher, 1997).

queer suffering. Simultaneously, a reproduction of defined perpetrator categories isolated queer cultural trauma from Nazi antisemitism. Implicitly, the Pink Triangle as a badge of inclusion also became a badge of exclusion, perpetuating artificial divides and obscuring intersectional analyses.

5.3 The women with[out] the Pink Triangle?

Looking at memory struggles inside queer organizations and investigating queer cultural memory of National Socialism, it is also possible to see how the Pink Triangle as a symbol also exacerbated tensions between gays and lesbians. Here, perpetrator categories are also at the center of the story, haunting the present and gatekeeping uses of the Pink Triangle in the second part of the twentieth century.[48]

During the last decade, historians have methodically proven how the Nazi regime oppressed queer women.[49] This follows several revolutionary works published decades prior.[50] However many queer male historians still act as gatekeepers

---

48 Part of this subchapter is the continuation of a reflection started in a blog post from 2020. See Sébastien Tremblay, "Wer zählt als Opfer? Einige Gedanken zu Gedächtnissymbolen und Legitimation." In *HISTORY | SEXUALITY | LAW Verschränkung von Recht und Sexualität im historischen Kontext*, November 10, 2020, https://hsl.hypotheses.org/1516.

49 Martin Lücke, "Die Verfolgung lesbischer Frauen im Nationalsozialismus: Forschungsdebatten zu Gedenkinitiativen am Beispiel des Frauen-Konzentrationslagers Ravensbrück," *Zeitschrift für Geschichtswissenschaft* 79, no. 5 (2022): 422–440; Laurie Marhoefer, "Lesbianism, Transvestitism, and the Nazi State: A Microhistory of a Gestapo Investigation, 1939–1943," *The American Historical Review* 121, no. 4 (2016): 1167–1195; Samuel Clowes Huneke, "The Duplicity of Tolerance: Lesbian Experiences in Nazi Berlin," *Journal of Contemporary History* 54, no. 1 (2019): 30–59; Jens Dobler, "Unzucht und Kuppelei: Lesbenverfolgung im Nationalsozialismus." In *Homophobie und Devianz: Weibliche und männliche Homosexualität im Nationalsozialismus*, ed. Insa Eschebach (Berlin: Stiftung Brandenburgische Gedenkstätten, 2012), 53–62; Anna Hájková, "Between Love and Coercion: Queer Desire, Sexual Barter and the Holocaust," *German History* 39, no. 1, Special Issue: Holocaust, Sexuality, Stigma (2020): 112–133. To fight against the overlooking of this literature, Anna Hájková compiled years of research in a significantly useful and easily accessible online bibliography on the lesbian and trans* history of National Socialism: "Sexuality, Holocaust, Stigma: Bibliography on lesbian and trans women in Nazi Germany," accessed January 24, 2023, https://sexualityandholocaust.com/blog/bibliography/.

50 Claudia Schoppmann is widely recognized as the instigator of research on lesbian suffering and oppression during National Socialism. She published her dissertation in the 1990s. Claudia Schoppmann, *Zeit der Maskierung: Lebensgeschichten lesbischer Frauen im "Dritten Reich"* (Berlin: Orlanda, 1993). Of note is her micro history of lesbian oppression: Claudia Schoppmann, "Elsa Conrad – Margarete Rosenberg – Mary Pünjer – Henny Schermann: Vier Porträts." In Eschebach, *Homophobie und Devianz*, 97–111.

(gaykeepers?), dismissing much of this research.⁵¹ One focus of these controversies is the existence of the Pink Triangle as a physical object, not only as symbol. The triangle's materiality is significant because the lack of visuals and knowledge about actual pink triangles worn by queer men in the camps has been overwhelmingly overshadowed by the discourse on the symbol and its recuperation in the 1970s. In return, the uncertainty cast on the original triangles makes it easy for queer men to dismiss claims of lesbian or queer female suffering.⁵²

So, what do we know about these pink triangles? Throughout this book and while researching in the archives, I have attempted to correct or answer contemporary claims about the symbol. For instance, I have been trying to learn if the pink triangle worn by these men really was bigger than other triangles for the SS guards to see '175ers' from afar, an opportunist idea that would have helped the torture of queer men in concentration camps.

After years of research, I have concluded that it is impossible to know for sure, and for clear material reasons. People in and outside of academia tend to visualize one famous poster when thinking about the various categories created by the Nazis: a poster from Dachau elaborating on all possible triangles juxtaposed or not with a Star of David and in multiple combinations. This is the document used by most memorials and museums across the world. I have also found copies of the poster in Richard Plant's papers.⁵³ This emphasis on the poster is misleading, as it falsely gives the idea that every concentration camp functioned the same way and

---

51 This dismissal evolved and merged into populist attacks on a queer scholarship of Nazi persecutions. Gay intellectuals are now staging themselves as the victims of a leftist cancel culture, denouncing the alleged dangers of a queer analysis of the era for academic freedom. Zinn is once again a great example of this current, coupling his refusal to engage with the literature in alarmist edited volumes on academic freedom or giving tendentious interviews with populist media. See Alexander Zinn, "Gefühlte Wahrheiten: Wie LGBTI-Aktivismus die Wissenschaftsfreiheit bedroht." In *Wissenschaftsfreiheit: Warum dieses Grundrecht zunehmend umkämpft ist*, ed. Sandra Kostner (Baden-Baden: Nomos, 2022), 165–182; Frederik Schindler, "'Queer' Opfer des Nationalsozialismus? ,Aus historischer Perspektive ist das Quatsch,'" *Welt+* (January 24, 2023). This opportunist course by Zinn is disappointing, as it not only fundamentally misunderstands historical analysis (in bad faith?), but discredits the historical discipline, giving rise to right-wing diatribes about the humanities as unserious and pseudo-sciences.
52 In this chapter, I deliberately use 'queer women' and 'lesbians.' I use queer women the same way I use it in the rest of the book, to underline the fluidity of sexualities and because I cannot be sure if these women were only having sex with women or if they would have given their sexualities a political identity. However, as the debates surrounding memory are also tied to the political aspect of 'lesbianism' and the gatekeeping of memory activism by gay historians, I consider it important to couple both concepts.
53 MS Richard Plants Papers: Series II. Writings, 1926–1996, Box 11, Folder 2. *The Pink Triangle – illustrations and documents, n.d.*, New York Public Library.

that a camp functioned the same way during its whole existence. Furthermore, it pushes the illusion that the Nazi Party was a well-functioning, well-organized, political totalitarian machine, when it was also chaotic, contradictory, and plagued with incompetence.[54]

This cliché of the organized Nazi regime hides the fact that some camps possibly had bigger pink triangles, also possibly only for part of the time. For instance, some queers were marked with a big "A" for *Arschficker*, 'ass fuckers,' and were branded later – or not at all – with pink triangles.[55] Some prisoners never saw the symbol or only understood much later what they meant. It is possible to work with written Nazi sources to find out who was sent to death, interned, or murdered for being a so-called antisocial element, sometimes with an extra mention of them being lesbian.[56] However the branding of lesbian and queer women could also have been just as chaotic. The point here is to relativize the certainty with which queer men define the Pink Triangle that they wield as a proof of their oppression while dismissing the structural persecution of lesbian and queer women.[57]

Indeed, similar assumptions have been made about the materiality of the triangle. To be clear: we know that queer men were persecuted, we know many of them were forced to wear pink triangles, and we know they were sent to death through forced labor. There are enough testimonies and sources to be sure. This book and others have shown how the voices of these men were silenced for decades after the events, and how this exclusion from official discourses on *Vergangenheitsbewältigung* destroyed many lives even up to this day. However, the appropriation of the symbol by a social movement is also paired with a certain misunderstanding of the historical research on the subject. Truly, we lack research on the visual materiality of the triangle, the scarcity of pink triangles from the camp, of tangible Pink Triangles. As shown in the previous chapters, the recu-

---

[54] In the case of sexuality, see Dagmar Herzog, *Sex after Fascism: Memory and Morality in Twentieth-Century Germany* (Princeton, NJ: Princeton University Press, 2005), 10–63.

[55] For an example see the account by Pierre Seel in his memoirs. Pierre Seel, *Moi, Pierre Seel, Déporté Homosexuel* (Paris: Calmann-Lévy, 1994). See also "We Were Marked With a Big 'A,'" *Jewish Bulletin* 143, no. 43 (November 4, 1994): 13.

[56] For the fate and memory of women considered to be anti-social elements and the memory of activists trying to uncover it, see Sigrid Jacobeit, "Zur Geschichte des Jugend-Konzentrationslagers Uckermark im Gesamtkonzept der Mahn- und Gedenkstätte Ravensbrück/Stiftung Brandenburgische Gedenkstätten." In *Das Mädchenkonzentrationslager Uckermark*, ed. Katja Limbacher et al. (Münster: Unrast, 2005), 271–279; Rosel Vadhera-Jonas, "Nach der Befreiung: Die zweite Geschichte des 'Jugendschutzlagers Uckermark.'" In Katja Limbacher et al *Das Mädchenkonzentrationslager Uckermark* (Münster: Unrast, 2005), 293–306.

[57] Müller, "Vergleichbarkeit der Lebenssituation," 49–60.

peration of the symbol on both sides of the Atlantic gave impulse to decades of necessary political change. But the number of actual triangles deposited in archives is quite low. Some archivists have communicated with each other behind the scenes to find out if a bequeathed pink triangle was a 'true' artefact or not.[58]

As mentioned in the last chapter the USHMM is in possession of one: from Josef Kohout, bequeathed to the museum by his lover. To the eye, this piece of cloth, hidden from sight for decades, is now more reddish than pink. Why does that matter? The fact that we do not know where pink triangles were produced – we do know where some of the Yellow Stars were produced – and the reality of a not-so-pink triangle together nuance the certainty that all queer men sent to camps because of their (alleged) sexuality were marked by this definite symbol, and that it was always pink.[59] Were red triangle bleached? Were Nazis using pink fabrics with different tones? These questions remain.

It is noteworthy that we are in possession of many more Pink Triangles created after the war, in memory of the men wearing the symbol in the camps. It shows how the discourse on the symbol became as important as the image itself. Hinting at a pink triangle that we so rarely possess as the basis for a whole political discourse on the Pink Triangle shows once again how images influence discourses as much as discourses influence them. Extensive research has shown how lesbians were not branded by pink triangles. Should we still block lesbians and queer women from walking on Pink Triangle bridges? Is it really an instrumentalization, or worse, falsification of history to aim for lesbian visibility and representation if we know that lesbians and queer women were structurally oppressed through the patriarchal and virilist structures of National Socialism?[60] As most of the early *Schwulenbewegung* was connected to the discovery of gay victims in the 1930s and 1940s, one question remains: Is victimhood only a legitimization if it comes with an official perpetrator category and colour on a poster? What does that mean for the legal status of lesbian persecution?

These debates are crystallized in a recent debate regarding the commemoration of lesbian and queer women tortured by the Nazis in the concentration camp of Ravensbrück. North of Berlin, Ravensbrück was the biggest women's concentration camp on German territory and consisted of a smaller camp for men after 1941. Until Liberation in April 1945, the authorities of the camp murdered around

---

58 E-Mail exchange between Jake W. Newsome and Albert Knoll (April 16, 2018). Shown to me by Albert Knoll during my visit to the archives.
59 In a factory in the Dutch town of Enschede. See Katja Happe, Michael Mayer, and Maja Peers. "Introduction." In *The Persecution and Murder of the European Jews by Nazi Germany 1933–1945*, eds. Katja Happe, Michael Mayer and Maja Peers (Oldenbourg: De Gruyter, 2022), 46.
60 Marhoefer, "Lesbianism, Transvestitism, and the Nazi State."

120,000 women and children, 20,000 men and 1,200 teenage girls. Ravensbrück became the theatre of many gendered aspects of Nazi violence during its years of existence.[61] From the sadism of 'scientific experiments' to sexual violence, from the coercive recruitment of female prisoners for camp brothels and German soldiers, the name of the camp is still associated with research and memory of Nazi misogyny and heteropatriarchal violence. Ground-breaking research in the 1990s and pilgrimages by lesbian women during the German Democratic Republic (GDR) established the importance of the camp in lesbian memory, like the significance of Sachsenhausen for gay men in West Berlin.[62]

Echoing the implicit rejection of intersectional experiences of victimhood discussed above in the case of non-Jewish and Jewish queer victimhood and memory, the recuperation of Pink Triangle after the war emphasized and reproduced categories of victimhood created by the perpetrators. For instance, historian Alexander Zinn opposed the "legend of lesbian persecution," arguing that no systematic legal persecution of lesbians took place.[63] He pointed to §175 StGB and the absence of such a paragraph in the penal code for lesbians or for queer women in general.[64]

---

[61] Helga Amesberger, Katrin Auer, and Brigitte Halbmayr, "Sexuelle Ausbeutung von Frauen in NS-Konzentrationslagern." In *Sexualisierte Gewalt: Weibliche Erfahrungen in NS-Konzentrationslagern*, ed. Helga Amesberger, Katrin Auer and Brigitte Halbmayr (Vienna: Mandelbaum Verlag, 2010), 101–162; Regina Mühlhäuser and Insa Eschebach, "Sexuelle Gewalt im Krieg und Sex-Zwangsarbeit in NS-Konzentrationslagern." In *Krieg und Geschlecht: Sexuelle Gewalt im Krieg und Sex-Zwangsarbeit in NS-Konzentrationslagern*, ed. Regina Mühlhäuser and Insa Eschebach (Berlin: Metropol, 2008), 11–34; Freya Klier, *Die Kaninchen von Ravensbrück. Medizinische Versuche an Frauen in der NS-Zeit* (Munich: Droemersche Verlagsanstalt, 1994).
[62] Maria Bühner, "Die Kontinuität des Schweigens: Das Gedenken der Ost-Berliner Gruppe Lesben in der Kirche in Ravensbrück," *Österreichische Zeitschrift für Geschichtswissenschaften* 28, no. 2 (2018): 111–131.
[63] Alexander Zinn, "Der Hang zu Opfererzählungen. Über Dramatisierung und selektive Wahrnehmung in Geschichtsschreibung und Erinnerungskultur zu Homosexuellen während der NS-Zeit," *Revue d'Allemagne et des pays de langue allemande* 53, no. 2 (2021): 331–346.
[64] While I disagree with Zinn analytically and find his persistence in discrediting factual scholarship on lesbian persecution beyond §175 StGB quite peculiar, the scope of his empirical research at the base of his main monograph is noteworthy. Alexander Zinn, *"Aus dem Volkskörper entfernt?" Homosexuelle Männer im Nationalsozialismus* (Frankfurt [Main]: Campus Verlag, 2018). He was not the only one. Many have already compiled biographies of the men with the pink triangle. See various biographies in Joachim Müller and Andreas Sternweiler, *Homosexuelle Männer im KZ Sachsenhausen* (Berlin: Verlag Rosa Winkel, 2000). For example, Rainer Hoffschildt, "'Nach der Befreiung wieder in Haft', Der bündische Widerstandskämpfer Paul Hahn." In *Homosexuelle Männer in KZ Sachsenhausen*, ed. Joachim Müller and Andreas Sternweiler (Berlin: Verlag Rosa WInkel, 2000), 354–358; Fred Brade, "‚Er war ein Hallodri' Der Tänzer Richard Barnack." In *Homosexuelle Männer in KZ Sachsenhausen*, 211–212.

5.3 The women with[out] the Pink Triangle? —— **153**

Using his position on the commission of experts of the Brandenburg Memorial Foundation, Zinn repeatedly blocked the inauguration of a memorial sphere in memory of queer women persecuted for being lesbians in Ravensbrück.[65] Rejecting claims of persecutions and opposing what he considered the siren call of identity politics and a falsification of historical facts, Zinn insisted on the importance of categories of victimhood.[66] Most of the research on the suffering of women desiring women under National Socialism argues beyond fixed identities, showing how new queer methodologies allow for better understandings of power structures during National Socialism beyond official victim categories.[67] Queer women fighting for the commemoration of lesbian and queer female suffering do not intend to create new categories of victimhood, but to democratize and open up our understanding of oppression during the Nazi dictatorship. Irmes Schwager, member of the *Initiative Autonome feministische FrauenLesben aus Deutschland und Österreich* 'Initiative for autonomous feminist women and lesbians from Germany and Austria' states: "I also don't understand why people have insisted for over four years that the commemoration [in Ravensbrück] is intended to create a category of imprisonment that didn't even exist. As an initiative, we have always made it very clear that this is not the point."[68] The episode of the commemorative sphere in Ravensbrück also brings to mind the story of the sphere of Dachau analysed in chapter four –

---

65 A quote attributed to the head of the Brandenburg Memorials Foundation underlines the importance of legal systemic persecutions. See Franziska Schulteß, "Gedenktafel soll an lesbische KZ-Häftlinge erinnern," *L-MAG* (21 September 2017), accessed August 4, 2021, https://www.l-mag.de/news-1010/gedenktafel-soll-an-lesbische-kz-haeftlinge-erinnern.html.
66 For Zinn's understanding of 'identity politics,' see Alexander Zinn, "Einfalt statt Vielfalt," *Frankfurter Allgemeine Zeitung* (March 16, 2021). Jennifer Evans offered a counter-perspective. Jennifer Evans, "Die queere Bewegung in Deutschland – eine vielstimmige Geschichte," *Der Tagesspiegel*, (April 16, 2021). It is to be noted that Zinn does not deny that lesbian women suffered during National Socialism. But he denies that they were directly persecuted because they were lesbians.
   Alexander Zinn, *"Aus Dem Volkskörper Entfernt"? Homosexuelle Männer im Nationalsozialismus* (Frankfurt [Main]: Campus Verlag, 2018.), 31. Zinn refers to Jens Dobler, "Unzucht und Kuppelei", 53–62. Lutz van Dijk and Alexander Zinn, "Zwischen Opfermythos und historischer Präzision," interview by Hanno Hauenstein, *Berliner Zeitung* (April 7, 2021). This interview was an answer to opposing pieces by the two: Alexander Zinn, "Schwule Helden." Lutz van Dijk, "Es ist an der Zeit, historische Forschung zu demaskieren," *Der Tagesspiegel* (February 4, 2021). As van Dijk argues for a structural analysis of oppression, Zinn continuously argues with §175 StGB, refusing to broaden his analysis beyond judicial persecutions.
67 Marhoefer, "Lesbianism, Transvestitism, and the Nazi State."
68 Aktivistinnen des lesbischen Gedenkens, "Anna Hájková und Birgit Bosold im Gespräch," 94. The German term *FrauenLesben* (WomenLesbians) is political and refers to the heterosexist construction of the category 'woman', hinting at the subversiveness of lesbianism inside the heteromatrix.

see section 4.2. This time, the group of victims blocking the inauguration of the monument were also queer. This story has its own happy yet long overdue ending. A provisionary monument was finally inaugurated in the spring of 2022, following an alliance of many gay and lesbian associations.[69]

In the camp, the violence against lesbian and queer women took many forms. Insa Eschebach, former head of the Memorial Museum Ravensbrück, also reminds us that beyond the reason behind these women's imprisonment, their everyday life in the camp was marked by openly lesbophobic/queerphobic hostility, not only from the *Schutzstaffel* 'the Nazi protection squadron' (SS), but also from fellow prisoners.[70] Anna Hájková's work investigates the intersectional aspects of this reality. She complicates these accounts of lesbophobia and demonstrates how they existed in parallel with sexual barter and complex relationships between victims and perpetrators.[71] Others have also contributed clear biographical evidence of this oppression.[72] The dismissal of the suffering of queer and lesbian women is thus not only a blatant rejection of the historiography, but also a persistence and an assertion of the correctness in using categories and laws created by the Nazis to commemorate Nazi victims. Similar conflicts startled the inauguration of the monument in *Tiergarten* at the turn of the century.[73]

Insa Eschebach, reflecting on the many conflicts surrounding the issue, frames these debates as a new wave of *Vergangenheitsbewältigung*, a democratization of the status of victim, an opening of categories.[74] The irony here is apparent. After

---

[69] 'Gedenkzeichen für die lesbischen Häftlinge im Frauen-Konzentrationslager Ravensbrück', Stiftung Brandenburgische Gedenkstätten: Mahn- und Gedenkstätte Ravensbrück. Meldungen, July 14, 2021, accessed January 20, 2022, https://www.ravensbrueck-sbg.de/meldungen/gedenkzeichen-fuer-die-lesbischen-haeftlinge-im-frauen-konzentrationslager-ravensbrueck/. See also Anna Hájková, 'Das verspätete Gedenken an lesbische NS-Opfer', *Der Tagesspiegel* (April 30, 2022) accessed January 20, 2022, https://www.tagesspiegel.de/gesellschaft/queerspiegel/langer-kampf-um-anerkennung-das-verspaetete-gedenken-an-lesbische-ns-opfer/28291076.html. The original sphere was accidentally damaged, and the real monument was unveiled later that year. A provisional plaque was first placed on site.
[70] Eschebach, "Queere Gedächtnisräume": 62.
[71] Hájková, "Between Love and Coercion: Queer Desire."
[72] Huneke, "Heterogeneous Persecution."
[73] Jennifer Evans, "Harmless kisses and infinite loops: Making space for queer place in twenty-first century Berlin." In *Queer Cities, Queer Cultures Europe since 1945*, ed. Jennifer Evans and Matt Cook (London: Bloomsbury Academic, 2014), 75–94; Tomberger, "Das Berliner Homosexuellen-Denkmal," 187–207; Stefanie Endlich, "Das Berliner Homosexuellen-Denkmal: Kontext, Erwartungen und die Debatte um den Videofilm." In Eschebach, *Homophobie und Devianz*, 167–186.
[74] Eschebach, "Queere Gedächtnisräume": 50–51; Aktivistinnen des lesbischen Gedenkens, "Anna Hájková und Birgit Bosold im Gespräch mit Ulrike Janz, Irmes Schwager und Lisa Steininger," *Invertito – Jahrbuch für die Geschichte der Homosexualitäten* 21 (2019): 89.

decades of exclusion of the men wearing pink triangles from official memory, gay men were in turn denying the recognition of the suffering of queer women. This time, the reason was different – this was not queerphobia *per se*. By having centered queer male suffering and legitimized its memory through the recuperation of a symbol created by the perpetrators, queer men were now faced with the slow erosion of these categories. This is not only a queer story. Recent debates about solidarity and conflict between victim groups have shown how the assertion of fixed categories of victimhood have been contested by victim organizations themselves.[75] Even Alexander Zinn has rearticulated the focus of his criticism, now arguing that a memory of Nazi queerphobia should leave behind debates about victimhood and rejecting victimization.[76] Yet the Pink Triangle has now become part of queer cultural memory of National Socialism. By focusing on the symbol for decades, activists have coupled victimhood and the historical wrongs of the past with a sense of belonging.

A new generation of queer historians have embraced the fluidity of queer methodologies for an analysis of the past. Beyond fixed categories and sexualities, they have attempted to revisit the atrocities committed by the Nazi regime and better understand the persecution of queerness. I am one of them. Revisiting the era also means reconsidering previous waves of *Vergangenheitsbewältigung*, examining the differences between various queer experiences of the dictatorship. For queer men, this could mean wearing pink triangles in concentration camps; for queer women, this could mean aggravating factors after being put in a camp, being branded as so-called antisocial element, or living in constant fear of denunciation.

The opening of these categories has also met with backlash.[77] The pink radicals of the 1970s are not responsible for contemporary historiographical debates, but the integration of cis gay suffering into the official memory of National Socialism and the various uses of the Pink Triangle throughout the second part of the twentieth century have semantically fixed categories of victimhood, an unfortunate case of collateral damage. Lacking a Pink Triangle, advocates for other queer victims of the Nazis are condemned as profiteers, instrumentalizing the past for contemporary

---

[75] See also my discussion of the event in Manuela Bauche Patricia Piberger, Sébastien Tremblay, and Hannah Tzuberi, "From Opferkonkurrenz to Solidarity: A Round Table," *Bulletin of the German Historical Institute London* 44, no. 2 – Special Issue Memory Culture 2.0: From Opferkonkurrenz to Solidarity (2022): 32–85.
[76] Alexander Zinn, "Abschied von der Opferperspektive: Plädoyer für einen Paradigmenwechsel in der schwulen und lesbischen Geschichtsschreibung," *Zeitschrift für Geschichtswissenschaft* 67, no. 11 (2019): 934–955.
[77] Lilli Mehne, "'Gefährliche Geschichtsfälschung' Die Wissenschaftlerin Dana Mahr erhält Drohungen, weil sie über trans Menschen im NS aufklärt," *Nd* (August 10, 2022).

aims.⁷⁸ Even if this was true – and it is not – it would brush over the fact that most of the legitimization and historicization of gay rights in the transatlantic world has been fought on the pretence of commemorating victims of National Socialism, identifying with them without having actually lived through the atrocities. Corinna Tomberger points out this irony, reminding gay activists and gay historians that denouncing a so-called lesbian instrumentalization of the monument in *Tiergarten* is peculiar, as the monument is in itself an instrumentalization of victimhood from the past to imagine a better world in the future.⁷⁹ All in all, the male queer subject was intrinsically tied to categories of the past and reinforced said categories in the present. By integrating official memory as a badge of inclusion, the Pink Triangle of the second part of the twentieth century also became a badge of exclusion.

5.4 Memory with or without solidarity

On June 24, 1995, local officials of the city of Cologne, home of one of West Germany most vocal queer communities, assembled next to the Hohenzollern Bridge crossing the Rhine near the Old City and inaugurated another sort of bridge, another stone in memory of the men forced to wear pink triangles in concentration camps. Situated on the bank of the river and near a popular gay cruising spot, this new monument consisted of two rosy wedges coming together to form a pink triangle with the inscription: *"Den schwulen und lesbischen Opfern des Nationalsozialismus,"* 'To the gay and lesbian victims of National Socialism.' [Figure 4] In the words of the artist responsible for the monument, Achim Zinkam, "pressure, back pressure and friction are prerequisites for overall cohesion. If one of the wedges is removed, at least one other loses its grip. The structure is destroyed [. . .] two trestles, two colors, two cuts, put together to form a whole. Men, women, lesbians, gays, leaning on each other, rubbing against each other, suspended in each other, conditioning each other."⁸⁰ The Cologne triangle is therefore a symbol of survivorship but also of queer solidarity. It commemorates queer suffering, but it also celebrates supports and recognition. What is more, the monument historicizes a queer present through narratives of victimhood, through an affirmation of survival. Here, survival, recognition, solidarity, and victimhood are not only linked, but co-dependent. As Zinkam writes, without each other every aspect of the story would collapse; the Pink Trian-

---

78 Franziska Schulteß, "'Schwule vs. Lesben?' – Streit um Gedenkkugel für lesbische NS-Opfer geht weiter," *Siegessäule* (October 12, 2018).
79 Tomberger, "Das Berliner Homosexuellen-Denkmal," 204.
80 Quoted from the artist in "Das Mahnmal zum Gedenken an schwule und lesbische Opfer des Nazi-Terros [sic] wird am 24. Juni im Rheingarten feierlich eingeweiht," *Box* (June 1995).

gle as a whole would break down. Without mentioning queer women, the artist says, the commemoration of queer men would fall apart. As this chapter demonstrates, this was and still is not always the case. Indeed, certain uses of the Pink Triangle intrinsically create(d) tensions and exclusions.

Figure 4: Two different views of the Pink Triangle monument in Cologne in 2017. Photos taken by the author.

6 A badge of universalization – Pink Triangles and the limits of Euro-American queer suffering

The second part of the 1980s led to a paradigm shift for the queer political memory of National Socialism in German-speaking countries. The first half of the decade had seen the inauguration of the commemorative plaque in the *Gedenkstätte* Mauthausen and Richard von Weizsäcker, the German Federal President, referred to "homosexuals" during his speech on May 8, 1985. Mainstream local newspapers were not only publishing pieces about the persecutions, but also covering events critical of the Adenauer era, validating years of activism and denunciation by the pink radicals.[1] Simultaneously, future prominent queer scholars were writing their canonical works on the Nazi era.[2] This inclusion to German *Vergangenheitsbewältigung* did not necessarily come hand in hand with political changes and direct benefits for victims of the Nazis; the period was also marked by frustration and anxiety. For instance, a look at the contemporary gay press shows how queers were concerned by the rise of neofascism in West Germany.[3] Queer organizations attentively dissected any news coming out of Bonn and Helmut Kohl's politics regarding reparations for other groups of victims.[4]

At the same time, gay and lesbian activists did not 'just' focus their memory politics on the commemoration of the men and women murdered by the Nazis. They also emphasized the destruction of the first emancipation movement at the beginning of the twentieth century. This new attention, given especially to Weimar Berlin, expanded the awareness of lesbian bars and organizations that were

---

[1] "Auch noch nach der 'Befreiung' verfolgt. VHS -Vortrag über 'Homosexuelle im Nationalsozialismus'- Mehr als 10 000 zu Tode geschunden," *Rhein-Neckar-Zeitung* (January 30, 1985).
[2] For example, in Münster, Burkhard Jelonnek was looking for first account witnesses and survivors for his dissertation on the topic. He published an advertising spot in *Die Zeit* in 1984. "Am Institut für Erziehungswissenschaft der Westfälischen Wilhelms-Universität Münster wird eine Dissertation über das Schicksal der Homosexuellen im Dritten Reich erarbeitet" *Die Zeit* (February 24, 1984). Jellonnek eventually published his work at the turn of the decade and was one of the first who did so on the topic after Rüdiger Lautmann. See Burkhard Jellonnek, *Homosexuelle unter dem Hakenkreuz* (Paderborn: Verlag Ferdinand Schöningh, 1990).
[3] See for example Michael Hunger, "'Kein schöner Land in dieser Zeit, . . .' oder sollten in der Bundesrepublik staatliche Gedenkfeiern verboten werden?," *Dorn Rosa Zeitung der demokratischen Lesben- und Schwuleninitiative* (December 1986): 4–5.
[4] For instance, Heike Mews, "Entschädigung ein 'Menschenrecht,'" *Dorn Rosa Zeitung der demokratischen Lesben- und Schwuleninitiative* (August 1987): 7–11.

destroyed by the Nazis, of the work of Magnus Hirschfeld, and of the persecution of non-heteronormative men prior to 1933.

This focus on destruction brings us back to the divided city of Berlin and to the start of another Pink Triangle journey. As Pink Triangle monuments were inaugurated beyond the grounds of former concentration camps, the symbol became the coat of arms of a broader international community. Pink Triangles narratives born in West Germany were universalized throughout the Euro-American world and eventually became the legitimization of queer international politics. This universalization of the Pink Triangle is a story of power, the power to carve one's narrative into stone and the power to canonize one national context in a global perspective, forcing other experiences of queerness to integrate or at least partake in dominant narratives coming out of Europe. Following on the previous chapter on the exclusions linked to the Pink Triangle's history, this sixth chapter analyzes the ways in which the symbol universalized one definition of queerness beyond the transatlantic world. It begins by discussing different Pink Triangle monuments in Germany, Italy, the Netherlands, and Spain to identify multiple Pink Triangle narratives and underline how they were built upon each other. It then examines the universalization of these narratives, pausing to reflect on the power asymmetries of Euro-American queer history.

6.1 Carving Pink Triangles in Schöneberg

Roland Hirsch and Ekkerhard Kunz of the *allgemeine homosexuellearbeitsgemeinschaft e.V.* (AHA) and the regional West Berlin group of the *Ökumenische Arbeitsgruppe Homosexuelle und Kirche e.V* (HuK), respectively, released a communiqué in the autumn of 1987 announcing their intention to pressure politicians into breaking their alleged silence about the persecutions of queerness during the Nazi regime. Arguing that the experiences at Mauthausen and Dachau (see chapter four) were examples of the importance of having a place of queer civic worship, they launched a fundraising campaign to create a Pink Triangle out of pink granite or marble with a Berlin twist on the (by then) well-known inscription: "Beaten to Death, Silenced to Death – To the homosexual victims of National Socialism from the homosexual initiatives of Berlin."[5] Both men also invited queers on November 22 of the same year to the official West Berliner memorial at *Stein-*

---

5 Letter and communiqué by *HuK and AHA* "Gedenktafel für die homosexuellen Opfer des Nationalsozialismus in Berlin-West October 20. 1987." Schwules Museum Berlin C Box Nr 196. *Gedenkorte der Homosexuellen Verfolgung / Berlin Nollendorfplatz*. This inscription is similar to the one used in Mauthausen and Dachau.

platz, in the borough of Charlottenburg, for a ceremony in memory of the men with the pink triangle.[6] The VVN supported the initiative and the endeavour also attracted the attention of local newspapers.[7]

Encouraged by the support they had received, the AHA and HuK-Berlin allied themselves with Raimund Bayer – a member of the Berlin House of Representatives for the *Sozialdemokratische Partei Deutschlands* (SPD) –, contacted the 38 parliamentary groups of the 12 Berlin boroughs –12 *Christlich Demokratische Union Deutschlands* 'Christian Democratic Union of Germany' (CDU), 12 SPD, 2 *Freie Demokratische Partei Deutschlands* (FDP), 2 *Alternative Liste*, 'Alternative List' – and encouraged them to petition their respective *Bezirksverordnetenversammlung*, 'borough assemblies.'[8] The *Alternative Liste*, the precursor of the Berlin Green Party, eventually introduced propositions in many district assemblies, as well as organizing the approval for the creation of a monument in Schöneberg, with the approval of the SPD and against the will of the CDU.[9] After numerous spots were considered and then rejected, the *Nollendorfplatz* at the center of Schöneberg was finally ratified.[10] Once the Senate of Berlin had dealt with the

---

6 Letter and communiqué by *HuK and AHA* "Gedenktafel für die homosexuellen Opfer des Nationalsozialismus in Berlin-West October 20. 1987."
7 "Letter Vereinigung der Verfolgten des Naziregimes Westberlin – Verband der Antifaschisten. November 3. 1987." Schwules Museum Berlin C Box Nr 196. *Gedenkorte der Homosexuellen Verfolgung / Berlin Nollendorfplatz*. In the letter, the VVN specifies that the topic did not concern any of its members (sic), but that it would gladly offer its support. The endeavor also gained the support of the *Landesvorstand of the Jungdemokraten* and the *Alternative Liste*. See letters from both political organizations in October 1987: Schwules Museum Berlin C Box Nr 196. *Gedenkorte der Homosexuellen Verfolgung / Berlin Nollendorfplatz*. See also "Gedenktafel für Homosexuelle NS-Opfer," *TAZ* (January 23, 1989) and "Opfer nicht rehabilitiert. Gedenktafel für homosexuelle NS-Opfer," *SPD Volksblatt* (May 7, 1988).
8 Borough assemblies are responsible bodies for the local administration of Berlin. The powers of the borough governments are limited, and the senate oversees their assigned tasks. In other words, Berlin is a city-state, and each borough is like a smaller town inside its walls.
9 HuK activists kept records of every discussion in every BVV and developed a strategy of lobbying local politicians. Proposed by the *Alternative Liste* and FDP in many BVV, motions were defeated in CDU strongholds and heavily discussed in others. Berlin-Schöneberg eventually proved to be the only BVV willing to pass the motion presented by the *Alternative Liste*, backed by the SPD, while the CDU abstained unanimously.
10 While developing their strategy and attending BVV meetings, queer activists in West Berlin drew lists of possible symbolic locations for their commemorative plaque. They dreamt of having one in Sachsenhausen or the Gedenkstätte Plötzensee in Tiergarten. They also suggested the S-Bahn station Beuselstraße for its connection with Sachsenhausen in the town Oranienburg, the former location of Magnus Hirschfeld's Institute in Tiergarten, one of the many bars raided during the Republic of Weimar, the grounds of the former concentration camp in Columbia-Haus in

unexpected opposition of the *Berliner Verkehrsbetriebe*, 'Berlin public transport company,'[11] the monument was inaugurated in June 1989, just in time for the twentieth anniversary of the liberalization of §175 StGB.[12] [Figure 5] Not everyone in Schöneberg welcomed the decision with open arms, with opposition still present in 1989 to any form of queer memory considering it as superfluous, unnecessary, and "pushy."[13] The heart of the so-called *Regenbogenkiez*, 'Rainbow Quarter,' was chosen for its importance for queer history. Numerous queer bars and meeting places were located in the area around *Nollendorfplatz* prior to the Nazi rise to power and many that had remained open afterward faced heavy surveillance and police raids. Reflecting on the location, the HuK drew parallels between state oppression during and after National Socialism, and the alleged uses of Nazi era documents for the surveillance of queer activists by the police in the long postwar period.[14]

Tempelhof or even the Prinz Albrecht Palais (today's *Topographie des Terrors* and the former headquarters of the Gestapo).

11 The Berliner Verkehrsbetriebe was afraid that the plaque on the U-Bahn station would draw a false connection between its operations and the deportation or persecutions of individuals during National Socialism. After hefty discussions and a correspondence involving members of the Berlin Lower Chamber, the Berlin Senator for Transport intervened directly and forced the *Berliner Verkehrsbetriebe* to give its authorization. The transport company didn't send any representative to the inauguration ceremony. In 2019, for the thirtieth anniversary of the inauguration, the *Berliner Verkehrsbetriebe* was not only invited, but commended for its swiftness in cleaning the monument every time it was vandalized, an unfortunate reality.

12 This is noteworthy. In his letter to the Berlin Senate concerning the *Berliner Verkehrsbetriebe* affair, Albert Eckert (mdA *Alternative Liste*) specified that the ceremony needed to take place before the Christopher Street Parade, tracing a direct link between the injustice of the past and the *Schwulenbewegung*. See the letter from June 14, 1989, in Schwules Museum Berlin C Box Nr 196. *Gedenkorte der Homosexuellen Verfolgung / Berlin Nollendorfplatz*.

13 Hans-Hermann Kotte, "'Schwimmer, Radfahrer, Homosexuelle': Endlich Gedenktafel ein Rosa Winkel den U-Bahnhof Nollendorffplatz (sic)" *TAZ* (June 16, 1989). The article quotes extensively the former director of the *Berliner Verkehrsbetriebe* Harro Sachße and his discontent. Sachße states that by accepting the monument, the Berlin senate opened the door for memorials for nothing and everything, for examples cyclists and swimmers. This kind of argument or opinion was common during debates about the inclusion of queer victims in the official memory of National Socialism later on during the decade.

14 "HuK Invitation letter to the inauguration June 11, 1989," Schwules Museum Berlin C Box Nr 196. *Gedenkorte der Homosexuellen Verfolgung / Berlin Nollendorfplatz*. So-called Pink Lists were registers of gay men at police and government agencies. Authorities long denied the existence of such lists, before documents regarding the HIV/AIDS crisis in Bavaria confirmed transfers of data between agencies. See for example " . . . Und was sagt Gauweiler dazu?," *Rosa Flieder* 49 (November 1986): 34.

Figure 5: The Schöneberg Triangle in 2023.

The *Nollendorfplatz*'s Pink Triangle, still hanging today on the walls of the underground station of the same name, began a new legacy of memory activism in the heart of the city as well as offering a template for other projects in the name of queer memory. The emphasis on the destruction of queer sites of pleasure and the placement of the monument shifted the discourse on queer memory of National Socialism. The Pink Triangle on the walls of the station served several purposes. It was both a reminder of queer survival throughout the twentieth century and a eulogy for the men forced to wear pink triangles in concentration camps. It is simultaneously an inscription of queer memory in the urban landscape, an appropriation of the space, and a statement of both visibility and resistance. By moving away from the general monument at Steinplatz to a community-based memorial site at *Nollendorfplatz*, queers had found a new space of commemoration exclusively for queer victims. They used it, for instance, for annual ceremonies before each year's

Christopher Street Parade.[15] The monument disrupted the silence surrounding the persecutions of the Adenauer era and called for an end to contemporary persecutions, or simply put, for excuses on behalf of the federal government. In this regard, it honours the men forced to wear pink triangles, but also uses their fate to legitimize other queer struggles toward emancipation. Again, we are faced with two triangles at once. This sedimentation of various layers of memory into one space offered queers a new place for the performance of memory, for acting out the cultural trauma at the core of the community's sense of belonging.[16] All these layers blurred the line between the present and the past and universalized the suffering under the Nazi regime. In other words, queer initiatives in the divided city had not only inaugurated a new memorial in the city, but they had also built in a new Pink Triangle bridge of granite outside of the perpetrator grounds, casting a new meta meaning for the symbol into tone, the sum of all queer memories based on a past of injury. Indeed, the Pink Triangle at *Nollendorfplatz* is still simultaneously a reference to German queer history and a permanent inscription of the victimhood narratives that started in the 1970s. Until the early 2000s and the creation of an official national monument for the 'homosexual persecuted during National Socialism' in Berlin's *Tiergarten*, the triangle in Schöneberg would retain this dual purpose of being both the Berlin memorial for the queer men oppressed and murdered by the Nazis, and a permanent reminder of what the dictatorship meant for the construction of queer collective identities, that is, the representation of struggle against queerphobia persisting throughout the twentieth century. Historicizing a symbol of the persecution of gay men, and its evolution as a symbol of the persecution of queerness more generally, was the first step toward the subjugation of many forms of queerness under one gay identity.

This story goes beyond West Berlin. The 1990s Pink Triangle monument by Achim Zinkam in Cologne echoed the one in Berlin Schöneberg. The Pink Triangle's constant occurrence in theatres of memory became synonymous with a particular narrative of victimhood and the universalization of one aspect of queerness, slowly eroding its fluidity toward fixation: being gay or being lesbian. Even in occurrences where the triangle does not seem to be present, one can find residues of its influence. For instance, a monument for the queer victims of National Socialism inaugu-

---

[15] See invitation to lay a wreath of flower by the HuK during the Christopher Street Parade in June. "Letter sent on April 21, 1997." Schwules Museum Berlin C Box Nr 196. *Gedenkorte der Homosexuellen Verfolgung / Berlin Nollendorfplatz*. This is still the case today during the annual Christopher Street Parade in Berlin.

[16] Jay Winter, "The Performance of the Past: Memory, History, Identity." In *Performing the Past: Memory, History and Identity in Modern Europe*, ed. Jay Winter, Karin Tilmans and Frank van Vree, (Amsterdam: Amsterdam University Press, 2010), 11–23.

rated in Frankfurt (Main) in 1997 consists of an angel with a broken neck. Yet one of the finalist projects consisted of a Pink Triangle. The winning design has since been criticized as being opaque and not easy to decipher.[17] For many, the historicization of gay and lesbian victimhood had to walk along Pink Triangle bridges. Historian and activist Günter Grau summarizes this idea in his speech during the inauguration of the Schöneberg Triangle mentioned in the introduction. By connecting one layer with the other, the symbol was the perfect narrative to anchor the present in the past and unveil the past in the present.

Gay and lesbian identities in West and eventually unified Germany are intrinsically linked to a reenactment of victimhood through the Pink Triangle. These interpretations of the past are not necessarily an instrumentalization; they are actually the result of an identification process between gay and lesbian subjects and their projection in the accepted history of a whole community: cultural trauma, queer postmemory, and utopic desires for a future devoid of queerphobia. In other words, the unveiling of Pink Triangles outside of the grounds of former concentration camps allowed the multilayered narratives of victimhood to enter political memory in a broader sense. Zinkam's triangle in Cologne – see section 5.4 – connects the past with the present, the need to remember which queer collective past was destroyed and where queer cultural trauma came from. This historicizing of queer suffering agglomerates a united lesbian and gay past into a common queer experience of National Socialism. By conflating different experiences of oppression, that is, the fate of the men accused under §175 StGB and the oppression of queer women by the Nazi regime, the monument also carves one understanding of the era into stone for posterity. The construction of these Pink Triangle bridges also illustrates the problematic nature of memorials *per se,* and the impossibility to represent all possible histories in their totality in one object.[18] If the symbol allows multiple discourses to haunt the present, influencing discourses as much as onlookers also ascribe a discourse upon it, the sedimentation

---

17 Stephan Balkenhol, "Entwurf für die Gestaltung eines 'Mahnmals Homosexuellenverfolgung' in Verbindung mit der Neugestaltung des Platzes an der Kreuzung Schäfergasse /Alte Gasse in Frankfurt a.M." Schwules Museum Berlin C Box Nr 197 *Gedenkorte Frankfurter Engel.* The Schwules Museum collected countless reportages about the monument, namely in the *FAZ,* the *Giessener Anzeiger, BILD Frankfurt.* Schwules Museum Berlin C Box Nr 197 *Gedenkorte Frankfurter Engel.*

18 Reinhart Koselleck, "Die Transformation der politischen Totenmale im 20. Jahrhundert." In *Zeitgeschichte als Streitgeschichte: Große Kontroverse nach 1945,* ed. Martin Sabrow, Ralph Jessen and Klaus Große Kracht (Munich: C.H. Beck 2003), 205–228; Lisa Regazzoni, "The Impossible Monument of Experience: A Story That Never Ends." In *Die Vergangenheit im Begriff. Von der Erfahrung der Geschichte zur Geschichtstheorie bei Reinhart Koselleck,* ed. Christophe Bouton, Jeffrey A. Barash and Servanne Jollivet (Baden-Baden: Verlag Karl Alber, 2021), 100–126.

of German queer suffering – that is, the various layers of memories piled on in one monument – eventually offers constraint to the plurality and fluidity of queerness.[19] Simply put, various memories and experiences of queerness are conflated into each other, into a gay and lesbian identity anchored in victimhood. The Pink Triangle becomes the vector and indicator of this process. What is more, the Pink Triangle eventually defined and fixed queerness in the Euro-American world and beyond.

6.2 Patent of nobility: The International Lesbian and Gay Association and the universalization of suffering

Following a meeting on transnational solidarity in the city of Coventry in 1978, gay and lesbian activists decided to create a new international association. Beginning as an alliance between various Western European and North American groups, the International Gay Association (ILGA)[20] evolved into a far-reaching worldwide nongovernmental organization that is now part of the Economic and Social Council of the United Nations with hundreds of daughter associations and support groups scattered across all continents except Antarctica. From its origins, the ILGA's rhetoric is intrinsically tied to the evolution of Pink Triangle narratives. Based in Brussels today, the first headquarters were in London, Cologne, New York, and Stockholm. The notable "Action Secretary," the structure responsible for the coordination of political actions, was hosted by the GLF in Cologne[21] and many of the activists mentioned so far in this book were linked at some point or the other to at least one ILGA network or decision committee.[22] One of the first pamphlets produced by the organi-

---

[19] Reinhart Koselleck, "Einleitung." In *Zeitschichten. Studien zur Historik* (Frankfurt [Main]: Suhrkamp, 2000), 9. See also Helge Jordheim, "Against Periodization. Koselleck's Theory of Multiple Temporalities," *History and Theory* 51, no. 2 (2012): 151–171; and John Zammito, "Koselleck's Philosophy of Historical Time(s) and the Practice of History," *History and Theory* 43, no. 1 (2004): 124–135.
[20] Changing its name to the International Lesbian and Gay Association in 1986. Today the ILGA still uses the same acronym, but calls itself the *International Lesbian, Gay, Bisexual, Trans and Intersex Association* (ILGA). As this subchapter goes back and forth between events of the early 1980s and the later parts of the decade, the later acronym (ILGA) will be used throughout. See Laura A Belmonte, *The International LGBT Rights Movement: A History* (London: Bloomsbury Academic, 2021).
[21] "Founding documents of the ILGA," MS International Gay Information Center Archives – Ephemera – Organizations, Box 10, Folder *ILGA*, New York Public Library.
[22] See for example the financial documents at the beginning of the 1980s. National Archive of Lesbian, Gay, Bisexual and Transgender History, Collection #121 "Dr. Harold Kooden Papers," Box 1, Folder 1: *ILGA [International Lesbian and Gay Association] Official Documents: Description, Constitution, etc.*

zation is very similar in rhetoric to the pink radicals in the FRG or North American actors at the centre of the last chapters. Appealing to the lessons of history to fight against queerphobia,[23] the ILGA started using the Pink Triangle. A pamphlet coupled the symbol with a Mercator projection of the world superimposed on a sonar image.[24]

Gaining traction in the 1980s across the Euro-American world and gaining standing through a campaign to petition the United Nations, the organization also exemplifies the intricacies of an imagined queer past of suffering and transatlantic communication networks. Anchored in transatlantic activism and therefore in the memory of the Nazi persecutions of queerness, the rhetoric of the ILGA highlights how German and North American Pink Triangle narratives were not only distinct, but also built on each other in a transnational perspective. As it gained recognition by international institutions, the association also started to perceive itself as the standard bearer of all non-heteronormative individuals around the globe. In doing so, ILGA members also universalized the story of the Pink Triangle. The German story of Nazi persecutions that had influenced queer activists in North America was now portrayed as a universal story for all non-heteronormative individuals, regardless of their cultural or local experience of queerness. The universalization of the Pink Triangle benefited from the presence of the ILGA on the world stage. The ILGA is not only a case study for international Pink Triangle narratives, but also one of the vectors of these narratives across the globe. My focus on the association is twofold. First, I trace a brief chronology of the ILGA's internal discussions about the asymmetries and power structures between its Euro-American origins and its international pretensions of solidarity. This brief summary of the association's intersectional history allows us to understand how the universalization of one aspect of queerness was constructed hand in hand with the erasure of other voices and realities outside of the Euro-American world. Second, I look at one episode at the end of the 1980s that illustrates how the ILGA Pink Triangle narratives were sanctioned by international bodies like the United Nations.

From the beginning, the goals of the organization were connected to its international pretensions. For instance, the group's foundational documents mention that queer men and women had learned from the "failure of the nations of the world to guarantee lesbian women and gay men full civil and political rights" and that there was therefore a "need for international solidarity in the face of univer-

---

23 "Official Pamphlet 1978" MS International Gay Information Center Archives – Ephemera –Organizations, Box 10, Folder *ILGA*, New York Public Library.
24 National Archive of Lesbian, Gay, Bisexual and Transgender History, Collection #121 "Dr. Harold Kooden Papers," Box 1, Folder 1: *ILGA [International Lesbian and Gay Association] Official Documents: Description, Constitution, etc.*

sal oppression."[25] The coverage in the gay press states that even during its early stages, the association outlined a plan for world action and an international fight against queerphobia (homophobia in the documents).[26] However, and this is the point, the first press releases of the ILGA still seemed unaware of the transatlantic perspective and origins of this rhetoric. That is, members of the ILGA were not necessarily conscious that they were embarking on a new crusade against queerphobia that would indirectly impose one narrative as the one true story of queerness around the globe. One of the early press releases states quite bluntly that a US liaison – probably the ILGA support group based at the Gay and Lesbian Centre in New York City – would "strive to inform Americans about conditions of Lesbians and Gay men in other countries and will issue alerts when the Secretariat calls for coordinated international action to emergency situations."[27] This kind of Euro-American centrism permeates most of the first decades of the ILGA. The association organized regional – read European – and international annual conferences where plans of actions were adopted. Any organization across the world paying for full membership was theoretically able to assist and vote for new propositions. Any individual could also pay and gain membership without the right to vote.[28] Browsing through documents and personal papers of some of its leading members, it is difficult to see if activists from outside Europe received any support to pay for transportation to these conferences or to obtain the necessary visas, but a quick look at the reports of these well-attended events seem to suggest that they somehow found the energy, money, and other resources to do so.[29] Nonetheless, most of these meetings took place in Western Europe and North America and were organized by associations in these regions. As the orders of business were mapped out by the hosts or by the Secretaries – General Secretaries, Information Secretaries, Actions Secretaries and Finance Secretaries – the power dynamics remained present in the agenda, even after the inclusion of

---

25 National Archive of Lesbian, Gay, Bisexual and Transgender History, Collection #121 "Dr. Harold Kooden Papers", Box 1, Folder 21: *Original UN-NGO Application and Papers.*
26 Robert Chesley, "New International Gay Association Outlines Plans for World Action," *Gaysweek* (October 16, 1978): 2.
27 "Press release of the ILGA,"MS International Gay Information Center Archives – Ephemera – Organizations, Box 10 Folder *ILGA*, New York Public Library.
28 "Financial documents at the beginning of the 1980s," National Archive of Lesbian, Gay, Bisexual and Transgender History, Collection #121 "Dr. Harold Kooden Papers," Box 1, Folder 1: *ILGA [International Lesbian and Gay Association] Official Documents: Description, Constitution, etc.*
29 "Reports from 1988," National Archive of Lesbian, Gay, Bisexual and Transgender History, Collection #121 "Dr. Harold Kooden Papers," Box 1, Folder 12: *ILGA Conference – 1988.*

members from around the world.[30] In the beginning, some members in Europe seem to have criticized their own Eurocentrism, but most of it was directed at the inclusion of more North American groups.[31] This is not to say that no one in the ILGA criticized this paternalistic approach to international solidarity. In an open letter in the mid-early 1980s, high-ranking members of the organization – the elected Secretaries – attacked the association on two fronts. First, they considered the fight between "radicals" and "pragmatic" forces in the ILGA to be futile and counter-productive.[32] One would be quick to notice a supranational transition of other fights already happening on the national level in countries like the FRG and the USA.[33] This discussion is also another example of the hybrid transformation of radical and institutionalized gay and lesbian politics, as well as the evolution of the Pink Triangle from a symbol of Marxist German queer liberation to an allegory for all struggles against queerphobia and the push for human rights. Second, the writers of the open letter tried to push for a more nuanced approach regarding the association's inclusion of the "Third World" and a greater differentiation of its universal claims.[34] The authors remind the reader in quite the exasperated and sarcastic tone that

> [a] few debate articles in the ILGA Bulletin, pointing to something 'disturbing' have missed the issue of mutual solidarity even on the lesbian and gay level. Some ILGA members have pointed to the existence of ILIS[35] as if this was 'something wrong' and an indication of a failure of the ILGA. The contrary is true. The world is a big place, with plenty of room for

---

30 "Reports from 1992," National Archive of Lesbian, Gay, Bisexual and Transgender History, Collection #121 "Dr. Harold Kooden Papers," Box 1, Folder 11: *ILGA Conference – 1992*.
31 MS International Gay Information Center Archives – Ephemera – Organizations, Box 10, Folder *ILGA*, New York Public Library.
32 "Some 'old-timers' talk about grass-roots and the advantage of having no real organization, while in reality they mean it is much more comfortable sitting in our little global closets, meeting for drinks and kisses once a year and pretending we are important" in "Open Letter to ILGA International Secretaries, International groups before the 1987 Oslo Conference: by Bill Schiller of the IGLA Information Secretariat," National Archive of Lesbian, Gay, Bisexual and Transgender History, Collection #121 "Dr. Harold Kooden Papers," Box 1, Folder 1: *ILGA [International Lesbian and Gay Association] Official Documents: Description, Constitution, etc.*
33 Benno Gammerl, *Anders Fühlen. Queeres Leben in der Bundesrepublik. Eine Emotionsgeschichte* (Munich: Hanser, 2021), 345–347.
34 "We need to stop thinking the world begins in New York and ends in San Francisco." "Open Letter to ILGA International Secretaries, International groups before the 1987 Oslo Conference: by Bill Schiller of the IGLA Information Secretariat," National Archive of Lesbian, Gay, Bisexual and Transgender History, Collection #121 "Dr. Harold Kooden Papers," Box 1, Folder 1: *ILGA [International Lesbian and Gay Association] Official Documents: Description, Constitution, etc.*
35 Acronym of the International Lesbian Information Service. It separated from the ILGA in 1980.

the ILGA, ILIS, IGLYO, European lesbian and gay writers, esperantists, Nordic homosexuals, Jews, Quakers and even an international organization of gay plumbers. The tragedy is not the number of worldwide homosexual organizations, but the lack of energy in keeping in touch with each other. This is part of our work for the future – both establishing a strong ILGA organization, reaching out to others, and promoting visibility to capture attention both in the homosexual and non-homosexual society.[36]

If the authors of these lines seem to embrace diversity, their understanding of queerness seems to be limited to homosexuality, to gay and lesbian realities, and a genealogy of queerness from the Euro-American world. Still, these discussions notably led to some changes in the organization, like the creation of Secretaries for women, and discussions on racism and sexism during conferences.[37] For example, participants were invited to workshops with titles such as "The problem of sexism between gay men." At the ninth annual conference in Helsinki in 1984, there was a full-day workshop on "isms." Browsing through the plenary discussion of the Paris conference in 1992, it is possible to identify some topics also relevant to this discussion: the experience of women of color, racism, neofascism, and the differences between "gay and lesbian cultures." Yet, most of the minutes show how these discussions centred on the broader society outside of the ILGA's membership, dismissing most of the organization's internal criticism.

This tendency can also be traced to the type of outreach undertaken by the ILGA during the 1980s and 1990s. Most of the association's work followed the same path: gathering information on the outskirts of Europe, deliberating on new possibilities and campaigns in Europe or North America, and then asking all members at the annual conference to vote on the actions. The "Eastern European Information Pool," initially situated in Berlin, was one of these organs. To put it bluntly, a rhetoric of gay liberation and a certain way to fight against queerphobia born in the Euro-American world was being forced upon queer members around the world in the name of solidarity.[38] Almost all of these leading members, for instance the Swedish *Riksförbundet för sexuellt likaberättigande* 'Federa-

---

[36] "Open Letter to ILGA International Secretaries, International groups before the 1987 Oslo Conference: by Bill Schiller of the IGLA Information Secretariat," National Archive of Lesbian, Gay, Bisexual and Transgender History, Collection #121 "Dr. Harold Kooden Papers," Box 1, Folder 1: *ILGA [International Lesbian and Gay Association] Official Documents: Description, Constitution, etc.*

[37] National Archive of Lesbian, Gay, Bisexual and Transgender History, Collection #121 "Dr. Harold Kooden Papers," Box 1, Folder 21: *Original UN-NGO Application and Papers*.

[38] "ILGA reports from 1987," National Archive of Lesbian, Gay, Bisexual and Transgender History, Collection #21 "Michael Weltmann Papers," Box 1, Folder 12, *ENGLAND & SCOTLAND, Letters & notecards: 1985–1990*.

tion for Gay and Lesbian Rights'[39] and the *Homosexuelle Initiative Wien* (HOSI Wien)[40] used the Pink Triangle as an official logo and referred to the fate of queer men in concentration camps to explain why a presupposed "international homosexual community" needed to band together against discrimination. These were also the same groups hosting various organs of the ILGA and pushing for this new collective identity for all non-heteronormative men and women, in effect an international homosexual identity based on the collective transatlantic memory of National Socialism. A closer look at the actions of the ILGA also identifies disparities between its rhetorical use of Nazi persecutions and the broader use of the Pink Triangle as an icon for the association's transnational fight against queerphobia. Indeed, the ILGA and its support groups organized actions in Argentina against Supreme Court decisions, in the United Kingdom against Section 28[41] or in Romania for the decriminalization of homosexuality.[42] This is not to say that the fate of the Nazis's victims were forgotten; German and non-German members continued to push for campaigns in that regard. The ILGA was prompt to draw on Homocaust narratives to campaign against queerphobia, but members were also actively fighting for a new European memory culture of fascism, for a memory of the Second World War including queer suffering. For example, during the annual conference in Paris in 1992, a group of activists held a symbolic action and demonstration in the city, renaming a street of the 16ᵉ Arrondissement 'sixteenth borough' – see section 2.5. In a speech accompanying the event, organizers said:

> So today, on the date marking the 50th anniversary of the first major deportation of Jew in France, we want to designate the "Rue du Triangle Rose" [. . .] to commemorate our gay brothers and lesbian sisters who died during the nazi [sic] dictatorship. We also want to show our serious concern about the rising of neo-facism [sic] in France, the violence and discrimination against lesbians and gays, immigrants and people of colour, and people with HIV/AIDS But not only in France the extreme-right raises its head again. In many countries around the world lesbians and gays have to face increasing oppression [. . .]. Gay and Lesbian rights are human rights.[43]

---

39 "Riksförbundet för sexuellt likaberättigande," National Archive of Lesbian, Gay, Bisexual and Transgender History, Collection #121 "Dr. Harold Kooden Papers," Box 1, Folder 11, *ILGA Conference – 1988.*
40 "Pamphlet from HOSI Wien," National Archive of Lesbian, Gay, Bisexual and Transgender History, Collection #121 "Dr. Harold Kooden Papers," Box 1, Folder 20, *ILGA Campaign Brochures.*
41 Section 28 of the Local Government Act of 1988 imposed a ban on the 'promotion' of homosexuality by local authorities in England and Wales.
42 National Archive of Lesbian, Gay, Bisexual and Transgender History, Collection #121 "Dr. Harold Kooden Papers," Box 1, Folder 17, *UN – Minority Report and Sub-Commission Info.*
43 An English translation was superposed to the French original. See "Parisian Action Flyer," National Archive of Lesbian, Gay, Bisexual and Transgender History, Collection #121 "Dr. Harold

Germany and the USA also remained targets of the ILGA; it was after all founded on the use of their national histories and an appeal to memory. During the same conference, the general assembly adopted two points concerning the FRG:

> A new letter of protest will be sent by this Conference to the Government of Brandenburg (Germany) concerning the building of an industrial estate on the site of a concentration camp. A copy will be sent to the Ministry of Social Affairs. It will be signed by the secretaries general as well as by representatives of the World Congress of Gay and Lesbian Jewish Organisations.[44]

> A letter of protest will be sent by this Conference to the German Commission of the Interior demanding the inclusion of homosexual victims of the Holocaust in a national memorial.[45]

Here, 'homosexual victims of the Holocaust' refers to the queer individuals persecuted by the Nazis and not necessarily to queer Jewish victims. The ILGA, following Homocaust narratives and North American traditions – see section 3.2 –, often conflated the Holocaust and other Nazi atrocities. The leading Euro-American members had read Richard Plant, had seen *Bent*, and had based their own coming to terms with this new collective memory on the creation of an international universalized experience of queerness with its roots in German queer history and in a transatlantic dialogue. The ILGA kept on referring to the fate of the men with the pink triangle; they printed flyers and press releases plastered with Pink Triangles. Rescuing queer victims from oblivion was the first step toward a worldwide "homosexual liberation" based on their own experience of queerness. This progressive narrative vision of an enlightened, paternalistic Euro-America fighting for non-European societies is not limited to queer history.[46] However, it would be anachronistic to frame this conversation as 'homonationalism' at this point in time, when the World Health Organization still regarded 'homosexuality' as a disease and no liberal democracies were using the rights of sexual minorities to push a sense of national pride, military intervention, a capitalist homosexual neoliberal market,

---

Kooden Papers," Box 1, Folder 11: *ILGA Conference – 1992*. The name of the street was changed in 2002 in memory of the antifascist and *Résistant* Jean Pierre Bloch. See M.C, "La rue Alexis-Carrel sera débaptisée," *Le Parisien* (March 12, 2002).
44 National Archive of Lesbian, Gay, Bisexual and Transgender History, Collection #121 "Dr. Harold Kooden Papers," Box 1, Folder 11: *ILGA Conference – 1992*.
45 National Archive of Lesbian, Gay, Bisexual and Transgender History, Collection #121 "Dr. Harold Kooden Papers," Box 1, Folder 11: *ILGA Conference – 1992*.
46 Sara R. Farris, *In the Name of Women's Rights: The Rise of Femonationalism* (Durham, NC: Duke University Press, 2017).

and structural racist biopolitics.⁴⁷ I come back to the whiteness of these framings in chapter eight – see section 8.1. If homonationalism in its current form was not yet at play however, power asymmetries were nonetheless an integral part of the ILGA. This disproportion in power between queer organizations on the world stage was at least made possible by the framing of memory and history in Euro-American terms. Even the draft of a report by the United Nations in 1988 on the discriminations suffered by "sexual minorities" hinted at this framework as a part of the ILGA:

> During Hitler's regime, under the 1935 Act on the 'protection of German blood and honour,' thousands of homosexuals (200,000 is the average figure cited) [sic] were interned in concentration camps, where they could be identified by the pink triangle they were required to wear.⁴⁸

and especially

> [b]y organizing along the lines of the trade union movement or the liberation movements, sexual minorities have been able to denounce the discrimination and even the persecution to which they are subjected. German homosexuals wore the *pink triangle* in the Nazi concentration camps, where they suffered just as much as Communists, G*psies,⁴⁹ uncompromising Christians and Jews, and, ever since then, their movement has had its *patent of nobility*, which it uses with assurance to claim its entitlement to the benefit of Universal Declaration of Human Rights.⁵⁰

The experts behind the report identified historical key moments relevant to the study of gay and lesbian liberation and their interpretation illustrates how the United Nations helped universalize the Pink Triangle. In this reading, gay liberation was one 'branch' of an international movement; there was an appeal to memorialize both Nazi German history and the riots from Stonewall as the foundations of a global movement, and queers – here in the form of homosexuals – were under-

---

47 Jasbir K. Puar, *Terrorist Assemblages: Homonationalism in Queer Times* (Durham, NC: Duke University Press, 2017); Jasbir K. Puar and David L. Eng, "Introduction: Left of Queer," *Social Text*, no. 145 – Special Issue: Left of Queer (2020): 1–25.
48 §45 of "Report of UN Economic and Social Council Sub-Commission on Prevention of Discrimination and Protection of Minorities." 13 June 1988, National Archive of Lesbian, Gay, Bisexual and Transgender History, Collection #121 "Dr. Harold Kooden Papers," Box 1, Folder 17, *UN – Minority Report and Sub-Commission Info*.
49 The word appears completely in the original.
50 §19 of "Report of UN Economic and Social Council Sub-Commission on Prevention of Discrimination and Protection of Minorities." 13 June 1988, National Archive of Lesbian, Gay, Bisexual and Transgender History, Collection #121 "Dr. Harold Kooden Papers," Box 1, Folder 17, *UN – Minority Report and Sub-Commission Info*. My emphasis.

stood as an international minority.⁵¹ In the late 1980s, the United Nations thus considered that there was such a thing as "the homosexual movement," that it had started in West Germany and North America, and that it had now expanded to the rest of the world.⁵² This was exactly the kind of rhetoric pushed by the ILGA and canonized by most of its Euro-American members. At the eleventh annual conference in Vienna, members were invited to visit the concentration camp of Mauthausen in Austria and reflect on the beginning of the struggle, standing on the very ground on which their actions were based, gazing at the Pink Triangle monument inaugurated by HOSI Wien.⁵³

Some of the ILGA's special committees responsible for lobbying the United Nations and based in New York followed this discourse as well. They petitioned the Economic and Social Council for membership in 1991 and then again in 1993, having failed the first time.⁵⁴ In their multifaceted strategy to appease both opposed voices like Greece, Oman and Libya as well as those more open to their issues like Sweden, France and the Netherlands – all members of the Council at the time – the ILGA presented queer men and women as an oppressed international minority united under the yoke of the same oppression. By accepting the ILGA as a consultative non-governmental organization, the Economic and Social Council would therefore, they alleged, be giving a voice and representation to every queer person on the planet, namely to every gay and lesbian person on the planet. This appropriation of worldwide queerness under the same roof was articulated in terms of

---

51 §§ 50–53 of "Report of UN Economic and Social Council Sub-Commission on Prevention of Discrimination and Protection of Minorities" 13 June 1988, National Archive of Lesbian, Gay, Bisexual and Transgender History, Collection #121 "Dr. Harold Kooden Papers," Box 1, Folder 17, *UN – Minority Report and Sub-Commission Info*.
52 §50 of "Report of UN Economic and Social Council Sub-Commission on Prevention of Discrimination and Protection of Minorities" 13 June 1988, National Archive of Lesbian, Gay, Bisexual and Transgender History, Collection #121 "Dr. Harold Kooden Papers," Box 1, Folder 17, *UN – Minority Report and Sub-Commission Info*.
53 MS International Gay Information Center Archives – Ephemera – Organizations, Box 10, Folder *ILGA*, New York Public Library.
54 This is a long story, but the ILGA lost its consultative position in 1994 because of the presence of a pederast/pedophile association ("Man/Boy Lover") among its ranks in the United States. The ILGA strongly condemned and expelled said organization. See the official statement: ILGA World, "ILGA and the ECOSOC Status controversy," accessed April 5, 2020, https://ilga.org/ilga-ecosoc-status-controversy. See also: "U.N. Suspends Group in Dispute over Pedophilia," *The New York Times* (September 18, 1994). Backstage, the condemnation was also a source of debates and harsh correspondence. See for example the open letter, "The Death of Gay Liberation?" by David Thorstad, MS International Gay Information Center Archives – Ephemera – Organizations, Box 10, Folder *ILGA* New York Public Library. In 2006, the ILGA petitioned the UN again and it finally regained its status in 2012.

human rights but also in terms of social reparations for the wrongs in a common past.⁵⁵ Simply put, the ILGA portrayed itself as an official international homosexual lobby, representing non-heteronormative men whether they lived in Bangladesh or in the United States. The fact that non-heteronormative men in Bangladesh might or might not use the same terminology or concepts as those in the Bay Area to describe their experience of queerness, their sexualities, or their gender identities did not stop the ILGA from integrating all non-heteronormative individuals under nomenclature used in the Euro-American world. At this point in time in the 1990s, the ILGA had members on many continents, active groups in numerous countries, and organs organized by and for peer groups across the world. Still, members of the organization adopted the same rhetoric and the same imagined virtual experience of the past linked to German history. A simple look at the members supports this premise: a group for people living with HIV/AIDS called Pink Triangle in Malaysia⁵⁶ or a newspaper called *Pink Triangle* in Tsim Sha Tsui, Hong Kong.⁵⁷ The universalization of Pink Triangle narratives can also be traced in memorial practices. Following ways that the Pink Triangle was being carved into stone across the transatlantic world, it is possible to write a genealogy of discourses concurring with the one of the ILGA, meaning a universalization of Euro-American gay and lesbian history, subsuming other experiences of queerness. This is the story of Pink Triangle monuments recalling the one in Schöneberg and appearing around the Euro-American world since the 1980s.

6.3 Pink Triangles against homophobia: International victimization in official political memorialization

On April 25, 1990, Italy's first and biggest queer organization, *Arcigay*, unveiled a marble Pink Triangle dedicated to "*Alle Vittime Omosessuali del Razzismo Nazifascista,*" 'the homosexual victims of Nazi-fascist racism,' placed in the grounds of the *Piazza di Porta Saragozza* at the centre of the college town of Bologna.⁵⁸ Present at the event were the general consul of the Federal Republic of Germany (FRG), the Mayor of Bologna, representatives of Italian Jewish and antifascist or-

---

55 National Archive of Lesbian, Gay, Bisexual and Transgender History, Collection #121 "Dr. Harold Kooden Papers," Box 1, Folder 18, *ILGA-UN: Minutes and Documents*.
56 National Archive of Lesbian, Gay, Bisexual and Transgender History, Collection #121 "Dr. Harold Kooden Papers," Box 1, Folder 11: *ILGA Conference – 1992*.
57 MS International Gay Information Center Archives – Ephemera – Organizations, Box 10, Folder *ILGA*, New York Public Library.
58 "Arriva l'omo-monumento," *La Repubblica* (February 9, 1990).

ganizations, as well as deportees and partisans.⁵⁹ The Italian press highlighted how Bologna was now host to the third monument of this kind around the world, after the ones on the grounds of the former concentration camp of Mauthausen and in Amsterdam. Notwithstanding their oversight of other monuments, such as the one in Schöneberg, this press coverage and the inauguration echo the Pink Triangle rhetoric of the ILGA.

Assembled in a famous gay club during a national congress in Bologna, regional delegates of *Arcigay* voted on a project by activist and architect Corrado Levi. What would become the Bologna Triangle was not the only decision that weekend. Having come together to discuss the future of queer politics in Italy, attendees also decided to pressure the municipality of Capri into unveiling a memorial for the queer victims of the former concentration camp of Fossoli.⁶⁰ The next year Franco Grillini, *Arcigay*'s founder, published a piece in the Italian magazine *Contatto* where he explained the idea behind the triangle, the significance of its inauguration on Liberation Day, and the importance of remembering queer victims of fascism.⁶¹ In his essay, Grillini portrayed events in a way that should by now sound familiar to readers of this book: how queer men where the lowest of the low in the camps' hierarchy "just below the Jews," how they had almost no chance of survival, and how their fate was erased after the war.⁶² Grillini also compares how pink triangles were similar to "yellow trriangles" [sic] worn by Jewish victims of the Nazis and emphasizes numerous times the martyrdom of "past homosexuals" during the Holocaust.⁶³ These mentions are not the only tropes drawn from Homocaust narratives. In another piece following Grillini's in the same issue of *Contatto*, the author parallels mentions of a hidden and forgotten Holocaust to the persecution of queerness on a grander scale after the war.⁶⁴ Both pieces revolve around the German-speaking context – §175 StGB, Dachau, Sachsenhausen, the Adenauer era, the HOSI memorial in Austria, etc. – jumping sporadically to the Italian situation to mention the raids and persecutions of the Italian gay and lesbian community during Mussolini's regime of terror.⁶⁵ Grillini's article also stresses how *Arcigay* worked with other political antifascist organizations to uncover police records surrounding the fate of the queer victims of Italian fascism. This back and forth is significant, as it transnationally entraps Italian queer strug-

---

59 Gianni Rossi Barilli, "Un monument alle vittime gay dei lager," *Il Manifesto* (April 26, 1990).
60 "Arriva l'omo-monumento," *La Repubblica* (February 9, 1990).
61 Franco Grillini, "Non solo un anniversario," *Contatto* (June–July 1991): 11–12.
62 Grillini, "Non solo un anniversario": 12.
63 Grillini, "Non solo un anniversario": 12.
64 Giovanni Dall'Orto, "Alcune Note Storiche sui 'Triangoli Rosa,'" *Contatto* (June–July 1991): 12.
65 Grillini, "Non solo un anniversario": 11–12.

gles of the 1990s and the memory of Italian fascism within the fight by queer associations in German-speaking countries. By internationalizing the Italian story, it expands local political memory with the transnational memory of the Second World War, it collectivizes queerness, and legitimizes *Arcigay*'s politics. The Bologna Triangle therefore represents much more than the memory of the men with the pink triangle, it also represents a broader Pink Triangle bridge between Germany, Austria, and Italy. As mentioned in the pages of *Contatto*, the triangle, "once a symbol of despair and the death of thousands of homosexuals was now a symbol of an international gay liberation, a symbol of pride and a warning from the past for the future."[66] On the other hand, these international connections and this discursive appeal to Homocaust narratives surprisingly came with brief references to historical research from abroad. Articles covering the inauguration of the Bologna Triangle also mention the work of Rüdiger Lautmann and his 1970s study of concentration camps.[67] Nevertheless, most of these accounts of historical research were also quick to point out the provisionary aspect of Lautmann's conclusions as well as the possibility of lost or hidden documents. These articles highlighted infamous book burnings at the end of the war when Nazis started to destroy evidence of their crimes against humanity.[68] Thus, the press offered readers an interesting hybrid of historical facts and debunked narratives lingering in Italy or in German-speaking countries. This Emilia-Romagna episode demonstrates how discourses around memory and the Pink Triangle echoed from Germany into neighboring countries that had also been affected by both fascism and the Holocaust. The struggle to integrate German *Vergangenheitsbewältigung* existed beyond the borders of Germany on the European continent, and Pink Triangle bridges were built on the Italian peninsula.

Elsewhere on the continent, these bridges were being created in ways concordant with the ILGA and not necessarily linked to the idea of coming to terms with Italian or German fascism. This next episode takes place in a country intrinsically linked to the international organization. Since the end of the 1970s, queer activists had juggled with the idea of creating a monument "against homophobia" in the Netherlands. Following a successful campaign by one of the oldest queer organizations in the world, *Cultuur en Ontspanningscentrum*, 'Culture and Leisure Center,' and funding by both private and public donors,[69] the Dutch capital unveiled

---

66 Dall'Orto, "Alcune Note Storiche," 12.
67 Barilli, "Un monument alle vittime."
68 Barilli, "Un monument alle vittime."
69 Régis Schlagdenhauffen, *Triangle Rose: La persécution nazie des homosexuels et sa mémoire* (Paris: Autrement, 2011), 190–211.

the first monument[70] to be erected anywhere in memory of the Nazi persecution of queerness in 1987, based on a proposition of artist Karin Daan.[71] The inauguration was well received back in the FRG[72] and eventually became one of Amsterdam's landmarks.[73] The *Homomonument*, as it became known, consists of three Pink Triangles. One of them descends into the waters of the *Keizersgracht* canal and acts as the commemorative space where wreaths of flowers are usually laid on Liberation Day and Remembrance Day. Two other triangles made from pink granite bricks form a bigger triangle connecting the neighboring streets. From this total of four triangles, one points toward the city's Dam Square and the National Monument in memory of the casualties of the Second World War and other armed conflicts, one points toward the headquarters of *Cultuur en Ontspanningscentrum*, and one points toward Anne Frank's house. Daan's *Homomonument* consequently offers a complex narrative mixing the ILGA universal fight against homophobia with a direct connection to the official memory of fascism. First, it is not only dedicated to the victims of the Nazis, but to every homosexual persecuted across the world.[74] It opens a bridge between the past and the present, between events that happened in Europe and a universal collective experience of queerness across the world. It presents the Netherlands as a progressive nation anchored in liberal values and invites the rest of the world to follow in its footsteps. To this end, the city's police forces are invited every year to pledge to fight against the evil of homophobia on the steps of the monument.[75] Second, one of Daan's triangles points toward one of the most recognized Holocaust memorial sites in the country: Anne Frank's house. On the triangle pointing toward the museum, visitors can see verses by gay Dutch Jewish poet Jacob Israël de Haan from his poem, "To a Young Fisherman": *"Naar Vriendschap Zulk een Mateloos Verlan-*

---

70 Outside a former concentration camp.
71 See the official German version of the COC pamphlet about the monument and its design. Schwules Museum Berlin C, Box 199, *Gedenk-Veranstaltungen Homosexuellen-Verfolgung Berlin-Sonstiges*.
72 Tommi Scheer, "Het Monument: Ein erstes Monument für die homosexuellen Opfer des Faschismus . . . oder die Reise zur Einweihung des weltweit ersten Mahnmals zum Gedenken der homosexuellen Opfer des Faschismus," *Dorn Rosa Zeitung der Demokratischen Lesben- und Schwuleninitiative* 9 (1987): 6–7.
73 It is now part of the *Madurodam* miniature park celebrating Dutch landmarks. Other Dutch cities have unveiled monuments for similar purposes. The one in Den Haag resembles a Pink Triangle even if it is not officially recognized. See Agence France Presse, "Denkmal für Homosexuelle," *Frankfurter Rundschau* (October 2, 1993).
74 Schwules Museum Berlin C, Box 199, *Gedenk-Veranstaltungen Homosexuellen-Verfolgung Berlin-Sonstiges*.
75 Schlagdenhauffen, *Triangle Rose*, 190–211.

gen," 'Toward an endless desire for friendship.'[76] The link between official Holocaust memory and queer victims of the Nazis is here apparent. More ambiguous is the use of this gay love declaration – "friendship" in this context – and the connection to Anne Frank. It can be understood as both a positive and empowering statement by a national gay Jewish hero with a tragic story or as a longing for official recognition and acceptance in canonical memory by other official victims. The *Homomonument* is therefore not only important as a precursor of queer memorial discourse, but also for carving into stone a clear perspective on queer persecutions entangled with the Holocaust.[77] Intriguingly, the monument is also used as a location for annual parties, to encourage the positive aspects of the queer community.[78] The injury linked to the Pink Triangle is then reinterpreted as liberation, a symbol of joy, of survival. It changes the urban space accordingly, inviting visitors to memorialize in certain ways, longing for queer utopias, reflecting on what it means to be gay, lesbian, queer, and to be part of an imagined international community.[79] This is not the only place in the Euro-American world that uses Pink Triangle bridges to transmute the negative aspects of the symbol into a call for a positive future. Contrary to the pink radical recuperation in the 1970s, this use of the Pink Triangle is mainly a call to action across the world. It is a celebration of the queer present to simultaneously evoke liberalism, democracy, and human rights. Following the ILGA and its rhetoric, this Pink Triangle connects the persecution of queerness under National Socialism with an assemblage of claims of regarding queer liberation and a universalist approach to queerness.

Pink Triangle bridges have left numerous traces around the Euro-American world. Beyond debates about Homocaust narratives, or the integration of queer

---

76 *Rozen zijn niet zoo schoon als uwe wangen,Tulpen niet als uw bloote voeten teer, En in geen oogen las ik immer meer, Naar vriendschap zulk een mateloos verlangen* (Roses are not as beautiful as your cheeks, Tulips not like your bare feet, And I never read in my eyes, For toward friendship such an endless desire). De Haan was a Jewish Dutch poet who eventually travelled to Palestine, found a Palestinian gay lover before being assassinated by Zionist activists. Gert Hekma, "Jacob Israël De Haan: Pederast Poet between Amsterdam and Jerusalem." In *Die andere Fakultät. Theorie, Geschichte, Gesellschaft*, ed. Florian Mildenberger (Hamburg: Männerschwarm, 2015), 90–110.
77 Martin Zebracki, "Homomonument as Queer Micropublic: An Emotional Geography of Sexual Citizenship," *Tijdschrift voor economische en sociale geografie* 108, no. 3 (2017): 261–364.
78 Homomonument Amsterdam, "Agenda," accessed July 20, 2019, https://www.homomonument.nl/agenda/.
79 See the roundtables on queer monuments and urban spaces published by QWIEN – Zentrum für schwul/lesbische Kultur und Geschichte and WASt – Wiener Antidiskriminierungsstelle für gleichgeschlechtliche und transgender Lebensweisen, *Zu spät?: Dimensionen des Gedenkens an homosexuelle und transgender Opfer des Nationalsozialismus* (Wien: Zaglossus, 2015).

memory of National Socialism on a national scale in the FRG, these selected episodes demonstrate how social and political actors navigated across a plurality of discourses on the Pink Triangle to push one universal storyline. First, Bologna exemplifies how other European organizations appealed to German interpretations of queer memory to make sense of their own local memory of the Second World War, inserting themselves in an international imagined community. Second, the *Homomonument* shows how official memory in a non-German context can further complicate our analysis of Pink Triangle bridges by effectively offering a hybrid of both the memorialization of a state-sanctioned narrative and a grassroots appeal to memories of National Socialism. These are of course not the only possibilities offered by the Pink Triangle. If one leaves Europe, one could look to Australia and its Pink Triangle memorial in Sydney, echoing the one in Amsterdam.[80] Even if one stays anchored in the Atlantic, it is possible to discover memorials using the Pink Triangle as a symbol against queerphobia without ever mentioning National Socialism. For instance, the Spanish city of Sitges unveiled a monument in 2006 to commemorate a riot during which police forces harshly repressed local queer activists. This monument against police brutality, a Pink Triangle, does not reference National Socialism directly.[81] Similarly, the Uruguayan capital's *Plaza de la Diversidad Sexual* reaffirms Montevideo's fight against discrimination, using the Pink Triangle without making a direct claim to the Nazi regime.[82] However, in Tel-Aviv, a 2014 Pink Triangle memorial outside the Municipal LGBT Community Centre obviously refers directly to the pink triangles in the camps.[83] It is by now clear that Pink Triangle bridges are plural, international, and that they offer different yet interconnected memorial discourses. Nonetheless, the petrification or carving into stone of one narrative over another and the appeal to victimhood offered by such monuments also affected the sometimes-difficult relations between members of queer communities, for example the distinctive fights and identification processes of gays and lesbians, the erasure of trans* realities, or the racism permeating white queer spaces. Pink Triangle bridges, from Germany to the United States, from Amsterdam to Montevideo, present a united front against queerphobia, but also universalize

---

[80] "Our Monument" Pamphlet for crowd funding project for the monument. Schwules Museum Berlin C, Box 199, *Gedenk-Veranstaltungen Homosexuellen-Verfolgung Berlin-Sonstiges.*
[81] Pink News Staff Write, "Monument against homophobia in Sitges" (October 11, 2006), accessed April 13, 2020, https://www.pinknews.co.uk/2006/10/11/monument-against-homophobia-in-sitges/.
[82] Joseph Orangias, Jeannie Simms, and Sloane Fremch, "The Cultural Functions and Social Potential of Monuments: A Preliminary Inventory and Analysis," *Journal of Homosexuality* 65, no. 6 (2018): 708.
[83] BBC, "Tel Aviv unveils first memorial to gay Holocaust victims" BBC (January 10, 2014), accessed January 20, 2023, https://www.bbc.com/news/world-europe-25687190.

Euro-American history. As an allegory, the Pink Triangle historicizes, but also universalizes queer struggles. However – as a symbol – the triangle offers still a third idiom, a way for queer activists to recognize each other, a 'patent of nobility' legitimizing and historicizing a quest for human rights. Nonetheless, this patent of nobility remains a badge of universalization, a badge of Euro-American history.

7 A badge of survival – AIDS activism, Pink Triangles, and an aesthetic of injury

San Francisco's high society got more than they had bargained as they entered the halls of the city's opera house in early autumn 1989. Having bought tickets for the premiere of Verdi's Falstaff, the audience was denied a comic and lyrical escapade from the times of the House of Lancaster and instead confronted with the abrupt presence of many residents of the Castro and Tenderloin districts, historically underprivileged neighborhoods and culturally significant for the queer community of the Bay Area.

This was at the height of the HIV/AIDS crisis on the West Coast and activists from the local chapter of the *AIDS Coalition to Unleash Power* (ACT UP) insisted on the emergency of the situation. Pouring through the venue during the overture, hundreds of AIDS activists bearing t-shirts emblazoned with Pink Triangles distributed leaflets and flyers all the while chanting epidemic related slogans. The audience were then further startled by the dropping of 10,000 pink paper triangles from a balcony onto the spectators.[1] Minutes later, the activists were gone. Their action was covered in every local newspaper the next morning.[2] The Bay Area's ACT UP activists were already infamous for their blockade of the Golden Bridge during rush hour nine months prior. While many San Franciscans opposed the action, some congratulated them, applauding the coalition for bringing a breath of fresh air in times of death and governmental inaction.[3] One reader of the *San Francisco Sentinel* even compared other established AIDS support groups to the *Judenrat*, 'Jewish Councils,' of Nazi Germany, linking the HIV/AIDS crisis to National Socialism and the Holocaust:

> ACT UP, like any other organization, makes its share of mistakes. However, their constant, dramatic, public actions have reminded the majority of us of the urgent necessity to demand a cure in the face of possible genocide. In the last Holocaust, two-thirds of the Jewish population of Europe were murdered. The unthinkable has happened once. It must never happen again.[4]

---

1 Gerard Koskovich, "San Francisco's Waiyde Palmer: No more Mr. Nice Guy," *The Advocate* (February 13, 1990): 4.
2 For example: "Opera Protest," *The San Francisco Chronicle* (September 12, 1989). For a reaction in the community, see an exchange of letters in the *Bay Are Reporter*. Mike Greathouse, "Don't Shut Up," *Bay Area Reporter* (September 28, 1989); Jim Smith, "Confrontation Doesn't Work," *Bay Area Reporter* (September 14, 1989).
3 Stanley Kern, "Chorus of Boos," *San Francisco Chronicle* (July 2, 1989).
4 Lee Heller, "Act Up Too Conservative," *San Francisco Sentinel* (July 6, 1989).

On the other side of the continent, AIDS activists had drawn similar conclusions in cities like New York, where they had founded the first chapter of ACT UP in 1987 and where the epidemic was at its most dire. There, ACT UP activists infiltrated the city's stock exchange in suits and ties – known to them as 'Wall Street drag' – chained themselves to the VIP balcony and paralysed the country's financial stronghold while being drowned in the queerphobic chants of traders down below.[5] During the same period, one of the group's estranged founders, Larry Kramer, published his first-person account of the crisis, entitled *Reports from the Holocaust*.[6]

ACT UP's style of AIDS activism found echoes across the continent as well as in Western Europe, where the coalition's tactics and in-your-face actions inspired political momentum in countries like Germany, France, and the Netherlands. The name ACT UP became a brand and their recuperation of the Pink Triangle as a symbol added another layer to the icon and its connection to a queer past of injury. It linked a remembrance of Nazi atrocities to a sense of emergency in the present. Focusing on more than just the persecutions to legitimate and historicize contemporary struggles that had been the raison d'être of the pink radicals in West Germany, queer AIDS activists emphasized survivorship, warning their community that the epidemic was a new genocide, a new battle that could also well be lost. This new recuperation of the Pink Triangle by queer AIDS activists simultaneously appealed to the utopic and dystopic nature of Pink Triangle bridges. On the one hand, ACT UP underlined tragedies of the past firmly anchored in the symbol since the first recuperations in the 1970s. In so doing, they highlighted the necessity to fight for a world denuded of queerphobia, a queer utopia. Yet they also foretold the death of their community in the case of political inaction, using examples from the queer past, from an archive of suffering, to call fellow queers to arms and to the barricades.

This genealogy of survival – from National Socialism to the HIV/AIDS crisis – is intimately connected with Euro-American queer memory, but also to the transmission of feelings and discourses through the power of images across the Atlantic. This chapter examines the story of ACT UP and Euro-American AIDS activism, focusing on the multilayered aspects of the Pink Triangle as a referent to genocide. Once again using the symbol as a prism, this chapter brings forward Pink Triangle bridges, that is, the link between history, memory, and the visual, com-

---

[5] David Handelman, "Act Up in Anger," *Rolling Stone* (March 8, 1990).
[6] Larry Kramer, *Reports from the Holocaust: The Story of an Aids Activist*, Updated and Expanded. ed. (New York, NY: St. Martin's Press, 1994).

bined through sensual political encounters – *politische sinnlichkeit*[7] 'political perception through the senses' – in the public space. The Pink Triangle is therefore central to the understanding of AIDS activism in the Euro-American world. By focusing on the symbol's trajectory, it is possible to appreciate the numerous activist connections between various regional spaces at the height of the HIV/AIDS crisis in Europe, the 1980s and the 1990s.[8]

Looking back at the incorporation of ACT UP's approaches in European AIDS activism, it is possible to see this evolution of the triangle's journey as a logical step. It originated on the same path as the *Homosexuelle Aktion Westberlin* (HAW) recuperation and parallels our discussion on the multidirectional memory of National Socialism in the Euro-American world – see section 3.1. At the time, scholars were already describing AIDS activism as a new social movement and analyzing it in terms that will sound familiar after our encounter with the HAW in the first chapter of this book – see section 1.2. Indeed, in a 1989-piece, sociologist Josh Gamson emphasized ACT UP's use and flaunting of gay campness as a political strategy. According to him, both the use of safe-sex sex positivity – "fuck me safe" t-shirts – and the use of the Pink Triangle instrumentalized the stigma of perversion and queerphobia to make a point about queerness.[9]

However, as much as this kind of recuperation of the symbol recalls the first reuse of the triangle in West Germany during the 1970s, I propose viewing this later usage of the Pink Triangle in a different light. For example, ACT UP chapters in Berlin and Cologne who printed the Pink Triangle on their mobilization material were not necessarily reproducing the same Pink Triangles as the one brand-

---

7 Reinhart Koselleck, "Die Transformation der politischen Totenmale im 20. Jahrhundert." In *Zeitgeschichte als Streitgeschichte: Große Kontroverse nach 1945*, ed. Martin Sabrow, Ralph Jessen and Klaus Große Kracht (München: C. H Beck, 2003), 205–228; Hubert Locher, "'Politische Ikonologie' und 'Politische Sinnlichkeit': Bild-Diskurs und historische Erfahrung nach Reinhart Koselleck." In *Reinhart Koselleck und die politische Ikonologie*, ed. Hubert Locher and Adriana Markantonatos (Munich: Deutscher Kunstverlag, 2013), 14–31. On Koselleck and the material turn, see Bettina Brandt, Britta Hochkirchen, and Thomas Thiel, *Reinhart Koselleck und das Bild: Begleitung Broschüre* (Herzebrock-Clarholz: Heinrich Eusterhus, 2018); Margrit Pernau, "Space and Emotion: Building to Feel," *History Compass* 12 (2014): 541–549.
8 I mention here "the heights of the crisis" to underline the ongoing nature of the crisis. HIV/AIDS may be less of an attention-grabbing topic than in the 1980s and 1990s, but the epidemic still kills thousands and its displacement toward other parts of the population or other geographical spaces should not be confused with an end of the epidemic. Queer historians have recently criticized a certain tendency in the historiography of HIV/AIDS that relegates the disease to the past and the preceding century. See John Petrus, "Discussing the Undiscussable: Reflecting on the 'End' of Aids," *GLQ: A Journal of Lesbian and Gay Studies* 25, no. 1 (2019): 67–72.
9 Josh Gamson, "Silence, Death, and the Invisible Enemy: AIDS Activism and Social Movement 'Newness,'" *Social Problems* 36, no. 4 (1989): 362.

ished by the HAW. As we will see, the Pink Triangle of ACT UP was only possible as a sum of the transatlantic episodes seen across the previous decades. What is more, its transatlantic voyage came full circle as the symbol travelled back to its origins in the Federal Republic of Germany (FRG), confronting local, political, and memorial, contexts in Germany with decades of North American memory and a story of queer internationalism. This importation of a new triangle in the homeland of National Socialism and the pink radicals was not only abstract. The triangle also concretely travelled from one continent to the other, from North America to Western Europe. Andreas Salmen, an important figure for this chapter and the creator of ACT UP Berlin, organized a bulk purchase of Pink Triangle t-shirts during a trip to New York City. Activists in Germany had until then organized shipping of Pink Triangle material through an ACT UP chapter in Edinburgh.[10]

This chapter investigates three points of analysis. First, North American AIDS activism was based partly on negative longings for the past and a queer memory of National Socialism. By this I mean that the core of AIDS activism and the rhetoric of AIDS activists were based on victimhood narratives connected to German history as it was received in the Euro-American world. This is not without comparisons to our discussion on the universalization of queerness through the Pink Triangle. Second, political activists fighting for governmental action, against repression, and for an end to the epidemic were crossing the same 'Pink Triangles bridges' that were built in the 1970s and 1980s and touched upon in the last chapter – see section 6.3. It is impossible to disentangle the Pink Triangle from its dialectical journey back and forth over the Atlantic. For example, during a 1987 demonstration in Bavaria against the repressive measures of the *Christlich-Soziale Union*, Christian Social Union, (CSU) concerning homosexuals and people living with HIV/AIDS, a demonstrator held a Pink Triangle sign facing downward, advocating for safer sex and denouncing governmental decisions in language reminiscent of the Nazi era – "Condoms instead of Gauweiler Pogroms."[11] This poster was possible due to memorial debates already touched upon in this book, as well as the discursive influences of the Pink Triangle relating to queer dystopias, an expectation of a queer demise

---

10 See annotated ACT UP/Los Angeles merchandise orders from ACT UP Edinburgh. Schwules Museum Berlin, Archive *Unsortiert Thematic Act UP*. The archives of the Schwules Museum in Berlin are in possession of nine boxes of unsorted material connected to ACT UP Berlin and other German chapters of the coalition. I went through all the material in 2019. Nothing had been catalogued yet.

11 Peter Gauweiler was a key figure behind the drastic prophylactic measures pushed forward by the Bavarian government in the late 1980s. See Tremblay, "Visual Collective Memories," 565; Henning Tümmers, *AIDS: Autopsie einer Bedrohung im geteilten Deutschland* (Göttingen: Wallstein Verlag, 2017); Sebastian Haus-Rybicki, *Eine Seuche Regieren. AIDS-Prävention in der Bundesrepublik 1981–1995* (Bielefeld: transcript, 2021).

ordered by the state. Finally, uses of the Pink Triangle were intrinsically linked to a double aesthetics of survival: Facing downward = National Socialism / facing upward = HIV/AIDS crisis. Lauren Berlant has investigated how reading and learning about the atrocities endured and survived by its perceived predecessors, a community can find a reason to fight for its own survival.[12] As a badge of survival, the Pink Triangle reinforced an international queer sense of belonging.

In the introduction of his canonical 2005 book on the global response to the HIV/AIDS crisis, Peter Baldwin opens his far-reaching examination of politics in an age of catastrophe and queer trauma with a statement about the historiography of a plague. In his words, "much has been written on AIDS, but much of it is journalistic and of the first generation. Little of it is broadly synthetic, most is restricted to evidence from one nation or in one language, and almost none applies a longer historical perspective."[13] During the last decade, historians have tackled the consequences of the disease for queer history, especially in discussion regarding the death of the archive and its sociological effects on promiscuity and lifestyles outside heteronormativity, including sex-negative and sex-positive commentaries of a now mythical "before AIDS" era. In other words, temporalizing HIV/AIDS meant creating the myth that life "before" was a life of pleasure and hedonism that was now no more. In a recent piece, Jim Hubbard mentions how this destruction of the queer archive through the many deaths due to the epidemic is connected to the loss of a generational transmission of memory.[14] Temporalizing the epidemic also meant rethinking sex and queer spaces. Activists like Rosa von Praunheim (in the FRG), Larry Kramer (in the USA), and Didier Lestrade (in France) platformed ideas against promiscuity, picturing barebacking and new possibilities offered by new medical treatments – such as PrEP[15] – as dangerous. This last example shows the

---

[12] Lauren Berlant, "Introduction: Affect in the Present." In *Cruel Optimism*, ed. Lauren Berlant (Durham, NC: Duke University Press, 2011), 1–22.
[13] Peter Baldwin, *Disease and Democracy: The Industrialized World Faces AIDS* (Berkeley, CA: University of California Press, 2005), 5.
[14] In other words, temporalizing AIDS meant creating the myth that life 'before' was a life of pleasure and hedonism, which was destroyed by the trauma of the disease. Jim Hubbard mentioned how this 'destruction' of the queer archive – through deaths due to the epidemic – is connected to the loss of a generational transmission of memory. Jim Hubbard "AIDS-Videoaktivismus und die Entstehung des 'Archivs.'" In *Queer Cinema*, ed. Dagmar Brunow and Simon Dickel (Mainz: Ventil Verlag, 2018), 82–105. For a good example – in French – of this new queer sex-negativity, see Didier Lestrade's interview with Thierry Ardisson in May 2004: INA Fr, "Didier Lestrade à 'Tout le Monde en Parle,'" YouTube, accessed October 20, 2020, https://www.youtube.com/watch?v=4dAqIBtT5Wc&t=239s.
[15] Pre-exposure Prophylaxis or PrEP implies the use of antiviral medication by someone who has not been exposed yet and does this preventively.

cleavage created by a traumatic moment in queer history. Survivors of the beginning of the HIV/AIDS crisis eventually opposed the behaviour of a new generation. This brings up a lot of questions not covered in this chapter. What does this mean for queer postmemory? How does the trauma of AIDS reshape desires and habits in queer spaces? Can we really talk about sex-negativity when analysing the traumatic reaction of survivors? Does this mean that desire or sex became traumatic for these men?

Recent essays have also pointed out that as the cartography of HIV/AIDS shifted outside of the northern Atlantic world, a new generation of – mostly – white gay men seem to talk about the disease as an eradicated plague. This historicizing of AIDS effectively renders the danger of relegating the present to an imaginary world where the crisis ended, a post epidemic era.[16] There is thus a paradox at the core of this chapter. It investigates the 'spectrability' of the disease – the AIDS ghosts of the past – in the queer present while also avoiding reducing the epidemic to a ghost haunting the pages of history books and the testimonies of those who remained. To put it differently, it must touch on the lingering effects of a traumatic queer past from the 1980s and 1990s without historicizing the disease so much as to ignore its contemporaneity. The following pages, therefore, need to be understood as an answer to both tasks awaiting queer historiography: mapping the entanglements of the HIV/AIDS crisis while anchoring the epidemic in its present. What is more, the object of study at the core of this chapter, that is, the link between queer memory, queer activism, and AIDS activism, should not obscure the multifaceted aspects of the disease, that is, the fact that it is far from being only a 'gay disease.'

7.1 Act up! coalitions, direct action and emancipation

In the spring of 1987, a tumultuous crowd gathered in the Lesbian and Gay Community Center in New York City. Those present were listening to a speech by activist, playwright, and agitator Larry Kramer, who galvanized the crowd with his ardent criticism of Gay Men's Health Crisis, the first worldwide association to help seropositive individuals. Kramer had co-founded Gay Men's Health Crisis following a meeting in his living room. Having left the group some years before, he was now denouncing its alleged institutionalization and inaction. Six years had passed since the *New York Times* first published their piece about a new and

---

16 Petrus, "Discussing the Undiscussable."

strange cancer afflicting homosexuals.[17] The government was ignoring the crisis. After years of a terrifying epidemic with no end in sight, significant delays in getting access to medication, and mainstream society openly talking about forced quarantine, the men amassed in Lower Manhattan had reached their breaking point. At the end of his speech, channelling his anger and the emergency of the situation, Kramer screamed at the crowd that they could all be dead the week afterward. Would they stay there and do nothing, or would they finally fight back? One week later, the AIDS Coalition to Unleash Power was created.[18] As in North America, German queers did not passively accept their fate; they organized. *Deutsche Aids-Hilfe*, 'German AIDS Service Organizations,' were created in the FRG. In Berlin, places like *Mann-O-Meter* in the district of Schöneberg were created in the mid-1980s to spread prevention and support for people living with AIDS. Communication networks inherited from previous decades were used to organize hotlines and to educate.[19]

During a time when a diagnosis seemed to be synonymous with a death sentence, when queers lived in fear of a phone call from an ex-affair, and when the previous decades of sexual liberation were now perceived as being the cause of their community's demise, governmental silence and media-spread hysteria seemed to be the last blow to the utopic aspirations of queer liberation. As the community tried to understand if it was responsible for its own destruction, the far right started pushing forward ideas of divine retribution[20] and mainstream news outlets reported on the so-called sexual perversion of society.[21] President Ronald Reagan deliberately took years to mention the epidemic and the federal government hindered any concerted effort on a national scale. During this period, activists were

---

17 Lawrence K. Altman, "Rare Cancer seen in 41 Homosexuals," *The New York Times* (July 3, 1981).
18 Here I somewhat romanticize the story. Larry Kramer was chastized many times for having taken credit for the founding of ACT UP. MS ACT UP: The AIDS Coalition to Unleash Power: Series III. Correspondence. Box 8, Folder 6, *ACT UP / NY*. April–June 1990, New York Public Library.
19 See, for example, the monthly advertisement campaigns for the *Rosa Telefon* in most issues of *Kellerjournal* in the 1980s.
20 Simon Watney, "The Spectacle of AIDS." In *October* 43 AIDS: Cultural Analysis, Cultural Activism (1988), 71–86; Eric A. Feldman and Ronald Bayer, *Blood Feuds: AIDS, Blood, and the Politics of Medical Disaster* (Oxford: Oxford University Press, 1999); Sebastian Haus, "Risky Sex: Risky Language HIV/AIDS and the West German Gay Scene in the 1980s," *Historical Social Research* 41, no. 1 (2016): 111–134; Christopher Castiglia and Christopher Reed, *If Memory Serves: Gay Men, AIDS, and the Promise of the Queer Past* (Minneapolis, MI: University of Minnesota Press, 2012).
21 Reactions in the population followed. See, for example, letters comparing homosexuals to Nazis in "Letters to Editors," *New York Post* (December 30, 1989).

screaming the names of their deceased loved ones at protests, fighting to get those in power to pay attention to what was happening.[22]

For example, Steven Rose, a person living with AIDS, wrote to the White House many times in the second half of the 1980s. When the First Lady laconically responded that he would be in her household's prayers, his riposte was snarky: "I sincerely thank you for writing and hope that I have introduced AIDS as a topic of family discussion at your house, as it is at mine."[23] Rose's tone is understandable when looking at the context of the era. As journalist – and later essayist – Richard Goldstein mentioned in an article in the *Village Voice*, HIV/AIDS not only created a stigmatized class of victims, it also took a stigmatized class of individuals – queers, people who inject drugs, sex workers, etc. – and made them victims of both the plague and society's answer to the plague.[24] When society discovered that queers and other 'undesirables' were not the sole victims of this affliction, widespread panic erupted in many countries.

In the words of Goldstein, "stigma is the reason an AIDS patient in North Carolina, being transferred from one hospital to another, arrived wrapped in a body bag with a small air tube protruding so he could breathe. Stigma is the reason a plane carrying demonstrators to the gay rights march on Washington was fumigated when the passengers departed."[25] As political forces in the Euro-American world refused to talk about safer sex in schools in order to avoid promoting "alternative lifestyles" and to "protect the youth,"[26] companies like Delta and Luf-

---

[22] See for example Cleve Jones's famous AIDS Quilt project: The AIDS Memorial Quilt (The NAMES Project Foundation, "History of the Quilt," accessed October 17, 2019, https://www.aidsquilt.org/about/the-aids-memorial-quilt.

[23] "Letter by Steven G. Rose to President Bush, September 10, 1989" and "Letter by Barbara Bush to Steven G. Rose on October 16, 1989." In Rose, G. Steven Major Subjects: AIDS Coalition to Unleash Power (ACT UP); AIDS Memorial Quilt; Johnson, Earvin 'Magic'; Maine; Medication/Treatment; Research/Funding. May 22, 1988–February 5, 1992; n.d. TS The Bush Administration and the AIDS Crisis: White House Office of Records Management: Alphabetical Files 200405, 103258, 298258, 76147, 91057. Answer to Barbara Bush's letter on October 20, 1989. In Rose, G. Steven Major Subjects: AIDS Coalition to Unleash Power (ACT UP); AIDS Memorial Quilt; Johnson, Earvin 'Magic'; Maine; Medication/Treatment; Research/Funding. May 22, 1988–February 5, 1992; n.d. TS The Bush Administration and the AIDS Crisis: White House Office of Records Management: Alphabetical Files 200405, 103258, 298258, 76147, 91057.

[24] Richard Goldstein, "AIDS and the Social Contract," *The Village Voice* (December 17, 1989): 14–16.

[25] Goldstein, "AIDS and the Social Contract," 16.

[26] In the United States Congress, Jesse Helms pushed legislation to block any form of funding for queer organizations and AIDS prevention tied to sexual education. In Bavaria, Peter Gauweiler passed repressive legislation against people living with AIDS (and especially queer men).

thansa refused service to people living with either the virus or the disease.[27] Governments seemed to be unwilling to react as long as the epidemic only appeared to target sexual misfits. For instance, August Lang, then Bavarian Minister of the Interior, complained that it would be career suicide to go to beer tents and *Schützenverein* – 'shooting clubs' – to explain why his party would be theoretically spending money on "faggots." At the same time, Bavarian tabloids warned their readers to stop using public razors in the country's train stations to avoid contracting the "gay disease."[28] In the FRG and in the USA, the gay press continued to cover an ongoing repressive climate. Denunciation campaigns were organized against anti-immigration measures targeting people living with AIDS by the Bush administration and articles were sharing information about treatments, the disease, and support groups. Housing committees were also formed in cities like Cologne, West Berlin, and on the east and west coasts of the United States.

7.2 AIDS activism and international knowledge transfers

As stipulated in its early beginning in New York, the goal of ACT UP was "to demonstrate our anger and frustration at this intolerable situation, create a critical mass of informed public opinion and influence our leaders to take constructive action."[29] The coalition's activists organized along horizontal political lines, meeting once a week in an assembly that could last for hours. These assemblies – known as "the Floor" – consisted of announcements, decisions about actions, and votes on various issues according to a one-person one-vote practice. Each member could also partake in one or more subcommittees responsible for specific tasks: budgeting, "zaps" – flash-mob-like actions to disrupt or create visibility, media, ad hoc specificities, etc. Over the years, these subcommittees also became affinity groups with special targets in mind, showcasing both the significance of the HIV/AIDS crisis and the diverse makeup of the organization: a women's committee, a so-called majority committee – a tongue-in-cheek name for the committee responsible for marginalized groups and racial issues, a committee for people who use drugs, etc. If it is true that a coordination committee was responsible for

---

[27] Both rules were challenged by activists and eventually abandoned by the respective companies following the protests.
[28] "Streit um 'Unzucht' im Maximilianeum," *Abendzeitung* (June 16/17, 1988); Barbara Bredl, "AIDS-Gefahr! Werden Miet-Rasierer am Hauptbahnhof verboten?," *BILD-München* (September 19, 1988).
[29] MS ACT UP: The AIDS Coalition to Unleash Power: Series II. Minutes Box 3, Folder 4. *ACT UP / NY Minutes, July 1987*, New York Public Library.

the organization of the meetings and the coordination of communications, it was clear from the start that the Floor made any possibility of having an elected board untenable. In fact, the coordination committee had no real power, adding another layer of bureaucracy to the organization. Such a system created a context in which great orators were in fact able to direct the group and power structures were concentrated in the hands of cis white middle-class men who became famous as a result. This core group of AIDS activists eventually gained national exposure.

Over time, the provocative attitude and anarchist in-your-face confrontations pushed by the coalition attracted the ire of others not only in New York, but also on a national scale.[30] Tensions among the 300 or so people present on the Floor each week also evolved into various conflicts based on intersectional issues like race, gender, and class. In this sense, ACT UP was a microcosm of the queer community at large. Media-savvy and using guerrilla art forms, ACT UP members managed to attract both the attention of the mainstream and queer press, as well as pushing the government to finally 'act up' in some ways, and pushing for affordable treatment. Along the way, these New Yorkers blocked Wall Street, disrupted municipal events, denounced the gay establishment, occupied the Center for Disease Control and Prevention and the National Institute of Health, shut down the Food and Drug Administration for a day,[31] occupied St. Patrick's Cathedral in Midtown to denounce the Catholic Church's stance on AIDS and homosexuality,[32] and thrown the ashes of AIDS victims onto the White House.[33]

ACT UP's presence in national events snowballed into a lasting national coalition of local organizations influenced by the deeds of their sisters and brothers in the Empire State. Taking part in the March on Washington for Lesbian and Gay

---

30 Following the third annual Lesbian and Gay Pride March in Provincetown, MA on July 23, 1989, a controversy splattered the local media for weeks. During a demonstration, one of the ACT UP activists present at the march had a sign stating: "Legalize Butt-Fucking." This irked some residents and other gay activists in the region. Open letters, speeches, and articles followed this small *éclat*. See MS ACT UP: The AIDS Coalition to Unleash Power: Series IV. Actions/Demonstrations/Zaps 1987–1995, Box 14, Folder 11 *Actions / Demonstrations / Zaps, Provincetown Gay Pride and Follow-Up, Provincetown, MA. July–August, 1989*, New York Public Library.
31 MS ACT UP: The AIDS Coalition to Unleash Power: Series IV. Actions/Demonstrations/Zaps 1987–1995, Box 13, Folder 1–3. *Demonstration master list 1987–1991, ACT UP / NY*, New York Public Library.
32 MS ACT UP: The AIDS Coalition to Unleash Power: Series IV. Actions/Demonstrations/Zaps 1987–1995, Box 15, Folder 1–2 *Stop the Church Action, ACT UP / NY*, New York Public Library.
33 MS ACT UP: The AIDS Coalition to Unleash Power: Series IV. Actions/Demonstrations/Zaps 1987–1995, Box 18, Folder 10 *Ashes, [Washington,] DC, 1992 Oct, ACT UP / NY*, New York Public Library.

Rights 1987,³⁴ ACT UP also became one of the leading groups behind the organization of the march, to the displeasure of some members on the Floor.³⁵ However, by lending some of their posters, material, and branding capacity to other groups partaking in this historic demonstration in the District of Columbia,³⁶ the New York militants managed to influence other activists in other parts of the country and to light the spark of a new form of activism. Most famously, activists banded together in Los Angeles, clearly stating in their initial outreach material how the New Yorkers, walking on the nation's capital side by side with them, had been a strong influence.³⁷

More than a simple organization, ACT UP became an international movement. Chapters inspired by – but not necessarily connected to – ACT UP New York started to use similar tactics and structures. Most of these chapters developed a national or transnational network of communication to keep in touch with each other, to share knowledge about the disease or the virus and to organize international campaigns.³⁸ For example, the Boston chapter covered part of the legal fees of the Californian activists who blocked the Golden Gate Bridge in the Bay Area³⁹ and in the

---

34 The March on Washington of 1987, also known as the Second National March on Washington for Lesbian and Gay Rights, was triggered by the HIV/AIDS crisis and the inaction and denial of the Reagan administration. It featured prominent AIDS activist groups and attracted national coverage. The symbol of the walk was a Pink Triangle with a silhouette of the Capitol building, home to the United States Congress. On the day following the march, activists unleashed a series of civil disobedience actions near the Supreme Court building.

35 Fed-up with ACT UP New York having to facilitate most of the march directives, one member declared during one assembly, "[w]e are not the coordination committee of the March of Washington!" Members were invited to take civil disobedience classes offered by ACT UP for the march and invited to bring huge Pink Triangle signs fixed on wooden poles. MS ACT UP: The AIDS Coalition to Unleash Power: Series II. Minutes Box 3, Folder 3 *ACT UP / NY Minutes, May – June 1987*, Folder 7 *ACT UP / NY Minutes, October 1987*, New York Public Library.

36 In the minutes of a meeting on July 27, 1987: "ACT UP voted to give the rights to March of Washington to use the SILENCE=DEATH buttons, exclusive of New York and exclusive of Washington D.C. during the March on Washington as a fund-raiser and that ACT UP attempt to use this to gain leverage with March on Washington." MS ACT UP: The AIDS Coalition to Unleash Power: Series II. Minutes Box 3, Folder 4 *ACT UP / NY Minutes, July 1987*, New York Public Library.

37 Press Release, "Action: Immigration and Naturalization Service (INS)-Los Angeles," ONE National Gay & Lesbian Archives, ACT UP Los Angeles Records: Actions and Events 1987–1997, Box 4, Folder 8. *ACT UP L.A. December 23 (1987). Actions and Events 1987–1997*.

38 For accounts of ACT UP chapters in Cologne, see Ulrich Würdemann, *Schweigen = Tod, Aktion = Leben: Act up in Deutschland 1989 Bis 1993* (Berlin: Thomas Michalak, 2017). For Paris, see Christophe Broqua, *Agir pour ne pas mourir!: ACT UP, les homosexuels et le sida* (Paris: Presses de la Fondation nationale des sciences politiques, 2005).

39 MS ACT UP: The AIDS Coalition to Unleash Power: Series IV. Chapters 1986–1993 (United States) Box 26, Folder 15 *Golden Gate, ACT UP / NY*, New York Public Library.

FRG, newly created chapters in Berlin and Cologne supported a Marlboro boycott organized by their US peers.[40]

Moreover, these various antennae of transatlantic AIDS activism reproduced some of their actions across both continents, spicing things up with a local flavor. Similar to the deeds of chapters on the east coast of the United States, various German chapters of ACT UP occupied the cathedral in Fulda, one of their better-known actions.[41] In Canada, a chapter in Montréal invited their comrades in the United States to help them storm the French Canadian metropolis's World Trade Center during an international conference in the city.[42] This last action in Montréal can also be considered as one of the sparks of an international AIDS activism, as it forced authorities to listen to people living with AIDS and grassroots organizations during their conventions on the epidemic.[43] As the planning of the next AIDS conferences later revealed, authorities ended up fearing the anger of ACT UP activists and dreading a repetition of the events in Montréal.[44] These fears eventually forced collaboration between activist circles and government agencies, giving the coalition a role of facilitator in the name of people living with AIDS. Simply put, ACT UP's success and standing was anchored in its internationalism.

---

40 Schwules Museum Berlin, Archive *Unsortiert Thematic: ACT UP*.
41 Like the action in the St. Patrick's Cathedral in New York City, the one during the German Bishop Conference was extremely controversial in Germany at the time. When Archbishop Dyba propagated the rumours that ACT UP activists had beaten up church attendees, activists from ACT UP Frankfurt (Main) sued him for defamation and lost. This court action by the Hessian chapter was central to its political activities for months after the events and financial support came from other regional chapters. See "Zivilklage gegen Dyba abgewiesen," *Fuldaer Zeitung*, (February 28, 1992); "Ermittlungen gegen Dyba eingestellt,"*Fuldaer Zeitung*, (February 21, 1992); "Presseerklärung von ACT UP Frankfurt zur Einstellung des Ermittlungsverfahrens gegen Bischof Dyba vom 20.02.1992 und zur Klageabweisung vom 27.02.1992," Schwules Museum Berlin, Archive *Unsortiert, Thematic: ACT UP*. For the crowdfunding campaign, see: "Protokoll des europäischen ACT UP Treffens in Berlin 16–17 Januar 1993" in Schwules Museum Berlin, Archive *Unsortiert, Thematic: ACT UP*.
42 MS ACT UP: The AIDS Coalition to Unleash Power: Series IV. Chapters 1986–1993 (International) Box 28, Folder 20 *Montréal, Québec, ACT UP / NY*, New York Public Library.
43 Ron Charles, "Huge AIDS meet overflows Palais," *Montreal Daily News* (June 5, 1989); Gabriel Girard et Alexandre Klein, "Les leçons de la conférence de Montréal de 1989 sur le sida," *Le Devoir* (5 June 2019); France Paradis, "Sida: reculer les frontières des croyances," *La Presse* (June 5, 1989); Alain Dubuc, "Le congrès sur le sida est devenu celui des sidéens," *La Presse*, (June 8, 1989).
44 "This year many delegates worried that San Francisco would be like Montreal only worse. ACT UP has grown in numbers and power and was planning to make a splash. One of its founders, Mr. Larry Kramer, had called for riots." "On the AIDS Barricades," *The Economist* (June 30, 1990): 79–81.

Mentions of international connections between different organizations who happen to share similar cognomens do not necessarily imply entanglements and similarities beyond the symbolic. The path chosen by European ACT UP chapters, while being part of an international fellowship of AIDS activists, was very much anchored in local contexts. For example, going beyond geographical differences, ACT UP Paris differed from ACT UP chapters in Germany and the United States. French activists developed their own reactions to the crisis and adopted the name of the coalition, but not necessarily similar political lines. Two members of ACT UP in Germany, Harry Hauck in Berlin and Helles Roth in Frankfurt (Main) spoke about the nuances of the coalition's international connections in a letter to the German gay magazine *Magnus* at the beginning of the 1990s: "We're not going to wait to get a certificate from the USA to call us Act Up. We understand ourselves in the tradition of these groups and are in contact with them."[45] Nonetheless, events on the future of ACT UP in the Federal Republic often seem to have given importance to panel discussions regarding the similarities and differences of the coalition in both its US origins and German manifestations.[46]

At the end of the 1980s, one member of the Berlin *Deutsche AIDS-Hilfe* published a piece in *Siegessäule*, 'Victory Column,'[47] about the accomplishments of ACT UP and the struggles of US Americans with the HIV/AIDS crisis. The author, Andreas Salmen, covered both the repression promoted by the legislative branch in Washington – for example, the actions of Congressman Jesse Helms – and ACT UP's focus on civil disobedience.[48] Tracing the history of civil disobedience from the abolition of slavery to the civil rights movement, Salmen simultaneously offered his readers a list of actions by AIDS activists in the United States. He closed his piece with a plea for the creation of something similar in the FRG, a way to go beyond bureaucracy with political action:

> What we need is not another council or board, but publicly visible actions. What is necessary is not a few witty lines, but the representation of our own interests in public space [. . .].

---

[45] Harry Hauck and Helles Roth, "Leserbrief an die Magnus Redaktion" in Schwules Museum Berlin, Archive *Unsortiert Thematic: ACT UP*.
[46] "Act Up Tagung in Akademie Waldschlösschen, 14–16 Februar 1992, Protokoll" in Schwules Museum Berlin, Archive *Unsortiert Thematic: ACT UP*.
[47] The magazine is named after a Prussian monument standing in the middle of *Großer Stern* 'big star,' a traffic square at the center of Tiergarten. Not far away from the monument is the *Löwenbrücke* 'the lion bridge,' a known cruising spot for queer men since the Wilhelmine era.
[48] A term he translated as *ziviler Ungehorsam*. Andreas Salmen, "Wie sich US-Schwule wehren," *Siegessäule* (March 1988): 6–8. The article even attracted the attention of members of ACT UP New York. MS ACT UP: The AIDS Coalition to Unleash Power: Series II. Minutes Box 3, Folder 14, *ACT UP / NY Minutes, July 1988*, New York Public Library.

> Many gay men are not only fighting for their lives in the United States, but also here in Berlin and the Federal Republic. What we need is not a new bureaucratic structure, but a gay action group in Berlin.[49]

Salmen also highlighted how Berlin, the German city with the most people living with AIDS in the 1980s, could also draw from its own political history in order to fight against the epidemic and force the government into action:

> Gays occupied houses in Berlin in the early 1980s, they took part in the great blockades of the US Army barracks during the Peace Movement in 1984, and they actively took part in the campaign boycotting the census. Why shouldn't we use these methods of nonviolent resistance for our issues and against increasing suppression of gay emancipation?[50]

In the following year, Andreas Salmen eventually went on to create ACT UP Berlin. Not only concerned with the fate of queer men, ACT UP Berlin, like its sisters and brothers from ACT UP New York, highlighted the dire situation of people who used drugs. It also tackled the discrimination of people living with AIDS on the job market and focused on the difficulties of people living with AIDS to access proper housing.[51] The chapter in Berlin was eventually joined by other sections in other cities, from Frankfurt (Main) to Cologne, and from Wiesbaden to Munich.[52] In the same vein, activists in Vienna, dissatisfied with the politics of *Homosexuelle Initiative Wien* (HOSI Wien) regarding the HIV/AIDS crisis, eventually created ACT UP Wien.[53] Although the groups did not necessarily reach the size of ACT UP New York, LA or Paris – ACT UP Berlin assembled only a handful of activists – their presence in the German gay press was constant. It is interesting to consider the various chapters of the coalition as a sort of ACP UP Germany or ACT UP in Germany. Indeed, when local groups had their weekly or bi-weekly 'Floors,' they released collaborative material and met to discuss policies.[54]

Yet behind the political flyers and campaigns, ACT UP in Germany gravitated toward political dialogs with health agencies, doctors, and governmental representatives. Where ACT UP in the United States and ACT UP Paris put pressure on

---

49 Andreas Salmen, "Burokratie oder Aktion," *Siegessäule* (March 1988): 8.
50 Salmen, "Burokratie oder Aktion": 8.
51 "ACT UP Berlin 'Wer wir sind, was wollen wir?'" Schwules Museum Berlin, Archive *Unsortiert Thematic: ACT UP*.
52 "ACT UP Gruppe Liste 24.07.1991" Schwules Museum Berlin, Archive *Unsortiert Thematic: ACT UP*.
53 "ACT UP Wien 'Wer Wir Sind'" Schwules Museum Berlin, Archive *Unsortiert Thematic: ACT UP*.
54 "ACT UP Tagung in Akademie Waldschlösschen, 14–16 Februar 1992, Protokoll" and "ACT UP Seminar Formen Gewaltfreien Widerstands in Akademie Waldschlösschen, 14–18, Oktober 1991, Protokoll", Schwules Museum Berlin, Archive *Unsortiert Thematic: ACT UP*.

governmental agencies and disrupted social peace to gain access to and force the hand of decision makers, ACT UP in Germany saw the politics envisioned by the likes of Salmen as too controversial.[55] In other words, ACT UP in the FRG was not in radical opposition to other support organizations already existing in the country even though it was committed to offering a grassroots answer to the HIV/AIDS crisis. It also did not act as a sort of direct action appendage to a more institutionalized wing of the queer community. In that sense, ACT UP in Germany is another German example of the false binary between radicalism and assimilationism touched upon in our discussion of the pink radicals in chapter one – see section 1.1. Still, it is possible to make many parallels between some of the political rhetoric from chapters in the USA and in the FRG,[56] the way ACT UP groups on both sides of the Atlantic used the media to gain attention,[57] and the presence of prominent cis white gay men at the forefront of the movement: an Andreas Salmen, a Larry Kramer, and Didier Lestrade.

Despite some differences, the direct connections between all these German chapters and their international counterparts are striking. First, most of these chapters continuously corresponded with each other. ACT UP New York, even if not the headquarters of the international coalition, intended to keep track of the various groups it had influenced. New Yorkers invited groups in Europe to keep in touch and keep some sort of statistics, a sort of ACT UP census to be shared with the rest of the other international chapters.[58] Like Andreas Salmen and his tendency to keep newspapers clippings of what was happening in the United States, the media committee of ACT UP New York kept track of activities in Europe.[59] It was then possible to coordinate activities and organize direct actions from a transnational perspective. For instance, chapters in Germany prearranged

---

55 Wolf-Jürgen Aßmus, "! Schweigen= Tod! Weltweite ACT UP Bewegung kämpft gegen Ignoranz," *Nürnberger Schwulenpost* (March 1991): 16.
56 See, for example, various flyers by ACT UP Berlin for a boycott of Marlboro products using the same language as ACT UP New York, Schwules Museum Berlin, Archive *Unsortiert Thematic: ACT UP*.
57 ACT UP Köln/Wärmer Leben used various "Media Pakete." They would send these documents to selected journalists to attract their attention beyond normal press releases. One of these still exists in its complete form: "Selbstdarstellung: Informationen für die Presse," Schwules Museum Berlin, Archive *Unsortiert Thematic: ACT UP*.
58 Correspondence between ACT UP Berlin and ACT UP New York (April 1990), Schwules Museum Berlin, Archive *Unsortiert Thematic: ACT UP*. According to the letters, this exchange also contained flyers and other forms of material ("enclosed together with some leaflets, buttons and other material").
59 MS ACT UP: The AIDS Coalition to Unleash Power: Series VI. Act up Chapters Box 28, Folder 22, *ACT UP Chapters, ACT UP Berlin, Germany*, New York Public Library.

concerted postal actions, planning to flood the White House with thousands of postcards to denounce the Bush administration.[60]

Second, international solidarity in the face of adversity became an unremitting topic for the various European chapters. ACT UP Berlin organized a solidarity boycott of the cigarette distributor Marlboro with other chapters, because the manufacturer Philipp Morris backed the re-election of senator Jesse Helms.[61] Supporting their comrades in San Francisco, German chapters compared the reactionary forces rallying behind Helms to the conservative forces at play in Bavaria; they compared Helms with Peter Gauweiler. This international solidarity is specifically apparent in the various concerted denunciations of immigration policies. From ACT UP LA's early focus on restrictive immigration reforms[62] to symbolic demonstrations at the *Platz der Luftbrücke* in Berlin condemning the Bush administration's ban on people living with AIDS entering the United States, discriminatory migration policies were also central to other groups around Europe. When the city of Berlin hosted the World AIDS Congress, alarmed North American groups asked their comrades in Berlin whether the city had developed similar laws to the Free State of Bavaria.[63] Eventually meeting up at the Technical University of Berlin, chapters from Munich, Berlin, Frankfurt (Main), New York, Amsterdam, and Barcelona organized joint actions and information stands for the Congress.[64] In the meantime, they had already established new contacts and helped each other financially.

Beyond the synchronicities mentioned above, these various chapters of ACT UP were also connected by their use of art for propaganda purposes.[65] Street art, logos, branding, shocking actions for the cameras – many have written about the importance of this media self-consciousness.[66] In the light of its communication networks, it is not surprising that the coalitions' methods followed a similar direc-

---

[60] Various "Call for action" from German ACT UP Chapters, Schwules Museum Berlin, Archive *Unsortiert Thematic: ACT UP*.

[61] Call to boycott Marlbroro by ACT UP Berlin, "Kennen Sie Jesse Helms? Aber Sie kennen Peter Gauweiler!," Schwules Museum Berlin, Archive *Unsortiert Thematic: ACT UP*.

[62] Sandy Dwyer, "ACT UP LA Targets INS," *The News* (December 11, 1987).

[63] Letter by ACT UP Berlin to ACT UP New York establishing the travel costs for the AIDS World Congress in Berlin, Schwules Museum Berlin, Archive *Unsortiert Thematic: ACT UP*.

[64] "Protokoll des europäischen Act Up Treffens in Berlin 16–17 January," Schwules Museum Berlin, Archive *Unsortiert Thematic: ACT UP*.

[65] Avram Finkelstein famously stated: "I'm not embarrassed to call what we do propaganda," MS ACT UP: The AIDS Coalition to Unleash Power: Series IV. Actions/Demonstrations/Zaps 1987–1995, Box 14, Folder 11 *Provincetown Gay Pride and Follow-Up, Provincetown, MA. July-August, 1989*, New York Public Library.

[66] Douglas Crimp, *AIDS Demo Graphic* (Seattle, WA: Bay Press, 1990); Avram Finkelstein, *After Silence: A History of AIDS through Its Images* (Oakland, CA: University of California Press, 2018).

tion. Various sections of ACT UP across both continents appealed to memories of National Socialism. They adopted a shared symbol, an equal motto. They related the HIV/AIDS crisis and its dystopic possible results to the persecution of queer men under National Socialism. This motto, SILENCE = DEATH and its various international translations were paired with a Pink Triangle facing upward. One episode from the 1990s exemplifies how AIDS activists crossed these Pink Triangle bridges and appealed to queer memories of National Socialism. In 1992, during the eighth International Conference on AIDS in Amsterdam, US chapters of the coalition from Boston, New York, LA, and San Francisco, co-sponsored a direct action with ACT UP Amsterdam to denounce travel restrictions afflicting people living with AIDS worldwide. Activists marched through the streets of the Dutch capital toward the US Embassy with 40 ceremonial coffins with the names and laws from various countries legislating against seropositive migrants. The procession started at the *Homomument*, the city's Pink Triangle.

7.3 A queer trivialization of genocide? Dystopian visions of an epidemic

Comparisons to Nazi atrocities were at the core of this new social movement during the 1980s and 1990s. In the early summer of 1987, the Floor of the then recently created first chapter of ACT UP New York passed a motion to create a float for the upcoming pride parade. Most of the discussion seemed to have revolved around possibilities of attracting attention to the epidemic and – echoing debates still present today – repoliticize the event.[67] The activists present on that day voted on a motion: for the float, they would recreate a mock concentration camp full of dying homosexuals. Their controversial wagon would be flanked by other ACT UP members wearing either fake SS uniforms or ACT UP apparel and they would distribute flyers to the crowd amassed for the parade. They also initially planned to throw condoms at St. Patrick's cathedral.[68] This rubber action was eventually abandoned to avoid shocking the public, but the concentration camp float did not seem to attract the same concerns. Indeed, one person opposed the topic and suggested a "graveyard theme" but their motion was almost unani-

---

67 MS ACT UP: The AIDS Coalition to Unleash Power: Series II. Minutes Box 3. Folder 3 *Minutes, ACT UP / NY Minutes, June 1987*, New York Public Library.
68 MS ACT UP: The AIDS Coalition to Unleash Power: Series II. Minutes Box 3. Folder 3 *Minutes, ACT UP / NY Minutes, June 1987*, New York Public Library.

mously rejected.⁶⁹ The prospect of re-enacting the genocide in a city with an important Jewish population did not seem to attract much unease, as the idea to recreate the "effective" float hovered around one year later during the same period.⁷⁰ Eventually, the Floor voted for another theme the following year, but the idea of a concerted genocide against homosexuals remained.

In the light of this macabre masquerade – and considering ACT UP's provocative deeds – it would be easy to brush such performances as a one-off action based on an emotional comparison. On the contrary, AIDS activists constantly appealed to National Socialism. The persecution of the men with the pink triangle was not simply one metaphor used among others, it was a major marker of identity for these men and women fighting against governmental abjuration, legislative indifference, the alarmingly slow pace of medical research, and the repression encountered.

In her 1988 meticulous deconstruction of AIDS hysteria afflicting the United States, *AIDS and its Metaphors*, Susan Sontag writes the genealogy of both the idea of plague as well as the scapegoating intertwined with epidemic panic.⁷¹ Drawing connections between the metaphorical language of plague and its presupposed retribution – political or divine – for transgressive behaviours, she also draws parallels between the idea of Europe – or in this case, North America – being infected by foreign diseases, for example the antisemitic tropes connected to the Black Death, and the xenophobic tropes presenting AIDS as an epidemic coming from outside.⁷² She interprets how this so-called filthy "outside realm" was present in depictions of Africa as the fertile ground for a possible contamination of the "pristine" West. Sontag links this racism with the xenophobic immigration measures voted for after the first outbreaks of HIV/AIDS among the heteronormative population. Still, this "outside contamination" also mirrored the idea of the queer other infecting the pristine realm of heterosexuality, the family, and eventually the "straight state," the nation.⁷³ Moreover, according to Sontag, "the persistence in the belief that illness reveals, and is punishment for moral laxity or turpitude can be seen in another way,

---

69 MS ACT UP: The AIDS Coalition to Unleash Power: Series II. Minutes Box 3. Folder 3 *Minutes, ACT UP / NY Minutes, June 1987*, New York Public Library.
70 MS ACT UP: The AIDS Coalition to Unleash Power: Series II. Minutes Box 4. Folder 12 *Minutes, ACT UP / NY Minutes, May 1988*, New York Public Library.
71 Susan Sontag, "Aids and Its Metaphors," *New York Review of Books* (October 27, 1988): 89–99.
72 The idea to deconstruct metaphorical discourses surrounding the concept of plague is not unique to Sontag. See, for example, articles in *Der Spiegel* and in the Gay Press. "Die großen Seuchen," *Der Spiegel* (September 23, 1985); Rüdiger Berg, "Meine Meinung," *Kellerjournal* (January 1988).
73 On the heteronormative potential and praxis of the state, see Margot Canaday, *The Straight State: Sexuality and Citizenship in Twentieth-Century America* (Princeton, NJ: Princeton University Press, 2009).

by noting the persistence of description of disorder or corruption as a disease."[74] Metaphors are a way to put the experience of AIDS into words, to historicize it, and to scan the past for possible warnings or reactions.

Queer AIDS activists dealt with repression by reinterpreting queer collective memories, cultural trauma, and the spectre of a new genocide echoing Homocaust narratives of the past. AIDS activism was an emotional fight and a constant marker for Manichean assertions, that is, the creation of definite enemies – the Church, the government, state agencies – recognized as evil. The struggle was also constantly branded as an ultimate fight for survival.[75] For many queer AIDS activists, the 1980s had a flavour of impending doom; it was two minutes to midnight. The prevalence of Homocaust narratives had taught many of these activists the necessity of preparing for the worst, for a dystopia in which AIDS was only the beginning. A collective letter to the *New York Times* by R-E-C-O-V-E-R Hotline illustrates the mistrust and fear of people living with AIDS, as well as the connection with National Socialism as a metaphor. The letter was brought up to the Floor of an ACT UP meeting in August 1987:

> The Jews in Germany at the beginning of the Nazi regime who went to establishment psychiatrists were treated for paranoia. Their disbelief and denial of the reality of Nazi Germany was so deep-seated that they thought there was something wrong with them [. . .]. Poor and minority people who are already accustomed to being blamed for the results of society's prejudice against them and neglect of them no longer trust society's messages about what this AIDS disease is, where it comes from, and what is being done about it for the poor and minorities. As a consequence, they have no reason to trust the information that the system is putting forth about AIDS.[76]

This ingrained mistrust in the state is entangled with preceding debates in the international queer community, discourses against the chimera of a possible integration into heteronormativity. The epidemic gave a face to the daunting idea that a repetition of traumata, of Nazi style persecution, was imminent. In Germany, a columnist in a special issue of *Kellerjournal* about AIDS and repression in Bavaria summarized this fear:

> Dachau and Auschwitz were not built in plain sight. The plans from the Interior Minister's drawers also shy away from public scrutiny – they should be dragged into the light, like all partisans for such plans, whether from the left or the right, scientists in working on AIDS or civil servants! What would such 'neo-fascists' say about the demand for registration and

---

74 Sontag, "Aids and Its Metaphors," 95–99.
75 Deborah B. Gould, *Moving Politics: Emotions and ACT UP's Fight Against AIDS* (Chicago, IL: University of Chicago Press, 2009).
76 "Letter August 24, 1987," MS ACT UP: The AIDS Coalition to Unleash Power: Series II. Minutes Box 3, Folder 5. *Minutes, ACT UP / NY Minutes, August 1987*, New York Public Library.

branding with tattoo of the letter 'N'? Are they not themselves a danger for Public Health? Examples of stories prove the opposite – they are more dangerous than any virus!⁷⁷

In the case of Germany, National Socialism was not only a metaphor, but a direct memory. Reporting on the Bavarian prophylactic measures, the gay magazine *Kellerjournal* reprinted the words of older members of the queer community. Michael Dursch stated: "I am not a scholar, but someone who is terribly afraid, because I suffer from the grace of being old and I therefore still remember how I was made to look away as a child on the street as the Jews were beaten and expelled from their homes."⁷⁸ One man, participating in a demonstration in Munich denouncing said measures held a poster on which a crude statement flanked a huge Pink Triangle facing downward: "Hey Bavaria! Have you already forgot about this?"⁷⁹

On the other side of the Atlantic, the comparison and link to National Socialism was more metaphorical. For example, a gay activist surviving AIDS in the 1990s mentioned how reading the works of Holocaust survivors had helped him find the necessary hope and strength to survive, concluding: "Maybe AIDS was a Holocaust of its own." For US AIDS activists, it was indispensable that people realize that they were not only supposedly awaiting genocide, but also already experiencing one. Countless flyers by various ACT UP chapters used this rhetoric to explain the emergency of the situation.⁸⁰ Other US AIDS activists were adamant about the issue stating: "Hopeless is an understatement, until we realize it's a holocaust. Holocaust survivors recognized early: GET OUT!"⁸¹ In an angry letter to the *New York Native* the activist and film historian Vito Russo stated:

> All those good and polite little boys and girls who have been whining about how ACT UP trashed its own party and how this wasn't the time or the place to zap the mayor are not activists, they're a bunch of politically naïve asswipes. [. . .]. These people are like the Jews who said: 'Don't throw rocks at the Nazis.' [. . .]. I am sickened by the spectacle of a group of lesbians and gay men who think that the AIDS crisis is a problem but not an emergency and

---

77 RS, "Die Macht (?) des Schicksals," *Kellerjournal* – Special Issue: Unser Bayern Heute (December 1986): 15.
78 For more information on the catalogue of extraordinary measures, see Tremblay, "Visual Collective Memories." See also Adrian Lehne, "Auseinandersetzung mit Recht in der westdeutschen Schwulenbewegung im Kontext von HIV/AIDS," Freie Universität Berlin (2022).
79 *Rosa Info* 4 (December & January 1987/1988): 4.
80 See for example: "This is Genocide," MS ACT UP: The AIDS Coalition to Unleash Power: Series XI. Ephemera, Flyers, Handbills by Act Up Box 203, Folder 1 *Ephemera, Flyers, Handbills by ACT UP, ACT UP Information / Resource Guide. 1988*, New York Public Library.
81 James Turcotte, "Letters to the Editors," *PWA Newsline* (December 1992): 6.

are willing to put political expediency before the lives of their friends. These prim and proper fans of gay history should take note. History will record that, like the Jews who did nothing during the Holocaust, they are the traitors and fools in our midst. Shame on them![82]

Meanwhile French ACT UP activists were also calling for a general wake-up drawn from a queer memory of National Socialism: "The homosexual community has been sorely wiped out by the AIDS epidemic. Today it is threatened by laws undermining its right to exist. However, the community does not consider it necessary to express its concern and anger. Will we have to wait for the crematoriums and the concentration camps before it finally thinks of going out on the street!"[83] Through flyers like this one, but also through direct action – the so-called zaps – and their use of street art, ACT UP chapters anchored their warnings about the future in negative longings from the past, namely queer memories of National Socialism. Raising the alarm about what had happened and what could possibly happen, they focused on mobilization. Their motto SILENCE = DEATH simultaneously denounced governmental inaction and conjured dystopic visions of doom. Yet it also evoked a path to survival through political action.

It is not simply fortuitous that the Pink Triangle appeared on most of the material created by the artist collective Gran Fury for the coalition. It was usually juxtaposed to or complementing this broader call-to-arms. If SILENCE = DEATH was a warning, the triangle temporalized, historicized, and legitimized the necessity of organizing to survive. In the words of Avram Finkelstein, member of Gran Fury, the idea of silence came from discussing the possible links between complicity and passivity during a crisis. The double meaning of silence was both a denunciation of top-down political erasure, and a denunciation of the alleged complicity of bystanders refusing to act against injustice.[84] The Pink Triangle facing upward completed this coded reference. Strangely, the story of the ACT UP Pink Triangle has been mostly ignored in queer historiography until today.[85] Elaborating on the concept in an interview with fellow ACT UP member and scholar Sarah Schulman, Avram Finkelstein explains:

---

82 Vito Russo, "Zapping the Mayor or Zapping Gay," *New York Native* (July 4, 1988): 6.
83 Flyer "Pédés, gouines, reveillez-vous!" MS ACT UP: The AIDS Coalition to Unleash Power: Series VI. Act up Chapters Box 28, Folder 21 *ACT UP Chapters, ACT UP Paris, France. 1989–1992*, New York Public Library.
84 Finkelstein, *After Silence*, 46.
85 Two exceptions are the sociologist-historian Regis Schlagdenhauffen and Jake Newsome. See Régis Schlagdenhauffen, Triangle Rose: La persécution nazie des homosexuels et sa mémoire (Paris: Autrement, 2011); Jake W. Newsome, *Pink Triangle Legacies: Coming out in the Shadow of the Holocaust* (Ithaca, NY: Cornell University Press, 2022).

> The pink triangle we hated because it intoned victimhood, obviously, but it seemed like it might have the most chance of being clear enough to the lesbian and gay community, more clear than the other images we were discussing that were abstract, and graphic enough to be intriguing, interesting, compelling, to people outside of the community who didn't know what it was. Then for a long time we thought about designing a new logo, a new image, for the lesbian and gay community, but realized as we talked about it, that would be a separate campaign. And people were dying, and we didn't feel comfortable doing that.[86]

It is here particularly interesting that Finkelstein mentions how the assembly of queer men loathed the symbol – its connection to victimhood – while acknowledging its importance for the community. In a way, this demonstrates how even the discourse about survival pushed forward by ACT UP was anchored in the victimhood aspects of a transatlantic queer memory. Finkelstein also discussed in more extensive terms the choice of the symbol in his memoirs:

> We liked the inclusiveness of the rainbow. But it also had a little hippie baggage, and its brightness seemed inappropriate and somehow lacking in gravitas. Ultimately, however, it was the graphics that disqualified it. We decided it would make an ugly poster. We preferred the feminist empowerment tonalities of the labrys, but we knew many men would be unacquainted with it, and it would be hard to connect to some of the issues at hand. We felt the lambda was not known well enough to younger lesbians and gay men. During this process, we became somewhat rattled by the lack of an agreed-on symbol for the lesbian and gay community. It seemed, in a way, as if this might be one of the roots of the issue. [. . .] [S]o we resigned ourselves to the use of the pink triangle.[87]

Not mentioned in this quote is the nature of the moment when Finkelstein and his peers decided to switch and reverse the triangle upside-down as a sign of hope. Later on in his memoirs, Finkelstein stipulates that a comrade had visited Dachau and thought they remembered the triangle was facing upward. Someone else supposedly in charge of verifying the information did not do their research properly and the triangle was printed on the original SILENCE = DEATH poster facing up.[88] [Figure 6] Remarkably, this alleged domino effect of history propelled analogies of National Socialism forward, as it doubled down on an aesthetics of survival already present in the triangle as a patent of nobility for queer liberation. Ironically, if the first recuperation of the Pink Triangle in the United States was based on a misunderstanding of the proportions of the persecutions of queerness during National Socialism, the second coming of the symbol during the HIV/ AIDS crisis came about from a second misunderstanding by a group of individuals appealing

---

86 Avram Finkelstein. "Interview # 108,"By Sarah Schulman. *Act Up Oral History Project*, MIX: The New York Lesbian & Gay Experimental Film Festival (2010).
87 Finkelstein, *After Silence*, 44–46.
88 Finkelstein, *After Silence*, 44–46.

Figure 6: Official SILENCE = DEATH Poster created by the collective Gran Fury for ACT UP New York. © Silence=Death Project, ACT UP New York, 1987.

to the first one. The triangle facing down was a now symbol of survival for queer legitimation, for victimhood and for the survival of queerness throughout the twentieth century. Almost at the turn of the millennium, the triangle facing up became a symbol of a second survival, a second annihilation.

It is peculiar that these men were self-conscious enough about the possible lack of empathy or ignorance of other gay men toward the labrys, while completely buying into the Pink Triangle as a symbol of gay and lesbian belonging. One could interpret this in two ways. First, the lesbians of the decade prior had not been vocal enough about their sentiment of exclusion from the symbolic of the Pink Triangle and their preference for another symbol like the Black Triangle. One could almost name this first perspective 'lesbian blaming.' Second, these men had bought into pretences of universalism analysed in chapter six –see section 6.2–, namely that the Pink Triangle was already a symbol conflating all experiences of queerness. In both cases, this can be seen as either another good example of lesbian erasure and gay hegemony, or a great indication of the transatlantic journey of the triangle and its all-encompassing discourse at the end of the 1980s.

In his own interview with the *Act Up Oral History Project*, Larry Kramer also mentions how he hated the symbol, but saw the possibilities offered by the comparison, not only with National Socialism but with the Holocaust.[89] He writes in the foreword to his 1994 memoirs that the "necessity" of such a comparison was plural. He dismissed accusations of antisemitism, counterarguing with his own Jewish identity.[90] Finkelstein also appealed explicitly to his Jewishness and his family's postmemory, closing his memoirs with a clear statement:

> As someone who feels a responsibility to history, AIDS [. . .] is disquietly similar to my father's efforts to situate himself within the attempt to make sense of the Holocaust, as an atheist Jew in the American Communist Party who was sent overseas by a country he was trying to dismantle [. . .] and he went because he never forgot the price his clan paid for its Jewishness. I wrote this book to map where I sit in a story I had a hand in but others have shaped, in the hope of helping remodel it into a toolbox for resistance in the future. [. . .] AIDS was, AIDS is, a political crisis. And silence was, silence is, packed with political meaning.[91]

More than a confirmation of the importance of postmemory and family memory, these closing remarks are a good summary of the aesthetic of survival of the Pink Triangle and its transatlantic journey. The gay son of a Jewish immigrant rebranded a symbol linked to National Socialism and a certain erroneous perspective on the era (Homocaust narratives). By doing so, he was partaking in the creation of new layers of meaning. The symbol which had been recuperated by queer men identifying with their "forefathers," had migrated over the ocean. Recuperated in New York, the triangle travelled once again across the Atlantic with the help of ACT UP activists in Germany and other European countries.

Compared to other posters by ACT UP in the USA that compared the Bush administration to Hitler, German uses of SILENCE=DEATH material might seem a less apparent comparison with National Socialism. Yet the constant marketing and rebranding of the design and its use in everyday life fixed the movement's identity in memories of the Nazi atrocities. The repetition, reproduction, and redistribution of Pink Triangle merchandise embodied this appeal to victimhood and generalized a connection between survival and queer memory. Indeed, after an initial first run of SILENCE = DEATH buttons, many minutes of the weekly

---

89 Larry Kramer. "Interview #35." By Sarah Schulman. *Act Up Oral History Project*, MIX: The New York Lesbian & Gay Experimental Film Festival (2003).
90 Kramer, *Reports from the Holocaust*, xii.
91 Finkelstein, *After Silence*, 220.

meetings usually mention one or two motions to order more buttons, print posters, create t-shirts, and even take part in museum exhibitions.[92] During the organization of the March on Washington for Lesbian and Gay Rights in 1987, again using the Pink Triangle for its logo, the Floor in New York – following discussions to patent the logo – decided to "lend" the rights to the SILENCE = DEATH design to the March organizers. They also "allowed" other chapters across the Atlantic to use the design as long as they complied with ACT UP's values and goals.[93] Many ACT UP groups in Germany complied. But does that mean that German activists were also comparing the HIV/AIDS crisis to National Socialism? I have shown that this was the case in Bavaria, but what about other places around the country? ACT UP Cologne and many other German chapters used the Pink Triangle in most of their material, thus making the same link between healthcare, national administration, state-sanctioned silence, and a form of genocide.

This is where the previous story of the Pink Triangle is significant. In Germany, the triangle pointing downward is a symbol of collective memory and of queer belonging from the 1970s, used by militant organizations from which ACT UP Germany inherited some of the rhetoric. If groups like ACT UP Cologne or Berlin were using the ACT UP Pink Triangle – pointing upward – were they automatically referring to National Socialism? Through its escapade across the Atlantic and back, had the triangle already become a broader symbol of queer struggles beyond its direct link with Nazi atrocities? As mentioned above, its designers, more or less accidentally, reversed the triangle as a symbol of hope. It is certainly not an issue of knowledge circulation, as I already established that ACT UP chapters in Germany read material from other North American members.[94] Once again, the triangle is multilayered; it encompasses multiple fragments of history and memory. ACT UP chapters in Germany may not have been referring to National Socialism but were clearly referring to a reference to National Socialism. This multitude at the heart of the symbol shows the impossibility of disentangling its transatlantic components.

---

92 MS ACT UP: The AIDS Coalition to Unleash Power: Series II. Minutes Box 3–4. Folder 1–19 *Minutes, ACT UP / NY Minutes, 1987–1988*, New York Public Library.
93 MS ACT UP: The AIDS Coalition to Unleash Power: Series II. Minutes Box 3. Folder 5. *Minutes, ACT UP / NY Minutes, August 1987*, New York Public Library.
94 On the potential and dangers of focusing on circulation and knowledge in global intellectual history, see: Christopher L. Hill, "Conceptual Universalization in the Transnational Nineteenth Century." In *Global Intellectual History*, ed. Andrew Sartori and Samuel Moyn (New York City, NY: Columbia University Press, 2013), 134–158; Kapil Raj, *Relocating Modern Science: Circulation and the Construction of Knowledge in South Asia and Europe, 1650–1900* (Houndmills: Palgrave Macmillan, 2007).

It is true that the symbol also became an icon of a transnational movement. During World AIDS day in the early 1990s, ACT UP Paris had planned to cover the pyramid at the Louvre with pink paint, effectively creating a gigantic SILENCE = DEATH installation at the centre of the city to attract attention to the epidemic. ACT UP Paris was known for its flair; they had famously (or infamously) covered the obelisk at *Place de la Concorde* with a giant pink condom. They never actually realized their "*Act Up Louvres contre le Sida*" project,[95] but it remains one of the possible examples of the use of the Pink Triangle for media-grappling purposes. Most of the time, these actions also included speeches and communiqués mentioning emergency and imagining Nazi-inspired dystopias for seropositive individuals and people living with AIDS.[96]

Back in the United States, some comparisons were more on the nose. In an "outing action"[97] in the 1990s, ACT UP Portland published flyers with the face of closeted queer Republicans who had voted "against the needs of the community." Next to their portraits and some severe denunciations, the group superposed a big Pink Triangle facing down, like the one worn by concentration camp inmates. In the words of the Portland activists, they were branding these traitors in the same way that their "fellow Nazis" would have branded them. That example illustrates how AIDS activists used the symbol in both ways – facing upward and downward – to make a point about their fear of death, their desire to survive, and what they considered an unapologetic fight for justice.

These selected examples of the uses of the Pink Triangle by ACT UP chapters across both continents demonstrate how the HIV/AIDS crisis exacerbated the needs of an imagined queer past of suffering as warning and legitimation. Surrounded by their dying lovers and their friends, activists dove into tropes already well established in queer collective memory and designed a logo that could express both their vision of a negative past and the need to reimagine the present. They were, in their words, "fighting back" to prevent an apocalyptic future. Visually, the Triangle – pointing up or down – was both iconic and indexical. It reminded activists of Homocaust narratives, of the dangers of genocide that had

---

[95] In French, ACT UP "Louvres pour le Sida" is a play on words. It simultaneously means that ACT UP and the Louvres are both positioning themselves regarding AIDS activism and that ACT UP "opens it" for AIDS, a sexual innuendo and an example of ACT UP's tongue-in-cheek attitude. MS ACT UP: The AIDS Coalition to Unleash Power: Series VI. Act up Chapters Box 28, Folder 21 *ACT UP Chapters, ACT UP Paris, France. 1989–1992*, New York Public Library.

[96] Open Letter, "Pédés Lesbiennes, réveillez vous!" MS ACT UP: The AIDS Coalition to Unleash Power: Series VI. Act up Chapters Box 28, Folder 21 *ACT UP Chapters, ACT UP Paris, France. 1989–1992*, New York Public Library.

[97] MS ACT UP: The AIDS Coalition to Unleash Power: Series IV. Series VI. Chapters, 1986–1993, Box 28, Folder 7 *Portland, Oregon*, New York Public Library.

never historically been, an inflated discourse on Nazi persecutions, but also a genocide that could eventually happen. The Triangle – pointing up or down – was a useful aesthetics of survival. In the 1970s, gay West German men born after 1945 had constructed a bridge between themselves and queer victims of the Nazis. In North America, ACT UP built a bridge from Nazi persecutions to an uncertain future, underlining the broader survival and the need to survive of a community, discussing the dangers of a "new Homocaust." According to ACT UP chapters in Germany, this bridge did not go as far, grabbing instead the attention of the mainstream by connecting governmental inaction to the sacred evils of history. In other words, German activists were discussing and drawing conclusions from the Nazi past without necessarily asserting the dangers of a Homocaust. Nonetheless, remembering the real or imagining mythical numbers of queers murdered in concentration camps, AIDS activists intended to survive.

It would maybe be tempting to dismiss these metaphors as another form of antisemitism. The reality is still more complicated. As we have seen in other chapters, Larry Kramer and Avram Finkelstein were not the only North American Jews to connect their contemporary struggles to postmemories of the Nazi era. For people growing up as children of Holocaust survivors, using such comparisons also meant finding an intersection between collective Jewish and collective queer memory.[98] Moreover – although distasteful for some – chapters of ACT UP were also aware of Holocaust relativizations, vehemently criticizing antisemitism and antisemitic comparisons. When a man in LA suggested picketing a Jewish Hospital to "remind the Jews that they are doing to us what happened to them," prominent figures of the region came together to push all Floors in California to condemn the proposition and denounce antisemitism.[99] However, they added a paragraph to their open letter underscoring the parallels between the HIV/AIDS crisis and National Socialism, stating that the action suggested in LA was antisemitic but that cross-referencing the Holocaust usually was not.[100] As for Germany, ACT UP chapters were not fond of Holocaust comparisons but other AIDS activists used coded languages and direct references to Nazi atrocities.[101]

Naturally, even if debunked discourses of a Homocaust and the cross-referential use of the Holocaust haunted its rhetoric, National Socialism was not the only political repertoire of AIDS activism. For instance, ACT UP New York pub-

---

98 Rick Landman, "Whose Holocaust? Letters to the Editors," *The Advocate* (January 20, 1998).
99 MS ACT UP: The AIDS Coalition to Unleash Power: Series VI. Act up Chapters (United States). Box 26, Folder 2 *Los Angeles, CA., August 24–November 15, 1990*, New York Public Library.
100 MS ACT UP: The AIDS Coalition to Unleash Power: Series VI. Act up Chapters (United States). Box 26, Folder 2 *Los Angeles, CA., August 24–November 15, 1990*, New York Public Library.
101 Tremblay, "Visual Collective Memories": 569.

lished material in *El Barrio* presenting the HIV/AIDS crisis as an immense hurricane engulfing the community, effectively targeting the dominant Puerto Rican population of the district with other metaphors.[102] Among the white non-Jewish (especially middle-class) population of New York, the haunting aspects of Nazi persecutions as presented in cultural magazines, plays, and literature were still seen as the best and most effective comparison. What is more, as part one of this book demonstrates, North American communities unaffected by National Socialism or by the HIV/AIDS were still using its atrocities as a referent. The horrors committed in Germany became the basis of discussions on the world stage and the backbone of the definition of crime against humanity. As I demonstrate in the next chapter – see section 8.1–, the importance of European history for queer memory remains embedded in white readings of queerness even though queer liberation has never been an exclusively white story.[103]

7.4 Still a badge of survival

This chapter has focused on ACT UP and leftist activists referring to the Pink Triangle's aesthetics of survival. As I write these lines, the world is still struggling on multiple levels to deal with the global pandemic of COVID-19. Many scholars have already shifted their focus from the state enforced quarantine to a long comparative analysis of the HIV/AIDS crisis and the present calamity.[104] Others have argued online about whether there is a possibility to either learn from reactions in the queer community during the highs of the HIV/AIDS crisis in the 1980s and

---

[102] "Huracan Sida" MS ACT UP: The AIDS Coalition to Unleash Power: Series X. Published and near Print Material Box 139, Folder 1. *Published and near Print Material, Media (1of 3), August 13–October 31, 1990*, New York Public Library.

[103] Dan Royles, *To Make the Wounded Whole: The African American Struggle against HIV/AIDS* (Chapel Hill, NC: University of North Carolina Press, 2020); E. Patrick Johnson, *No Tea, No Shade: New Writings in Black Queer Studies* (Durham, NC: Duke University Press, 2016); Darius Bost, *Evidence of Being: The Black Gay Cultural Renaissance and the Politics of Violence* (Chicago, IL: The University of Chicago Press, 2019); Jennifer Brier, Jim Downs, and Jennifer L. Morgan, *Connexions: Histories of Race and Sex in North America*, (Urbana, IL: University of Illinois Press, 2016).

[104] For an example of a mainstream approach, see Paul M. Renfro, "Coronavirus is different from AIDS," *The Washington Post* (April 6, 2020); Edmund White, "Fear, Bigotry and Misinformation – this Reminds me of the 1980s AIDS Pandemic" *The Guardian* (April 6, 2020). For the perspective of a German scholar, see Adrian Lehne, "Ein Virus ist immer mehr als nur ein Virus. Gedanken zu HIV/AIDS und COVID-19," *Hypotheses.org* (April 14, 2020), https://hsl.hypotheses.org/1353.

1990s or by referring back to Susan Sontag's essay on plague.[105] Even the famous AIDS-quilt has now been re-purposed to create protection masks for the US population.[106]

These troubled and uncertain times also involve ACT UP and the creation of new 'Pink Triangle bridges.' Following debates surrounding the US federal reaction to the COVID-19 pandemic and the disproportionate effects of the virus on marginalized communities, ACT UP New York has re-imagined its famous SILENCE = DEATH poster. Instead of a Pink Triangle facing up, an orange triangle appeared next to the words TRUMP = DEATH, a chromatic tongue-in-cheek association with the forty-fifth US president's apparent love for tanning salons. The words are a reference to the lack of testing and deficient handlings of the pandemic in the United States under the Trump administration. In this case, the poster is so iconic that changing the Pink Triangle to orange, a colour never used in the Nazi murder apparatus, does not erase the connection with a queer past of suffering or with other layers of memory surviving through times. It remains a badge of survival, a call-to-arms, a warning.

This kind of recuperation of the symbol is not exclusive to the Left. In the summer of 2000, the libertarian activist Doug Krick founded the Pink Pistols, an organization allegedly present in more than 30 US states, opposing firearms regulation and preaching militia ideology. Their official logo consists of a gun wielding figure on a Pink Triangle facing down, appealing more to the National Socialist atrocities than to the HIV/AIDS crisis, to the first "genocide" and not to the second.[107] According to spokesperson Gwen Patton, who usually refuses interviews, "we don't want people to hurt us, we want people to run away from us, and the best way we have found to do that is to be armed."[108] Since the election of Donald Trump and the Orlando shootings at the Pulse Nightclub in June 2016, their membership has sup-

---

105 Henning Tümmers, "Forum: Corona-Lektüre – Henning Tümmers über Susan Sontag," *H/Soz/Kult* (April 15, 2020), accessed January 20, 2023, https://www.hsozkult.de/debate/id/diskussionen-4970?utm_source=hskhtml&utm_medium=email&utm_term=2020-4&utm_campaign=htmldigest.
106 Julian Shen-Berro, "Extra Fabric from AIDS Memorial Quilt Used for Coronavirus Masks," *NBC News* (April 14, 2020), accessed January 20, 2023, https://www.nbcnews.com/feature/nbc-out/extra-fabric-aids-memorial-quilt-used-coronavirus-masks-n1183501.
107 The Pink Pistols, "About the Pink Pistols," accessed April 16, 2020, http://www.pinkpistols.org/about-the-pink-pistols/.
108 Hollie Mckay, "Gay Gun activists: Growing LGBT Push to Support the Second Amendment," *Fox News* (October 1, 2014), accessed April 16, 2020, https://www.foxnews.com/entertainment/gay-gun-activists-growing-lgbt-push-to-support-the-second-amendment.

posedly increased to over 9,000 members.[109] Discussions on their online forum are emblazoned with the usual alarmist rhetoric known to fringe militia groups.[110]

By using the Pink Triangle, the group draws a connection to one reading of a queer past of injury, and weaponizes trauma. It appeals to a traditional antifascist memory of 'never again' connected to the Pink Triangle facing downward. By denouncing and refusing passivity in the face of adversity – here queerphobia – and by calling other queers to arm themselves, the Pink Pistols are also far more connected to the triangle pointing upward, refusing to be silent, violent if necessary, fighting to survive. The use of the symbol by the Pink Pistols reminds us that the key moments of an icon's journey are not necessarily linear. It also demonstrates that the meaning of a symbol can be both synchronic and multiple, that every use of the Pink Triangle is embedded in its transatlantic journey and cannot be disentangled from the various significations ascribed to it.

---

109 Matt Kwong, "Trump 'gave hate groups a megaphone': Gun sales surge among LGBT, minorities in the U.S.," CBC News (April 2, 2017), accessed April 16, 2020 https://www.cbc.ca/news/world/texas-gun-lgbt-firearms-trump-1.4046334.

110 I have browsed through the General Discussion section of the forum. The Pink Pistols, "Forum," accessed April 16, 2020, http://forum.pinkpistols.org/index.php?board=1.0.

8 A badge of temporalities – European time and asynchronous Pink Triangle modernities

It has almost become a cliché to connect the queer past with two mythological stories: with the biblical metaphor of Lot's wife turned into a pillar of salt for looking back at the destruction of Sodom and Gomorrah; and second, with Orpheus losing the love of his life to the pits of Hades for daring to look back. In both cases, by looking back at the injury or trying to save the past, the protagonists face horrendous consequences. They are either paralyzed on their way to emancipation – turned into a pillar of salt – or they lose a part of who they are – losing Eurydice. Under this trope, queer history – like queer activism – seems to focus on distancing oneself from the injury, to come out. Apparently, in a fight for emancipation, queers had to let go of the persecutions of the past to find pride, to reach the utopian future.[1] What are we to do then with Pink Triangle connections to the past? What can shame and pain bring to the table? How are the temporalities of the Pink Triangle including and excluding members of the queer community? Queer scholars have condemned this bondage of the "gay affirmative" and underscored the necessity of criticizing progressive narratives in gay, bisexual, and lesbian history. Others have criticized the normative aspect of coming-out narratives as a form of universalizing biographical marker.[2] Even those defining aspects of their lives as 'before' and 'after' coming-out would agree that the act of unveiling queerness in a heteronormative world is a perpetual one; one is often coming-out daily, to new friends, colleagues, or to strangers. In this sense, queer theory disrupts gay, bisexual, or lesbian narratives of pride and unidirectional temporality. Heather Love states that "the politics of gay pride will only get us so far. Such an approach does not address the marginal situation of queers who experience the stigma of poverty, racism, AIDS, gender dysphoria, disability, immi-

---

[1] On queer utopia, one cannot escape the wonderful prose of José Esteban Muños on the potential of the queer future. José Esteban Muñoz, *Cruising Utopia: The Then and There of Queer Futurity* (New York: New York University Press, 2009).
[2] On the complexity of framing coming-out narratives, see Ellen Samuels, "My Body, My Closet: Invisible Disability and the Limits of Coming-out Discourse," *GLQ: A Journal of Lesbian and Gay Studies* 9, no. 1–2 (2003): 233–255. On alternatives for the closet – here the checkpoint – and for another intersectional critique of visibility and coming-out narratives, see Jason Ritchie, "How Do You Say 'Come out of the Closet' in Arabic?: Queer Activism and the Politics of Visibility in Israel-Palestine," *GLQ: A Journal of Lesbian and Gay Studies* 16, no. 4 (2010): 557–575.

gration, and sexism [. . .] the assertion of pride does not deal with the psychic complexity of shame, which lingers on well into the post-Stonewall era."[3]

Tracing the journey of the Pink Triangle in the Euro-American world, this book has so far discussed the negative, the injury, and suffering, demonstrating their significance for the queer subject in Germany and in North America in different albeit entangled ways. In her book, *Feeling Backward* Heather Love considers different ways of looking backward at difficult moments of history. Going beyond the usual stories of Orpheus and Eurydice,[4] she touches the reimagination of the present through a confrontation with the past. The queer past, she writes, is a spectre haunting history. However, the ghosts of the past are not paralyzing but a potential. Inspired, scared, or defined by what came before, the queer present opens for opportunities, dreams, or legitimation. By reimagining themselves and projecting themselves into the past, queer activists are weaving connections and disconnections with actors of the past, creating new senses of belonging. For example, the imagined glorious years of Weimar Berlin made sense through their destruction. Pink radicals from the 1970s looking back at Weimar were not paralyzed by the suffering of their imagined ancestors, but longed for a utopian future, for a possibility coming out of destruction. Recuperating the Pink Triangle, they situated their present, defined their future, and remembered the past.

Queer history is indeed composed of constant longing for what was or what could have been, a feeling backward, a lesson of failures, an impossible mission to save the past and rescue the sexual misfits who dared to think of a future they could not imagine outside of utopianism.[5] This is also a methodological danger if the impulse becomes a constant longing for "ancestral genealogies" where queer historians try to "touch across time" to save other misfits of the past.[6] By looking for people with whom they can identify in the past, queer activists and queer

---

[3] Heather Love, *Feeling Backward: Loss and the Politics of Queer History* (Cambridge, MA: Harvard University Press, 2009): 147.
[4] Even though Love does use both parables in her introduction.
[5] On the potential of failure, see Jack J. Halberstam, *The Queer Art of Failure* (Durham, NC: Duke University Press, 2011). Carla Freccero suggests in her *Queer/Early/Modern* that queer history could offer a form of 'queer spectrality,' never forgetting the dead, never mourning them. This spectrability would imply looking at the past to imagine the future, without creating a master narrative and a gay and lesbian periodization of time anchored in the violence of history. See Carla Freccero, *Queer/Early/Modern* (Durham, NC: Duke University Press, 2006).
[6] Freccero, *Queer/Early/Modern*, 37; for Dinshaw, see Carolyn Dinshaw, "Touching on the Past." In *The Boswell Thesis: Essays for the Twenty-Fifth Anniversary of John Boswell's Christianity, Social Tolerance, and Homosexuality*, ed. Matthew Kuefler (Chicago, IL: University of Chicago Press, 2006), 57–73.

scholars reach across time to give a voice, to reveal, to name, to list.⁷ This was also the case of early queer activism and at the centre of the memory activism of the pink radicals. The impulse to look back is also a paradox engrained in queer history, as tracing these ancestral genealogies to historicize categories of the present also means fixing categories of analysis in the past, a venture at odd with the fluidity at the heart of queer theory.⁸

As this chapter shows, Pink Triangle bridges are a great example of the necessity to focus on queer temporalities. Beyond being a multilayered symbol of memory and political rhetoric, the Triangle defined what the queer subject was, is, and eventually would be. It shaped the ways in which queer activists understood their relation to history in the Euro-American world and the way they referred to and still discuss time. Therefore, as a historical concept, a vector, and finally an indicator of historical change the Pink Triangle not only channels various memorial discourses, but also conceptions of time. Conflated together, these multiple temporal aspects of the symbol are entangled in racialized framings and procedures of othering.

Looking simultaneously at queer temporalities and the whiteness of Pink Triangle bridges is a necessary endeavor if one wants to understand how the act of feeling backward can also produce exclusions. In terms of discursive and affective practices, Love's conceptualization of 'feeling backward' encompasses not only the past but also the present, emphasizing the use of historical awareness to counteract any oppressive imaginings that may arise within contemporary queer politics. Love's negative longings are not a plea for stagnation. We are, indeed, not turned into a statue of salt for looking at the Nazi persecutions of queerness and there is potential in organizing based on what has happened and imagining what could still happen. Hence, a longing for the negative past invites a new perspective beyond optimistic progress narratives and the lionization of past political gains. Liberating us from the prevailing narratives of the present, which falsely assert that the struggle for queer rights has been successfully concluded and no longer necessitates our ongoing activism, Love's feeling backward is not about being chained to the past but imagining alternative chronologies beyond mainstream narratives of queer history to understand the present differently. As I will

---

7 The practice of naming, listing, and uncovering intellectual thought is not just a queer endeavor. It is also a very important aspect of Black feminisms. See Terrion L Williamson, *Scandalize My Name: Black Feminist Practice and the Making of Black Social Life* (New York, NY: Fordham University Press, 2016); Brittney C Cooper, *Beyond Respectability: The Intellectual Thought of Race Women* (Urbana, IL: University of Illinois Press, 2017).
8 Laura Doan, "Queer History / Queer Memory: The Case of Alan Turing," *GLQ: A Journal of Lesbian and Gay Studies* 23, no. 1 (2017): 127.

show in this chapter, underlining how the past has shaped contemporary queer politics in Germany through Pink Triangle bridges enables the deconstruction of white centered narratives and queer genealogies untouched by race.

This chapter brings together the various Pink Triangle bridges examined throughout this book with the discussion on universalism at the heart of chapter six – see section 6.2. It shows how uses of the Pink Triangle have cemented a particular conception of queer time. Adding to a rich literature on queer temporalities, it highlights how the universalization of Euro-American queer memory is broadly used to frame (one?) European modernity in opposition to a so-called 'premodern' non-European space.[9] As I investigate the role of the symbol regarding European Time in the German queer community, I consider the whiteness of Pink Triangle bridges and their connection with an ethnonationalist understanding of what it means to be German. To make sense of this assemblage and export of time, memory, and discourse on national belongings, I then coin and discuss the term 'homosynchronism.'

8.1 Looking back at whiteness in the Euro-American world

In her book, *The Renaissance of Lesbianism in Early Modern England*, Valerie Traub sets herself the task of understanding the impulse and reason behind many projects by gay and lesbian historians to "look at themselves in the mirror."[10] The story of the Pink Triangle underlines how this mirror can have distorting effects and dire consequences on the framings of an imagined community, especially regarding the erasure of race and the obscuring of whiteness. The problem is not necessarily looking in this mirror *per se*, but how one looks in it. Scholars working on the first German emancipation movement – often considered the first 'homosexual movement' – have highlighted how from its early stages, German queer thinkers and activists shaped their understanding of queerness as "unmarked by race," pointing out the consequences, as "this allow[ed] for a queer politics that was unconcerned with racism and [. . .] made the homosex-

---

9 On queer temporalities, see Carolyn Dinshaw, Lee Edelman, Roderick A. Ferguson, Carla Freccero, Elizabeth Freeman, Judith/Jack Halberstam, Annamarie Jagose, Christopher S. Nealon, and Tan Hoang Nguyen, "Theorizing Queer Temporalities: A Roundtable Discussion" *GLQ: A Journal of Lesbian and Gay Studies* 13, no. 2–3 (2007): 177–195.
10 Valerie Traub, *The Renaissance of Lesbianism in Early Modern England* (Cambridge: Cambridge University Press, 2002).

ual subject implicitly, functionally white."[11] Revisiting the era and focusing on visual aspects of the first emancipation movement, recent scholarship has also demonstrated how race as a category of analysis was not necessary absent from the early writings of fin de siècle and Weimar Berlin queer intelligentsia, but how actually a highly racialized discourse glorifying whiteness created the idea of a white queer subject.[12]

Similarly, the erasure of kinship across racial lines at the centre of early queer activism and sexual science also helped to shape the world of queerness as a white story.[13] The framing of the movement as raceless – and therefore white – implied that the destruction and persecution of queerness was an attack on whiteness. As a symbol echoing the destruction of the first emancipation movement by the Nazis and the persecution of queerness by the regime, the recuperation of the Pink Triangle is entangled with these white framings, sticking to it.[14] Chapter one has shown how this discourse was slow to evolve in the second part of the twentieth century – see section 1.1. The community's main communication networks erased racialized experiences and voices from domestic discussions, relegating their existence to the pages concerned with tourism, the exotic, and the erotic.[15] The recuperation of the triangle by the pink radicals in the 1970s and its appearances in queer printed media of the subsequent decades was then also semantically anchored in whiteness, as both the signifier and the signified referred to and represented the idea of white suffering, white continuities, and white remembrance.

---

11 Laurie Marhoefer, "Was the Homosexual Made White? Race, Empire, and Analogy in Gay and Trans Thought in Twentieth-Century Germany," *Gender & History* 31, no. 1 (2019): 98.
12 Javier Samper Vendrell has analyzed the glorification of whiteness in the writings of Adolf Brand. See Javier Semper Vendrell, "Photography and the Homoerotics of Race in Adolf Brand's Rasse und Schönheit." In *Queer Media in the German Speaking World – New Approaches to Print Sources*, ed. Christopher Ewing and Sébastien Tremblay (London: Palgrave Macmillan, [forthcoming]). For a broader investigation of these magazines, see Javier Semper Vendrell, *The Seduction of Youth: Print Culture and Homosexual Rights in the Weimar Republic* (Toronto, ON: Toronto University Press, 2020).
13 Laurie Marhoefer, *Racism and the Making of Gay Rights: A Sexologist, His Student, and the Empire of Queer Love* (Toronto, ON: University of Toronto Press, 2022).
14 See Ahmed's discussion on the stickiness of feelings to objects. Sara Ahmed, "Happy Objects." In *The Affect Theory Reader*, ed. Melissa Gregg and Gregory J. Seigworth (Durham, NC: Duke University Press, 2010), 29–51.
15 Christopher Ewing, "Color Him Black: Erotic Representations and the Politics of Race in West German Homosexual Magazines, 1949–1974," *Sexuality & Culture* 21, no. 2 (2017): 382–403.

My point here is not to say that Jewishness – particularly in Germany – was not a fundamentally racialized experience.[16] Nor is it to say that queerness in Germany was a white experience. Both these statements would be false and have been brilliantly debunked by others.[17] Some of the recent literature on the history of sexualities also regularly includes race as an indispensable category of analysis, often examining racial segregation in communities, illustrating the input and role played by marginalized and racialized queer communities.[18] Black German Studies have underlined the presence of Black thoughts and Black culture in Germany throughout the centuries, anchoring experiences of racism in the present and connecting them with the construction of whiteness.[19]

There is still a latent whiteness to the Pink Triangle and a racial dimension to Pink Triangle bridges in the Euro-American world.[20] Regarding narratives of queer survival, the AIDS Coalition to Unleash Power (ACT UP) is again a great point of departure. ACT UP New York was representative of the grassroots movement in the city, denuded of the elitist aspects of some other organizations in the five boroughs of the metropolis, and succeeded at building alliances beyond structures of desire.[21] Heteronormative and non-heteronormative people using injection drugs, sex workers, and others fought the state for better access to medication. Reading leaflets and browsing through ACT UP's material in not only New York, but also in LA or other

---

16 Gregor Hufenreuter, "Rassenantisemitismus." In *Handbuch des Antisemitismus*, vol 3 – Begriffe, Theorien, Ideologien, ed. by Brigitte Mihok (Berlin: De Gruyter, 2011), 272–273. Ascribing whiteness to the Jewish experience has been criticized by historians. See Eric L. Goldstein, *The Price of Whiteness: Jews, Race, and American Identity* (Princeton, NJ: Princeton University Press, 2006). One should also not dismiss Black Jewish experiences. See Janice W. Fernheimer, *Stepping into Zion: Hatzaad Harishon, Black Jews, and the Remaking of Jewish Identity* (Tuscaloosa, AL: University of Alabama Press, 2014).

17 Black women were already writing their own history in the 1980s, focusing on the *longue durée* of Black German experiences. See Katharina Oguntoye, May Ayim (Opitz), and Dagmar Schultz, *Farbe bekennen: Afro-Deutsche Frauen auf den Spuren ihrer Geschichte* (Berlin: Orlanda Frauenverlag, 1986). For a more recent example, see Sara Lennox *Remapping Black Germany: New Perspectives on Afro-German History, Politics, and Culture* (Amherst, MA: University of Massachusetts Press, 2016).

18 See for example Fatima El-Tayeb, *European Others: Queering Ethnicity in Postnational Europe* (Minneapolis, MN: University of Minnesota Press, 2011).

19 The German Quarterly published a wonderful forum on the matter in the Fall of 2022: Priscilla Layne and Kira Thurman, "Introduction: Black German Studies," *The German Quarterly* 95, no. 4 (2022): 359–371.

20 This statement is not exclusive to the use of the triangle by Black artists in the USA. The Black filmmaker and poet Marlon Riggs used the symbol in his work on AIDS. I would still argue that he was mainly influenced by the uses of ACT UP.

21 Russo also compared Vito Russo, "Zapping the Mayor or Zapping Gay," *New York Native* (4 July 1988): 6.

cities, it is possible to identify different struggles beyond white cis gay male struggles, a real effort on the part of the Floor to push actions that focused on poverty, on structural violence, and marginalization. Still, whiteness permeated most of the structures of the coalition. The archives are filled with episodes that shed light on the discrimination experienced by Black, Indigenous, or other racialized members of the coalition. One example is the open letter written by an anonymous woman in May 1990 explaining why she was quitting her local chapter.[22] In her message, she describes harassment by fellow comrades during the sale of SILENCE = DEATH t-shirts, names episodes of racism during her time as a member and denounces instances of tone policing and control.[23] Black ACT UP activists also wrote pieces directed toward their white comrades. Indeed, fellow white members who were vocal about their anti-racism had apparently managed to monopolize the majority committee, the group in place to fight racism in and outside of ACT UP.

These two examples, part of a broader structural problem in ACT UP, are not chosen to negate the efforts of many members of the coalition to fight against racial discrimination and white settler's colonialism within the ranks of the coalition's various chapters. This not only affected local US chapters, particularly in segregated urban centers, but also affected European chapters' framing of international politics.[24] In Germany, an analysis of queer media underlines how dominant AIDS activists framed queerness according to white narratives of suffering.[25] Like the lionization of some individuals in the press, the media savvy aspects of AIDS activism, far from being only beneficial, ended up playing a double game: attracting attention while pushing narratives that were respectable for mainstream society.[26] Selling the story by making it more palatable eventually also centred whiteness.

---

[22] "An Open Letter to the Members of Act Up: Monday 20th May 1990 One Day After my Racial Harassment at GMHC's AIDS Walk," MS ACT UP: The AIDS Coalition to Unleash Power: Series III. Correspondence Box 8, Folder 6 *Correspondence, ACT UP / NY, April-June, 1990*, New York Public Library.
[23] "An Open Letter to the Members of Act Up: Monday 20th May 1990 One Day After my Racial Harassment at GMHC's AIDS Walk."
[24] Dan Royles, *To Make the Wounded Whole: The African American Struggle against HIV/AIDS* (Chapel Hill, NC: University of North Carolina Press, 2020), 165–194; Michael J. Bosia, "AIDS and Postcolonial Politics: Acting up on Science and Immigration in France." *French Politics, Culture & Society* 27, no. 1 (2009): 69–90.
[25] Christopher Ewing, "Highly Affected Groups: Gay Men and Racial Others in West Germany's AIDS Epidemic, 1981–1992" *Sexualities* 23, no. 1–2 (2020): 201–223.
[26] Like the portrayal of New York activist Peter Stanley in David Handelman, "Act Up in Anger," *Rolling Stone* (March 8, 1990).

Using the Pink Triangle and metaphors of the Holocaust brought the same paradox. As seen in the previous chapters, many queer activists in national and international organizations presented the memories of the persecution of queerness as a collective story with roots in Europe and connected to North America – see sections 3.1 and 6.2. Imagining the Euro-American as white, white queers framed queer liberation as a white model of liberation that had inspired the rest of the world. Activists in the Euro-American world appropriated queerness internationally through organizations such as the International Lesbian and Gay Association (ILGA) and articulated their struggle in terms of human rights, but also in terms of historical social justice.[27] Again, the Pink Triangle is the patent of nobility of this assemblage; it anchored queer survival in white narratives of European history, for example, in the suffering of white queer males in concentration camps. All in all, imagining and associating queer suffering with whiteness, queer activists in the second part of the twentieth century also navigated the waters of a culture of remembrance not only defined by whiteness, but also associated with whiteness.[28]

8.2 A badge of European modernity?

At the end of the twentieth century, paradigm shifts regarding *Vergangenheitsbewältigung* slowly facilitated a transfer to a new national discourse on memory where remembering the atrocities of the Nazi past became the German reason of state.[29] This shift enabled a certain chauvinism among German intellectuals, where being German ironically became synonymous with a new sort of Enlightenment, working through the horrors of the past.[30] This also had repercussions beyond Europe, as North American scholars eventually also started to credulously praise German *Vergangenheitsbewältigung* as an instruction manual for other instances of national atonement.[31]

---

27 National Archive of Lesbian, Gay, Bisexual and Transgender History, Collection #121 "Dr. Harold Kooden Papers," Box 1, Folder 18, *ILGA-UN: Minutes and Documents*.
28 Sébastien Tremblay, "Apocryphal Queers and Gay Orthodoxy." In *The New Fascism Syllabus* (2021), accessed January 23, 2023, newfascismsyllabus.com/opinions/apocryphal-queers-and-gay-orthodoxy/.
29 Mirjam Sarah Brusius, "Introduction," *Bulletin of the German Historical Institute London* 44, no. 2 Special Issue Memory cultures 2.0: From Opferkonkurrenz to Solidarity (2022): 3–20.
30 Maha El Hissy, "Die Erinnerung an den Holocaust gehört nicht einer weißen, deutschen Mehrheit", *Berliner Zeitung* (May 7, 2022): 12–13.
31 These think pieces are usually written by US Americans drawing a very simple portrait of *Vergangenheitsbewältigung* and presenting it as a success. Susan Neiman, *Learning from the Ger-*

However, these uncritical understandings of the last decades as a sort of German memorial Enlightenment have veiled a broader conceptualization of German identity and its connection to temporalities and migration. Queer scholars have demonstrated how European whiteness frames change and the evolution of European societies as they confront their past and reinvent themselves. In comparison, spaces outside of European epistemologies are portrayed as static, perpetual outsiders to European modernity, incapable of adaptation.[32] Migrants are then presented as agents of pre-modernity roaming free in an enlightened Europe. The queer community, unmarked by race, opposes this conception of European modernity to the potential and alleged dangers of the migrant other.[33] This does not exclude an eroticization of migrants and the erasure of queer migrants.[34]

Racialized European citizens are also not spared the stickiness of the migration experience and its concurring exclusion of European modernity. Fatima El-Tayeb and Jin Haritaworn have written on the European *Dominanzgesellschaft*'s, 'dominant society's,' conceptualization of migration as a perpetual experience.[35] Presented as never completely arrived but simultaneously always arriving, racialized communities never belong to European Time up to the nth generation.[36] This has regrettably dismal repercussions when the reason of state is connected to

---

mans: Race and the Memory of Evil (New York, NY: macmillan Publishers, 2019); Clint Smith, "Monuments to the Unthinkable," *The Atlantic* (November 14, 2022).

32 The tension is still present today in discussions about European framings of historicity regimes and debates regarding centres and peripheries. One can read in parallel both debates and identify tropes referring to modernity. See François Hartog, "Chronos, Kairos, Krisis: The Genesis of Western Time," *History & Theory* 60, no. 3 (2022): 425–439 and Monica Juneja, "Viewing Europe, or Where and What Is the 'Outside.'" In *Why Europe, Which Europe* (2022), accessed January 23, 2023, https://europedebate.hypotheses.org/1462.

33 Fatima El-Tayeb, "'Gays Who Cannot Properly Be Gay': Queer Muslims in the Neoliberal European City," *European Journal of Women's Studies* 19, no. 1 (2012): 79–95; Sébastien Tremblay, "Homosynchronism and the Temporal-Memory Border: Framing Racialized Bodies, Time, and Mobility in German Queer Printed Media," *SCRIPTS Working Papers* 21 (Berlin: Cluster of Excellence 2055 "Contestations of the Liberal Script [SCRIPTS]," 2022).

34 Jin Haritaworn, *Queer Lovers and Hateful Others: Regenerating Violent Times and Places* (London: Pluto Press, 2015); Ulrike Schaper, Magdalena Beljan, Pascal Eitler, Christopher Ewing, and Benno Gammerl, "Sexotic: The Interplay between Sexualization and Exoticization," *Sexualities* 23, no. 1–2 (2020): 114–126.

35 Jin Haritaworn, "Queer Injuries: The Racial Politics of 'Homophobic Hate Crime' in Germany," *Social Justice* 37, no. 1 (2010): 69–89; Fatima El-Tayeb, "'Blood Is a Very Special Juice': Racialized Bodies and Citizenship in Twentieth-Century Germany," *International Review of Social History* 44, no. 7 (1999): 149–169.

36 Fatima El-Tayeb, "'The Birth of a European Public': Migration, Postnationality, and Race in the Uniting of Europe", *American Quarterly* 60, no. 3 (2008): 653.

memory and the educational aspects of the past.[37] Indeed, this state of eternal arrival artificially cuts migrants and people framed as migrants from a link to the German contaminated past. Without a link to the perpetrators' bygone era, they are excluded from 'Germanness.'[38] Having access to German citizenship or being born German is not enough. As Dan Diner correctly states, "in this sense, *ius sanguinis* is being prolonged by the rituals of memory and remembrance."[39] On one hand, racialized people living in Germany, migrants or not, are not able to take part in the atonement for the past, they are excluded from the reason of state. However, they are constantly reminded that this rejection and marginalization cut them off from the professed enlightenment of the crimes committed by the family of those *mit Nazihintergrund*, 'with a Nazi background.'[40]

This repercussion of European Time on memory practices in Germany is ironic. On one hand, it ties the German past and German memory culture to the condition of *Täterschaft*, 'the act of perpetration,' and whiteness, therefore using *Vergangenheitsbewältigung* to exclude marginalized voices and reimagining a multiracial Germany as a novelty, even if Black and racialized Germans have a long history. On the other hand, it also centers whiteness over Black, Jewish, and other racialized voices in a conversation on racist, antisemitic, and queerphobic atrocities.[41]

As shown throughout this book, this is also true for the significance of victimhood for the queer community and the use of the Pink Triangle. Already as a badge of continuities, the symbol allowed the queer community to build Pink Triangle bridges to the past, identifying with the queer men persecuted by the Nazis. Anchored in these wounded attachments, queer activists belonged to Germany. They were victims of the perpetrators, they were 'there,' they shared the same regime of historicity. Walking on Pink Triangle bridges, they were and remained Germans. Remembering and ritualizing their commemoration of the Nazi past, queer activists trapped German queer politics in a corner, chaining it perpetually

---

[37] Manuela Bauche, Patricia Piberger, Sébastien Tremblay, and Hannah Tzuberi, "From Opferkonkurrenz to Solidarity: A Round Table," *Bulletin of the German Historical Institute London* 44, no. 2 – Special Issue Memory Culture 2.0: From Opferkonkurrenz to Solidarity (2022): 32–85.
[38] Dan Diner, "Nation, Migration, and Memory: On Historical Concepts of Citizenship," *Constellations* 4, no. 3 (1998): 303.
[39] Diner, "Nation, Migration, and Memory": 303.
[40] Saskia Trebing, "Künstlerin Moshtari Hilal: 'Kritik ist das Gegenteil von Gleichgültigkeit,'" *Monopol: Magazin für Kunst und Leben* (7 May 2021), accessed May 9, 2022, https://www.monopol-magazin.de/moshtari-hilal-menschen-mit-nazi-hintergrund-kritik-ist-das-gegenteil-von-gleichgueltigkeit.
[41] Sa'ed Atshan, and Katharina Galor, *The Moral Triangle. Germans, Israelis, Palestinians* (Durham, NC: Duke University Press, 2020).

to the past of injury. Unfortunately, this longing for the negative past is linked to similar whitewashed framings as those denounced from El-Tayeb to Marhoefer; looking back at a past of injury this way meant and still means creating and reproducing whiteness. Racialized queers living in Germany – with or without an experience of migration – are denied a walk on the same bridges. Different to the rainbow flag's inclusive pride promising a place for everyone, the Pink Triangle is not only anchored in the potential of the negative for the creation of new sense of queer belongings, but also a transmitter of whiteness, a reproduction of European Time, and the othering of racialized queerness. It defines who was supposedly there and whose story is told.

8.3 A badge of homosynchronism

This story has repercussions beyond the Euro-American world. As the patent of nobility of the struggle against queerphobia, the Pink Triangle is not only the vector but also an indicator of this problem. Indeed, by linking their struggles for rights and inclusion to the persecutions and injustices committed before, during, or after the war, queer activists have legitimized their struggles by using Nazi atrocities committed against queer men.[42] As the iconic journey of the Pink Triangle demonstrates, walking across Pink Triangle bridges had a cohesive effect for the queer community on both sides of the Atlantic. But with the Pink Triangle being a badge of survival and a badge of universalism, a European queer regime of historicity was imposed on the rest of the world, where the past, a European one, was overcome.[43] The rest of the world is then either imagined as inherently queerphobic and premodern, or on its way to being enlightened. Eurocentrism is an affair of time, and the rest of the world is the past of Europe's present.

Paired with false binaries between Europe and non-Europe, or modern and non-modern, a liberal script forces spaces outside of Europe onto a timeline that centres Nazi persecutions of queerness.[44] Defined, framed, and trapped in a European Time-matrix, non-European Time is outside of progress.[45] While the space

---

42 Women are seldom at the center of such narratives.
43 François Hartog, "Régimes d'historicité: Présentisme et expériences du temps" (Paris: Éditions du Seuil, 2012).
44 Tanja Börzel and Michael Zürn, "Contestations of the Liberal Script: A Research Program" *Scripts Working Papers* (Berlin: Cluster of Excellence 2055 "Contestations of the Liberal Script – SCRIPTS," 2020).
45 Recent examples inside of Europe make it clear how this discourse is malleable. See for example the framing of Hungary as almost outside of Europe during debates regarding the queerpho-

outside of Europe is portrayed as premodern, the European space reinterpreted injuries of the past as a lesson and a warning, echoing once again El-Tayeb's argument that Europe only frames European Time as being malleable and suitable for change. The official monument for the queer victims of the Nazi regime in Berlin's *Tiergarten* park is connected to this appeal. The inscription on the path leading to the Memorial to the Persecuted Homosexuals under National Socialism reminds passers-by that the German state has a "responsibility to actively oppose the violation of gay men's and lesbians' human rights. In many parts of the world, people continue to be persecuted for their sexuality, homosexual love remains illegal, and a kiss can be dangerous." Linked to the German past, but now allegedly a reality situated beyond the borders of modern-day Germany, this mission, this German responsibility to fight queerphobia links *Vergangenheitsbewältigung* and the mission at the core of the liberal script, opposing a liberal 'here' with an illiberal 'there.'

By pretending that racialized queers, with a personal experience of migration in their biography or not, were both absent from the founding myth of their progressive narrative, and by therefore implying that they were not part of the community of injury, white German queers implicitly subtracted migrant and racialized German communities from their new crusade for a better status and for human rights. In her seminal work, *Terrorist Assemblages*, Jasbir Puar refers to an assemblage of practices and discourses where the rights of sexual minorities are politically instrumentalized to push forward patriotic and often xenophobic positions. She coined the term "homonationalism" to describe this.[46]

---

bia of the Hungarian state. Andreas Glas, "Die CSU erstrahlt in Regenbogenfarben," *Süddeutsche Zeitung* (June 24, 2021); Karoline Meta Beisel, "'Dieses ungarische Gesetz ist eine Schande': Die EU-Kommission geißelt Diskriminierung durch die Regierung in Budapest," *Süddeutsche Zeitung* (June 24, 2021); Ulrich Krökel, "Der Regenbogenstreit ist nur der Anfang," *Frankfurter Rundschau* (June 26, 2021).

[46] See Jasbir K. Puar, *Terrorist Assemblages: Homonationalism in Queer Times* (Durham, NC: Duke University Press, 2010); Omisoore H. Dryden and Suzanne Lenon, *Disrupting Queer Inclusion: Canadian Homonationalisms and the Politics of Belonging* (Vancouver, BC: University of British Columbia Press, 2015). Uses of the concept are still rare in German academic contexts. See Laura Egemann, "Zur Kritik der Homonationalismus-Kritik." In *Feministische Kritiken und Menschenrechte: Reflexionen auf ein produktives Spannungsverhältnis*, ed. Imke Leicht, Nadja Meisterhans, Christine Löw and Katharina Volk (Opladen: Verlag Barbara Budrich, 2016), 75–94. It is useful to investigate contemporary issues and German social realities. See Zülfukar Çetin, "Der Schwulenkiez. Homonationalismus und Dominanzgesellschaft." In *Dominanzkultur Reloaded. Neue Texte zu gesellschaftlichen Machtverhältnissen und ihren Wechselwirkungen*, ed. Iman Attia, Swantje Köbsell, Nivedita Prasad (Bielefeld: transcript, 2015), 35–46.

One can think of the recent debates on the "one-love armbands" during the 2022 World Cup in Qatar.[47] Following calls for a boycott and denunciations regarding the rights of queer Qatari, but still mainly focusing on queer football fans traveling to the host countries in the winter of 2022, German media manufactured a scandal when the national team, particularly captain Manuel Neuer, refrained from wearing an item symbolizing queer solidarity, an armband emblazoned with a rainbow echoing the rainbow flag.[48] The team decided against wearing the armband, afraid to be punished during the tournament. The media sensation climaxed when the federal Interior Minister of Germany, Nancy Faeser, proudly showed the armband on her body while posing in a Qatari stadium.[49] As an important political symbol, the armband will now be housed in the vaults of the House of History in Bonn, one of Germany most important museums.[50]

If the Pink Triangle is a warning of the past and a reminder that Europe has learned from its mistakes, or that a premodern world is entrenched in queerphobia away from the lessons of history, the one-love armband is a symbol of the alleged modernity of Europe. It is also connected to negative longings of the past, but is mainly focused on the future, on the teachings of Europe. Here the irony will not be lost that most of the atrocities committed by the Nazis, namely the industrial slaughter of six million Jews, were not estranged from a European history of modern thought.

Similar stories also exist inside the European Union and demonstrate how the construction of the European script – of what is Europe – does not necessarily follow the timeline of European integration. Once again, football is at the center of the story as international competitions offer an ideal space for national identity and socio-political debates on the world stage.[51] As the prime minister of Hungary, Viktor Orbán, passed new discriminatory measures into law and criminalized supposed "queer propaganda," German media started questioning the place of some Eastern European countries in the Union.[52] This conversation happened during the UEFA European Football Championship in 2020. The Munich Allianz Arena, a stadium with an integrative light system usually illuminated in red or blue, the col-

---

[47] "'Die Fifa verdient Verachtung' – Pressestimmen zur 'One-Love'-Binde," *Der Spiegel* (November 22, 2022).
[48] "DFB-Kapitän Manuel Neuer spielt ohne 'One-Love'-Binde," *Der Spiegel* (November 21, 2022).
[49] "Ministerin Faeser trägt in Katar 'One Love'-Binde," *Der Spiegel* (November 23, 2022).
[50] "Faesers 'One-Love'-Binde soll ins Haus der Geschichte," *Der Spiegel* (November 24, 2022).
[51] Jonas Bens, Susanne Kleinfeld, and Karoline Noack, *Fußball. Macht. Politik: Interdisziplinäre Perspektiven auf Fußball und Gesellschaft* (Bielefeld: transcript, 2014).
[52] Marie Julie May, "Ungarn hat in der EU nichts mehr zu suchen," *Der Spiegel* (June 24, 2021); Laurenz Schreiner, "Bundesregierung wirft Ungarn Verstoß gegen EU-Werte vor," *Der Spiegel* (June 22, 2021).

ours of the local teams, was instead draped in rainbow colours.[53] German politicians, usually far from being allies to the queer community in Germany, also supported the idea.[54] They allegedly showed their support, prompting Hungary to remember the binding status of "European values."[55] Echoing Puar, it is possible to appreciate how queer rights again became the benchmark on which to measure integration to a broader range of European values. Using the rainbow flag, politicians once again defined European Time, defined what was Europe and what had not yet caught up, what was not there yet. In this case, the use of symbols did not make use of the negative past; it was a marker of Europe, of modernity.

Like the armband or the various iterations of the rainbow, the Pink Triangle is a badge of negative European modernity. By highlighting 'where Europe has been,' the Pink Triangle is not only a warning to queers in the Euro-American world, but supposedly shows how Europe is in a position to instruct the 'non-European space.' Like the monument in *Tiergarten*, it echoes European history and integrates spaces outside of the European liberal script into European memory, paralleling oppression inside and outside European Time with the ultimate evil of the twentieth century that was the Nazi regime.[56]

As these parallels are not always expressed in patriotic or nationalist terms, Puar's homonationalism is not ideal to describe these assemblages. I have named this amalgam between European Time and the liberal script *homosynchronism*.[57] Similar to homonationalism, homosynchronism is an assemblage of public memory and political rhetoric validated through collective identities, discussions about queerness, and the desire to both save 'non-European' queers allegedly trapped in the premodern abroad while fearing and demonizing racialized queers domestically. By attaching European queer history to European Time, homosynchronists have fixed queerness in European history. Recalling the ways queerness is read through European understandings of gender and sexuality as discussed in chapter six – see section 6.2–, homosynchronism reveals veiled Eurocentrism in the disguise of universalism. Homosynchronism is a paradox. It universalizes the past – it is synchronic – while reinforcing multiple temporal hierarchies through the liberal script – it is diachronic. The 'never again' of German *Vergangenheitsbewältigung*

---

53 Andreas Glas, "Die CSU erstrahlt in Regenbogenfarben."
54 Glas, "Die CSU erstrahlt in Regenbogenfarben."
55 Laurenz Schreiner, "Bundesregierung wirft Ungarn."
56 Maria Brock and Emil Edenborg, "'You Cannot Oppress Those Who Do Not Exist' Gay Persecution in Chechnya and the Politics of in/Visibility," *GLQ: A Journal of Lesbian and Gay Studies* 26, no. 4 (2020): 673–700.
57 For a longer discussion on the uses of the concept, see Tremblay, "Homosynchronism," 5–6.

travels through the Pink Triangle to places where the 'again' does not necessarily makes sense.

A Badge of Injury has demonstrated how the Euro-American world is overflowing with Pink Triangle bridges built from one side of the Atlantic to the other, following the symbol as a badge of continuities, narratives, injury, inclusion, and exclusion. As a badge of temporality, the triangle is a memorial prosthetic, affixed to the collective memory of political struggles outside of European Time. Thus, understanding the Pink Triangle in a global perspective not only means provincializing visual concepts of Euro-American queerness, but also underlining entanglements, exchange, and power asymmetries. To put it another way, it means understanding that queer struggles in a space beyond Europe are haunted by foreign European memories.

The Pink Triangle as badge of temporality is different to the rainbow flag, yet both symbols complement each other. One is a symbol of pride that overcame shame; the other is a symbol of shame recuperated to make a political statement. As shown throughout the book, the Pink Triangle eventually also became a symbol of pride, an icon to put forward. The pink radicals even used it as a badge against "straight-passing." If the rainbow flag was created in the USA and disseminated across the world through cultural power structures and communication networks anchored in Global North and Global South dynamics, the case of the Pink Triangle is different. If both the rainbow flag and the Pink Triangle can both be a vector of homosynchronism, only the Pink Triangle is automatically a badge of temporality. Pink Triangle bridges not only accompany coming-out stories and visualize the overcoming of shame. They are also attached to the past, they give sense to the present and the future. They always remain in connection to shame, to the negative, to the injury. In this regard, using the symbol to make a statement in the present automatically integrates local time with the German past, with European Time.

8.4 Different timelines, same triangle

The David France film, *Welcome to Chechnya,* received the Panorama Audience Award for best documentary at the International Berlin Film Festival 2020. France was already linked to the Pink Triangle through his documentary, *How to Survive a Plague,* on the HIV/AIDS crisis and ACT UP, where the symbol noticeably plays a central role. His *Welcome to Chechnya* portrays the abuse of human rights by the Chechnyan government and the allegations of concentration camps for queer citizens in the small Caucasian republic.⁵⁸ The Russian activists at the centre of the film were present at the Berlinale's 2020 Teddy Awards – the festival's prestigious queer awards' ceremony – to receive the Teddy Activist Award and wore Pink Triangles for the occasion.⁵⁹ Many activists and artists trying to attract attention to the situation in Chechnya have also worn the symbol.⁶⁰ In his discussion of the uses of queerphobia in Putin's Russia as a rallying battle cry against "western values," Dan Healey presents Russian state-sponsored queerphobia as a sort of counter-liberal script.⁶¹ Pitching homonationalism against queerphobia, the Russian state places Russian history in its own distinct timeline. Presented as "western" and as "propaganda of non-traditional sexual relations," queerness becomes an agent of decadent modernity in traditional Russia. Putin in Moscow or Kadyrov in Grozny are therefore able to portray themselves as bulwarks against European Time, against the decadence of "the West." By wearing Pink Triangles, Russian activists and their allies are weaponizing homosynchronism, linking a European past of injury to their present, denouncing the misuse of time by the Russian government. The Russian example exemplifies a moment where homosynchronism offers a utilitarian rhetoric beyond its Eurocentrism.

Across the Atlantic, contemporary uses of the Pink Triangle also carry a similar appeal, separating the world into different timelines. These uses of the Pink Triangle bring us to California and a political art project that began in the 1990s. Every year since 1996, the Pink Triangle Project installs a giant fabric Pink Triangle atop Twin Peaks during Pride weekend in San Francisco, the traditional epicentre of queer politics on the West Coast. 200 feet across, nearly an acre in size, the symbol can be seen "from 20 miles afar" according to the official website.⁶² Every year, the organizers of this "symbolic commemoration" invite congressio-

---

58 David France, "Welcome to Chechnya," 107 Minutes. USA: HBO Films, 2020.
59 Teddy Awards (@teddyaward), "This year's #TeddyAward was the first edition to introduce the TEDDY ACTIVIST AWARD. The prize recognizes the leadership of individuals who strive to uphold the rights of sexual and gender minorities using visual media," Instagram photo, March 1, 2020, https://www.instagram.com/p/B9MlN3MnLD-/.
60 For example, see the performance by Daniel Donigan (@bigandmilky) "'big queer hug' arms long enough to hug everyone near and far until our right to hug vanishes," Instagram Photo, https://www.instagram.com/p/BivgR2ZDs0m/.
61 Dan Healey, *Russian Homophobia from Stalin to Sochi* (London: Bloomsbury Academic, 2017), 131–147.
62 The Pink Triangle Project, "why is the Pink Triangle installed each year," accessed April 13, 2020, http://www.thepinktriangle.com/about/why.html.

nal elected officials and celebrities to attend their ceremony.[63] San Francisco is also no stranger to the Pink Triangle as a symbol. California granite pylons in the Pink Triangle Park in the Castro are reminders of the persecutions under National Socialism and subsequent oppression in the early years of the Federal Republic of Germany (FRG). The artists behind the monument invite visitors to "pause for a moment to reflect upon the moral, ethical, and spiritual aspects of that time, and to embrace the individual responsibilities all people share as citizens of a democracy."[64] This international appeal to global democracy evokes the crusade of the International Lesbian and Gay Association (ILGA). The Pink Triangle Project takes the discourse further, linking human rights and liberal ideals of state-sanctioned protection. It also classifies countries according to their treatment of sexual minorities. In this narrative, Germany is almost forgiven for its atrocities as it has 'progressed' to the right side of history. At the same time, outside of European Time – or outside of the liberal script – other countries are implicitly compared to National Socialism, the evil of history:

> The test of any democracy is how well it treats its minorities. The Third Reich demonstrates how easily a government can devise minority scapegoats. Branding homosexuals as criminals let most Germans feel comfortable looking the other way while the Nazis went about their persecution. Germany is today one of the gay-friendliest places on Earth with true safeguards for LGBTs, however tactics used there so long ago still occur today in other places. While most nations are continually progressing, dozens others are ever more oppressive, less and less tolerant and less inclusive, and are violators of human rights. Many LGBTs in those areas will spend the unforeseen future living in utter fear.[65]

This kind of rhetoric is deceitful as most of the countries denounced by the group have inherited their discriminatory laws from European colonialism or as a result of missionary activities launched from Europe or North America. In other words, what is presented as premodern is a result of European modernity. It also omits the voting habits of some members of Euro-American societies – like in Germany – who actively give their voice to queerphobic parties, pushing queerphobic policies.[66] This is another reminder that the liberal script is more "an idea of

---

63 For more information and interviews with the organizers, please refer to Jake Newsome, "Homosexuals after the Holocaust: Sexual Citizenship and the Politics of Memory in Germany and the United States, 1945–2008," State University of New York at Buffalo, 2016.
64 The Pink Triangle Park, "Pink Triangle Memorial," accessed April 13, 2020, https://pinktrianglepark.org/.
65 The Pink Triangle Project, "why is the Pink Triangle installed each year," accessed April 13, 2020, http://www.thepinktriangle.com/about/why.html.
66 Tania Witte, "Andersrum ist auch nicht besser: Homo Afdensis," *Zeit Online* (April 26, 2017); Patrick Wielowiejski, "Identitäre Schwule und bedrohliche Queers: Zum Verhältnis von Homona-

how a society should be organized and not a description of how a society is organized."[67] 'Homemade' queerphobia is therefore a product of free speech and a necessary evil in the marketplace of ideas as opposed to a presupposed premodern illiberal queerphobia on a different timeline. The point here is not to deny the human rights abuses of various states across the globe or to completely dismiss a group of queer activists who care about other individuals they identify with. Still, there is a connection between the uses of a negative longing to the past and Pink Triangle whataboutism.

Overall, the journey of the Pink Triangle is not only connected to history, to memory, to the past, and to possible future. By designating who belongs, the inclusive and exclusive aspects of the symbol are also markers of time. In this chapter I have discussed three ways in which the Pink Triangle's temporalities shape the queer present. First, by looking at the past of injury, queer activists legitimizing and historicizing their struggles with the horrors of Nazi queerphobia have also reproduced narratives of whiteness. In this sense, the symbol also indirectly reproduces some exclusionary aspects of *Vergangenheitsbewältigung* and memory culture in Germany. As a result, associations using the Pink Triangle in the Euro-American world partake in the same reproduction of whiteness. Second, linked to its international resonance, the Pink Triangle also becomes a symbol of homosynchronism in the sense that it forces places outside of the European space to adapt to European history. The Pink Triangle as a badge of temporality forces us to discuss multiple temporalities and the way provincializing European Time allows historians to unveil power asymmetries in queer history, in this case in the way queer persecutions are framed beyond the borders or at the margins of the Euro-American world. A global history of the Triangle as a badge of modernity does not reinforce a false dichotomy beyond centres and peripheries but highlights how global integrations in the second part of the twentieth century also echo colonial structures of the past. Third, the Pink Triangle and discussions on temporalities underscore ways in which queer realities are instrumentalized beyond queer activism, as state actors and political organizations use Pink Triangle narratives to legitimize their agenda.

---

tionalismus und Anti-/G/Enderismus im Nationalkonservatismus." *Feministische Studien* 36, no. 2 (2018): 347–356.
67 Daniel Drewski and Jürgen Gerhards, "The Liberal Border Script and Its Contestations. An Attempt of Definition and Systematization," *Scripts Working Papers* 4 (Berlin: Cluster of Excellence 2055 "Contestations of the Liberal Script – SCRIPTS," 2020): 4.

9 A badge of visibility – Branding Pink Triangles for emancipation

In the summer of 1990, *Christopher Street* published an interview with famous writer and child of Holocaust survivors, Lev Raphael. Most of the interview focused on his own identity as a queer Jewish man in the USA and how he translated these intersections into his writing.[1] In the subsequent pages, the magazine reprinted one of his short stories unapologetically addressing the same topic, *Abominations*. Raphael's piece relates the story of a Jewish assistant professor of history named Brenda during her temporary tenure at Michigan State University, and follows her dismay after she discovers vehement white queerphobic graffiti during one of her morning walks on campus.[2] Freshly transplanted from the East Coast, Brenda reflects on the significance of homophobic violence in the United States while considering the fate of her brother Nat, excluded from their orthodox congregation for being queer. She is then personally drawn to fight for her brother's survival, as one of her anodyne answers to an on-campus interview ends up outing Nat, prompting a series of arson attacks and his temporary disappearance.

As he writes Brenda's story, Raphael waltzes simultaneously between the Jewish memory of the Holocaust and the aftermath of queer liberation. With the focus on Brenda – the heterosexual protagonist dealing with her brother's queerness – Raphael offers an allegory for the inner struggles inside Jewish communities regarding queerness and clearly compares the persecution and murder of the European Jewry with queerphobia at the end of the twentieth century. Indeed, Brenda's reflections on her antisemitic colleagues annoyed by "too much" Holocaust memory and her brother's ostracism are paralleled with the repeated imagery of smoke, fire, and reminiscences of Europe's many pogroms. A particular scene evokes this dark hour of European history. Arriving at his sister's apartment, an exhausted Nat informs Brenda that his car has been stolen and his dorm room burned to the ground as an act of retribution for his recently discovered homosexuality. Offering her brother support, Brenda is alarmed by the smell of smoke emanating from his clothing and engulfing her: "she was suddenly flooded by all the terrible films she'd seen of Germany in the thirties, with *Juden Raus* [. . .] whitewashed across Jewish-owned storefronts, synagogues collapsing in flame, religious Jews beaten, bloody, dead."[3] Brenda's role as a heterosexual Jewish historian

---

[1] Ronald Gans, "An Interview with Lev Raphael," *Christopher Street* (August 1990): 28–33.
[2] Lev Raphael, "Abominations," *Christopher Street* (August 1990): 34–42.
[3] Raphael, "Abominations": 41.

is not innocent. She is the warrant of Jewish past, teaching history, remembering suffering while she is herself challenged by her brother's queer and Jewish present and is, interestingly, never mentioning the persecutions of queer men during National Socialism directly.

The end of Raphael's piece directly tackled the power and history of the Pink Triangle's transatlantic journey. The only thing Nat could salvage from the fire is his Pink Triangle button given to him by his partner Mark, a symbol fervently disapproved by Brenda: "But you're Jewish, too! [. . .] Don't you hate that they use something from the camps? You never see Jews wearing yellow stars in a parade!"[4] Moments later, she recalls past arguments with Mark when he confronted her with the positive appeal of shock value offered by using the symbol in the Jewish community. Distracted from her brother's narrative of events, she pictures again the destruction of Jewish apartments in Germany before and during the war years. Raphael finally concludes his story with an appeal to the Jewish heterosexual community to support their queer brothers and sisters, remembering their own experience of National Socialism. As the story ends, Brenda gets in her car and pauses, convincing herself one last time that her parents would support their child if they could smell the fire and the familiar odor of burning synagogues. She takes the Pink Triangle button given to her by Nat and considers "how the King of Denmark had worn a yellow star when the occupying Nazis started persecuting Danish Jews."[5] She then uses her rear-view mirror to pin the Pink Triangle on her dress.

This final chapter underlines the affirmative aspects of the Pink Triangle as an object. It reflects on the materiality of the triangle and the significance of capitalism for queer transfers of knowledge. Examining merchandizing and the branding of political groups using the symbol, it links Pink Triangle bridges with art, outreach campaigns, and literature on the so-called material turn in the writing of history.[6]

---

4 Raphael, "Abominations": 41–42.
5 Raphael, "Abominations": 42.
6 See for example the coupling of a history of emotions with the material turn in Margrit Pernau, "Celebrating Monsoon Feelings: The Flower-Sellers' Festival of Delhi." In *Monsoon Feelings: A History of Emotions in the Rain*, ed. Margrit Pernau, Imke Rajamani and Katherine Butler Schofield (New York, NY: Niyogi Books, 2018), 379–407. Historians have also reflected on the work of Reinhart Koselleck and the power of the visual. See Bettina Brandt and Britta Hochkirchen, "Bilder als Denk- und Erfahrungsraum möglicher Geschichten im Werk Reinhart Kosellecks." In *Reinhart Koselleck als Historiker. Zu den Bedingungen möglicher Geschichten*, ed. Manfred Hettling and Wolfgang Schieder (Göttingen: Vandenhoeck & Ruprecht, 2021), 248–275. Historians can also look toward art history and its analysis of visuals and concepts. One very good example is Hannah Baader, "Das Objekt auf der Bühne: Diamanten, Dinge und Johann Melchior Dinglingers Imaginationen einer Geburtstagfeier in Agra." In *Synergies in Visual Cultures – Bildkulturen im*

After having investigated the journey, the history, and the influences of the symbol as an icon, a metaphor, and a concept, this last small essay invites you to grasp, touch, feel, find, collect and lose Pink Triangle memorabilia, pausing for a moment like Brenda in Raphael's story and considering the importance of the Pink Triangle as an object, a portable *Geschichtsdinge* 'objects that trigger history' subject to the artist's whims and the market.[7] In this regard, I am echoing the work of pioneering queer historians who collected manifestations of queerness and mundane objects that now allow the writing of books such as this one.[8]

9.1 Branding Pink Triangle bridges: Capitalism

In 2018, Nike released a new collection of sneakers intended for "homosexuals who knew their history,"[9] the so-called BETRUE collection consisting of white and black sneakers emblazoned with Pink Triangles pointing upward. According to the company's website, "the Nike BETRUE 2018 collection celebrates colors and symbols that have been reclaimed and historically repurposed by the LGBTQ community."[10] This capitalization of queer history is significant for a variety of reasons. First, the name of the campaign – BETRUE – implies that the essence of queer liberation is to be "true to oneself." Completely overlooking ideas of revolution, desires, and sex, Nike invites non-heteronormative individuals to declare whom they are, to take a stand, by literally crossing a Pink Triangle bridge with their feet, bringing Pink Triangles wherever they go. In this narrative, buying a shoe is an act of resistance; the marketability of oneself equals an opportunity to

---

Dialog, ed. Manuela de Giorgi, Annette Hoffmann and Nicola Suthor (Paderborn: Brill, 2013), 269–284.
7 See Lisa Regazzoni's work on monuments as *Geschichtsdinge* and her epistemological analysis of historical objects. Lisa Regazzoni, *Geschichtsdinge: Gallische Vergangenheit und französische Geschichtsforschung im 18. und frühen 19. Jahrhundert* (Oldenbourg: De Gruyter, 2020), 15–20.
8 The archives of the Schwules Museum in Berlin possess a rich collection of material from the 1970s due to Michael Holy. Holy reflected on his own act of collecting *Geschichtsdinge*. See Michael Holy, "Bewegungsgeschichte und Sammelleidenschaft: Zur Entstehungsgeschichte der 'Sammlung Holy.'" In *Politiken in Bewegung. Die Emanzipation Homosexueller im 20. Jahrhundert*, ed. Andreas Pretzel and Volker Weiß (Hamburg: Männerschwarm, 2017), 193–235.
9 Nike, "BeTrue 2018 Collection," accessed April 16, 2020, https://news.nike.com/news/nike-betrue-2018-collection.
10 Nike, "BeTrue 2018 Collection."

be true, to belong, to be distinct, to be queer through consumption and to move across space reproducing and carrying the statement with you.[11]

Nike's campaign ran in conjunction with pride and queer history month in the United States and echoes other episodes of capitalist recuperation where queerness has been not only reduced to a distinct identity, but also to a well-defined and marketable social group.[12] Here, visibility is good and visibility is the goal at the end of a long procedure of coming-out. Like any form of coming-out in a heteronormative world, it focuses on the queer subject telling the world that there is something 'other' about them, demarcated by the norm.[13] In other words, by separating the queer subject from the murkiness and intangibility of queerness and by desexualizing liberalization, Nike allows gay, lesbian, trans*, or other queers to categorize themselves individually, using a symbol historically used by the gay community to universalize its own experience of queerness. In a way, the campaign allows Nike to use history to reduce queerness to a market niche. Of course, one could also argue that heteronormative individuals could buy the shoes as an act of solidarity, but it would also imply that solidarity is connected to one's visibility and self-marketing. Central to the themes at the core of this book, the communication potential of these shoes is particularly noteworthy. Do they allow queer buyers to message each other? Are they a new form of hanky code?[14] Do they show that queer men are part of a community that survived and remembers? Is this form of commercialization of history the end of queer through commercialization? Would the collection be the same with a rainbow flag? Building on this campaign and recent scholarship on the formative aspects of what is now known as pink capitalism, I want to use the BETRUE collection as an entry point

---

11 On pink washing as a criticism of nation-states, see Koray Yılmaz-Günay and Salih Alexander Wolter, "Pinkwashing Germany? German Homonationalism and the 'Jewish Card.'" In *The Queer Intersectional in Contemporary Germany: Essays on Racism, Capitalism and Sexual Politics*, ed. Christopher Sweetapple (Gießen: Psychosozial-Verlag, 2018), 183–199. Here I am mainly voicing a critique not of nation-states, but of capitalism. See Philipp Köpp, "Liebe Unternehmen, wie sieht das ab dem 01. Juli dann eigentlich bei euch mit Pride aus?," *Esquire* (June 1, 2022).
12 For recent debates on the connection between capitalism, identity creation, and the queer community, see: Katherine Sender, "The Gay Market Is Dead, Long Live the Gay Market," *Advertising & Society Quarterly* 18, no. 4 (2017).
13 On how the conceptualization of sexualities also affects heteronormativity and how scholars should reach beyond sexual binaries, see: Heiko Stoff, "Heterosexualität." In *Was ist Homosexualität?*, ed. Florian Mildenberger, Jennifer Evans, Martin Lücke, Rüdiger Lautmann and Jakob Pastötter (Hamburg: Männerschwarm, 2014), 73–104.
14 The Hanky Code was a way to show sexual preferences by displaying handkerchiefs of a certain color. See Chris Thomas, "Untucking queer history colourful hanky code," *OUT* (June 19, 2017).

for a necessary discussion on the commercialization of Pink Triangle bridges and the potential of the symbol for the visibility and circulation of queerness in the second part of the twentieth century up to the twenty-first century. Although provocative, it is possible to see connections between capitalist ventures and Pink Triangle memorabilia, like t-shirts and buttons, created and disseminated by AIDS activists. In other words, chapters of the AIDS coalition to Unleash Power (ACT UP) were not acting so differently when they created new Pink Triangle bridges, mixing fundraising necessities and outreach efforts. Knowing that ACT UP New York vehemently condemned the campaign by Nike in 2018, I ask: was the commercialization of the triangle during their actions, through the sale of t-shirts, buttons, and logos, different?

Let us first go back to the connection between ACT UP New York, Gran Fury and the original choice to use the Pink Triangle. If the SILENCE = DEATH poster created by the collective became its most well-known artistic intervention, the self-proclaimed propaganda ministry of the coalition[15] also created other illustrious pieces of art later seen in zaps and on flyers.[16] Gran Fury is therefore an important part of the entangled history and art history of AIDS activism. Reading news outlets of the time, ACT UP had indeed transformed New York into one massive open air exhibition raising awareness about the disease.[17] Incorporated in museums[18] they also blurred the lines between art activism, the street, and the world of art. They were not alone. Other artists such as Keith Haring also created material used by ACT UP and featuring Pink Triangles before dying himself of health complications due to AIDS.[19] His name is on the long list of New Yorkers who became famous for their art and their militancy concerning the epidemic: David Wojnarowicz, Peter Hujar, etc.

This moment in art history also had impacts overseas. Organized by students of art history in the Lower Saxon capital of Hannover, an exhibit of the collective's better-known pieces made its way to Germany, confronting queer activists

---

15 See Section 8.3 in this book.
16 Manuscripts and Archives Division, The New York Public Library. "The government has blood on its hands. One AIDS death every half hour." *New York Public Library Digital Collections*, accessed November 1, 2021. http://digitalcollections.nypl.org/items/510d47e3-3ebe-a3d9-e040-e00a18064a99.
17 Karrie Jacobs, "Up against the wall!: The lively art of political posters," *Utne Reader* (March & April 1991): 89–93. Robert Atkins, "Art = Life," *7 Days* (May 24, 1989): 67–68.
18 ACT UP New York created a committee (mainly members of Gran Fury) for an exhibit curated by the New Museum in NYC. MS ACT UP: The AIDS Coalition to Unleash Power: Series II. Minutes Box 3, Folder 8 *Minutes, ACT UP / NY Minutes, November – December 1987*, New York Public Library.
19 Ruth Bass, "Keith Haring," *Art News* (March 1989).

in the Federal Republic of Germany (FRG) with agitative art from the east coast of the United States.[20] In October 1990, Andreas Salmen communicated by mail with the backers of the exhibition at Leibniz University and asked for permission to bring the material to Berlin.[21] The show opened at Mann-O-Meter, a community space in the Berlin borough of Schöneberg in March 1991.[22] It brought forward iconology already in use by ACT UP Berlin at the time, namely hands covered in blood and the Pink Triangle.[23] Parallel to the exhibition, students in Hannover also translated the introduction of Douglas Crimp's 1990 influential *AIDS Demo Graphic*, introducing Germans to AIDS activist art from North America.[24] The *Deutsche AIDS-Hilfe* republished the results, familiarizing a broader audience with Crimp's thoughts, including the German translation in a volume on AIDS activism edited by Salmen.[25] In the text, Crimp comes back to the events behind the creation of the SILENCE = DEATH poster, reflecting on the meanings and uses of an allegory such as the Pink Triangle. In his opinion, the comparison with National Socialism and the Holocaust was admittedly problematic, but he considered the matter almost irrelevant in comparison to the potential of using the symbol and the intent behind its provocative aspects.[26]

This utilitarian focus echoes two aspects of the Pink Triangle after Gran Fury. On one hand, the collective – and in a grander scheme, the coalition as a whole – knew how the appeal of the Holocaust, of Homocaust narratives, and of National Socialism were meaningful, useful, and confrontational. The words of Avram Finkelstein in chapter seven reminds us that these artists recognized what they were doing – see section 7.3. ACT UP chapters also organized events and workshops to discuss the importance of using mainstream media to their advantage while working with peoples' symbolic and popular understanding of history and mem-

---

20 Brigitte Werneburg, "Kunst gegen Positive Babys," *TAZ* (December 11, 1990).
21 Letter exchange between Andreas Salmen and Lutz Hieber, Schwules Museum Berlin. Archive *Unsortiert Thematic: ACT UP*. For more on Andreas Salmen see Sébastien Tremblay, "Visual Collective Memories of National Socialism: Transatlantic HIV/AIDS Activism and Discourses of Persecutions," *German History* 40, no. 4 (2022): 563–582.
22 ACT UP Berlin, "Katalog. Bilderschock: Aids und Kunst: Arbeiten von Act Up-Künstlern aus New York," Schwules Museum Berlin. Archive *Unsortiert Thematic: ACT UP*.
23 Poster, "Bilderschock," Schwules Museum Berlin. Archive *Unsortiert Thematic: ACT UP*.
24 Letter, 26.09.1990 by Lutzt Hieber to Andreas Salmen and German Translation of Douglas Crimp's famous book, Schwules Museum Berlin. Archive *Unsortiert Thematic: ACT UP*. Douglas Crimp, *AIDS Demo Graphic* (Seattle, WA: Bay Press, 1990).
25 Salmen and *Deutsche Aids-Hilfe*'s correspondence about the book also included a back-and-forth with prominent activists and artists from New York, for example with David Wojnarowicz. Schwules Museum Berlin. Archive *Unsortiert Thematic: ACT UP*.
26 Crimp, *AIDS Demo Graphic*, 14–15.

ory. Crimp gives a good example of this use of camp popular knowledge and tongue-in-cheek politics in his introduction.[27] During an action targeting City Hall, activists wore t-shirts with the face and name of singer and gay icon Cher. When asked by the media what Cher's name had to do with AIDS, they replied that it meant: "Commie Homos Engaged in Revolution."[28] In other words, ACT UP knew how to attract attention from both journalists and the community. In this sense, their use of Pink Triangles might have been primarily functional. On the other hand, the appeal to Pink Triangle bridges was anchored in queer collective memory. In Paris, one of the most influential members of the collective in the 1990s joined the group after seeing members during a pride parade wearing Pink Triangle *SILENCE = MORT* t-shirts, one of the first public appearances of the Paris chapter.[29] He was moved by the possibility that queer men could be facing a new form of genocide.[30] Similarly, a Californian reader of the *San Francisco Sentinel* voiced his support for the Golden Gate Bridge action in the 1980s, when AIDS activists blocked the famous Californian landmark, stating that from now on he would wear a Pink Triangle button, that he had understood that his silence in the face of oppression meant death. He stated, "I wonder if the German civilians on trains which were temporally side-tracked because trains carrying Jews to Dachau took the rail priority felt inconvenienced also . . ."[31] These examples illustrate the two results of ACT UP's Pink Triangle. First, it shows ways in which the coalition agitated the community but allowed the past to move others into action, a bit like Brenda in Raphael's story. Second, the portative aspect of the t-shirt and buttons – selling well in both North America and in Europe –[32] allowed Pink Triangle bridges to be mobile. In other words, queers did not have to go to places of remembrance like the monument in Schöneberg or secular queer places of worship like in Sachsenhausen to experience and especially feel queer memory, queer injury, cultural trauma, and the endued queer forms of belonging. They could be walking on the street, they could be driving their car, they could be at a festive event, and see other men and women wearing attire echoing the haunting allu-

---

27 Susan Sontag, "Notes on 'Camp,'" *Partisan Review* 31, no. 4 (1964): 515–530.
28 Crimp, *AIDS Demo Graphic*, 20.
29 Christophe Broqua, *Agir pour ne pas mourir!: ACT UP, les homosexuels et le sida* (Paris: Presses de la Fondation nationale des sciences politiques, 2005), 70–71.
30 Broqua, *Agir pour ne pas mourir!*, 70–71.
31 John-Michael Olexy, "Bill, Bob and Terry," *San Francisco Chronicle* (July 2, 1989).
32 Looking at the minutes of ACT UP New York, one can observe how often buttons and t-shirts were being reprinted. See for example: MS ACT UP: The AIDS Coalition to Unleash Power: Series II. Minutes Box 3, Folder 15 *Minutes, ACT UP / NY Minutes, August 1988*, New York Public Library. For the various paper slips and calls to order merchandize from the United States by activists in Germany and Europe, see Schwules Museum Berlin, Archive *Unsortiert Thematic: ACT UP*.

sions to the Homocaust. Wearing Pink Triangles bridges reminded queers that their history had been hidden; it drew a parallel between silences imposed prior to queer liberation and the silence on the AIDS epidemic. This is of interest, because it also forcibly included other heteronormative people living with AIDS in queer history and it included lesbians in an overarching gay narrative, even if not all lesbians connected themselves with the triangle. Once again, the badge of visibility was also a badge of inclusion and exclusion.

9.2 Pictorial agency

Recent scholarship on the history of emotions has also tackled the importance of objects for the transmission of feelings, as the pictorial turn[33] of the last decades made space for a broader material turn interested in the connection between objects, their materiality, and the history of concepts. In this sense, by using, reprinting, and selling the triangle and encouraging fellow activists to consume it, ACT UP indirectly gave birth to yet another new episode in the symbol's journey. This era of Pink Triangles sold on mugs and t-shirts is not an end of meaning; it is a new way to cross Pink Triangle bridges, to carry, wear, and distribute injuries of the past, warnings for the future, and comparisons in the present. To put it another way, since the 1990s, drinking coffee in a SILENCE = DEATH cup or wearing Pink Triangle earrings can trigger various layers of the symbol depending on the context where the memorabilia is seen and by whom. Naturally, the intentions of Gran Fury were not necessary the same as Nike, and ACT UP was not the first group to reproduce Pink Triangle. One can recall the *Arbeitsgruppe Homosexualität Braunschweig*'s anecdote in chapter one regarding the heterosexual employee who had wrongly reprinted Pink Triangle stickers – see section 1.5. Nonetheless, thanks to ACT UP, Pink Triangle memorabilia not only invited queers to historicize, legitimize in the present, or compare their struggles with the past. The Pink Triangle of ACT UP was also mobile across spaces, across time, and across meanings.

In an article for the *Intellectual History Review*, Jennifer Miliam and Alan Maddox plead for new forms of visual and aural intellectual histories where a picture, a painting, a sonata or a symphony could constitute a visual-text and musical-text for

---

[33] Bettina Brandt, "Politik im Bild? Überlegungen zum VerhäLtnis von Begriff und Bild." In *Politik: Situationen eines Wortgebrauchs im Europa der Neuzeit*, ed. Wilibald Steinmetz (Frankfurt [Main]: Campus, 2007), 41–71.

the sake of intellectual history.³⁴ They write that intellectual historians should go beyond musicology and art history and look at musical composition and the world of art in general as new springs of sources, using them to see how ideas travel through different mediums. In so doing, they give as examples various "play scenes" by Jean-Honoré Fragonard during the Rococo and how the confrontation with the playful scenes in his painting helped the new dissemination of the concept of play at the time.³⁵ The same can be done with the Pink Triangle, as the symbol affected and still affects experiences and bodily practices, but also commemorations and interpretations of the politics, the identity, as well as the everyday life of queers in the Euro-American world. Indeed, Sumathi Ramaswamy was already making the case with Martin Jay that images and the reception of images through our senses were implicit to our understanding of empire and race in her introduction to *Empires of Vision* in 2014.³⁶ Ramaswamy and Jay argue that our relation to objects "is a two-way street in which it is impossible to distinguish where the agency lies."³⁷ Indeed, visuals not only have their role to play in our material interpretation of the world, but our practices and our memories of said practices are also all entangled.³⁸ By looking and recognizing the Pink Triangle through our bodily senses – our eyes –, we trigger experiences, interpretations and memories or learned collective history that is considered a shared memory in a given collective – in this case an imagined and felt queer community.³⁹ The view of the Triangle triggers experiences, or 'virtual' experiences linked to certain senses of belonging. It appeals to certain expectations. But which kinds of experiences? What can the Triangle conjure for someone who identified as gay in the 1970s or 2020 and who did not experience the death or concentration camps of the Nazi regime? What inspires young queers to ironically tattoo Pink Triangles on their bodies

---

34 Jennifer Milam and Alan Maddox, "Visual and Aural Intellectual Histories: An Introduction," *Intellectual History Review* 27, no. 3 (2017): 285–298.
35 Milam and Maddox, "Visual and Aural Intellectual Histories": 289.
36 Martin Jay and Sumathi Ramaswamy, "Introduction." In *Empires of Vision: A Reader*, ed. Martin Jay and Sumathi Ramaswany (Durham, NC: Duke University Press, 2014), 1–22.
37 This argumentation goes along the line of a trend-defining article by Keith Moxey on visual studies. Keith Moxey, "Visual Studies and the Iconic Turn," *Journal of Visual Culture* 7, no. 2 (2008): 134.
38 Jeffrey Escoffier offered an interesting queering of visual culture in 2017, demonstrating how an analysis of gay porn could offer different narratives on our understanding of the HIV/AIDS crisis. See Jeffrey Escofier, "Sex in the Seventies: Gay Porn Cinema as an Archive for the History of American Sexuality," *Journal of the History of Sexuality* 26, no. 1 (2017): 88–113.
39 For the link between conceptual interpretations, expectations, and the material world, see Imke Rajamani, "Pictures, Emotions, Conceptual Change: Anger in Popular Hindi Cinema." In *Global Conceptual History: A Reader*, ed. Dominic Sachsenmaier and Margrit Pernau (London: Bloomsbury Academics, 2016), 307–335.

when the symbol originally branded queer men in concentration camps against their will?[40] What could prompt would-be travellers to sign up for gay cruises advertised with Pink Triangles or buy Pink Triangle insurances or shop at Pink Triangle florists?[41] Georges Didi-Huberman writes in his 2002 book, *L'image Survivante*, that Aby Warburg's theory of *Nachleben*, 'survival,' has been too easily discarded in art history. The French art historian's uses of *Nachleben* conjure the multiple layers of meanings of a particular image.[42] I have already connected the Pink Triangle to aesthetics of survival but surviving layers of meanings inside all aesthetics of the symbol are noteworthy mechanisms of mobilization. Using Warburg's *Nachleben*, historians can not only look at the visual intellectual history of the triangle, but also reconcile visual culture with Reinhart Koselleck's idea of the contemporaneity of the non-contemporaneous.[43] Mixing Warburg and Koselleck, it is possible to make a visual conceptual history of the multiple layers of meaning of the triangle. Each level of meaning either comes from the use of the symbol or the discourse and tradition ascribed to it: a two-way street. These various layers survive as phantoms through time and can manifest themselves in different ways and at various moments throughout history, depending on who looks at the triangle and depending on the context in which the triangle encounters the eyes of a given individual. The image has the agency to affect either independently of its origins or directly connected to its origins.[44] It can be an image suggesting a fight, pride, or a given memory. It can include or exclude.[45] The sale of Pink Triangle memorabilia and the use of the symbol by activist groups or a new form of pink industry remains connected to the transmission of collective memories and a connection to the past, the

---

40 The pink triangles in the camps were not branded on the skin.
41 "We're not just roses. The Gay Rose," *The Advocate* (April 20, 1993); "World's Biggest Gay Party," *The Advocate* (December 29, 1992).
42 Georges Didi-Huberman, *L'image survivante: Histoire de l'art et temps des fantômes selon Aby Warburg* (Paris: Les Éditions de Minuit, 2002). See also Georges Didi-Huberman, *Remontages du temps subi. L'œil de l'histoire* (Paris: Les Éditions de Minuit, 2010). The idea to use Didi-Huberman comes from the work by Milam and Maddox. Writings out of Bielefeld inspired this hybrid of Warburg, Didi-Huberman and Koselleck: Hubert Locher et al., *Reinhart Koselleck und die politische Ikonologie* (Berlin Deutscher Kunstverlag, 2013).
43 Niklas Olsen, *History in the Plural: An Introduction to the Work of Reinhart Koselleck* (New York: Berghahn Books, 2012), 151.
44 Alfred Gell, *Art and Agency: An Anthropological Theory* (Oxford: Clarendon Press, 2007). Maybe agency is not the best word in this context. I would preconize the German *Handlungsmacht*.
45 The new monument for the homosexual victims of the National Socialist regime in the Bavarian capital of Munich (2017) is a good example, as it ahistorically mixes up various symbols together in an iconological mishmash, pretending to include all members of the LGBTQ community. Wolfgang Görl, "Denkmal enthüllt: Die Zeichen lesen," *Süddeutsche Zeitung* (June 27, 2017).

present, and the future. It underscores the effects of capitalism on the creation of the queer subject.[46]

The constant use of the coalition's iconology made the symbol irremediably omnipresent in the gay press. A look at *The Advocate* in the 1990s provides a good example of the uses of the Triangle in all possible manners. Suddenly, the community was confronted with Pink Triangles in ad spots for veteran support, hotels, and even clothing.[47] Also noteworthy, the colour of the symbol became independent of the meaning. Publicity in the gay press was clearly aimed at the community and often printed only in black and white for reasons of economy; triangles presented within these pages were not then necessarily part of a new tendency to push for lesbian proponents of the Black Triangle. By the end of the century, a black triangle in a magazine next to a queer – especially gay – advertisement was coded pink; it was intended to be read as pink. Transcending colours, triangles were now queer if read in a queer context.

9.3 The potential of objects

Like the rainbow flag, the sheer numbers of Pink Triangles means that they have reached almost all circles of queer life, at least in North America, Europe, and Australia. This negative longing of the Pink Triangle completes the positive solidarity of the rainbow flag. As Heather Love tells us, the boundaries and temporalization created by this negative longing for the past had the potential to cement collective identity, that is, the Pink Triangle was both recuperation and resistance. It was an aesthetics of survival for the community, but also a proof that activists had done their homework, knew their history, were wary of possible futures. It reminded fellow queers of the danger that allegedly united them and reproduced discourses about a hidden Homocaust. This is obviously a paradox, as brandishing the triangle to prove one "knew about history" also meant using a symbol recuperated from and based on debunked narratives and misplaced genocide comparisons.

---

46 David K. Johnson has written about collective affirmations through capitalism, focusing on North American magazines. See David K. Johnson, *Buying Gay: How Physique Entrepreneurs Sparked a Movement* (New York, NY: Columbia University Press, 2019); David K. Johnson, Justin Bengry, Katherine Parkin, Katherine Sender, and Edward Timke, "Author Meets Critics: Buying Gay: How Physique Entrepreneurs Sparked a Movement," *Advertising & Society Quarterly* 20, no. 3 (2019).
47 "Support our Gay Troops! T-Shirt," *The Advocate* (February 23, 1993); "Triangle Inn," *The Advocate* (April 20, 1993); "H.I.M.,"*The Advocate* (February 9, 1993).

Groups like *Amnesty International* also joined in, creating their own Pink Triangle t-shirts.[48] Indeed, in searching for the Pink Triangle while researching this book, I have encountered innumerable forms of Pink Triangle memorabilia: From the kitsch of Irish American leprechaun badges with a Pink Triangle to the cringe of Pink Triangle mascots, from the "I have voted" Democrat buttons with Pink Triangles to the Pink Triangle used by Voices4, a direct-action group for queer solidarity with various chapters in London or Berlin.[49] The drag queen Cheddar Gorgeous even walked down the runway in a Pink Triangle outfit on the fourth season of *Ru Paul's Drag Race UK*. The runway theme of the episode was "Tickled Pink" and Gorgeous walked in a black and pink outfit echoing the SILENCE = DEATH poster.[50] Other drag queens of the franchise later commented the outfit, reminding their audience how Gorgeous was giving "a sign of where we come from."[51] As I write these lines, I am myself propelled back in the archives as I look at an antifascist Pink Triangle button bestowed on me at the Bishop's Institute in London. Pathos aside, the cohesive aspect of the symbol might also be intrinsically linked to its reproduction. Repeating the motive obviously emphasized its importance through repetition.

The scale of these Pink Triangles also plays a role.[52] As Brita Hochkirchen writes, "every change of perspective in reception has a direct effect on the perceptibility of the size of the medium. This means that the scaling, its perceptibility, and effect are mutually changeable and regulable."[53] Referring to the position of encounter also echoes the political aspect of our senses and their mediation of knowledge and history, what Koselleck calls *politische Sinnlichkeit*. Hochkirchen concludes that "consequently history and its cognition are not independent of

---

48 "Amnesty International Gay Pride T-Shirt," Washington D.C. 1996, *Forum Queeres Archiv München e.V.*

49 Their use of the pink triangle in Berlin is therefore quite interesting as it echoes more of a North American or British tradition on German soil. Here historians could research the impact of mobility and migration on the use of memory symbols.

50 Cheddar Gorgeous profile, accessed January 26, 2023, https://rupaulsdragrace.fandom.com/wiki/RuPaul%27s_Drag_Race_UK_(Season_4).

51 "FASHION PHOTO RUVIEW: RuPaul's Drag Race UK Season 4 – Tickled Pink," 4m57, accessed January 26, 2023, https://www.youtube.com/watch?v=81pKx-S48EM.

52 Carlos Spoerhase, "Skalierung. Ein ästhetischer Grundbegriff der Gegenwart," *Zeitschrift für Ästhetik und allgemeine Kunstwissenschaft* 18 – Ästhetik der Skalierung (2020): 5–16.

53 Britta Hochkirchen, "Skalierung von Geschichte und historischer Erkenntnis. Annäherung und Distanzierung durch Reinhart Kosellecks Figurensammlung." In *Vom Ding und Unding der Geschichte: Annäherung an die Figurensammlung Reinhart Koselleck*, ed. Lisa Regazzoni (Bielefeld: Bielefeld University Press, 2023), 99–122.

scaling, but deeply influenced by the size of its medium."⁵⁴ In other words, through the act of collecting, buying, wearing, and reproducing Pink Triangles in various shapes or forms, queer activists have mediated history, they have made it portable, shareable, and valuable.

One anecdote from the gay and lesbian German press synthesizes the idea of reproduction, scale, and the mobility of Pink Triangle bridges. In 1987, a young German man named Tommi was driving on the motorway, when he stopped at a gas station and ended up in conversation with two lesbian women he had just met. Tommi's car had attracted their attention with its larger-than-life Pink Triangle painted on the hood. Notified by the artwork, the two women had recognized him as a member, or at least a sympathizer, of the queer community. After exchanging contacts, they all joined an activist group in Düsseldorf.⁵⁵

The Pink Triangle has not always been such a signifier. At the start of the decade, the Pink Triangle by itself did not suffice. For example, HAW members distributing flyers in Berlin in 1975 not only carried pink cardboard triangles, but also collectively spelled the word *Schwul* by holding triangular placards, each of them emblazoned with one letter and forming the word when held side-by-side.⁵⁶ As Craig Griffiths points out, the rediscovery of the Nazi stigma would have been too recent to carry meaning without the written signifier.⁵⁷ When the group RotZschwul, 'Red (Cell) Gay,' distributed small Pink Triangles to passers-by in the Hessen metropolis of Frankfurt (Main), they also took the time to write *Schwul* on each and single one of them.⁵⁸ A decade later, through the journey covered in this book, the Pink Triangle had been distributed, collected, reproduced, and mentioned enough that it now encompasses years of activism, decades of history and a plurality of meaning.

---

54 Hochkirchen, "Skalierung von Geschichte und historischer Erkenntnis," 99–122.
55 Tommi Scheer, "Was nicht so alles geschehen kann . . . wenn man einen Rosa Winkel auf dem Auto kleben hat . . . .," *Dorn Rosa: Zeitung der demokratischen Lesben- und Schwulen-Initiative* (Oktober 1987): 25.
56 See Section 1.0 in this book.
57 Craig Griffiths, *The Ambivalence of Gay Liberation: Male Homosexual Politics in 1970s West Germany* (Oxford: Oxford University Press, 2021), 153. Here further research is necessary on the colour pink and its association with persecutions. Dominique Grisard has written about it. See Dominique Grisard, "Pink Prisons, Rosy Futures? The Prison Politics of the Pink Triangle." In *Queer Interventions: Queer Futures: Reconsidering Ethics Activism and the Political,* ed. Elahe Haschemi Yekani, Eveline Kilian, Beatrice Michaelis (Farnham: Ashgate, 2016), 83–97; Dominique Grisard, "Rosa: Zum Stellenwert der Farbe in der Schwulen- und Lesbenbewegung." In *Rosa Radikale: Die Schwulenbewegung der 1970er Jahre,* ed. Andreas Pretzel and Volker Weiß (Hamburg: Männerschwarm, 2012), 177–98.
58 See Section 1.0, ft 6 in this book.

Writing this book meant touching, grasping, and searching for Pink Triangles. Reading countless queer written media also mean annotating, photographing, and scanning a vast number of Pink Triangles. As I reorganized them in my own private archive, rotating them, facing downward, upward, and then again downward, I experienced first-hand the multilayered aspect of the symbol. My own act of collecting and mapping the symbol in Berlin or New York reminded me of the symbol's journey as activists reproduced it on both sides of the Atlantic. Echoing Andreas Salmen, my Pink Triangles travelled in my luggage, on my external hard drives. I exchanged them with other researchers, misplaced them, and gazed at them while writing. Friends started sending me Pink Triangles and I became quite astute at noticing Pink Triangle stickers.[59] In these few years of assembling and archiving my collection, I was also overwhelmed by the amount of data, losing some early artefacts and pictures in the bowels of my computer files or the vaults of old phones and cameras. The power of the Pink Triangle is therefore not only symbolic. Its materiality triggers our sense and forces us to ask questions, to remember, to write, to connect. The triangle's multiple iterations, living side-by-side with each other, are as many entry-points in the imaginary of a community, fighting for its survival, historicizing its emancipation, and making sense of the past, present, and future.

---

59 I have also started to exchange Pink Triangle material or information with Jake W. Newsome and Craig Griffiths.

Epilogue – The Pink Triangle in homonationalist times

The public historian Jake Newsome publishes aspects of his brilliant research on the queer memory of National Socialism almost daily on his Instagram account. Besides quotes by historical actors central to his book, *Pink Triangle Legacies*, he also compiles and shares his followers' impressions of the symbol.[1] The testimonies vary greatly from "the reversal of what they tried to mark us as a dishonour, for a symbol of Pride And [sic] unity" to another answer stating how the symbol is a "[v]isual equivalent of reclaiming slurs like f*g or d*ke [censored in the original]. Can never be co-opted into [rainbow emoji] Capitalism."[2] One user even asserts that "the pink triangle is our crucifix. It's our most radical symbol compared to the pride flag."[3] This book has shown how the Pink Triangle has indeed been co-opted by capitalist ventures. I have also argued that the symbol goes beyond a simple transition from shame to pride, proving that the Pink Triangle highlights the power of longing backward at a past of injury. Yet as I have shown in this book, statements like these are examples of commonly expressed views and opinions that arise when discussing the Pink Triangle. I am therefore grateful for Newsome's labour, compiling queer voices and archiving these contemporary perspectives on the symbol. Regarding the so-called radical aspects of the symbol, most probably experienced by the respondent through queer politics, I have also demonstrated over the last nine chapters how the Pink Triangle did not always neatly fit into a binary division between radical or assimilationist politics and how its uses not only included but excluded, even universalizing certain aspects of queer history.[4] Messy and complex, the Pink Triangle's journey still conveys a contemporary sense of "knowing one's history." To conclude, I wish to revisit the topics at the core of *A Badge of Injury* and reflect on the link between the Pink Triangle and the rainbow flag to underscore how, through its connection to Euro-American amalgams and hegemony, the Pink Triangle is not so different from the flag as a badge of memory.

---

[1] Jake W. Newsome, @wjnewsome, *Instagram*, accessed January 23, 2023.
[2] Jake W. Newsome, @wjnewsome, *Instagram*, accessed January 23, 2023, see "Story Highlights."
[3] Jake W. Newsome, @wjnewsome, *Instagram*, accessed January 23, 2023, see "Story Highlights."
[4] Benno Gammerl, *Anders Fühlen. Queeres Leben in der Bundesrepublik. Eine Emotionsgeschichte* (Munich: Hanser, 2021), 24–25.

10.1 Many Pink Triangles

Berlin was not the only city in 2019 to organize a special event, like the conference introduced at the start of this book where colleagues proudly showed me their Pink Triangle badges. New York City – epicenter of the Stonewall narrative and supposedly the birthplace of modern queer liberation in the Euro-American world – hosted the 2019 *WorldPride*, renamed *Stonewall 50 – WorldPride NYC 2019* for the occasion.[5] Millions of visitors attended a series of events taking place across the metropolis. Parallel to these, an organization calling itself the *Reclaim Pride Coalition* decided to create a counter-event denouncing the liberalization and commercialization of Pride and hold its own queer demonstration to commemorate the Stonewall anniversary. These alternative festivities were also paired with vigorous uses of the Pink Triangle on all merchandise, crowdfunding campaigns, and mobilization material before, during, and after the event.[6] The Triangle was also used in other recent political festivities and demonstrations. In Cologne, the official program of the city's 2017 *Christopher Street Demonstration* – usually abbreviated to CSD – used the symbol paired with the Black Triangle.[7]

The symbol is also connected to the memory of the murder of queer men and women across fascist Europe, including but not limited to German fascism. The award-nominated *Bones of Contention*, Andrea Weiss's 2017 documentary on Francoist Spain, touches on the persecution of gay men under Spain's fascist regime and its apparent erasure in the long postfascist era. One of her central protagonists, an activist fighting for legal reparations for queer men, wears a Pink Triangle pinned on his outfit throughout the film.[8] In 2014, the city of Tel-Aviv in Israel unveiled a Pink Triangle monument in memory of the victims of the Nazi regime "who were persecuted because of their sexual orientation or gender identity."[9] In 2022, a Pink Triangle column for the queer male victims of §175 StGB was inaugurated on the grounds of the former concentration camp of Flossenbürg, one of the camps where Josef Kohout had been interned.[10]

---

[5] Karma Allen, "About 5 million people attended WorldPride in NYC, mayor says," *ABC* (July 2, 2019).
[6] Reclaim Pride Coalition, "Store," accessed January 2, 2023, https://teespring.com/stores/queer-liberation-march.
[7] Cologne Pride, "Das Programmheft," accessed January 2, 2023, https://www.colognepride.de/de/2017/06/11/das-programmheft-2017/.
[8] Andrea Weiss, "Bones of Contention," 75 min: Jezebel Productions and Icarus Films, 2017.
[9] "Tel Aviv unveils memorial to gay Holocaust victims," *The Times of Israel* (January 10, 2014).
[10] Bayerischer Landtag and Stiftung Bayerische Gedenkstätten, *Gedenkakt 2022 – Flossenbürg* (January 26, 2022).

These examples show how the symbol is still in use today and how various key moments of its journey across the Atlantic all merge into one another, both in the queer community and in the public sphere. In this book, I have focused on the key moments of the Pink Triangle throughout the second half of the twentieth century and shown how its history was linked not only to the memories of Nazi persecutions of queer men and women, but also to the political reinterpretations of these atrocities in collective memory, focusing on the east and west coasts of North America and important urban centres in the Federal Republic of Germany (FRG). Separating this journey thematically and pointing out the inclusions and exclusions entrenched in the uses of the Pink Triangle, I have also mapped the entanglements of the tropes and narratives surviving within the symbol, including the idea of a Homocaust, the push for a universalized experience of queerness based on Euro-American gay liberation, a legitimization of queer rights based on Nazi persecutions in the past, and the dystopic referents of AIDS activism. Through this cartography, I have demonstrated how the symbol is tied to a transregional circulation of knowledge. This knowledge, sometimes based on facts and sometimes part of an imagined queer past, is at the core of a collective queer memory in the Euro-American world.

As a badge of injury, the Pink Triangle not only accompanied and illustrated the knowledge and creation of a collective memory of National Socialism but was also both an indicator and a factor of historical change for the queer community. It was first an indicator, as it became a go-to symbol for political groups in the FRG and the USA. Here the pink radicals in West Germany covered in the first chapter come to mind – see section 1.4 –, as well as various groups in the United States who adopted the symbol after identifying with the victims of the Nazi regime. For these groups, the use of a similar symbol was an important indicator of cohesion for the memory, and eventually the identity, of gays and lesbians on both sides of the Atlantic. The Pink Triangle was also a factor of change, a vector of historicization and legitimization for the queer community across the Euro-American world. The creation of Pink Triangle bridges in stone and on paper and the construction of the queer subject through the visual aspects of the symbol enabled the inclusion of the queer subject into official memory – *Vergangenheitsbewältigung* comes to mind. It also universalized one experience of queerness beyond the Euro-American world – a so-called patent of nobility – excluding other queer realities during National Socialism. For example, it erased the structural oppression of queer women, forcing them to either conceive their identity through a similar symbol – a Black Triangle – or adopt a mainly gay story to attract attention to specific forms of lesbian erasure and lesbophobic oppressions. Reflecting on the temporalities of the symbol and criticizing tropes of *Vergangenheitsbewältigung*, *A Badge of Injury* has likewise offered contemplations on the whiteness of the Pink Triangle and underlined a tendency of using National Socialism –or the Holocaust– rhetorically in non-Jewish queer circles.

An investigation of the Pink Triangle as a visual concept substantiated how the Euro-American queer memory culture of National Socialism anchored the construction of the queer subject in a negative longing for the past, in injury, and in narratives of victimhood. This is also identifiable in the ways that the Pink Triangle offered a visual culture of survival for the community in both the long postwar era and for subsequent struggles. AIDS activism and its discursive connections to the atrocities committed by the Nazis influenced memory on both continents, showing how the icon even transposed ideas of the Homocaust to places where such comparisons were frowned upon.

Entwined in our nine thematical stops while following our Pink Triangle aircraft's metaphorical journey on both sides of the Atlantic, this book also shed lights on four overarching topics: the writing of gay history; the importance of visual culture beyond the textual; the dialogue between queer and global history; and the necessity of provincializing gay history.

10.2 Memory culture and victimhood in the transatlantic world

The creation and evolution of a Euro-American queer collective was and still is anchored in a transregional cultural memory of National Socialism, and in many cases, the fantasy of atrocities that were not committed in the ways that they were imagined to have been after 1945. Through the Pink Triangle, queer men and women conflated various Homocaust narratives. For instance, they alleged that non-Jewish queer men shared a fate more horrendous than Jewish, Roma, and Sinti victims of the Nazis or that millions of people had been sent to their death because of §175 StGB. From the idea that queer history had been hidden evolved the idea that other victims of German fascism had stolen the spotlight in the marketplace of memory.

Our discussion on comparative and multidirectional memory in the third chapter – see section 3.1 – contextualized this appeal to memory in queer circles. It demonstrated paradoxically how the memory of the Holocaust was voided of its Jewish component in a North American context while an appeal to the murder of the European Jewry also became a universal sacred evil to which political communities and minorities started to connect their own oppression, forcing people in power to "learn from the lessons of history." This Americanization of the Holocaust – a focus on survivor witnesses, a sacralised evil, and the idea of learning from the past – eventually became a transregional phenomenon. North American queer activists further conflated the Holocaust with other Nazi atrocities, for example the persecution of queerness by the regime. In this context, not only was the Holocaust emptied of its Jewishness to make parallels with other moments of history, but the queer community also paradoxically accused Jewish voices of taking up too much space in the public sphere. In other words, non-Jewish queer activists considered the Holocaust to be a global icon to be referred to, but they also considered that the Holocaust was discussed too much.

In Germany, the emphasis was mainly on the cultural trauma at the base of the North American queer fascination for National Socialism. Looking at this cultural trauma under the scope of postmemory, virtual experience, and adopted memory, it is possible to expose the reasons behind the appeal of Homocaust narratives for queer activists – from the pink radicals onward – in the 1970s and 1980s. (Re)discovering the very real atrocities committed against gays and lesbians by the so-called Third Reich, queer communication networks propagated similitudes and continuities between Nazi politics and ideologies of the long postwar era. This led to an identification process where the queer subject (re)imagined itself as a victim of German fascism from the 1970s onward. As discussed in the first chapter – see section 1.3 –, this is one of the reasons behind the recuperation of the Pink Triangle by the pink radicals and the main argument behind the uses of the symbol in North America.

The focus of this book was not an ethical analysis of these recuperations or comparisons. As shown throughout the book, historians – even some of the scholars at the source of Homocaust narratives in the early days of queer liberation – have debunked historical exaggerations and researched Nazi persecutions of queerness beyond the scope of historical fallacy. However, by looking at the entanglements of all these perspectives and discourses about a presupposed Homocaust, this book has demonstrated how these narratives and cultural traumata were at the core of the construction of a Euro-American queer collective. In the case of queer women, the erasure of their story by queer men also enabled the adoption of another symbol connected to the horrors committed by the regime: the Black Triangle. This implies that a queer cultural memory of National Socialism in the Euro-American world is both a story of integration of the collective to official memory – *Vergangenheitsbewältigung* – but also exclusion within the queer collective itself. The Pink Triangle is therefore not only an indicator of the importance of National Socialism for the creation of the queer subject. The symbol also framed the discussion and the appeal of this cultural memory. Walks on Pink Triangle bridges were conditional as gatekeepers blocked – and are still obstructing – access to Pink Triangle memories by certain members of the queer community who are not cis and male.[11]

10.3 A visual history of the Pink Triangle

The Pink Triangle offers the possibility of using images and symbols as third idioms in order to trace the circulation of memory and knowledge. Other scholars working on queer memory culture have tackled some of the aspects mentioned above, looking comparatively at the history of gay and lesbian activism on both side of the Atlantic.[12] *A Badge of Injury* has presented a new and unique perspective on the history of the Euro-American queer subject, North American and German queer liberation, as well as the collectivization of queer memory in the Euro-American world, by looking at visual culture and at concepts going beyond the textual. The nine chapters of this book have shown how historians of sexualities can analyze the intellectual history of social movements and map the transfer of ideas without necessarily finding the same semantic viewpoints by looking at visual concepts, in this case the Pink Triangle.

Visual symbols carry many layers that accumulate over time and convey a multitude of narratives. In this regard, *A Badge of Injury* has underlined the role of bodily encounters, focusing on vision. Through a myriad of case studies, it has displayed how the Pink Triangle is a discursive two-way street; how images can be a representation of a discourse, and how their various layers and significations can affect their viewers according to context, space, and time. Queer activists looking at Pink Triangle monuments or memorabilia could walk on Pink Triangle bridges connecting them with the past and new possible utopias. In other words, the experience and context of one viewer looking at, for example, the Pink Triangle at *Nollendorfplatz*, could connect the plaque to various moments of queer history and allow them to imagine utopian futures devoid of homophobia. Queer injuries of the past therefore haunt the present, surviving as phantom pain. A visual conceptual history of the Pink Triangle cannot consequently be detached from a reflection on queer temporalities. Indeed, numerous key moments of the symbol's journey are all simultaneously existing, appearing, and disappearing as vectors of memory and cultural belonging depending on the viewer and the con-

---

11 Alexander Zinn, "Gefühlte Wahrheiten: Wie LGBTI-Aktivismus die Wissenschaftsfreiheit bedroht," In *Wissenschaftsfreiheit: Warum dieses Grundrecht zunehmend umkämpft ist*, ed. Sandra Kostner (Baden-Baden: Nomos, 2022), 165–182.
12 Jake W. Newsome, *Pink Triangle Legacies. Coming out in the Shadow of the Holocaust* (Ithaca, NY: Cornell University Press, 2022).

text in which the image is being viewed and used. This analysis of the Pink Triangle is intrinsically linked to the emancipatory negative emotions such as shame and with the inward and outward impulses of victimhood. Some have called this the agency of images; this book has highlighted how it is a form of conceptual interpretation triggered by our senses and through bodily encounters. The first recuperations of the triangle by the pink radicals in the 1970s are therefore linked to the branding of the symbol as an icon of survival by other groups like ACT UP, and even to the sale of Pink Triangle memorabilia at the turn of the millennium.

Last, this book has displayed how the study of icons and images is necessary to understand the various discourses at the core of social movements. For instance, certain German gay historians pretend that lesbian women are now falsifying history by appealing to the persecution of queer women by the Nazis. The second and third parts of this book have dived into these troubled waters and some of the more political aspects of queer historiography, dealing with the materiality of the Pink Triangle and the implicit exclusions entrenched in the symbol. Through such an investigation of the materiality of the triangle, it has been possible to demonstrate how the core of the symbol's story is not based on tangible objects. Museums and archives do not possess many Pink Triangles created before the end of the Second World War. This is not to dismiss in any ways the seriousness of the fate with of the men who were murdered wearing a pink triangle, but to nuance the idea that victimhood needs to be paired with perpetrator categories and the symbols they used. Hence, using visual history, *A Badge of Injury* has exposed tensions in gay and lesbian historiography, showing not only how the Pink Triangle became a collective symbol of queer memory, but how its adoption influenced the construction of historical identities within the queer collective in the Euro-American world.

10.4 Global queer history and provincialized gayness

This story of memory and cultural traumata is implicitly transregional. Tracing various key moments of the Pink Triangle through the writings and correspondences of scholars like James Steakley, Rüdiger Lautman, and Richard Plant or cultural productions like Martin Sherman's *Bent*, the story of the Pink Triangle was always a discussion between at least two continents. Because of the power structure of the Euro-American world in international organizations, for example, in and through the International Lesbian and Gay Association (ILGA), this transatlantic communication was internationalized and presented as universal. Through the circulation of knowledge from Euro-American activists to the world stage, for example, the United Nations, the Pink Triangle became a patent of nobility for homosexuality as a worldwide expression of queerness. *A Badge of Injury* has focused mainly on queer communication networks on both continents and the accumulation and circulation of knowledge between queer activists in the second part of the twentieth century.

Through many episodes, the book has opened a much-needed dialogue between queer history and global history and acts as an incitement to bring conceptual history and queer theory to the same table. The various case studies have shown how difficult it is to disentangle the Pink Triangle from its transatlantic journey. As the first part of the book has demonstrated, various national actors were part of a transregional conversation on the symbol and on memory, influencing the construction of a queer collective memory on both sides of the ocean. This back and forth between local queer communities moulded both a cultural memory of homosexualities and the bases for an international generalization of Euro-American queerness. *A Badge of Injury* has therefore highlighted the problems of writing national queer histories without taking the transregional transfers of ideas into consideration. If it has shown how local or national contexts are still relevant to the interpretation of discourses and symbols, this book has also exhibited how these national contexts cannot be isolated. It is thus necessary to go beyond the nation-state and look at broader communication networks, especially while writing a history establishing the fluidity of queerness. Taking for example, the AIDS activism at the core of chapter seven, it was possible to identify the local particularities of each section of the AIDS Coalition to Unleash Power (ACT UP) while appreciating the unifying factors of the movement's symbolic and connection to a queer memory of National Socialism – see section 7.3 –. To put it another way, following Jennifer Evans's call to queer German history, the nine chapters of this book have established how scholars should begin to think of queer German or North American history through the global turn.

Furthermore, understanding global networks and the transfer of ideas helps scholars and activists alike to assess power asymmetries in queer communities. Chapter six has shown how the broader adoption of the Pink Triangle is connected to the importance given to Euro-American narratives in the writing of queer history – see section 6.3. By mainly prioritizing queer origin stories in "the west," scholarship has so far reproduced a very Eurocentric understanding of queer history. *A Badge of Injury* has tackled these narratives, uncovering their construction in the transatlantic world. This focus was both an invitation to rethink Euro-American queer history as just one aspect of the global history of non-heteronormative sexualities and identities, and a way to look at gay and lesbian history horizontally, without essentializing its importance for the rest of the world.

My goal in writing this book was therefore to provincialize gay history. In other words, by showing the construction of the queer subject and the connection of the Pink Triangle with gay narratives, I show gay history as one aspect among many, uncovering the power structures that made this history seem universal. Other scholars have decided to highlight lesbian or trans* history, both highly necessary endeavors as a focus on gay frameworks of queerness still dominates queer scholarship. I have chosen to provincialize the mundane aspect of gay history to present it as what it is, one part of the LGBTQIA+ experience in the Euro-American world and one of the many experiences of queerness at the planetary scale. Throughout *A Badge of Injury*, I have mainly shed light upon episodes of gay history, while connecting the case studies and the importance of the Pink Triangle to other experiences of queerness. As I have demonstrated, the prevalence of gay power structures in the community and the emphasis put on aspects of the triangle's journey – §175 StGB, categories created by perpetrators, male-centered narratives, etc. – have contributed to the erasure of queer female realities or forced queer women to frame their liberation through gay structures. Similarly, the whiteness of this Euro-American journey can only be understood as a simultaneous erasure or silencing of racialized narratives.

Finally, I wrote this book for those who still needed more proof of the relevance of queer analysis and queer history for global history. As I have written, the Pink Triangle cannot be disentangled from its transatlantic journey. Global historians are here confronted with a case study that offers both new foci for a global history of social movements and identifies new ways to look at the global exchange of ideas. Beyond the visual culture analysis mentioned above, this book has demonstrated how a queer analysis can be a useful tool to global historians. Suggesting new conceptions of temporalities and possibilities to look at the fluidity and multilayered aspects of identity and memory, queer theory is useful for the creation of global semantic fields or for the cartography of social movements and cultural memory. *A Badge of Injury* was therefore a first step toward both a global history of queer and a queering of global history.

10.5 Beyond homonationalist triangles? Beyond the rainbow?

Much is still to be done to fully understand the impacts of the Pink Triangle and of Pink Triangle bridges. I have been able to trace the symbol's journey throughout the Euro-American world in a global perspective, but studies have yet to focus on lesser-known parts of this space, for example, the Midwest or the use of the symbol in the German Democratic Republic. Expanding the story of the Pink Triangle would also be necessary to even better understand the push of an international homosexual identity as a barometer for queerness beyond the Euro-American world. While writing *A Badge of Injury*, archivists from Australia generously contacted me to share examples of Pink Triangles appearing at the Sydney Mardi Gras during the early 1970s, simultaneous with their appearance in North America. Tracing the communication networks 'down under' would certainly be useful to understanding the icon's evolution. Furthermore, if Pink Triangles can be found in the South Pacific, expanding this research to Asia and Africa would be the next logical step to also understand the power asymmetry between queer NGOs coming from Europe and North America and grassroots organizations in the rest of the world. Simply put, one also needs to write the Pink Triangle's journey beyond the foci of this book. Beyond Australia, I have also found the symbol in China, Brazil, Japan, and Nigeria.

This new and complementary endeavour would also benefit recent scholarship on homonationalism. I have tackled the uses of queer politics by liberal democracies in chapter six and in chapter eight – see sections 6.2 and 8.2. Coined by Puar and re-interpreted by many, the concept is worth a final reflection. As illustrated by the *Pink Triangle Project* in San Francisco, the idea that "the west" has learned from decades of queerphobia and is now able to preach the values of tolerance and acceptance to the rest of the world is difficult to swallow.[13] Many of the countries seen as champions of queer rights do not always hold up to their own pretensions. Homonationalism and pink washing are interrelated. The first defines an assemblage of national racialized discourses on humanitarian interventions and patriotism on the back of certain members of the queer community or queer jingoist discourses of white supremacy masquerading as progress; that is, white queer activists excusing their own racism through progressive narratives.[14] Pink washing describes the purpose of public marketing campaigns or diplomatic missions that exaggerate aspects of one's nation or business venture regarding the liberal acceptance of queer individuals, usually only those deemed respectable enough. Underlining some aspects of this acceptance, for example, same-sex marriage or the inclusion of trans* soldiers in a national army, are then used to 'wash' away other human rights abuses, even silencing the voices of Black, Indigenous and queers of colour.[15] Canada is a good example. Ignoring the

---

[13] See Daniel Segal, "Rassismus im Schwulen Museum? Infowand sorgt für Kritik," *Siegessäule* (February 25, 2019).

[14] Jin Haritaworn and Jen Petzen, "Invented Traditions New Intimate Publics. Tracing the German 'Muslim Homophobia' Discourse," In *Islam in Its International Context. Comparative Perspectives*, ed. Stephen Hutchings, Chris Flood, Galina Miazhevich and Henri Nickels (Newcastle upon Tyne: Cambridge Scholars Publishing, 2011), 48–64.

[15] Ryan Conrad, *Against Equality: Queer Revolution Not Mere Inclusion* (London: AK Press, 2014).

fact that the 2010 Olympic Games in Vancouver were taking place on unceded Indigenous land and ignoring the call by various Indigenous groups to demonstrate against the event,[16] the Canadian press decided to focus on the so-called Pride House available for queer athletes during the games. Presenting Canada as the bastion of tolerance and following decades of Canadian pink washing of immigration policies despite the pleas of queer refugees,[17] magazines like *Xtra* presented the Pride House as the ultimate achievement of a long struggle against queerphobia that had now come to an end in the Nordic country. During the opening ceremony, members of various groups could be seen wearing a Pink Triangle as a badge.[18]

We are then, indeed, always coming back to the Pink Triangle. As mentioned in the introduction and in my use of the term homosynchronism, the rainbow flag and the Pink Triangle complement each other. One is a symbol of pride; the other is a symbol of shame recuperated to politically legitimize and historicize queer struggles. As shown throughout this book, the Pink Triangle eventually also became a symbol of pride, an icon to put forward, as the historicization of a past injury and the legitimization of a battle cry only made sense within a typical coming-out narrative. In other words, the Pink Triangle was conflated with the rainbow flag through homosynchronist and homonationalist amalgams, albeit as a symbol associated with history, with the past, and with survival. If the rainbow flag aims to bring queer community together highlighting the link between kinship and differences, the Pink Triangle, a symbol of legitimization, ironically became the vector of hegemony.

---

[16] See Scott Lauria Morgensen, "Settler Homonationalism: Theorizing Settler Colonialism within Queer Modernities," *GLQ: A Journal of Lesbian and Gay Studies* 16, no. 1–2 (2010): 105–131.

[17] In 2019, the Canadian Federal government pushed a new narrative presenting the Liberal Party of Justin Trudeau as the direct descendant of Pierre-Elliott Trudeau's decision to repeal laws criminalizing sodomy in 1969. Historians Tom Hooper and Gary Kinsman have deconstructed this narrative in the media, examining the various manners in which homosexuality kept on being punished after 1969. See their extensive analysis on the campaign's website, accessed 20 November, 2022 https://anti-69.ca/faq/. See also Sébastien Tremblay and Christopher Ewing, "Zündstoff" *Siegessäule* (October 2019); Gary William Kinsman and Patrizia Gentile, *The Canadian War on Queers: National Security as Sexual Regulation*, Sexuality Studies Series, (Vancouver: UBC Press, 2010); Gary William Kinsman, "Policing Borders and Sexual/Gender Identities: Queer Refugees in the Years of Canadian Neoliberalism and Homonationalism." In *(Neo)Colonialism, Neoliberalism, Resistance and Hope*, eds. Nancy Nicol, Adrian Jjuuko, Richard Lusimbo, Nick J. Mulé, Susan Ursel, Amar Wahab and Phyllis Waugh (London: School of Advanced Study, University of London, Institute of Commonwealth Studies., 2018), 97–129.

[18] Heather Sykes and Jeff Lloyd, "Gay Pride on Stolen Land: Homonationalism, Queer Asylum and Indigenous Sovereignty at the Vancouver Winter Olympics," 2012, http://hdl.handle.net/1807/32972.

Both symbols gained international traction. If the rainbow flag was created in the USA and disseminated across the world through cultural power structures and communication networks anchored in Global North and Global South dynamics, I still claim that the case of the Pink Triangle is different. A patent of nobility for Euro-American queer liberation, it is anchored in Euro-American history. Understanding its dissemination across the world therefore brings new dimensions to the study of homonationalism and pink washing by unveiling the various transregional entanglements of universalization and nuancing tropes of diffusionism. To put it differently, to understand the global power structures behind the Pink Triangle, it is first necessary to understand other layers of its transregional story. The Pink Triangle invites provincialization.

On its Telegram channel, the group Voices4 Berlin sends daily push alerts and notifications regarding queer politics: demonstrations, events, articles, and films. Describing itself as an "inclusive, non-violent direct-action group of LGBTQIA+ individuals for queer liberation [rainbow emoji]" the group's logo is composed of two triangles, one pink facing down and one in rainbow colours facing up and emerging from the former one. As I receive information on upcoming actions, meetings, and events, I often ponder whether this combination of so many layers of queer history offers possibilities to reframe our understanding of queerness and show solidarity with other experiences, or if it limits our political framings in narratives from the Euro-American world.

Through the Pink Triangle, Euro-American queer liberation has successfully fixed gay history and homosexual collective memory in a history of victimhood and injury. It is then not surprising that queer associations in 'the west' are now using their own collective memory of this past of persecution to analyse the world they live in. In this case, assumptions or behaviours of some institutions like the Human Rights Campaign in the United States of America or the *Lesben- und Schwulenverband Deutschlands* in Germany are different to the cynical pink washing tactics of governments and conglomerates.

Understanding the queer subject in other parts of the world as part of one big international community and writing Eurocentrist gay history as a universal story do not have to go hand-in-hand. The Pink Triangle did not automatically lead to cultural imperialism and eventually homonationalism. Such a claim would be teleogical. What I am pleading for here is a new scrutiny of homonationalism and its connection to queer memory and identity. Provincializing gay history and especially gay Euro-American history means deconstructing homonationalist discourses, writing the history of queer movements across the world, and finally translating and sharing the work of queer scholars of other parts of the globe, observing that queer experiences elsewhere – especially if they are connected to discrimination and persecution – do not necessarily have anything to do with a transatlantic memory of the Holocaust.

Having shown the merits of provincializing gay history through its symbols, the next step would be to deprovincialize experiences of queerness from elsewhere in the world for our understanding of queer history and particularly queer global history. This would imply confronting the false binaries of the Euro-American world with a rich understanding of genders and sexualities from elsewhere, but also questioning queer timelines of the Global North anchored in the transcendence of shame through pride. The Pink Triangle has shown how its journey nuances normative tropes in the Euro-American world. Comparing, opposing, and challenging the Pink Triangle with another history of queerness beyond the Euro-American world could show the limiting aspects of Pink Triangle bridges by showing other perspectives on time, on queerness, on memory. Queers in the Euro-American world have found their patent of nobility, have built bridges between injuries of the past and possible utopias. In doing so, they have understood and framed their experiences of queerness and their place in the world and worn history and memory as a badge. What does a badge of memory look like when it manifests positive longings of the past? Does a badge of memory necessarily have to be a badge of injury? Would a badge of happiness, of queer joy, have the same potential? Would it include, exclude, and underline survival in a similar way?

Bibliography

Unpublished Source Material

Canada

The ArQuives (formerly known as Canadian Lesbian and Gay Archives) [Toronto, ON]
Digital Poster Collection from the Canadian Lesbian and Gay Archives.

Federal Republic of Germany

Forum queeres Archiv München (formerly known as Forum Homosexualität München e.V.) [Munich]
Folder HAG/HAM 1974–1980.
Folder VSG 1974–1980.
Folder Schwulen Themen AIDS.
Folder 80er Zeitungsauschnittsammlung.
Folder 70er Zeitungsauschnittsammlung.

KZ-Gedensktätte Dachau / Stiftung Bayerische Gedenkstätten (DaA) [Dachau]
Albert Knoll Personal Papers.
Sammlung Dachau VSG Schwule Gruppe.
Sammlung Homosexuelle u. Gedenktafel.
Sammlung Schwule u. Faschismus.

Archives of the Schwules Museum Berlin [Berlin]
Sammlung Michael Holy.
Unsortiert Thematic, ACT UP.
SM E Schauspielkritiken, Martin Sherman.
SM C Denkmal Debatte NS-Zeit.
SM C Erinnerung an Nationalsozialistische Homosexuellen-Verfolgung 1977–2008.
SM C Gedenken an die Homosexuellen Häftlinge in Sachsenhausen.
SM C Gedenkorte der Homosexuellen Verfolgung Berlin Nollendorfplatz.
SM C Gedenkorte der Homosexuellen Verfolgung Frankfurter Engel.
SM C Gedenk-Veranstaltungen Homosexuellen-Verfolgung Berlin-Sonstiges.

United States of America

Beinecke Rare Book & Manuscript Library [New Haven, CT]
Larry Kramer Papers, 1920–2008.

Gay, Lesbian, Bisexual, and Transgender Historical Society [San Francisco, CA]
Allan Berube Papers, 1946–2007.

George H.W. Bush Library Center [College Station, TX]
The Bush Administration and the AIDS Crisis: White House Office of Records Management.
Subject Files, AIDS Coalition to Unleash Power (ACT UP): AIDS Memorial Quilt.

Lesbian Herstory Archives [Brooklyn, NY]
Subject Files, Feminism International, Lesbian Movement.
Subject Files, Holocaust.
Subject Files, Jewish Lesbians.
Subject Files, Lavender Menace.
Subject Files, Spinsters-Youth.
Subject Files, Symbols.

National Archive of Lesbian, Gay, Bisexual and Transgender History [New York, NY]
Collection #24, Michael Weltmann Papers, 1968–1992.
Collection #45, New York Boycott Colorado Papers, 1993.
Collection #65, Congregation Beth Simchat Torah Records, 1973–2000.
Collection #84, Jonathan Ned Katz Papers, 1919–1997.
Collection #121, Dr. Harold Kooden Papers, 1980–1996.

Manuscripts and Archives Division, The New York Public Library [New York, NY]
MssCol 10, ACT UP New York Records 1969, 1982–1997.
MssCol 1483, International Gay Information Center 1959–2000, Ephemera files – Organizations.
- Committee on Lesbian and Gay History CLGH.
- Gay Liberation Chicago.
- International Gay and Lesbian Association ILGA.
- Jewish Lesbian Daughters of Holocaust Survivors.
- Lavender Hill Mob.
- Lavender Left.
- Pink Triangle Alliance.

- Pink Triangle Coalition.
- Pink Panthers.
- Publishing Triangle.
- Radical Women.
- Red Butterfly.

MssCol 1482, International Gay Information Center 1959–2000, Ephemera files – Individuals.
- Reagan, Ronald.
- Rothenberg, David.
- Sherman, Martin.
- Shewey, Don.
- Thorstad, David.
- Ulrichs, Karl Heinrich.
- Vidal, Gore.
- Von Praunheim, Rosa.

MssCol, 3648 Gran Fury Collection.
MssCol, 4374 Richard Plant Papers, 1910–1998.

ONE National Gay and Lesbian Archives at the USC Libraries [Los Angeles, CA]
ACT UP / Los Angeles records, 1987–1997.
Twice Blessed Collection, circa 1966–2000.

Newspapers Corpus

- *Christopher Street* 1976–1992.
- *Dorn Rosa. Zeitung der demokratischen Lesben- und Schwulen Initiative* 1986–1994.
- *Du & Ich* 1970–1987.
- *Emanzipation / Homosexuelle Emanzipation* 1975–1980.
- *GLF-Infos* 1971–1980.
- *HAW-Infos* 1972–1975.
- *HuK-Infos* 1981–1988.
- *Kellerjournal* 1980–1987.
- *Magnus* 1989–1997.
- *New York Native* 1980–1995.
- *Rosa Info* 1987–1997.
- *Rosa Flieder* 1977–1989.
- *The Advocate* 1970–1999.
- *The Body Politic* 1971–1987.
- *Schwuchtel* 1975–1977.
- *Siegessäule* 1984–1999 (including time as Berlin-Annex for *Magnus*)
- *Südwind* 1987–1991.

Films and other Broadcastings

France, David. 2012. How to Survive a Plague. GathrFilms.
France, David. 2020. Welcome to Chechnya. HBO Films.
Hick, Jochen. 2017. Mein wunderbares West Berlin. Galeria Alaska Productions.
Hubbard, Jim. 2012. United in Anger: A History of ACT UP. Independant.
Recht, Peter, Christiane Schmerl, and Detlef Stoffel. 1975–1976. Rosa Winkel? Das ist doch schon lange vorbei ... Fakültät für Soziologie Universität Bielefeld.
Weiss, Andrea. 2017. Bones of Contention. Jezebel Productions and Icarus Films.

Interviews

ACT UP Oral History Project

Barr, David. 2007. Interview #73 'ACT UPs Sprung Up Around the Country.' In *Act Up Oral History Project (MIX: The New York Lesbian & Gay Experimental Film Festival)*, edited by Sarah Schulman.
Christenson, Kim. 2010. Interview #122 'Drawing Lessons from the Past.' In *Act Up Oral History Project (MIX: The New York Lesbian & Gay Experimental Film Festival)*, edited by Sarah Schulman.
Crimp, Douglas. 2007. Interview #74 'Complexity into Sloganeering.' In *Act Up Oral History Project (MIX: The New York Lesbian & Gay Experimental Film Festival)*, edited by Sarah Schulman.
Fidelino, Jose. 2004. Interview #57 'A Conscience in ACT UP.' In *Act Up Oral History Project (MIX: The New York Lesbian & Gay Experimental Film Festival)*, edited by Sarah Schulman.
Finkelstein, Avram. 2010. Interview # 108 'Silence = Death.' In *Act Up Oral History Project (MIX: The New York Lesbian & Gay Experimental Film Festival)*, edited by Sarah Schulman.
Goldberg, Ron. 2003. Interview #32 'The ACT UP Timeline.' In *Act Up Oral History Project (MIX: The New York Lesbian & Gay Experimental Film Festival)*, edited by Sarah Schulman.
Guerrero, Elias. 2004. Interview #51 'AIDS Remains a Political Struggle.' In *Act Up Oral History Project (MIX: The New York Lesbian & Gay Experimental Film Festival)*, edited by Sarah Schulman.
Huff, Bob. 2007. Interview #79 'That Amazing Poster.' In *Act Up Oral History Project (MIX: The New York Lesbian & Gay Experimental Film Festival)*, edited by Sarah Schulman.
Kalin, Tom. 2004. Interview #42 'A Room Bristling with Ideas and Energy.' In *Act Up Oral History Project (MIX: The New York Lesbian & Gay Experimental Film Festival)*, edited by Sarah Schulman.
Katz, Sandy. 2004. Interview #58 'Ronald Reagan – Murderer!' In *Act Up Oral History Project (MIX: The New York Lesbian & Gay Experimental Film Festival)*, edited by Sarah Schulman and Jim Hubbard.
Kramer, Larry. 2003. Interview # 35 'ACT UP's Greatest Achievement.' In *Act Up Oral History Project (MIX: The New York Lesbian & Gay Experimental Film Festival)*, edited by Sarah Schulman.
Manhoff, Ira. 2013. Interview #152 'Zaps!' In *Act Up Oral History Project (MIX: The New York Lesbian & Gay Experimental Film Festival)*, edited by Sarah Schulman.
MaxZine, Weinstein. 2004. Interview #59 'Challenging Homophobia.' In *Act Up Oral History Project (MIX: The New York Lesbian & Gay Experimental Film Festival)*, edited by Sarah Schulman.
Nesline, Michael. 2003. Interview #14 'T-Shirts.' In *Act Up Oral History Project (MIX: The New York Lesbian & Gay Experimental Film Festival)*, edited by Sarah Schulman.
Northrop, Ann. 2003. Interview #27 'Strong and Angry.' In *Act Up Oral History Project (MIX: The New York Lesbian & Gay Experimental Film Festival)*, edited by Sarah Schulman.

O'Dwyer, Paul. 2015. Interview #174 'The HIV Ban.' In *Act Up Oral History Project (MIX: The New York Lesbian & Gay Experimental Film Festival)*, edited by Sarah Schulman.
Philbin, Ann. 2003. Interview #11 'ACT UP & the Art World.' In *Act Up Oral History Project (MIX: The New York Lesbian & Gay Experimental Film Festival)*, edited by Sarah Schulman.
Rolston, Adam. 2008. Interview #101 'ACT UP Graphics.' In *Act Up Oral History Project (MIX: The New York Lesbian & Gay Experimental Film Festival)*, edited by Sarah Schulman.
Staley, Peter. 2006. Interview #67 'Invading the New York Stock Exchange.' In *Act Up Oral History Project (MIX: The New York Lesbian & Gay Experimental Film Festival)*, edited by Sarah Schulman.
Wolfe, Maxine. 2004. Interview #43 'People, People, You Have to Listen.' In *Act Up Oral History Project (MIX: The New York Lesbian & Gay Experimental Film Festival)*, edited by Jim Hubbard.

Archiv der anderen Erinnerungen

Lauinger, Wolfgang. 2015. Lauinger. In *Archiv der anderen Erinnerungen*, edited by Michael Bochow, Karl-Heinz Steinle and Daniel Hübner: Bundesstiftung Magnus Hirschfeld.

Published Source Material

Beck, Gad. *An Underground Life : Memoirs of a Gay Jew in Nazi Berlin*. Madison, WI: The University of Wisconsin Press, 2000.
Consoli, Massimo. *Homocaust*. Milan: Kaos, 1991.
Finkelstein, Avram. *After Silence: A History of AIDS through Its Images*. Oakland, CA: University of California Press, 2018.
Heger, Heinz. *Die Männer mit dem rosa Winkel*. 4. ed. London: GMP Publ. 2001. Original Edition, 1974.
Kramer, Larry. *Faggots*. New York, NY: Plume, 1987.
Kramer, Larry. *Reports from the Holocaust : the Story of an AIDS Activist*. Updated and Expanded. ed. New York, NY: St. Martin's Press, 1994.
Lively, Scott, and Kevin Abrams. *The Pink Swastika Homosexuality in the Nazi Party*. 3. ed. Keiser, OR: Founders Publisher, 1997.
Mass, Lawrence D. *Confessions of a Jewish Wagnerite*. New York, NY: Cassell, 1994.
Monette, Paul. *Borrowed Time: An AIDS Memoir*. San Diego, CA: Harcourt Brace Jovanovich, 1988.
Plant, Richard. *The Pink Triangle: The Nazi War Against Homosexuals*. New York City, NY: Henry Holt and Company, 1988.
Popp, Wolfgang. „Auf den Spuren einer Schwulen Identität: Vorbemerkungen." In „*Ein erfülltes Leben trotzdem": Erinnerungen Homosexueller 1933-1945*, edited by Lutz van Dijk, i–v. Hamburg: Rowohlt, 1992.
Rector, Frank. *The Nazi Extermination of Homosexuals* New York City, NY: Stein & Day, 1981.
Seel, Pierre. *Moi, Pierre Seel, déporté homosexuel*. Paris: Calmann-Lévy, 1994.
Sherman, Martin. *Bent*. New York, NY: Avon Books, 1980.
Shilts, Randy. *And the band played on: Politics, People, and the AIDS Epidemic*. New York, NY: St. Martin's Press, 1987.
Thorstad, David, and John Lauritsen. *The Homosexual Rights Movement (1864-1935)*. Washington, NJ: Times Change Press, 1973.

Wojnarowicz, David. *Close to Knives: A Memoir of Desintegration*. New York City, NY: Vintage, 1991.
Würdemann, Ulrich. *Schweigen = Tod, Aktion = Leben: ACT Up in Deutschland 1989 bis 1993*. Berlin: Thomas Michalak, 2017.

Secondary Literature

Ahmed, Sara. *The Cultural Politics of Emotion*. Edinburgh: Edinburgh University Press, 2004.
Ahmed, Sara. *Queer Phenomenology: Orientations, Objects, Others*. Durham, NC Duke University Press, 2006.
Ahmed, Sara. "Happy Objects." In *The Affect Theory Reader*, edited by Melissa Gregg and Gregory J. Seigworth, 29–51. Durham, NC: Duke University Press, 2010.
Aktivistinnen des lesbischen Gedenkens. "Anna Hájková und Birgit Bosold im Gespräch mit Ulrike Janz, Irmes Schwager und Lisa Steininger." *Invertito: Jahrbuch für die Geschichte der Homosexualitäten* 21 (2019): 74–97.
Alexander, Jeffrey C. "On the Social Construction of Moral Universals. The 'Holocaust' from War Crime to Trauma Drama." *European Journal of Social Theory* 5, no1 (2002): 5–85.
Alexander, Jeffrey C. *Cultural Trauma and Collective Identity*. Berkeley, CA: University of California Press, 2004.
Alexander, Jeffrey C. "Toward a Theory of Cultural Trauma." In *Cultural Trauma and Collective Identity*, edited by Alexander Jeffrey, Ron Eyerman and Bernard Giesen, 1–30. Berkeley, CA: University of California Press, 2004.
Alexander, Jeffrey C., and Martin Jay. *Remembering the Holocaust: A Debate*. Oxford; New York: Oxford University Press, 2009.
Amesberger, Helga, Katrin Auer, and Brigitte Halbmayr. "Sexuelle Ausbeutung von Frauen in NS-Konzentrationslagern." In *Sexualisierte Gewalt: Weibliche Erfahrungen in NS-Konzentrationslagern*, edited by Helga Amesberger, Katrin Auer and Brigitte Halbmayr, 101–162. Vienna: Mandelbaum Verlag, 2010.
Assmann, Aleida. *Erinnerungsräume: Formen und Wandlungen des kulturellen Gedächtnisses, C. H. Beck Kulturwissenschaft*. München: C. H. Beck, 1999.
Assmann, Aleida. "Canon and Archive." In *Cultural Memory Studies: An International and Interdiscipinary Handbook*, edited by Astrid Erll, Ansgar Nünning and Sara B. Young, 97–108. Berlin: Walter de Gruyter, 2008.
Assmann, Aleida. "The Holocaust: A Global Memory? Extensions and Limits of a New Memory Community." In *Memory in a Global Age: Discourses, Practices and Trajectories*, edited by Aleida Assmann and Sebastian Conrad, 97–117. Basingstoke: Palgrave Macmillan, 2010
Assmann, Aleida. "Re-Framing Memory: Between Individual and Collective Forms of Constructing the Past." In *Performing the Past: Memory, History, and Identity in Modern Europe*, edited by Jay Winter, Karin Tilmans and Frank van Vree, 35–50. Amsterdam: Amsterdam University Press, 2010.
Assmann, Aleida. *Das neue Unbehagen an der Erinnerungskultur: Eine Intervention*. Munich: C. H. Beck, 2013.
Assmann, Aleida, and Sebastian Conrad. "Introduction." In *Memory in a Global Age: Discourses, Practices and Trajectories*, edited by Aleida Assmann and Sebastian Conrad, 1–16. Basingstoke: Palgrave Macmillan, 2010.
Atshan, Sa'ed, and Katharina Galor. *The Moral Triangle. Germans, Israelis, Palestinians*. Durham, NC: Duke University Press, 2020.

Baader, Hannah. "Das Objekt auf der Bühne. Diamanten, Dinge und Johann Melchior Dinglingers Imaginationen einer Geburtstagfeier in Agra." In *Synergies in Visual Cultures – Bildkulturen im Dialog*, edited by Manuela de Giorgi, Annette Hoffmann and Nicola Suthor, 269–284. Paderborn: Brill, 2013.

Bal, Mieke. "Introduction." In *Acts of Memory: Cultural Recall in the Present*, edited by Mieke Bal, Jonathan V. Crewe and Leo Spitzer, vii–xvii. Hanover, NH: University Press of New England, 1999.

Barthes, Roland. *La chambre claire: note sur la photographie, Cahiers du cinéma*. Paris: Gallimard, 1980.

Bauche, Manuela, Patricia Piberger, Sébastien Tremblay, and Hannah Tzuberi. "From Opferkonkurrenz to Solidarity: A Round Table." *Bulletin of the German Historical Institute London* 44, no. 2 – Special Issue Memory Culture 2.0: From Opferkonkurrenz to Solidarity (2022): 32–85.

Bayramoğlu, Yener. *Queere (Un-)Sichtbarkeiten: Die Geschichte der queeren Repräsentationen in der türkischen und deutschen Boulevardpresse*. Bielefeld: Transcript-Verlag, 2018.

Beemyn, Genny. *A Queer Capital: A History of Gay Life in Washington, D.C.* New York, NY: Routledge, 2015.

Beljan, Daniela, and Mathias N. Lorenz. "Weizsäcker-Rede." In *Lexikon der ‚Vergangenheitsbewältigung' in Deutschland: Debatten- und Diskursgeschichte des Nationalsozialismus nach 1945*, edited by Torben Fischer and Matthias N. Lorenz, 253–256. Bielefeld: transcript, 2015.

Bens, Jonas, Susanne Kleinfeld, and Karoline Noack. *Fußball. Macht. Politik: Interdisziplinäre Perspektiven auf Fußball und Gesellschaft*. Bielefeld: transcript, 2014.

Bentley, Jerry H. "One Regional Histories, Global Processes, Cross-Cultural Interactions." In *Interactions: Transregional Perspectives on World History*, edited by Jerry H. Bentley, Renate Bridenthal and Anand A. Yang, 1–13. Honolulu, HI: University of Hawai'i Press, 2005.

Berlant, Lauren. "Introduction: Affect in the Present." In *Cruel Optimism*, edited by Lauren Berlant, 1–22. Durham, NC: Duke University Press, 2011.

Blackwood, Evelyn. "Native American Genders and Sexualities: Beyond Anthropological Models and Misrepresentations." In *Two-spirit People: Native American Gender Identity, Sexuality, and Spirituality*, edited by Sue-Ellen Jacobs, Wesley Thomas and Sabine Lang, 284–296. Champaign, IL: University of Illinois Press, 2005.

Boehm, Gottfried. *Wie Bilder Sinn erzeugen: Die Macht des Zeigens*. Berlin: Berlin University Press, 2008.

Boehm, Gottfried and Sebastian Egenhofer. *Was ist ein Bild?: Antworten in Bildern: Gottfried Boehm zum 70. Geburtstag*. München: Wilhelm Fink, 2012.

Börzel, Tanja, and Michael Zürn. *Contestations of the Liberal Script. A Research Program, SCRIPTS Working Paper Series*. Berlin: Cluster of Excellence 2055. "Contestations of the Liberal Script – SCRIPTS" (Freie Universität Berlin). 2020.

Bos, Pascale R. "Adopted Memory: The Holocaust, Postmemory, and Jewish Identity in America." In *Diaspora and Memory: Figures of Displacement in Contemporary Literature, Arts and Politics*, edited by Marie-Aude Baronian, Stephan Besser and Yolande Jansen, 97–108. Amsterdam: Brill, 2016.

Bosia, Michael J. "AIDS and Postcolonial Politics: Acting Up on Science and Immigration in France." *French Politics, Culture & Society* 27, no. 1 (2009): 69–90.

Bost, Darius. *Evidence of Being: The Black Gay Cultural Renaissance and the Politics of Violence*. Chicago, IL: The University of Chicago Press, 2019.

Brade, Fred. "'Er war ein Hallodri' Der Tänzer Richard Barnack." In *Homosexuelle Männer im KZ Sachsenhausen* edited by Joachim Müller and Andreas Sternweiler, 211–212. Berlin: Verlag Rosa Winkel, 2000.

Brandt, Bettina. "Politik im Bild? Überlegungen zum Verhältnis von Begriff und Bild." In *Politik: Situationen eines Wortgebrauchs im Europa der Neuzeit*, edited by Wilibald Steinmetz, 41–71. Frankfurt (Main): Campus, 2007.

Brandt, Bettina, and Britta Hochkirchen. "Bilder als Denk- und Erfahrungsraum möglicher Geschichten im Werk Reinhart Kosellecks." In *Reinhart Koselleck als Historiker. Zu den Bedingungen möglicher Geschichten*, edited by Manfred Hettling and Wolfgang Schieder, 248–275. Göttingen: Vandenhoeck & Ruprecht, 2021.

Brandt, Bettina, Britta Hochkirchen, and Thomas Thiel. Reinhart Koselleck und das Bild. Begleitung Broschüre. Herzebrock-Clarholz: Heinrich Eusterhus, 2018.

Braukman, Stacy. "Epilogue: Anita Bryant and Florida's Culture Wars." In *Communists and Perverts Under the Palms: The Johns Committee in Florida 1956–1965*, edited by Stacy Braukman, 193–208. Gainesville, Tallahasse, FL: University Press of Florida, 2013.

Brier, Jennifer, Jim Downs, and Jennifer L. Morgan. *Connexions: Histories of Race and Sex in North America*. Urbana, IL: University of Illinois Press. 2016.

Brillon, Susan. "Trauma Narratives and the Remaking of the Self." In *Acts of Memory: Cultural Recall in the Present*, edited by Mieke Bal, Jonathan V. Crewe and Leo Spitzer, 39–54. Hanover, NH: University Press of New England, 1999.

Britt, Lory, and David Heise. "From Shame to Pride in Identity Politics." In *Self, Identity, And Social Movements*, edited by Sheldon Stryker, Timothy J. Owens and Robert W. White, 252–268. Minneapolis, MN: University of Minnesota Press, 2000.

Brock, Maria, and Emil Edenborg. "'You cannot oppress those who do not exist' Gay Persecution in Chechnya and the Politics of In/visibility." *GLQ: A Journal of Lesbian and Gay Studies* 26, no. 4 (2020): 673–700.

Broqua, Christophe. *Agir pour ne pas mourir! : ACT UP, les homosexuels et le sida*. Paris: Presses de la Fondation nationale des sciences politiques, 2005.

Brown, Wendy. "Wounded Attachments: Late Modern Oppositional Political Formations." In *The Identity in Question*, edited by John Rajchman, 199–228. New York, NY: Routledge, 1995.

Brusius, Mirjam Sarah. "Introduction." *Bulletin of the German Historical Institute London* 44, no. 2 – Special Issue Memory cultures 2.0: From Opferkonkurrenz to Solidarity (2022): 3–20.

Bühner, Maria. "Die Kontinuität des Schweigens. Das Gedenken der Ost-Berliner Gruppe Lesben in der Kirche in Ravensbrück." *Österreichische Zeitschrift für Geschichtswissenschaften* 29, no. 2 (2019): 111–131.

Canaday, Margot. *The Straight State: Sexuality and Citizenship in Twentieth-century America*. Princeton, NJ.: Princeton University Press, 2009.

Carruthers, Susan L. *The Good Occupation: American Soldiers and the Hazards of Peace*. Cambridge, MA: Harvard University Press, 2016.

Caruth, Cathy. *Unclaimed Experience: Trauma, Narrative, and History*. Baltimore, MD: Johns Hopkins University Press, 1996.

Castiglia, Christopher, and Christopher Reed, *If Memory Serves: Gay Men, AIDS, and the Promise of the Queer Past*. Minneapolis, MN: University of Minnesota Press, 2012.

Catlin, Jonathon. "'A New German Historians' Debate? A Conversation with Sultan Doughan, A. Dirk Moses, and Michael Rothberg." *Journal of the History of Ideas Blog*. https://jhiblog.org/2022/02/02/a-new-german-historians-debate-a-conversation-with-sultan-doughan-a-dirk-moses-and-michael-rothberg-part-i/. 2022.

Chaumont, Jean-Michel. *La concurrence des victimes: Génocide, identité, reconnaissance*. Paris: Éditions la Découverte, 1997.

Conrad, Ryan. *Against Equality: Queer Revolution Not Mere Inclusion*. London: AK Press, 2014.

Cooper, Brittney C. *Beyond Respectability: The Intellectual Thought of Race Women*. Urbana, IL: University of Illinois Press, 2017.

Crimp, Douglas. *AIDS Demo Graphic*. Seattle, WA: Bay Press, 1990.
Didi-Huberman, Georges. *L'image survivante: Histoire de l'Art et temps des fantômes selon Aby Warburg*. Paris: Les Éditions de Minuit, 2002.
Didi-Huberman, Georges. *Quand les images prennent position: L'oeil de l'Histoire 1*. Paris: Les Éditions de Minuit, 2009.
Didi-Huberman, Georges. *Remontages du temps subi. L' oeil de l'histoire*. Paris: Les Éditions de Minuit, 2010.
Diner, Dan. "Nation, Migration, and Memory: On Historical Concepts of Citizenship." *Constellations* 4, no. 3 (1998): 293–462.
Dinshaw, Carolyn. "Touching on the Past." In *The Boswell Thesis: Essays for the Twenty-Fifth Anniversary of John Boswell's Christianity, Social Tolerance, and Homosexuality*, edited by Matthew Kuefler, 57–73. Chicago, IL: University of Chicago Press, 2006.
Doan, Laura. "Queer History / Queer Memory: The Case of Alan Turing." *GLQ: A Journal of Lesbian and Gay Studies* 23, no. 1(2017): 113–136.
Dobler, Jens. "Unzucht und Kuppelei: Lesbenverfolgung im Nationalsozialismus." In *Homophobie und Devianz: Weibliche und männliche Homosexualität im Nationalsozialismus*, edited by Insa Eschebach, 53–62. Berlin: Stiftung Brandenburgische Gedenkstätten, 2012.
Drewski, Daniel, and Jürgen Gerhards. *The Liberal Border Script and its Contestations. An Attempt of De nition and Systematization*. Vol. 4, *SCRIPTS Working Paper*. Berlin: Cluster of Excellence 2055 "Contestations of the Liberal Script – SCRIPTS," 2020.
Dryden, OmiSoore H., and Suzanne Lenon. *Disrupting Queer Inclusion: Canadian Homonationalisms and the Politics of Belonging*. Vancouver, BC: University of British Columbia Press, 2015.
Duberman, Martin. *Has the Gay Movement Failed?* Oakland, CA: University of California Press, 2018.
Duchaine-Guillon, Laurence, *La vie juive à Berlin après 1945*. Paris: CNRS Editions, 2011.
Egemann, Laura. "Zur Kritik der Homonationalismus-Kritik." In *Feministische Kritiken und Menschenrechte. Reflexionen auf ein produktives Spannungsverhältnis*, edited by Imke Leicht, Nadja Meisterhans, Christine Löw and Katharina Volk, 75–94. Opladen: Verlag Barbara Budrich, 2016.
Elman, R. Almy. 1996. "Triangles and Tribulations." *Journal of Homosexuality* 30, no. 3 (1996): 1–11.
Endlich, Stefanie. "Das Berliner Homosexuellen-Denkmal: Kontext, Erwartungen und die Debatte um den Videofilm." In *Homophobie und Devianz. Weibliche und männliche Homosexualität im Nationalsozialismus*, edited by Insa Eschebach, 167–186. Berlin: Metropol, 2012.
Eschebach, Insa. "Queere Gedächtnis. Zivilgesellschaftliches Engagement und Erinnerungskonkurrenzen im Kontext der Gedenkstätte Ravensbrück." *Invertito: Jahrbuch für die Geschichte der Homosexualitäten* 21 (2019): 49–73.
Escofier, Jeffrey. "Sex in the Seventies: Gay Porn Cinema as an Archive for the History of American Sexuality." *Journal of the History of Sexuality* 26, no. 1 (2017): 88–113.
Evans, Jennifer. "Harmless kisses and infinite loops. Making space for queer place in twenty-first century Berlin." In *Queer Cities, Queer Cultures Europe since 1945*, edited by Jennifer Evans and Matt Cook, 75–94. London: Bloomsbury Academic, 2014.
Evans, Jennifer. *The Queer Art of History: Queer Kinship after Fascism*. Durham, NC: Duke University Press, 2023.
Evans, Jennifer. "Why Queer German History?" *German History* 34, no. 3 (2016): 371–384.
Evans, Jennifer. "Seeing Subjectivity: Erotic Photography and the Optics of Desire." *American Historical Review* 118, no. 2 (2013): 430–462.
Ewing, Christopher "Highly affected groups: Gay men and racial others in West Germany's AIDS epidemic, 1981–1992." *Sexualities* 23, no. 1–2 (2020): 201–223.

Ewing, Christopher, and Sébastien Tremblay. "Introduction. Queer Imprint." In *Queer Media in the German Speaking World – New Approaches to Print Sources*, edited by Christopher Ewing and Sébastien Tremblay. London: Palgrave Macmillan, [Forthcoming 2024].

Farris, Sara R. *In the Name of Women's Rights: The Rise of Femonationalism*. Durham, NC: Duke University Press, 2017.

Feldman, Eric A., and Ronald Bayer, *Blood Feuds: AIDS, Blood, and the Politics of Medical Disaster* Oxford: Oxford University Press, 1999.

Fernheimer, Janice W. *Stepping Into Zion: Hatzaad Harishon, Black Jews, and the Remaking of Jewish Identity*. Tuscaloosa, AL: University of Alabama Press, 2014.

Flanzbaum, Hilene. "Introduction: The Americanization of the Holocaust." In *The Americanization of the Holocaust*, edited by Hilene Flanzbaum, 1–17. Baltimore, MD: Johns Hopkins University Press, 1999.

Flanzbaum, Hilene. "The Imaginary Jew and the American Poet." In *The Americanization of the Holocaust*, edited by Hilene Flanzbaum, 18–32. Baltimore, MD: Johns Hopkins University Press, 1999.

Florvil, Tiffany N. *Mobilizing Black Germany. Afro-German Women and the Making of a Transnational Movement*. Champaign, IL: University of Illinois Press, 2020.

Florvil, Tiffany N., and Sina Speit. "Intellektuelle des Alltags. Die afro-deutsche Frauenbewegung – ein Gespräch." *Geschichte der Gegenwart*, July 18. https://geschichtedergegenwart.ch/intellektuelle-des-alltags-die-afro-deutsche-frauenbewegung-ein-gespraech/. 2021.

Fortunati, Vita, and Elena Lamberti. "Cultural Memory: A European Perspective." In *Cultural Memory Studies: An International and Interdisciplinary Handbook* edited by Astrid Erll, Ansgar Nünning and Sara B. Young, 127–140. Berlin: Walter de Gruyter, 2008.

Freccero, Carla. *Queer/early/modern*. Durham, NC: Duke University Press, 2006.

Fried, Michael. "Barthes's Punctum." *Critical Inquiry* 31, no. 3 (2005): 539–574.

Fritzsche, Peter. *Stranded in the Present: Modern Time and the Melancholy of History*. Cambridge, MA: Harvard University Press, 2004.

Fuchs, Martin. "Reaching out or Nobody Exists in One Context Only Society as Translation." *Translation Studies* 2, no. 1 (2009): 21–40.

Games, Alison. "Beyond the Atlantic: English Globetrotters and Transoceanic Connections." *The William and Mary Quarterly* 63, no. 4 (2006): 675–692.

Gammerl, Benno. *Anders fühlen. Queeres Leben in der Bundesrepublik. Eine Emotionsgeschichte,*. Munich: Hanser, 2021.

Gamson, Josh. "Silence, Death, and the Invisible Ennemy: AIDS Activism and Social Movement 'Newness.'" *Social Problems* 36, no. 4 (1989): 351–367.

Gell, Alfred. *Art and Agency: An Anthropological Theory*. Oxford: Clarendon Press. 2007. Original edition, 1998.

Gilroy, Paul. *The Black Atlantic: Modernity and Double Consciousness*. Cambridge, MA: Harvard University Press, 1994.

Gilroy, Paul. *Against Race: Imagining Political Culture Beyond the Color Line*. Cambridge, MA: Belknap Press of Harvard University Press, 2000.

Goldstein, Eric L. *The Price of Whiteness: Jews, Race, and American Identity*. Princeton, NJ: Princeton University Press, 2006.

Gould, Deborah B. *Moving Politics: Emotions and ACT UP's fight against AIDS*. Chicago, IL: University of Chicago Press, 2009.

Griffiths, Craig. „Konkurrierende Pfade der Emanzipation: Der Tuntenstreit (1973–1975) und die Frage des ‚respektablen Auftretens.'" In *Rosa Radikale: Die Schwulenbewegung der 1970er Jahre*, edited by Andreas Pretzel and Volker Weiß, 143–159. Hamburg: Männerschwarm Verlag, 2012.

Griffiths, Craig. *The Ambivalence of Gay Liberation: Male Homosexual Politics in 1970s West Germany.* Oxford: Oxford University Press, 2021.
Griffiths, Craig. "Die Ambivalenz der Schwulenemanzipation der 1970er Jahre." *Invertito – Jahrbuch für die Geschichte der Homosexualitäten* 23 (2021): 136–145.
Grisard, Dominique. "Rosa: Zum Stellenwert der Farbe in der Schwulen- und Lesbenbewegung." In *Rosa Radikale: Die Schwulenbewegung der 1970er Jahre* edited by Andreas Pretzel and Volker Weiß, 177–198. Hamburg: Männerschwarm, 2012.
Grisard, Dominique. "Pink Prisons, Rosy Futures? The Prison Politics of the Pink Triangle." In *Queer Interventions: Queer Futures: Reconsidering Ethics Activism and the Political*, edited by Elahe Haschemi Yekani, Eveline Kilian and Beatrice Michaelis, 83–97. Farnham: Ashgate, 2016.
Häberlen, Joachim C., and Jake P. Smith. "Struggling for Feelings: The Politics of Emotions in the Radical New Left in West Germany, c.1968–84." *Contemporary European History* 23, no. 4 (2014): 615–637.
Hájková, Anna. "Den Holocaust queer erzählen." In *Jahrbuch Sexualitäten*, edited by Janin Afken, Jan Feddersen, Benno Gammerl, Rainer Nicolaysen and Benedikt Wolf, 86–110. Göttingen: Wallstein Verlag, 2018.
Hájková, Anna. "Between Love and Coercion: Queer Desire, Sexual Barter and the Holocaust." *German History* 39, no. 1 – Special Issue: Holocaust, Sexuality, Stigma (2020): 112–133.
Hájková, Anna. *Menschen ohne Geschichte sind Staub: Homophobie und Holocaust.* Wallstein Verlag. Göttingen, 2021.
Hájková, Anna. 2021. "Introduction: Sexuality, Holocaust, Stigma." *German History* 39, no. 1 – Special issue Holocaust Sexuality, Stigma (2020): 1–14.
Halberstam, Jack J. *The Queer Art of Failure.* Durham, NC: Duke University Press, 2011.
Halperin, David M. *How to be Gay.* Cambridge, MA: Belknap Press of Harvard University Press, 2012.
Hamilton, Rosa. "The Very Quintessence of Persecution. Queer Anti-fascism in 1970s Western Europe." *Radical History Review* 138 (2020): 60–81.
Hamilton, Rosa. "A Clarification." *Radical History Review* 141 (2021): 221–223.
Happe, Katja, Michael Mayer, and Maja Peers. "Introduction." In *The Persecution and Murder of the European Jews by Nazi Germany 1933-1945*, edited by Katja Happe, Michael Mayer and Maja Peers, 13–75. Oldenbourg: De Gruyter, 2022.
Haritaworn, Jin, and Jen Petzen. "Invented traditions new intimate publics. Tracing the German 'Muslim Homophobia' discourse." In *Islam in its International Context. Comparative Perspectives*, edited by Stephen Hutchings, Chris Flood, Galina Miazhevich and Henri Nickels, 48–64. Newcastle upon Tyne: Cambridge Scholars Publishing, 2011.
Hartog, François, *Régimes d'Historicité: Présentisme et expériences du temps.* Paris: Éditions du Seuil. 2012. Original edition, 2003.
Hartog, François. "Chronos, Kairos, Krisis: The Genesis of Western Time." *History & Theory* 60, no. 3 (2020): 425–439.
Haus, Sebastian. "Risky Sex: Risky Language HIV/AIDS and the West German Gay Scene in the 1980s." *Historical Social Research* 41, no. 1 (2016): 111–134.
Haus-Rybicki, Sebastian. *Eine Seuche regieren. AIDS-Prävention in der Bundesrepublik 1981-1995.* Bielefeld: transcript, 2021.
Healey, Dan. *Russian Homophobia from Stalin to Sochi.* London: Bloomsbury Academic, 2017.
Heinrich, Elisa. *Intim und respektabel. Homosexualität und Freundinnenschaft in der deutschen Frauenbewegung um 1900* Göttingen: Vandenhoeck & Ruprecht, 2022.

Hekma, Gert. "Jacob Israël de Haan: Pederast poet between Amsterdam and Jerusalem." In *Die andere Fakultät. Theorie, Geschichte, Gesellschaft*, edited by Florian Mildenberger, 90–110. Hamburg: Männerschwarm, 2015.

Herrn, Rainer. *Der Liebe und dem Leid. Das Institut für Sexualwissenschaft 1919–1933*. Berlin: Suhrkamp, 2022.

Herzog, Dagmar. *Sex after Fascism: Memory and Morality in Twentieth-Century Germany*. Princeton, NJ: Princeton University Press, 2005.

Hill, Christopher L. "Conceptual Universalization in the Transnational Nineteenth Century." In *Global Intellectual History*, edited by Andrew Sartori and Samuel Moyn, 134–158. New York City, NY: Columbia University Press, 2013.

Hirsch, Marianne. *Family Frames: Photography, Narrative, and Postmemory*. Cambridge, MA: Harvard University Press, 1997.

Hirsch, Marianne. "Projected Memory: Holocaust Photographs in Personal and Public Fantasy." In *Acts of Memory: Cultural Recall in the Present*, edited by Mieke Bal, Jonathan V. Crewe and Leo Spitzer, 2–23. Hanover, NH: University Press of New England, 1999.

Hirsch, Marianne. *The Generation of Postmemory: Writing and Visual Culture After the Holocaust*. New York, NY: Columbia University Press, 2012.

Hirsch, Marianne, and Leo Spitzer. "Testimonial Objects Memory, Gender and Transmission." In *Diaspora and Memory: Figures of Displacement in Contemporary Literature, Arts and Politics*, edited by Marie-Aude Baronian, Stephan Besser and Yolande Jansen, Testimonial Objects Memory, Gender and Transmission, 137–163. Amsterdam: Brill, 2016.

Hochkirchen, Britta. "Skalierung von Geschichte und historischer Erkenntnis. Annäherung und Distanzierung durch Reinhart Kosellecks Figurensammlung." In *Vom Ding und Unding der Geschichte Annäherung an die Figurensammlung Reinhart Koselleck*, edited by Lisa Regazzoni, 99–121. Bielefeld: Bielefeld University Press, 2023.

Hoffschildt, Rainer. "'Nach der Befreiung wieder in Haft' Der bündische Widerstandskämpfer Paul Hahn." In *Homosexuelle Männer in KZ Sachsenhausen*, edited by Joachim Müller and Andreas Sternweiler, 354–358. Berlin: Verlag Rosa Winkel. 2000.

Holy, Michael. "Der entliehene rosa Winkel." In *Der Frankfurter Engel, Mahnmal Homosexuellenverfolgung: Ein Lesebuch*, edited by Initiative Mahnmal Homosexuellenverfolgung, 74–87. Frankfurt (Main): Eichborn, 1997.

Holy, Michael. "Jenseits von Stonewall: Rückblicke auf die Schwulenbewegung in der BRD 1969–1980." In *Rosa Radikale: Die Schwulenbewegung der 1970er Jahre* edited by Andreas Pretzel and Volker Weiß, 39–79. Hamburg: Männerschwarm Verlag, 2012.

Holy, Michael. "Bewegungsgeschichte und Sammelleidenschaft. Zur Entstehungsgeschichte der ‚Sammlung Holy.'" In *Politiken in Bewegung. Die Emanzipation Homosexueller im 20. Jahrhundert*, edited by Andreas Pretzel and Volker Weiß, 193–235. Hamburg: Männerschwarm, 2017.

HomoMonument, Initiative. *Der homosexuellen NS-Opfer gedenken*. Berlin: Heinrich Böll Stiftung, 1999.

Hooper, Tom. "'Enough is Enough:' The Right to Privacy Committee and Bathhouse Raids in Toronto, 1978–83." PhD diss, York University, 2016.

Horstkotte, Silke. "Recollective Processes and the 'Topography of Forgetting' in W.G. Sebald's Austerlitz." In *Diaspora and Memory: Figures of Displacement in Contemporary Literature, Arts and Politics*, edited by Marie-Aude Baronian, Stephan Besser and Yolande Jansen, 193–202. Amsterdam: Brill, 2016.

Hubbard, Jim. "AIDS-Videoaktivismus und die Entstehung des 'Archivs.'" In *Queer Cinema*, edited by Dagmar Brunow and Simon Dickel, 82–105. Mainz: Ventil Verlag, 2018.

Hufenreuter, Gregor. "Rassenantisemitismus." In *Handbuch des Antisemitismus* edited by Brigitte Mihok, 272–273. Berlin: De Gruyter, 2011.

Huneke, Samuel Clowes. 2019. "The Duplicity of Tolerance: Lesbian Experiences in Nazi Berlin." *Journal of Contemporary History* 54, no. 1 (2019): 30–59.

Huneke, Samuel Clowes. "Heterogeneous Persecution: Lesbianism and the Nazi State." *Central European History* 54, no. 2 (2021): 297–325.

Huneke, Samuel Clowes. *States of Liberation: Gay Men between Dictatorship and Democracy in Cold War Germany* Toronto, ON: Toronto University Press, 2022.

Ingebretsen, Edward. "Gone Shopping: The Commercialization of Same-Sex Desire." *International Journal of Sexuality and Gender Studies* 4 (1999): 125–148.

Jackman, Michael Connors, and Nishant Upadhyay. "Pinkwatching Israel, Whitewashing Canada: Queer (Settler) Politics and Indigenous Colonization in Canada." *Women's Studies Quarterly* 42, no. 3–4 (2014): 195–210.

Jackson, Edward, and Stan Persky. *Flaunting it! A Decade of Gay Journalism From the Body Politic: An Anthology*. Toronto, ON: Pink Triangle Press, 1982.

Jacobeit, Sigrid. "Zur Geschichte des Jugend-Konzentrationslagers Uckermark im Gesamtkonzept der Mahn- und Gedenkstätte Ravensbrück/Stiftung Brandenburgische Gedenkstätten." In *Das Mädchenkonzentrationslager Uckermark*, edited by Katja Limbacher, Maike Merten and Bettina Pfefferle, 271–279. Münster: Unrast, 2005.

Jacobs, Sue-Ellen. "Is the « North American Berdache » Merely a Phantom in the Imagination of Western Social Scientist?" In *Two-Spirit People: Native American Gender Identity, Sexuality, and Spirituality*, edited by Sue-Ellen Jacobs, Wesley Thomas and Sabine Lang, 21–44. Champaign, IL: University of Illinois Press, 2005.

Jellonnek, Burkhard. *Homosexuelle unter dem Hakenkreuz* Paderborn: Verlag Ferdinand Schöningh, 1990.

Jensen, Erik N. "The Pink Triangle and Political Consciousness: Gays, Lesbians, and the Memory of Nazi Persecution." *Journal of the History of Sexuality* 11, no. 1 (2002): 319–349.

Jensen, Erik N. "The Pink Triangle and Political Consciousness: Gay, Lesbians, and the Memory of Nazi Persecution." In Sexuality and German Fascism, edited by Dagmar Herzog, 319–349. New York, NY: Berghahn, 2004.

Johnson, David K., Justin Bengry, Katherine Parkin, Katherine Sender, and Edward Timke. "Author Meets Critics: Buying Gay: How Physique Entrepreneurs Sparked a Movement." *Advertising & Society Quarterly* 20, no. 3 (2019).

Johnson, E. Patrick. *No Tea, no Shade: New Writings in Black Queer Studies*. Durham, NC: Duke University Press, 2016.

Jordheim, Helge. "Against Periodization: Koselleck's Theory of Multiple Temporalities." *History and Theory* 51, no. 2 (2012): 151–171.

Juneja, Monica. "Viewing Europe, or Where and What is the 'Outside.'" *Why Europe, Which Europe*. 2022. Accessed January 24, 2023, https://europedebate.hypotheses.org/1462.

Katz, Jonathan Ned. *Daring Life and Dangerous Times of Eve Adams*. Chicago, IL: Chicago Review Press, 2021.

Kiesling, Elena. 2017. "The Missing Colors of the Rainbow: Black Queer Resistance." *European Journal of American Studies* 11, no. 3 (2017). Accessed January 26, 2023, doi.org/10.4000/ejas.11830.

Kinsman, Gary William. "Policing borders and sexual/gender identities: queer refugees in the years of Canadian neoliberalism and homonationalism." In *(Neo)colonialism, Neoliberalism, Resistance and Hope*, edited by Nancy Nicol, Adrian Jjuuko, Richard Lusimbo, Nick J. Mulé, Susan Ursel, Amar Wahab and Phyllis Waugh, 97–129. London: School of Advanced Study, University of London, Institute of Commonwealth Studies, 2018.

Kinsman, Gary William, and Patrizia Gentile. *The Canadian War on Queers: National Security as Sexual Regulation*. Vancouver, BC: University of British Columbia Press., 2010.

Kirchknopf, Johann Karl. "Die strafrechtliche Verfolgung homosexueller Handlungen in Österreich im 20. Jahrhundert." *Zeitgeschichte* 43, no. 2 (2016): 68–84.

Kissi, Edward, Tom Lawson, Ulrike Lindner, and Mirjam Zadoff. "A European Vergangenheitsbewältigung? New Entanglements of Holocaust and Colonial Histories." In *Colonial Paradigms of Violence: Comparative Analysis of the Holocaust, Genocide, and Mass Killing*, edited by Michelle Gordon and Rachel O'Sullivan, 217–242. Göttingen: Wallstein, 2022.

Klävers, Steffen. "Kollektive Erinnerung: ein kompetitives Nullsummenspiel? Michael Rothbergs Theorie multidirektionaler Erinnerung im Spannungsfeld von Holocaust- und Postcolonial Studies." In *Decolonizing Auschwitz? Komparativ-postkoloniale Ansätze in der Holocaustforschung*, edited by Steffen Klävers, 133–177. Oldenbourg: De Gruyter Oldenbourg, 2019.

Kleinberg, Ethan. *Haunting History: For a Deconstructive Approach to the Past*. Stanford, CA: Stanford University Press, 2017.

Klier, Freya. *Die Kaninchen von Ravensbrück. Medizinische Versuche an Frauen in der NS-Zeit* Munich: Droemersche Verlagsanstalt, 1994.

Knoll, Albert. "'Die Vergessenen' und die 'ausgeschlossenen Opfer' – Spurensuche nach homosexuellen Überlebenden des Konzentrationslagers Dachau." In *Ohnmacht und Aufbegehren. Homosexuelle Männer in der frühen Bundesrepublik*, edited by Andreas Pretzel and Volker Weiß. Hamburg: Männerschwarm Verlag, 2010.

Knoll, Albert, and Burghard Richter. "Initiative zu dem Rosa-Winkel-Gedenkstein." In *Der Rosa-Winkel-Gedenkstein: Die Erinnerung an die Homosexuellen im KZ Dachau*, edited by Albert Knoll, 39–55. Munich: Forum Homosexualität München, 2015.

Kogon, Eugen. *Der SS-Staat: das System der deutschen Konzentrationslager*. München: Heyne. 1981. Original Edition, 1946.

Koselleck, Reinhart. "Einleitung." In *Zeitschichten: Studien zur Historik* edited by Reinhart Koselleck. Frankfurt (Main): Suhrkamp. 2000.

Koselleck, Reinhart. "Erinnerungsschleusen und Erfahrungsschichten: Der Einfluss der beiden Weltkriege auf das Soziale Bewußtsein." In *Zeitschichten: Studien zur Historik*, edited by Reinhart Kosselleck, 265–284. Frankfurt (Main): Suhrkamp, 2003.

Koselleck, Reinhart. "Die Transformation der politischen Totenmale im 20. Jahrhundert." In *Zeitgeschichte als Streitgeschichte. Große Kontroverse nach 1945*, edited by Martin Sabrow, Ralph Jessen and Klaus Große Kracht, 205–228. Munich: C. H Beck, 2003.

Labov, Jessie. *Transatlantic Central Europe: Contesting Geography and Redefining Culture beyond the Nation*. Budapest: Central European University Press, 2019.

LaCapra, Dominick. *Representing the Holocaust*. Ithaca, NY: Cornell University Press, 1996.

LaCapra, Dominick. *History in Transit: Experience, Identity, Critical Theory*. Ithaca, NY: Cornell University Press, 2004.

Landsberg, Alison. *Prosthetic Memory: The Transformation of American Remembrance in the Age of Mass Culture*. New York, NY: Columbia University Press, 2004

Lautmann, Rüdiger, Winfried Grikschat, and Egbert Schmidt. "Der rosa Winkel in den nationalsozialistischen Konzentrationslagern." In *Seminar: Gesellschaft und Homosexualität*, edited by Rüdiger Lautmann, 325–365. Frankfurt (Main), 1977.

Leggewie, Claus, and Erik Meyer. *Ein Ort, an den man gerne geht: Das Holocaust-Mahnmal und die Geschichtspolitik nach 1989*. Munich: Carl Hanser Verlag, 2005.

Lemmey, Huw, and Ben Miller. *Bad Gays: A Homosexual History*. London: Verso, 2022

Lennox, Sara. *Remapping Black Germany: New Perspectives on Afro-German history, Politics, and Culture*. Amherst, MA: University of Massachusetts Press, 2016.

Levy, Daniel, and Natan Shnaider. *The Holocaust and Memory in the Global Age*. Philadelphia, PA: Temple University Press, 2006.

Levy, Daniel C., and Natan Sznaider. "Memory Unbound: The Holocaust and the Formation of Cosmopolitan Memory." *European Journal of Social Theory* 5, no. 1 (2002): 87–106.

Lewis, Martin W., and Kären E. Wigen. *The Myth of Continents. A Critique of Metageography*. Berkeley, CA: University of California Press, 1997.

Lim, Jie-Hyun. "Victimhood Nationalism in Contested Memories: National Mourning and Global Accountability." In *Memory in a Global Age: Discourses, Practices and Trajectories*, edited by Aleida Assmann and Sebastian Conrad, 138–162. Basingstoke: Palgrave Macmillan, 2010.

Locher, Hubert. "'Politische Ikonologie' und 'Politische Sinnlichkeit': Bild-Diskurs und historische Erfahrung nach Reinhart Koselleck." In *Reinhart Koselleck und die Politische Ikonologie*, edited by Hubert Locher and Adriana Markantonatos, 14–31. Munich: Deutscher Kunstverlag, 2013.

Locher, Hubert, Adriana Markantonatos, Daniela Bohde, Dennis Janzen, Deutsches Dokumentationszentrum für Kunstgeschichte – Bildarchiv Foto Marburg, and Tagung Reinhart Koselleck (1923–2006) Politische Ikonologie. Berlin u.a.: Dt. Kunstverlag, 2010.

Lotto-Kusche, Sebastian. *Der Völkermord an den Sinti und Roma und die Bundesrepublik: Der lange Weg zur Anerkennung 1949–1990*. Oldenbourg: De Gruyter, 2022.

Love, Heather. *Feeling Backward: Loss and the Politics of Queer History*. Cambridge, MA: Harvard University Press, 2009.

Love, Heather. *Underdogs: Social Deviance and Queer Theory*. Chicago, IL: The University of Chicago Press, 2021.

Lücke, Martin. "Die Verfolgung lesbischer Frauen im Nationalsozialismus: Forschungsdebatten zu Gedenkinitiativen am Beispiel des Frauen-Konzentrationslagers Ravensbrück." *Zeitschrift für Geschichtswissenschaft* 79, no. 5 (2022): 422–440.

Marhoefer, Laurie. *Sex and the Weimar Republic: German Homosexual Emancipation and the Rise of the Nazis*. Toronto, ON: University of Toronto Press, 2015.

Marhoefer, Laurie, "Lesbianism, Transvestitism, and the Nazi State: A Microhistory of a Gestapo Investigation, 1939–1943." *The American Historical Review* 121, no. 4 (2016):1167–1195.

Marhoefer, Laurie. "Was the Homosexual Made White? Race, Empire, and Analogy in Gay and Trans Thought in Twentieth-Century Germany." *Gender & History* 31, no. 1 (2019): 91–114.

Marhoefer, Laurie. *Racism and the Making of Gay Rights: A Sexologist, His Student, and the Empire of Queer Love*. Toronto, ON: University of Toronto Press, 2022.

Menakem, Resma. *My Grandmother's Hands: The Bloodline of Racialized Trauma and the Mending of Our Bodies and Hearts: Racialized Trauma and the Pathway to Mending Our Hearts and Bodies*. Buffalo, NY: Central Recovery Press, 2017.

Meyer, Gabi. *Offizielles Erinnern und die Situation der Sinti und Roma in Deutschland : der nationalsozialistische Völkermord in den parlamentarischen Debatten des Deutschen Bundestages*. Wiesbaden: Springer VS, 2013.

Milam, Jennifer, and Alan Maddox. "Visual and Aural Intellectual Histories: An Introduction." *Intellectual History Review* 27, no. 3 (2017): 285–298.

Mildenberger, Florian. *Schwulenbewegung in München 1969 bis 1996*. Vol. 5, *Materialien zur Geschichte der Homosexuellen in München und Bayern*. Munich: Forum Homosexualität und Geschichte München e.V., 2000.
Mitchell, W. J. T. *Picture Theory: Essays on Verbal and Visual Representation*. Chicago, IL: University of Chicago Press, 1994.
Mitchell, W. J. T. *What do Pictures Want?: The Lives and Loves of images*. Chicago, IL: University of Chicago Press, 2005.
Mitchell, W. J. T. *Image Science: Iconology, Visual Culture, and Media Aesthetics*. Chicago, IL: University of Chicago Press, 2015.
Morgensen, Scott Lauria. "Settler Homonationalism: Theorizing Settler Colonialism within Queer Modernities." *GLQ: A Journal of Lesbian and Gay Studies* 16, no. 1–2 (2010): 105–131.
Moses, Dirk. *The Problems of Genocide: Permanent Security and the Language of Transgression*. Cambridge: Cambridge University Press, 2021.
Moxey, Keith. "Visual Studies and the Iconic Turn." *Journal of Visual Culture* 7, no. 2 (2008): 131–146.
Moyn, Samuel, and Andrew Sartori. "Approaches to Global Intellectual History." In *Global Intellectual History*, edited by Samuel Moyn and Andrew Sartori, 3–30. New York, NY: Columbia University Press, 2013.
Mühlhäuser, Regina, and Insa Eschebach. "Sexuelle Gewalt im Krieg und Sex-Zwangsarbeit in NS-Konzentrationslagern." In *Krieg und Geschlecht: Sexuelle Gewalt im Krieg und Sex-Zwangsarbeit in NS-Konzentrationslagern*, edited by Regina Mühlhäuser and Insa Eschebach, 11–34. Berlin: Metropol, 2008
Müller, Joachim. "Unnatürliche Todesfälle: Vorfälle in den Außenbereichen Klinkerwerk, Schießplatz und Tongrube." In *Homosexuelle Männer im KZ Sachsenhausen*, edited by Joachim Müller, Schwules Museum (Berlin) and Andreas Sternweiler, 216–263. Berlin: Verlag Rosa Winkel. 2000.
Müller, Joachim, and Andreas Sternweiler. *Homosexuelle Männer im KZ Sachsenhausen*. Berlin: Verlag Rosa Winkel, 2000.
Munier, Julia Noah. "Die Homophilenbewegung im deutschen Südwesten der 1950er und 1960er Jahre als Akteurin der Anerkennung." *Invertito – Jahrbuch für die Geschichte der Homosexualitäten* 22 (2020): 77–112.
Muñoz, José Esteban. *Cruising Utopia: The Then and There of Queer Futurity, Sexual Cultures*. New York: New York University Press, 2009.
Munt, Sally. *Queer Attachments the Cultural Politics of Shame, Queer Interventions*. Aldershot Ashgate, 2008.
Neiman, Susan. *Learning from the Germans: Race and the Memory of Evil*. New York, NY: macmillan Publishers, 2019.
Nesselbauf, Jonas. "Was Sie schon immer über Pornographie wissen wollten, aber nie zu fragen wagten: Eine Annäherung in sechs Schritten." In *Ästhetik(en) der Pornographie: Darstellungen von Sexualitäten im Medienvergleich*, edited by Norbert Lennartz and Jonas Nesselbauf, 7–74. Baden-Baden: Nomos, 2021.
Newsome, Jake W. "Homosexuals after the Holocaust: Sexual Citizenship and the Politics of Memory in Germany and the United States, 1945–2008." PhD diss, Department of History State University of New York at Buffalo, 2016.
Newsome, Jake W. *Pink Triangle Legacies. Coming Out in the Shadow of the Holocaust*. Ithaca, NY: Cornell University Press, 2022.
Nicolaysen, Rainer. "Entwürdigt – Die Aberkennung von Doktortiteln im »Dritten Reich« Homosexuelle Opfer der Hamburger Universität." In *Gewinner und Verlierer: Beiträge zur*

Geschichte der Homosexualität in Deutschland im 20. Jahrhundert, edited by Norman Domeier, 45–61. Göttingen: Wallstein, 2015.
Novick, Peter. *The Holocaust in American Life*. Boston, MA: Houghton Mifflin, 1999.
Nunn, Zavier. "Trans Liminality and the Nazi State." *Past & Present* 260, no. 1 (2023): 123–157.
Oholi, Jeannette. "Forum: On Black German Studies – Literaturgeschichte stören. BPoC Literature in Deutschland relational lesen." *The German Quarterly* 95 no. 4 (2022): 414–417.
Olick, Jeffrey K. "From Collective Memory to the Sociology of Mnemonic Practices and Products." In *Cultural Memory Studies: An International and Interdisciplinary Handbook* edited by Astrid Erll, Ansgar Nünning and Sara B. Young, 151–162. Berlin: Walter de Gruyter, 2008.
Olsen, Niklas. 2012. *History in the Plural: An Introduction to the Work of Reinhart Koselleck*. New York: Berghahn Books.
Orangias, Joseph, Jeannie Simms, and Sloane Fremch. "The Cultural Functions and Social Potential of Monuments: A Preliminary Inventory and Analysis." *Journal of Homosexuality* 65, no. 6 (2018): 705–726.
Ostrowska, Joanna, Joanna Talewicz-Kwiatkowska, and Lutz van Dijk. *Erinnern in Auschwitz. Auch an sexuelle Minderheiten*. Berlin: Querverlag, 2020.
Oxman, Elena. "Sensing the Image: Roland Barthes and the Affect of the Visual." *SubStance* 39, no. 2 (2010): 71–90.
Paul, Gerhard. "Das Mao-Porträt. Herrscherbild, Protestsymbol und Kunstikone." *Contemporary History* 6, no. 1 (2009): 58–84.
Paul, Gerhard. *Bilder einer Diktatur: Zur Visual History des* "Dritten Reiches". Göttingen: Wallstein, 2020.
Pernau, Margrit. "Space and Emotion: Building to Feel." *History Compass* 12 (2014): 541–549.
Pernau, Margrit. 2016. "Provincializing Concepts: The Language of Transnational History." *Comparative Studies of South Asia, Africa and the Middle East* 36, no. 3 (2016): 483–499.
Pernau, Margrit. "Celebrating Monsoon Feelings: The Flower-sellers' Festival of Delhi." In *Monsoon feelings: A History of Emotions in the Rain*, edited by Margrit Pernau, Imke Rajamani and Katherine Butler Schofield, 379–407. New York, NY: Niyogi Books, 2018.
Pernau, Margrit. "The Time of the Prophet and the Future of the Community Temporalities in Nineteenth and Twentieth Century Muslim India." *Time & Society* 30, no. 4 (2021): 477–493.
Pernau, Margrit, and Imke Rajamani. "Emotional Translations: Conceptual History Beyond Language." *History and Theory* 55 (February 2016): 46–65.
Pernau, Margrit, and Sébastien Tremblay. "Dealing with an Ocean of Meaninglessness: Reinhart Koselleck's Lava Memories and Conceptual History." *Contribution to the History of Concepts* 15, no. 2 (2020): 7–28.
Petrus, John. "Discussing The Undiscussable: Reflecting on the 'End' of AIDS." *GLQ: A Journal of Lesbian and Gay Studies* 25, no. 1(2019): 67–72.
Phelan, Shane. *Sexual Strangers: Gays, Lesbians, and Dilemmas of Citizenship*. Philadelphia, PA: Temple University Press, 2001.
Pretzel, Andreas. "Wiedergutmachung unter Vorbehalt und mit neuer Perspektive – Was homosexuellen NS-Opfern verweigert wurde und was wir noch tun können." In *Ohnmacht und Aufbegehren. Homosexuelle Männer in der frühen Bundesrepublik* edited by Andreas Pretzel and Volker Weiß, 91–113. Hamburg: Männerschwarm. 2010.
Pretzel, Andreas, and Volker Weiß. "Die Schwulenbewegung der 1970er Jahre: Annäherungen an ein legendäres Jahrzehnt." In *Rosa Radikale: Die Schwulenbewegung der 1970s Jahre*, edited by Andreas Pretzel and Volker Weiß, 9–28. Hamburg: Männerschwarm, 2012.

Puar, Jasbir K. *Terrorist Assemblages:: Homonationalism in Queer Times*. Durham, NC: Duke University Press, 2017.

Puar, Jasbir K., and David L. Eng. "Introduction: Left of Queer." *Social Text* 145 – Special Issue: Left of Queer (2020): 1–25.

Pugach, Sara. "Forum: On Black German Studies – African Voices in German colonial Sources." *The German Quarterly* 95, no. 4 (2020): 437–439.

Pyryeskina, Julia. "'A remarkable dense historical and political juncture,' Anita Bryant, The Body Politics, and the Canadian Gay and Lesbian Community in January 1978." *Canadian Journal of History / Annales canadiennes d'histoire* 53, no. 1 (2018): 58–85.

Quadrio, Carolyn. "Family Therapy with Families of Holocaust Survivors." *Journal of Aggression, Maltreatment & Trauma* 25, no. 6 (2016): 618–634.

QWIEN, and WASt, *ZU SPÄT?: Dimensionen des Gedenkens an homosexuelle und transgender Opfer des Nationalsozialismus* Wien: Zaglossus, 2015

Raj, Kapil. *Relocating Modern Science: Circulation and the Construction of Knowledge in South Asia and Europe, 1650–1900*. Houndmills: Palgrave Macmillan, 2007.

Rajamani, Imke. "Pictures, Emotions, Conceptual Change: Anger in Popular Hindi Cinema." In *Global Conceptual History: A Reader*, edited by Dominic Sachsenmaier and Margrit Pernau, 307–335. London: Bloomsbury Academics, 2016.

Raphael, Samuel. *Past and Present in Contemporary Culture, Theatres of Memory*. London: Verso, 1996.

Reading, Anna. *The Social Inheritance of the Holocaust: Gender, Culture and Memory*. Houndmills: Palgrave Macmillan, 2002.

Regazzoni, Lisa. *Geschichtsdinge: Gallische Vergangenheit und französische Geschichtsforschung im 18. und frühen 19. Jahrhundert*. Oldenbourg: De Gruyter. 2020.

Regazzoni, Lisa. "The impossible monument of experience: A story that never ends." In *Die Vergangenheit im Begriff. Von der Erfahrung der Geschichte zur Geschichtstheorie bei Reinhart Koselleck*, edited by Christophe Bouton, Jeffrey A. Barash and Servanne Jollivet, 100–126. Baden-Baden: Verlag Karl Alber, 2021.

Reichel, Peter, Harald Schmid, and Peter Steinbach. "Die 'zweite Geschichte' der Hitler-Diktatur." In *Der Nationalsozialismus – die zweite Geschichte*, edited by Peter Reichel, Harald Schmid and Peter Steinbach, 7–21. Munich: C. H. Beck, 2009.

Riedle, Andrea. "Georg Tauber: an 'Asocial' Prisoner in the Dachau Concentration Camp and his futile struggle for recognition as a Nazi Victim." In *Catalogue of the Special Exhibition: Evidence for Posterity. The Drawings of the Dachau Survivor Georg Tauber*, edited by Stefanie Pilzweger-Steine and Andrea Riedle, 13–35. Berlin: Metropol, 2016.

Ritchie, Jason. "HOW DO YOU SAY 'COME OUT OF THE CLOSET' IN ARABIC?: Queer Activism and the Politics of Visibility in Israel-Palestine." *GLQ: A Journal of Lesbian and Gay Studies* 16, no. 4 (2010): 557–575.

Rosello, Mireille, and Sudeep Dasgupta. "Introduction Queer and Europe: An Encounter." In *What's Queer about Europe? Productive Encounters and Re-enchanting Paradigms*, edited by Mireille Rosello and Sudeep Dasgupta, 1–26. New York City, NY: Fordham University Press, 2014.

Rosenkranz, Bernhard, and Gottfried Lorenz. *Hamburg auf anderen Wegen: Die Geschichte des schwulen Lebens in der Hansestadt*. Hamburg: Lambda, 2005.

Rothberg, Michael. *Multidirectional Memory: Remembering the Holocaust in the Age of Decolonization, Cultural Memory in the Present*. Stanford, CA: Stanford University Press, 2009.

Rothberg, Michael, and Mirjam Sarah Brusius. "'Victimhood is a Tricky Terrain to Negotiate': Michael Rothberg in conversation with Mirjam Sarah Brusius." *Bulletin of the German Historical Institute*

London 44, no. 2 – Special Issue Memory cultures 2.0: From Opferkonkurrenz to Solidarity (2022): 21–31.

Rothberg, Michael, and Yasmin Yildiz. "Memory Citizenship. Migrant Archives of Holocaust Remembrance in Contemporary Germany." *Parallax* 17, no. 4 (2011): 32–48.

Rottmann, Andrea. *Queer Lives Across the Wall: Desire and Danger in Divided Berlin, 1945–1970*. Toronto, ON: University of Toronto Press. 2023.

Royles, Dan. *To Make the Wounded Whole: The African American Struggle against HIV/AIDS*. Edited by Dan Royles. Chapel Hill, NC: University of North Carolina Press, 2020.

Safaian, Dorna. "Why Images? The Role of Visual Media in Protest Movement Research." *History | Sexuality | Law. Blog für Beiträge zu Verschränkungen von Recht und Sexualität in historischen Kontexten*. October 26, 2019. Accessed December 20, 2022, https://hsl.hypotheses.org/995.

Safaian, Dorna, and Susanne Regener. "Lebenswelten als Protest. Fotografische Praktiken der deutschen und dänischen Schwulenbewegung seit den 1970er Jahren." *Beiträge zur Geschichte und Ästhetik der Fotografie. (Sonderheft: Protestfotografie)* 39, no. 154 (2019): 15–24.

Samudzi, Zoe. "Paradox of Recognition: Genocide and Colonialism." *Postmodern Culture* 31, no. 1–2 (2020). Accessed December 20, 2022, doi:10.1353/pmc.2020.0028.

Samudzi, Zoe. "In Absentia of Black Study." *New Fascism Syllabus*. May 31, 2021. Accessed January 28, 2023, http://newfascismsyllabus.com/opinions/in-absentia-of-black-study/.

Samuels, Ellen. "MY BODY, MY CLOSET: Invisible Disability and the Limits of Coming-Out Discourse." *GLQ: A Journal of Lesbian and Gay Studies* 9, no. 1–2 (2003): 233–255.

Sartori, Andrew. "The Resonance of Culture: Framing a Problem in Global Concept History." In *Global Conceptual History: A Reader*, edited by Dominic Sachsenmaier and Margrit Pernau, 227–258. London: Bloomsbury Academics, 2016.

Schappach, Beate. "Geballte Faust, Doppelaxt, rosa Winkel: Gruppenkonstituierende Symbole der Frauen-, Lesben- und Schwulenbewegung." In *Linksalternative Milieus und Neue Soziale Bewegungen in den 1970er Jahren*, edited by Cordia Baumann, Sebastian Gehrig and Nicolas Büchse, 259–283. Heidelberg: Universitätsverlag Heidelberg, 2011.

Schlagdenhauffen, Régis. *Triangle rose : La persécution nazie des homosexuels et sa mémoire, Collection Mutations*. Paris: Autrement, 2011.

Schmidt, Siegfried J. "Memory and Remembrance: A Constructivist Approach." In *Cultural Memory Studies: An International and Interdisciplinary Handbook* edited by Astrid Erll, Ansgar Nünning and Sara B. Young, 191–202. Berlin: Walter de Gruyter, 2008.

Schoppmann, Claudia. *Zeit der Maskierung: Lebensgeschichten lesbischer Frauen im "Dritten Reich"*. Berlin: Orlanda Frauenverlag, 1993.

Schoppmann, Claudia. "Elsa Conrad – Margarete Rosenberg – Mary Pünjer – Henny Schermann: Vier Porträts." In *Homophobie und Devianz. Weibliche und männliche Homosexualität im Nationalsozialismus*, edited by Insa Eschebach, 97–111. Berlin: Metropol, 2012.

Schretter, Lukas. "Anmerkungen zum WInkelrelief im Internationalen Mahnmal der KZ-Gedenkstätte Dachau." In *Der Rosa-Winkel-Gedenkstein*, edited by Albert Knoll, 30–38. Munich: Forum Homosexualität und Geschichte e.V., 2015.

Schwartz, Michael. "'Herrschaft der Homosexuellen': Die Röhm-Skandale 1932 und 1934 als öffentliche Provokation." In *Homosexuelle, Seilschaften, Verrat*, edited by Michael Schwartz, 160–211. Oldenbourg: De Gruyter Oldenbourg, 2019

Sedgwick, Eve Kosofsky. *Touching Feeling: Affect, Pedagogy, Performativity*. Durham, NC: Duke University Press, 2006.

Sender, Katherine. 2017. "The Gay Market is Dead, Long Live the Gay Market." *Advertising & Society Quarterly* 18, no. 4 (2017). Accessed December 20, 2022, doi:10.1353/asr.2018.0001.

Sharples, Caroline. "In Pursuit of Justice: Debating the Statute of Limitations for Nazi War Crimes in Britain and West Germany during the 1960s." *Holocaust Studies: A Journal of Culture and History* 20, no. 3 (2015): 81–108.

Spitzer, Leo. "Back Through the Future: Nostalgic Memory and Critical Memory in a Refuge from Nazism." In *Acts of Memory: Cultural Recall in the Present*, edited by Mieke Bal, Jonathan V. Crewe and Leo Spitzer, 87–104. Hanover, NH: University Press of New England, 1999.

Spoerhase, Carlos. "Skalierung. Ein ästhetischer Grundbegriff der Gegenwart." *Zeitschrift für Ästhetik und Allgemeine Kunstwissenschaft* 18 – Ästhetik der Skalierung (2020): 5–16.

Steakley, James D. *The Homosexual Emancipation Movement in Germany*. New York City, NY: Arno Press, 1975.

Steakley, James D. "Selbstkritische Gedanken zur Mythologiserung der Homosexuellenverfolgung im Dritten Reich." In *Nationalsozialistischer Terror gegen Homosexuelle: Verdrängt und ungesühnt*, edited by Burkhard Jellonek and Rüdiger Lautmann, 55–68. Padeborn: Verlag Ferdinand Schöningh, 2002.

Stern, Frank. *Im Anfang war Auschwitz: Antisemitismus und Philosemitismus im deutschen Nachkrieg*. Gerlingen: Bleicher Verlag, 1991.

Sternweiler, Andreas. *Frankfurt, Basel, New York: Richard Plant*. Berlin: Verlag Rosa Winkel, 1996

Stoff, Heiko. "Heterosexualität." In *Was ist Homosexualität?*, edited by Florian Mildenberger, Jennifer Evans, Martin Lücke, Rüdiger Lautmann and Jakob Pastötter, 73–104. Hamburg: Männerschwarm, 2014.

Straub, Julia. "Introduction: Transatlantic North American Studies." In *Handbook of Transatlantic North American Studies*, edited by Julia Straub, 1–20. Berlin: De Gruyter, 2016.

Sutton, Katie. "Sexology's Photographic Turn: Visualizing Trans Identity in Interwar Germany." *Journal of the History of Sexuality* 27, no. 3 (2018): 442–479.

Sykes, Heather and Jeff Lloyd, "Gay Pride on Stolen Land: Homonationalism, Queer Asylum and Indigenous Sovereignty at the Vancouver Winter Olympics." (2012). Accessed January 20, 2022, http://hdl.handle.net/1807/32972

Sznaider, Natan. *Fluchtpunkte der Erinnerung: Über die Gegenwart von Holocaust und Kolonialismus*. Munich: Hanser, 2022.

Tinsley, Omise'eke Natasha. "BLACK ATLANTIC, QUEER ATLANTIC: Queer Imaginings of the Middle Passage." *GLQ: A Journal of Lesbian and Gay Studies* 14, no. 2–3 (2008): 191–215.

Tomberger, Corinna. "Das Berliner Homosexuellen-Denkmal: Ein Denkmal für Schwule und Lesben?" In *Homophobie und Devianz. Weibliche und männliche Homosexualität im Nationalsozialismus*, edited by Insa Eschebach, 187–207. Berlin: Metropol, 2012.

Tomkins, Silvan S., and Eve Kosofsky Sedgwick. *Shame and its Sisters: A Silvan Tomkins Reader*. Durham, NC: Duke University Press, 1995.

Traub, Valerie. *The Renaissance of Lesbianism in Early Modern England*. Cambridge: Cambridge University Press, 2002.

Tremblay, Sébastien. "'Ich konnte ihren Schmerz körperlich spüren.' Die Historisierung der NS-Verfolgung und die Wiederaneignung des Rosa Winkels in der westdeutschen Schwulenbewegung der 1970er Jahre." *Invertito Jahrbuch für die Geschichte der Homosexualitäten* 21 (2019): 179–202.

Tremblay, Sébastien. "Visual Collective Memories of National Socialism: Transatlantic HIV/AIDS Activism and Discourses of Persecutions." *German History* 40, no. 4 (2022): 563–582.

Tremblay, Sébastien. *Homosynchronism and the Temporal-Memory Border: Framing Racialized Bodies, Time, and Mobility in German Queer Printed Media, SCRIPTS Working Papers*. Berlin: Cluster of Excellence 2055. "Contestations of the Liberal Script (SCRIPTS)." 2022.

Tremblay, Sébastien. "Der Rosa Winkel: vielschichtige Symbolik und Erinnerung in der Schwulenbewegung beiderseits des Atlantiks / The Pink Triangle: Multilayered Symbolism and Memory in the Queer Atlantic." In *Queer Lives 1900-1950*, edited by Karolina Kühn and Mirjam Zadoff, 328–341. Munich: Hirmer Verlag, 2023.

Tümmers, Henning. *AIDS: Autopsie einer Bedrohung im geteilten Deutschland*. Göttingen: Wallstein Verlag, 2017.

Tzuberi, Hannah. "'Reforesting' Jews: The German State and the Construction of 'New German Judaism.'" *Jewish Studies Quarterly* 27, no. 3 (2020): 199–224.

Vadhera-Jonas, Rosel. "Nach der Befreiung: Die zweite Geschichte des 'Jugendschutzlagers Uckermark.'" In *Das Mädchenkonzentrationslager Uckermark*, edited by Katja Limbacher, Maike Merten and Bettina Pfefferle, 293–306. Münster: Unrast, 2005.

van Alpen, Ernst. "Symptoms of Discursivity: Experience, Memory, and Trauma." In *Acts of Memory: Cultural Recall in the Present*, edited by Mieke Bal, Jonathan V. Crewe and Leo Spitzer, 24–38. Hanover, NH: University Press of New England, 1999.

van Dijk, Lutz. "Die Folgen des Schweigens: für unmittelbar Betroffene, die historische Forschungsowie jüngere Generationen von Schwulen und Lesben." In *Nationalsozialistischer Terror gegen Homosexuelle: verdrängt und ungesühnt*, edited by Burkhard Jellonek and Rüdiger Lautmann, 389–396. Paderborn: Schoeningh, 2002.

Vendrell, Javier Semper. "Photography and the Homoerotics of Race in Adolf Brand's Rasse und Schönheit." In *Queer Media in the German Speaking World - New Approaches to Print Sources*, edited by Christopher Ewing and Sébastien Tremblay. London: Palgrave Macmillan [Forthcoming 2024].

Vendrell, Javier Semper. *The Seduction of Youth: Print Culture and Homosexual Rights in the Weimar Republic*. Toronto, ON: Toronto University Press, 2020.

Whisnant, Clayton J. *Queer Identities and Politics in Germany: A History 1880-1945*. New York, NY: Harrington Park Press, 2016.

Wiedemann, Charlotte. *Den Schmerz der Anderen begreifen: Über Erinnerung und Solidarität – Ein Plädoyer für eine empathische Erinnerungskultur*. Berlin: Ullstein, 2022.

Wielowiejski, Patrick. "Identitäre Schwule und bedrohliche Queers: Zum Verhältnis von Homonationalismus und Anti-/G/enderismus im Nationalkonservatismus." *Feministische Studien* 36, no. 2 (2018): 347–356.

Winter, Jay. "The Performance of the Past: Memory, History, Identity." In *Performing the Past: Memory, History and Identity in Modern Europe*, edited by Jay Winter, Karin Tilmans and Frank van Vree, 11–23. Amsterdam: Amsterdam University Press, 2010.

Zebracki, Martin. "Homomonument as Queer Micropublic: An Emotional Geography of Sexual Citizenship." *Tijdschrift voor economische en sociale geografie* 108, no. 3 (2017): 261–364.

Zelizer, Barbie. *Visual Culture and the Holocaust*. New Brunswick, N.J.: Rutgers University Press, 2001.

Zelizer, Barbie. "Journalism's Memory Work." In *Cultural Memory Studies: An International and Interdisciplinary Handbook*, edited by Astrid Erll, Ansgar Nünning and Sara B. Young, 379–388. Berlin: Walter de Gruyter, 2008.

Zinn, Alexander. *'Aus dem Volkskörper entfernt?' Homosexuelle Männer im Nationalsozialismus*. Frankfurt (Main): Campus Verlag, 2018.

Zinn, Alexander. "Abschied von der Opferperspektive: Plädoyer für einen Paradigmenwechsel in der schwulen und lesbischen Geschichtsschreibung." *Zeitschrift für Geschichtswissenschaft* 67, no. 11 (2019): 934–955.

Zinn, Alexander. "Der Hang zu Opfererzählungen. Über Dramatisierung und selektive Wahrnehmung in Geschichtsschreibung und Erinnerungskultur zu Homosexuellen während der NS-Zeit." *Revue d'Allemagne et des pays de langue allemande* 53, no. 2 (2021):331–346.

Zinn, Alexander. "Gefühlte Wahrheiten: Wie LGBTI-Aktivismus die Wissenschaftsfreiheit bedroht." In *Wissenschaftsfreiheit: Warum dieses Grundrecht zunehmend umkämpft ist*, edited by Sandra Kostner, 165–182. Baden-Baden: Nomos, 2022.

Zumbusch, Cornelia. *Wissenschaft in Bildern. Symbol und dialektisches Bild in Aby Warburgs Mnemosyne-Atlas und Walter Benjamins Passagen-Werk*. Berlin: Akademie-Verlag, 2004.

zur Nieden, Susanne. "Der homosexuelle Staatsfeind: Zur Radikalisierung eines Feindbildes im NS." In *Homophobie und Devianz: Weibliche und männliche Homosexualität im Nationalsozialismus*, edited by Insa Eschebach, 23–34. Berlin: Metropol, 2012.

Index

ACT UP 181–184, 186–187, 189–208, 26, 225
- ACT UP Berlin 184, 192–194, 196, 205, 234
- ACT UP Cologne 205
- ACT UP Los Angeles 191, 196, 207, 216
- ACT UP New York 186–187, 189–199, 201–205, 207, 216, 232–233
- ACT UP Paris 193, 206, 235
Advocate (The) 100, 132–134, 239
AIDS Coalition to Unleash Power. See ACT UP
AIDS Activism 7, 25–26, 56, 181–211, 217, 233–234, 245–250
Allgemeine Homosexuelle Arbeitsgemeinschaft e. V. (AHA) 52, 159, 160
Americanization of the Holocaust 88–93
Amsterdam 89, 176–180, 196–197
Ancestral Genealogies 212–213
Arbeitsgruppe Homosexualität Braunschweig (AHB) 46–47, 50–51
Arcigay 174–176
Autonome feministische FrauenLesben aus Deutschland und Österreich 153–156

Beck, Gad 144
Bent. See Martin Sherman
Bergman, David 106–107, 146
Berliner Verkehrsbetriebe 161
Bierwagen, Greta 79–83
Black Triangle 15, 18, 79–81, 83, 102, 108–111, 123, 138, 203, 239, 244–247
Body Politic (The) 59–65
Bologna (Monument) 174–179
Bundestag 120, 126–129
Bryant, Anita 101–104

Chechnya 26, 225–226
Christopher Street (Magazine) 55, 62, 66, 72–73, 97, 103, 229
Christopher Street Parades 163, 244
Cologne (Monument) 156–157, 163
Comité International de Dachau (CID) 51, 108–110, 117
Congregation Beth Simchat Torah (CBST) 139–147
Contatto 175–176

Cultural Trauma 37–51, 91–93, 97–99, 122–124, 143–148, 163–164, 199, 235, 247–249
Cultuur en Ontspanningscentrum 176–177

Dachau 44, 48–51, 60, 64–65, 70, 80, 88, 107–124, 145–153, 169, 175, 199, 202, 235, 257, 270–275
Dade County 103–105
de Haan, Jacob Israël 177–178
Deutsche Aids-Hilfe 193, 197, 234

Emanzipation (Magazine) 30–32, 44, 47, 50–53, 73
European Time 211–228

Faeser, Nancy 223
Feministenpapier. See *Homosexuelle Aktion Westberlin*
Finkelstein, Avram 196, 201–204, 207
Football 223–224
Frank, Anne 87–91, 104, 177–178
Frankfurt Engel 163–164

Gauweiler, Peter 184–196
Gay Liberation Front (Cologne) 27, 48–49, 165
Gay Synagogue News. See Congregation Beth Simchat Torah
Geto, Ethan. See Dade County.
Global Memory of the Holocaust 93–95
Gran Fury. See Silence = Death

Helms, Jesse 191, 196
Hirschfeld, Magnus 59, 96, 159
Holocaust Remembrance Day 137, 177, 141–142
Homocaust 1, 15, 60–88, 97–102, 117–122, 130–134, 145, 170–178, 199, 204–207, 234–239, 245–247
Homomonument 176–180, 197
Homonationalism 14, 171–172, 222–226, 251–256
Homophile 12–13, 29
Homosexuelle Aktion Westberlin (HAW) 28–38, 44–50, 54, 58, 69, 99, 183–184, 241
Homosexuelle Emanzipation. See *Emanzipation* (Magazine)

Homosexuelle Initiative Linz 138
Homosexuelle Initiative Wien 114–117, 170, 173, 175, 194
Homosynchronism 26, 214, 224–228, 253

International Lesbian and Gay Association (ILGA) 165–178, 218, 227, 249
Institut für Sexualwissenschaft. See Hirschfeld, Magnus

Jewish Lesbian Daughters of Holocaust Survivors 141

Kellerjournal 50, 199–200
Kinship 22, 54–56, 215
Kohout, Josef 31–32, 39, 42, 45, 54, 135, 142, 151, 244
Kramer, Larry 182, 185–187, 192, 195, 204, 207

Labrys 82, 141, 202–203
Lambda 140–143, 202
Landman, Rick 132–133
Lautmann, Rüdiger 61, 65, 70, 78, 122, 138, 158
Lesbian Erasure 15, 21, 79–81, 179, 245

Mann-O-Meter 187, 234
March on Washington 133–134, 188, 190–191
Mauthausen 114–120, 124, 159, 175
Monette, Paul 86–87
Montréal AIDS Conference 192
Müller, Klaus 133–136
Multidirectional Memory 91–96, 104, 183, 246

Nollendorfplatz 160–163, 248

Ökumenische Arbeitsgruppe Homosexuelle und Kirche e.V (HuK) 49, 79, 119–123, 159–163
Operation Soap. See Police Repression

Pictorial Turn 16, 236
Pink Capitalism 230–239
Pink Radicals 29–52, 54, 58, 61, 68, 78, 87, 96–97, 130–134, 155, 158, 166, 178, 182–184, 212–215, 225, 24–249
Pink Pistols 209–210

Pink Triangle
– Bridges 19–20, 130, 136, 139, 144, 151, 164, 176–185, 197, 209, 213–216, 220–221, 225, 230–255
– Day 101–102
– Narratives 25, 63, 134, 159, 165–166, 174
– As Negative Symbol 2, 36, 143, 178
– Pointing Downwards 46, 60, 184–185, 200, 205–206, 210, 242
– Pointing Upwards 197, 201–206, 210, 231, 242
– Press 44, 59, 101
Pink Washing 252–254
Plague (Metaphors) 198, 209
Plant, Richard 55–61, 71–78, 149, 171, 249
Police Repression 59, 102, 124, 161, 179
Politische Sinnlichkeit 183, 240
Postmemory 15–16, 40–45, 95–96, 135, 144, 164, 186, 204–207, 247
Prophylactic Measures 200
Prosthetic Memory 16, 93, 225

Queer Temporalities 211–214
Queer Shame 35–36, 54

Raphael, Lev 229–235
Rainbow Flag 2, 20, 37, 99, 221–225, 232, 239, 243, 253–254
Ravensbrück 80, 109, 138, 151–154
Röhm, Ernst 9
Rose, Steven 188
Rosa Telefon 50
Rosa Winkel Wuppertal 47
Rosa Winkel: das ist doch schon lange vorbei 27

Sachsenhausen 44, 48, 60, 72, 107, 110–114, 121, 122–124, 137–138, 152, 160, 175, 235–237
Sacred Evil 88–96
Salmen, Andreas 184, 193–195, 234, 242
Scaling 240–241
Schermann, Henny (Jenny) 80, 135
Schwule Aktion Köln (SAK) 48–49
Section 175 (§175 StGB) 9–10, 27–35, 54, 59, 61, 65, 71–73, 79, 112, 137–139, 152–153, 161–164, 175, 244–246, 251
Sherman, Martin 57, 63–64, 66–71, 78, 142, 249

Siegessäule 193
Silence = Death 197, 201–206, 217, 233–236
Steakley, James D. 1, 24, 56–65, 70–78, 249
Steinplatz 162
Stockholm Declaration 94
Stonewall 3, 59, 63, 101, 133, 172, 212, 244

Tel Aviv 179, 244
Tiergarten 154–156, 163, 22–24
Thorstadt, David 95–96
Topographie des Terrors 131–132
Tuntenstreit. See *Homosexuelle Aktion Westberlin*

United Nations Economic and Social Council. See International Lesbian and Gay Association
The United States Holocaust Memorial Museum 100, 106–108, 133–135, 143, 146, 151

Verein für sexuelle Gleichberechtigung (VSG) 49–50, 113–120
Vergangenheitsbewältigung 21, 25, 37, 125, 130–131, 154–155, 176, 218–224, 228, 247
Verjährungsdebatte 52
Versöhnungskirche 113, 119–120
Vidal, Gore 87, 98
Visual Concepts 5–6, 18, 56, 78, 85, 139, 225, 236–238, 246–251
Vereinigung der Verfolgten des Naziregimes 42, 52–53, 79, 11–113, 124, 160
Vergessenen (Die) 111

Winkelrelief 108–110

Yad Vashem 147

www.ingramcontent.com/pod-product-compliance
Lightning Source LLC
Chambersburg PA
CBHW060351190426
43201CB00044B/1983